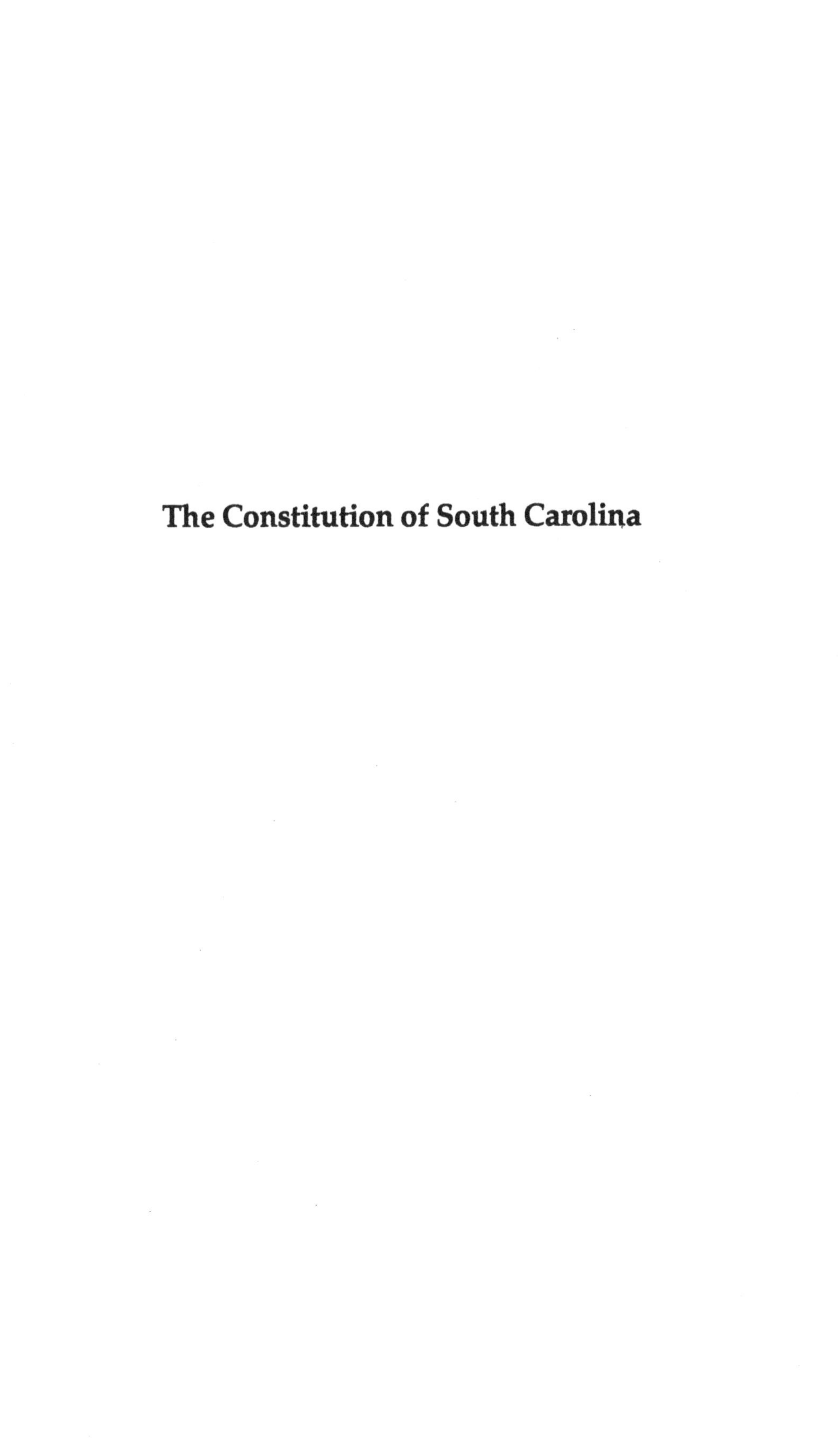

The Constitution of South Carolina

THE CONSTITUTION OF SOUTH CAROLINA

Volume III: Church and State, Morality and Free Expression

By James Lowell Underwood

UNIVERSITY OF SOUTH CAROLINA PRESS

Published in Columbia, South Carolina, by the
University of South Carolina Press

23 22 21 20 19 6 5 4 3 2

Library of Congress Cataloging-in-Publication Data
(Revised for volume 3)

Underwood, James L.
The Constitution of South Carolina.

Includes bibliographies and index.
Contents: v. 1. The relationship of the legislative, executive, and judicial branches
–v. 2. The journey toward local self-government
–v. 3. Church and state, morality and free expression.
1. South Carolina–Constitutional law.
I. Title.
KFS2202.U53 1986 342.757'029 86-1709
347.570229
ISBN 0-87249-443-8 (v. 1)
ISBN 0-87249-636-8 (v. 2)
ISBN 0-87249-833-6 (v. 3, alk. paper)

BUT IT DOES ME NO INJURY FOR MY NEIGHBOR TO SAY THAT THERE ARE TWENTY GODS, OR NO GOD. IT NEITHER PICKS MY POCKET NOR BREAKS MY LEG.

Thomas Jefferson

I Dumas Malone, *Jefferson and His Time, Jefferson The Virginian* 275 (1948).

CONTENTS

PREFACE

This series is an exploratory voyage into the allocation of power under the Constitution of South Carolina. It takes its bearings from three Constitutional promotories: (1) the balance of power among the statewide branches, (2) the relationship of the state government to its political subdivisions, and (3) the sanctuary afforded the civil rights of the people from intrusion by state and local governments. The first two topics were discussed in volumes I and II. In South Carolina history, two major focal points in the struggle to protect civil liberties have been: (a) the relationship of church and state and its impact on freedom of conscience and the ability to use forms of expression believed by many to have an adverse impact upon the moral strength of the community, and (b) the quest for equal political rights, especially with regard to the right to vote. This volume concentrates on the first of the focal points: the balance between church and state, between spiritual and secular power. In addition to examining the constitutional doctrines against the establishment, and in favor of the free exercise of religion, this volume considers the regulation of forms of expression such as obscene and indecent speech that pose questions with regard to the extent to which government should seek to control not only physically dangerous behavior but also the moral purity of thought. To some observers, government regulations to raise the moral standards of the people are a futile attempt to lock a God-given soul in a man-made box of legal imperatives. To others, it appears equally futile to attempt to separate thought and behavior. Each has an impact on the other and true safety of the community can be achieved only by regulation of both. This work explores this debate from historical and contemporary perspectives, beginning with early colonial regulations and extending to modern constitutional doctrine. As in the previous volumes in the series, this book blends legal, historical and social science materials rather than relying upon any one as the sole source of useful insight. South Carolina has a lengthy and unique history with respect to the problems discussed in this volume. Even though this volume uses historical materials where they help illuminate legal concepts, it is a constitutional law work and not a history or theology book. However, I hope that it will be useful to anyone interested in freedom of conscience issues no matter what professional discipline he or she pursues.

Because of the incorporation doctrine by which federal civil rights guarantees are applied to the states, beginning with the middle of the twentieth century, we see an intense interaction between state and federal constitutional standards with the federal standards steadily growing in influence. This volume deals with a dynamic area and the debate concerning the proper relationship between church and state, morality and free expression, state and federal law, will continue. Perhaps the present debate will be better understood when it is linked with its antecedents as this book seeks to do.

J.L.U.

ACKNOWLEDGMENTS

The picture of the solitary author toiling in his remote garret sustained only by fortitude and an occasional sliver of cheese may retain some validity, but modern life is a story of interdependence. No one can hope to accomplish much without the goodwill, assistance and advice of a great many people. The complex problems addressed in this series and the length of time required to complete the research and writing of each volume mean that I am especially grateful to those who have provided valuable aid. I would like to thank the administration of the University of South Carolina Law School, especially Dean John Montgomery and Associate Deans Nathan Crystal and Philip Lacy for their support. The able staff of the Law School library, including Joseph Cross, Steve Huang, Mary E. "Prue" Goolsby, Mary McCormick and Diana Osbaldiston, all operating under the benign dictatorship of Director Bruce Johnson, have been of great help in locating elusive research materials. The staffs of the State Department of Archives and History and the South Caroliniana Library of the University of South Carolina helped in locating historical material while the State Library furnished contemporary documents.

An active squad of student research assistants rendered valuable help. Cathy Hazelwood and Barbara Price conducted extremely difficult portions of the final citation check. Also contributing significant assistance in research, editing or citation checking were Scott Robinson, Laura Rummans Potts, Ross Hall, Gamble Hartzell, and Brana Williams. Wayne Edwards and Michele Bateman, who did such excellent work in the closing phases of Volume II, helped start the research on Volume III.

The Law School's intrepid secretarial staff typed numerous drafts with boundless patience and skill. Those participating were Laura Long, Director, Frances Donnelly, Nancy Shealy, Doris Cooper, DeAnna Sugrue and Belinda Davis.

Professor Robert Wilcox of the Law School read the manuscript and gave me the benefit of his sage advice.

Officials of the South Carolina Baptist Convention, the United Methodist and Lutheran Churches were very helpful in making available back copies of their denominational newspapers or convention resolutions. I greatly appreciate their willingness to contribute to the public debate on the significant issues discussed in this volume.

J.L.U.

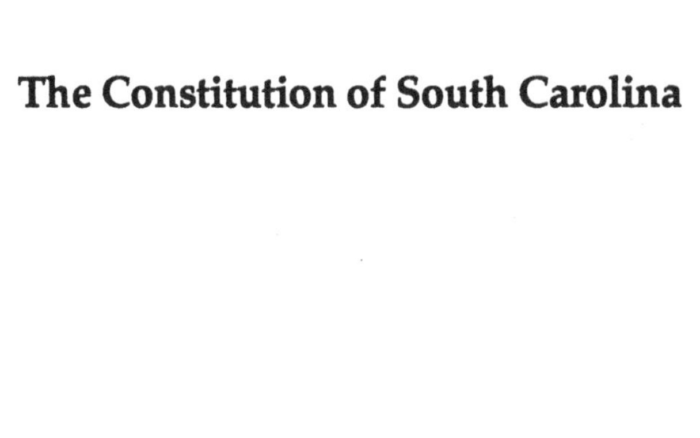

The Constitution of South Carolina

INTRODUCTION

The history of the relationship of government to religion demonstrates a recurring vacillation between two polar opposite approaches: a view that religion is one of several means of social control by which the state can keep the population meekly in check, and the view that religion represents a highly personal approach by an individual to God that cannot be dictated by the state. The philosophy that government can use religion as a device for curbing the excesses of the people masks widely divergent views. Religion can be used as a subordinate tool for a regime that merely wishes to maintain itself in power, or it can be a manifestation of a more fundamental view that government itself is ordained by divine power and thus its laws must reinforce religiously mandated moral standards. The practical nature of government, deeply influenced by economic necessity and political reality, dictates that these philosophies can not survive in pure form in real life. Compromise and constant redefinition of a consensus are essential.

The history of South Carolina illustrates the ambivalent embracing and spurning of the polar opposite views of religion as an instrument of social control and as a personal rite of passage for the conscience. In addition, the history of South Carolina demonstrates the compromises demanded by the scramble for economic growth. An established church gives way to the need to attract settlers, many of whom are fleeing from the pressure for religious conformity in Europe. The privileged position of the Church of England crumbles in the face of the need to unify the population in the revolutionary struggle for separation from England. The long-entrenched system of Sunday Blue Laws, after centuries of sacrosanct status, eventually withers under the competitive demands of a modern economy. The umbrella of religious freedom contracts and expands fitfully, inviting those with a variety of beliefs to settle in the colony, then demanding conformity, especially from those in positions of political leadership, then expanding again to include Catholics and Jews but within a legal atmosphere that leaves little doubt that Protestant Christianity retains the inner circle of influence and that freedom must never become license.

The earliest colonial documents reveal the uneasy coexistence of toleration and conformity, of religion as a social control device and mode of individual expression. The provisions of the first Charter display these tensions.

CHAPTER ONE

THE CHARTERS AND THE FUNDAMENTAL CONSTITUTIONS: THE TOLERATION OF FREEDOM WITHIN LIMITS

In 1663, Charles II granted a Charter for Carolina to the Lords Proprietor, a group of men to whom he was indebted for their assistance in regaining the throne that was lost after the execution of his father, Charles I.[1] The Charter reveals a view that control over religion can be an ownership right that is an incident to the grant of land. The Charter includes among the powers granted to the Lords Proprietor the following:

> And Furthermore, the Patronage and Advowsons of all the Churches and Chapels which, as Christian Religion shall increase within the Country, Isles, Islets, and Limits aforesaid, shall happen hereafter to be erected; Together with licence and power to Build and found Churches, Chapels, and Oratories in convenient and fit places within the said Bounds and Limits, and to cause them to be Dedicated and Consecrated according to the Ecclesiastical Laws of our Kingdom of England . . . .[2]

Thus the proprietors received a licensing authority to create churches but within the broad circumference of the laws of England. The Charter betrays a belief that churches should not spring up in spontaneous serendipity but only through official certification.

The pivotal religious freedom provision of the Charter displays a need to tolerate a variety of religious beliefs and practices in order to attract settlers, but it describes such freedom as a revocable boon rather than a firmly established right. The Charter states:

> And because it may happen that some of the People and Inhabitants of the said Province cannot in their private opinions Conform to the Public Exercise of Religion according to the Liturgy, forms, and Ceremonies of the Church of England, or take or subscribe the Oaths and Articles made and established in that behalf; And for that the same, by reason of the remote distances of those Places, Will, as We hope, be no breach of the *unity and uniformity established in this Nation*:
>
> Our Will and pleasure, therefore, is, And We Do, by these presents, for us, our heirs and Successors, Give and Grant unto the said Edward, Earl of Clarendon; George, Duke of Albemarle; William, Lord Craven; John, Lord Berkley; Anthony, Lord Ashley; Sir George Carterett; Sir William Berkley; and Sir John Colleton, their heirs and Assigns, full and free Licence, liberty, and Authority, by such legal ways and means as they shall think fit, to give and grant unto such Person and Persons inhabiting and being within the said Province, or any part thereof, Who really in their Judgments, and for Conscience sake, cannot or shall not conform to the said Liturgy and Ceremonies, and take and Subscribe the Oaths; and Articles aforesaid, or any of them, such Indulgences and Dispensations in that Behalf, *for and during such time and times, and with such limitations and restrictions*, as they, the said Edward, Earl of Clarendon; George, Duke of Albemarle; William, Lord Craven; John, Lord Berkley; Anthony, Lord Ashley; Sir George Carterett; Sir William Berkley; and Sir John Colleton, their heirs or Assigns, shall, *in their discretions*, think fit and reasonable;
>
> And with this express Proviso and Limitation also; that such Person and Persons to whom such Indulgences or Dispensations shall be granted, as aforesaid, do and shall, from time to time, Declare and continue all fidelity, Loyalty, and Obedience to us, our heirs and Successors; and be subject and obedient to all other the Laws, Ordinances, and Constitutions of the said Province, in all matters whatsoever, as well Ecclesiastical as Civil; And do not

> in any wise disturb the Peace and safety thereof, or scandalize or reproach the said Liturgy, forms, and Ceremonies, or any thing relating thereunto, or any Person or Persons whatsoever for, or in respect of, his or their use or exercise thereof, or his or their obedience or conformity thereunto.[3]

These provisions no doubt struck an appealing note to potential settlers laboring under the heavy hand of religious oppression in England and Europe but they formed an unstable basis for religious freedom because:

(1) whether or not such freedom was granted was entirely within the discretion of the proprietors and could be withdrawn by them at any time,

(2) freedom of worship was not to be carried to the extreme that it scandalized or reproached the liturgy of the Church of England,

(3) freedom of worship could exist only to the extent that it was consistent with allegiance to the King,

(4) freedom of worship was tolerable in the colony only because its remote distance from England made it unlikely that such freedom would undermine "unity and uniformity" in the parent country. If such freedom was ever found to be destructive of religious unity in England, it would be subject to revocation.

On June 30, 1665, a Second Charter was granted to the Lords Proprietor.[4] The primary purpose of the new Charter was to enlarge the territory of the grant but the scope of religious freedom also received at least a theoretical broadening.

A key provision defining the boundaries of freedom of conscience and worship declared:

> And that no person or persons unto whom such liberty shall be given shall be any way molested, punished, disquieted, or called in question for any differences in opinion or practice in matters of Religious concernment, who do not actually disturb the Civil Peace of the Province, County, or Colony that they shall make their abode in; but all and every such Person and Persons may, from time to time, and at all times, freely and quietly have and enjoy his and their Judgements and Consciences in matters of Religion throughout all the said Province or Colony, they behaving themselves peaceably and [not] using this liberty to licentiousness, nor to the civil Injury or outward disturbance of others; Any law, Statute, or Clause, contained or to be contained, usage or Custom of Our Realm of England to the contrary hereof in any wise notwithstanding.[5]

Under this provision religious freedom would seem to be more securely guaranteed and less subject to the whim of the proprietors. Religious freedom was to be curtailed when it resulted in the disturbance of the "Civil Peace." The 1663 Charter permitted intrusion on religious freedom when there was no breach of peace but merely critical language that scandalized or reproached the liturgy of the Church of England. This generous ambit of religious freedom was less hemmed in by the laws applicable in the parent country since the 1665 Charter provision announced that the freedom was granted despite any "usage or Custom of Our Realm of England to the contrary hereof in any wise notwithstanding."[6] However, such impressive rhetoric guaranteeing religious freedom often means little when those manipulating the levers of power are determined to use control of religion as a means of fortifying their position.

Reality may have been more clearly reflected in documents issued by the direct governing authority, the proprietors themselves, than in the lofty rhetoric of the King. On January 7, 1665, after issuance of the First Charter and shortly before the promulgation of the Second Charter, the Lords Proprietor entered into a concessions and agreement with a group of settlers under the leadership of Major John Yeamans. This document contained concrete promises made by the proprietors to the would-be colonists in order to attract settlers. Item Eight of the concessions contains a liberal grant of religious freedom in language that closely resembles that used later that year in the Second Charter.[7] However, this provision was preceded in Item Seven by a reservation of authority in the proprietors to revoke freedoms granted in the concessions and agreement. Orders withdrawing freedoms would be applicable to settlers arriving after the revocation notice but would not abrogate the freedom of the existing settlers who migrated in reliance upon the earlier generous grant of freedom.[8] The retention of such revocation power by the proprietors may have betrayed a fear of the unknown. Future settlers might espouse more dangerous beliefs than those who were signatories to the concessions and agreements. This approach raised the specter of an unworkable system under which different groups of settlers would have different rights depending on their date of arrival. The Second Charter seemed to envision less discretion on the part of the proprietors but the language is vague enough to permit a variety of approaches.

Another part of the concessions and agreement indicated how the proprietors would exercise their charter powers to create and license churches and ministers. The proprietors pledged that they would not use the authority as a cloak under which they would make encroachments upon "the General clause of Liberty of Conscience."[9] Item Nine delegated to the legislative assemblies that were to be created in each county the power to establish churches and provide for their maintenance from public funds. This power to appoint ministers and create churches that would enjoy government support was not to be exercised in a monopolistic fashion. Liberty was given "to any person or persons to keep and maintain what preachers or Ministers they please."[10] This provision was at once generous and discriminatory. It permitted the voluntary creation of ministries that might more closely reflect the views of a particular group of settlers than would those established by the county assemblies but it strongly implied that such unofficial churches must fend for themselves financially. Thus, they would be at a competitive disadvantage with the officially supported ministries. However, the county assemblies were admonished not to use their power to create and support ministries or any other legislative authority in a manner that would be "against the Article for Liberty of Conscience."[11]

The concessions and agreement constitute a contract between the proprietors and a specific group of settlers. A more far-reaching influence on the climate of religious freedom in South Carolina is found in the Fundamental Constitutions. These basic documents allocate government power and define the rights and freedoms of various segments of society.[12] Because the Fundamental Constitutions attempted to reestablish a nearly medieval society composed of an hereditary nobility and a serflike class of "leetmen" who were tied to the land, they were rejected by the people and never fully implemented.[13] Authorship of these documents is sometimes attributed to the political philosopher John Locke. However, some scholars believe the contents were heavily influenced by the wishes of the proprietors.[14] Even though the Fundamental Constitutions were never fully effectuated, they formed the textual ammunition which various sides in religious freedom controversies hurled at one another. In addition, some provisions of the Fundamental Constitutions furnished direct antecedents for later documents. For example, Article 90 of the first version of the Fundamental Constitutions lists the beliefs that must be espoused before a group of worshipers can be officially recognized as a church.[15] This provision foreshadows similar requirements that must be met in order to be a governmentally sanctioned church under the Constitution of 1778. Because of their significant impact on the nature of church-state relations in early South Carolina, the provisions of the Fundamental Constitutions dealing with religion will be considered in some detail. The approach of the Fundamental Constitutions to religious freedom was to cast the net of toleration broadly enough to attract numerous settlers who would undoubtedly have a diversity of beliefs but to insist on agreement with certain bedrock principles without which it was believed government could not endure. The July 21, 1669, version illustrates these characteristics.[16] Article 86 states that:

> No man shall be permitted to be a Freeman of Carolina, or to have any Estate or habitation within it, that does not acknowledge a God, and that God is publicly and Solemnly to be worshipped.[17]

This language does not insist on belief in a Church of England version of God or even a Christianized God but it does insist on acceptance of a higher being as a predicate to life in a civilized society.

The basic document then delineated a broad-gauged doctrine of religious tolerance, but it did so not out of a philosophical commitment to freedom but in pursuit of the pragmatic self-interest of the proprietors. Potential settlers must not be frightened away by inhospitable religious rules. To populate a remote colony, a necessarily diverse lot of migrants must be enlisted. Peace could most easily be maintained among such a varied lot by not attempting to force everyone into the same narrow mold. To these ends Article 87 stated:

> But since the Natives of that place, who will be concerned in our Plantations, are utterly Strangers to Christianity, whose Idolatry, Ignorance, or mistake gives us no right to expel or use them ill; and those who remove from other parts to Plant there will unavoidably be of different opinions concerning matters of Religion, the liberty whereof they will expect to have allowed them, and it will not be reasonable for us, on this account, to keep them out, that Civil peace may be maintained amidst the diversity of opinions, and our agreement and compact with all men may be clearly and faithfully observed, the violation whereof, upon what pretence soever, cannot be without great

> offence to Almighty God, and great Scandal to the true Religion that we profess; and also, that heathens, Jews, and other dissenters from the purity of Christian Religion may not be Scared and kept at a distance from it, but, by having an opportunity of acquainting them selves with the truth and reasonableness of its Doctrines, and the peaceableness and inoffensiveness of its professors, may, by good usage and persuasion [originally preservation], and all those convincing Methods of Gentleness and meekness Suitable to the Rules and design of the Gospel, be won over to embrace and unfeignedly receive the truth: Therefore, any Seven or more persons agreeing *in any Religion* shall constitute a church or profession, to which they shall give Some name to distinguish it from others.[18]

The economic imperative to grant religious tolerance as a magnet to settlers to populate the colony was tinged with a missionary flavor. Such tolerance set a proper Christian example of gentle persuasion that was most likely to attract native Indians, Jews and ". . . other dissenters from the purity of Christian Religion" to that faith. If religious freedom is not viewed as a worthy end in itself but is considered to be merely a useful tool to achieve the economic goals of entrepreneurs, the missionary ends of the church, and the peace-keeping goals of the church, it may be flouted when it is perceived as no longer serving those ends. As we shall see, a later version of this provision is less broadly tolerant and more endorsing of the Church of England as the only one deserving of government fiscal support.

The provision permitting seven or more people who have reached a consensus concerning doctrine to form a new church of "any Religion" demonstrated that the proprietors would continue the approach they had followed in the concessions and agreement: their power to create and maintain churches would not be exercised in a monopolistic fashion. However, Article 90 stipulated that those seeking to form a new church avow that they (1) believed in God, (2) that God was publicly to be worshipped and (3) that their written communion contained some means by which adherents who gave testimony as witnesses could swear before God that their assertions were true. Tolerance should not be carried to the extreme of indulging those who could not be trusted to honestly perform the duties of citizenship, such as giving evidence, in a truthful manner. Instead, religious standards should be used as a means of producing good citizens. Religious assemblies not meeting the requirements set by Article

90 were declared by Article 99 to be unlawful meetings that could be punished as riots.[19]

The July 21, 1669, version of the Fundamental Constitutions sought to establish a ranking among several important but clashing values. The security of the government was most highly valued, followed by freedom of worship and freedom of speech, in that order. Freedom of speech was treated not so much as an independent value but as a practice that should not be indulged to the jeopardy of the other values. The paramount position of government security was seen in Article 94 which stated that:

> No person whatsoever shall speak anything in their Religious assembly Irreverently or Seditiously of the Government or Governors or state matters.[20]

The Fundamental Constitutions took the approach that a varied population with diverse religions could not live in peace if rough, brawling doctrinal debates were permitted. Accordingly, Article 97 stated that "[no] person shall use any reproachful, Reviling, or abusive language against the Religion of any Church or Profession, that being the certain way of disturbing the public peace. . . ."[21]

This provision was fortified by Article 100 which declared that "[n]o person whatsoever shall disturb, molest or persecute another for his speculative opinions in Religion or his way of worship."[22] These provisions bespeak a government obligation to not only avoid interfering in freedom of worship unless the mode of worship threatened the security of the government or the public peace, but an affirmative duty for the authorities to act to prevent private individuals from interfering with the worship of others. Remnants of this philosophy will later be seen in state statutes and case law protecting religious assemblies from rowdy detractors.

Even slaves were to enjoy freedom of worship and religious affiliation but within more restrictive limits. Article 98 stated that:

> Since Charity obliges us to wish well to the Souls of all men and Religion ought to alter nothing in any man's civil Estate or Right, It shall be lawful for Slaves, as all others, to enter them selves and be of what church any of them shall think best, and therefore be as fully members as any freemen. But yet, no Slave shall hereby be exempted from that civil dominion his Master has

> over him, but be in all other things in the same State and condition he was in before.[23]

The Fundamental Constitutions emphasized the point that religious freedom of the slave was not to result in physical and economic freedom by reiterating in Article 101 of the July 21, 1669, version that "[e]very Freeman of Carolina shall have absolute Authority over his Negro Slaves, of what opinion or Religion soever."[24] In other words, religious freedom for the slave was fine, it might even serve to distract the slave from his condition, but such freedom was to be entirely psychological. It could not undermine in any way the slave's status as mere property. It is difficult to maintain one freedom in isolation without other freedoms to fortify it.

Overall, however, the July 21, 1669, version of the Fundamental Constitutions granted a wide latitude for religious freedom, especially in view of the practice elsewhere during the colonial era. For example, the 1624 Regulations for colonists in New Amsterdam stated that:

> [The colonists] shall practice no other form of divine worship within their territory than that of the Reformed religion as presently practiced here in this country, and, in so doing, by their Christian life and conduct, lead the Indians and other blind people to the Knowledge of God and of His Word, without, however, persecuting anyone because of his faith, but leaving to everyone the freedom of his conscience. But, if anyone among them or within their jurisdiction should wantonly revile or blaspheme the name of God or of our Savior Jesus Christ, he shall be punished by the commander and his council according to the circumstances.[25]

An absolute inner freedom of conscience can be a meaningless sop unless accompanied by the freedom to choose an outward mode of worship so long as the form of worship does not disturb the civil peace. Perhaps the grant of religious freedom contained in the July 21, 1669, draft of the Fundamental Constitutions had a broader scope than was comfortable to the proprietors. On March 1, 1670, a new version of the Fundamental Constitutions was promulgated.[26] Article 95 of this new document continued the requirement present in Article 86 of the earlier draft that no one could be a freeman in Carolina unless he believed in God. New Article 96 sharply reined in religious diversity. It declared that:

> As the Country comes to be sufficiently Planted and Distributed into fit Divisions, it shall belong to the Parliament to take care for the building of Churches and the public Maintenance of Divines, to be employed in the Exercise of Religion according to the Church of England, which, being the only true and Orthodox, and the National Religion of all the King's Dominions, is so also of Carolina, and therefore, it alone shall be allowed to receive public Maintenance by Grant of Parliament.[27]

By endorsing the Church of England as the only "true" religion, this provision sent a message that those who wanted to advance socially, politically and economically would be well advised to become adherents to the Church of England. By giving Parliament a leading role in building churches and maintaining ministers, the incentive for voluntary private efforts that would be likely to lead to greater diversity was reduced. By making the Church of England the only church entitled to public funds, it was given a strong competitive advantage over its rivals. One commentator has noted that the July 21, 1669, version of the Fundamental Constitutions in John Locke's handwriting did not contain any provision comparable to the later Article 96.[28] Locke and his patron Lord Ashley were believed to favor broader toleration.[29] Locke later remarked that Article 96 was inserted in the new version at the insistence of other proprietors.[30]

Two revised drafts of the Fundamental Constitutions were issued in 1682. The January 12, 1682, version renumbered as Article 94 the requirement that in order to be a freeman in Carolina, one must believe in and acknowledge the existence of God and that God is publicly to be worshipped. It further insisted that the would-be freeman also avow that ". . . there is a future being after this Life."[31] This standard received further refinement as Article 100 of the August 17, 1682, version which stated that those seeking freeman status must not only espouse a belief in God, that God is publicly and solemnly to be worshipped, and that there is a future life after this one, but also that the after life can be a state of "... happiness or misery," depending, presumably, upon one's conduct on earth.[32] Thus the freeman qualifications evolved from broad standards that left much room for exploration by each individual's conscience to an increasingly more specific litany.

The establishment of the Church of England which was found in Article 96 of the 1670 edition of the Fundamental Constitutions was retained with only cosmetic changes in the first 1682 version as Article 95. The second 1682 edition lightens the yoke placed by the establishment of the Church of England on the backs of the taxpayers. It states:

> 101 As the Country comes to be sufficiently planted and distributed into fit divisions, it shall belong to the parliament to take care of the building of churches and the public maintenance of divines, to be employed in the exercise of Religion according to the Church of England, which being the religion of the government of England, it alone shall be allowed to receive public maintenance by grant of parliament; *which said public maintenance is to arise out of lands or rents assigned voluntarily, contributions, or such other ways whereby no man shall be chargeable to pay out of his particular Estate that is not conformable to the church as aforesaid, but every church or Congregation of Christians, not of the communion of the Church of Rome, shall have power to lay a tax on its own members, not exceeding a penny per acre on their Lands and twelve per head per annum, for the maintenance of their public ministers; and of all money so paid and disbursed they shall keep an account, which the grand council, or any authorized by them shall have liberty from time and time to Inspect.*[33]

Thus voluntary contributions replaced coerced taxes as the means for maintaining the Church of England. Only adherents were expected to contribute to it. This provision obviously was not a complete charter of religious freedom, although it did make a diversity of beliefs easier to achieve. Other denominations use their own administrative machinery, rather than parliament, and tax their own members. However, the constitution still assumes that everyone must be a member of some church and he must support it whether he chooses to or not. Although the colonist is relieved of the necessity of supporting someone else's religion, he cannot influence the direction of his own sect by choosing to withdraw support or reduce or increase the level of contributions. The constitution controls the growth of Church of England rivals by placing a ceiling on the amount of tax that they can impose. The "Church of Rome" is denied the privilege of taxing its members presumably because it is regarded as the servant of the Papal State, a foreign power that could undermine the control of England over its colony. The church was to be the instrument of the government rather than the government the tool of the church, even if that church were the Church of England rather than the more foreign-influenced Church of Rome. To that end, Article 102 of the

August, 1682, version of the Fundamental Constitutions decreed that "[n]o ordained minister, or that receives any maintenance of any congregation or Church, shall be member of parliament, or have any civil office, but wholly attend his ministry."[34]

A final version of the Fundamental Constitutions was promulgated on April 11, 1698. The provision establishing the Church of England became Article 26. It turned its back on the voluntary contribution approach to maintaining the Church of England that was the liberal hallmark of the August, 1682, Constitution. The wording was almost identical to the infamous Article 96 of the March, 1670, draft. The obligation was placed on Parliament to provide for the construction of churches and payment of the salaries of ministers; and the Church of England was endorsed as the ". . . only true and orthodox, and the National religion of the King's Dominions . . ." including Carolina. As such, it is the only religion permitted to receive fiscal support from Parliament.[35]

The various drafts of the Fundamental Constitutions vacillated between broad tolerance of all settlers who believed in the public worship of God and a rigid establishment of the Church of England. However, the overall impression, created especially by the July 21, 1669, version, was that settlers with a wide diversity of beliefs would be welcome in the colony. One historian of the Jewish faith has observed that the Fundamental Constitutions served as a beacon that attracted settlers of that religion who were fleeing oppression in the Old World.[36] Barnett Elzas commented concerning the 1669 Fundamental Constitution that:

> This Constitution of John Locke (1669) was a veritable Magna Charta of Liberty and tolerance. South Carolina started right. Our chief concern being with the Jews of South Carolina, it would be well to note carefully Article 87 of this wise and far-seeing Constitution.
>
> . . . .
>
> Little wonder, then, that the persecuted Jew, like the persecuted Huguenot and German Palatine, soon came here to find a haven of rest. To be undisturbed in the possession of 'life, liberty, and the pursuit of happiness,' and to enjoy the privilege of worshipping God as his conscience dictated--these have ever been the ideals of the Jew, even as they were the ideals upon which the great Republic was established. For by far the greater part of his history, in every country, some or all of these 'inalienable rights of man' have been denied him. Here he could have them all, and in fullest measure. South

> Carolina welcomed him, welcomed him as a man and as a citizen, and the Jew showed himself worthy of the confidence that was reposed in him.[37]

As we shall note in later discussions of the clash between Jewish merchants and Sunday closing-law proponents, as well as controversies between Jewish leaders and governors issuing Christian-oriented Thanksgiving Day proclamations, this shining vision of the peaceable kingdom has not always been realized. However, the earliest version of the Fundamental Constitutions did strike a tolerant note. Robert St. John has noted that although Article 90 outlawed atheism for freemen and Article 91 required that all persons above seventeen must select a church in order to be eligible for places of honor and profit, much scope still remained for individual decisions. He further noted that although the posture of tolerance was in part adopted for the dubious reason of gently persuading the non-Christian to adopt that faith, the document still encouraged a climate of tolerance.[38]

The attractiveness of South Carolina as a magnet for a religiously diverse group of settlers was enhanced by legislation. Most significant among these early laws was an act passed during the 1696-97 legislative session which extended the same property rights and rights before the courts to settlers, no matter what their country of origin, as were enjoyed by inhabitants born of English parents within the colony.[39] The preamble to the act was worded in such a manner as to make it clear that the statute was intended, in part, as a reward to those who had fled religious oppression to settle in Carolina and had proved to be loyal subjects of the King. Historians of the Jewish religion have noted that the liberal property ownership and equal justice provisions were particularly attractive inducements to Jewish settlers.[40] However, it is notable that the act's religious freedom provisions, although generous for the time, spoke of ". . . full, free and undisturbed . . ." worship for ". . . all Christians" and limited even that grant to non-papists.[41]

CHAPTER ONE—NOTES

NOTES

1. NORTH CAROLINA CHARTERS AND CONSTITUTIONS 1578-1698 at 76 (M. PARKER ed. 1963) [hereinafter cited as M. PARKER].

2. M. PARKER at 77.

3. M. PARKER at 88-89 (emphasis added).

4. M. PARKER at 90.

5. M. PARKER at 104.

6. M. PARKER at 104.

7. M. PARKER at 114-15.

8. M. PARKER at 114-15.

9. M. PARKER at 114.

10. M. PARKER at 114.

11. M. PARKER at 115.

12. M. PARKER at 128-240. *See* THE FUNDAMENTAL CONSTITUTIONS OF CAROLINA, reprinted in 1 S.C. STATUTES AT LARGE 43-56 (Cooper 1836). Because it contains a more complete account of the succeeding versions of the Fundamental Constitutions most citations to the text of documents will be to NORTH CAROLINA CHARTERS AND CONSTITUTIONS 1578-1698.

13. *See* R. WEIR, COLONIAL SOUTH CAROLINA, A HISTORY 55-73 (1983) [hereinafter cited as R. WEIR] and 2 D. RAMSAY, THE HISTORY OF SOUTH CAROLINA FROM ITS FIRST SETTLEMENT IN 1670, TO THE YEAR 1808 122-124 (1809) [hereinafter cited as 2 D. RAMSAY].

14. 2 D. RAMSAY at 122 notes that Locke's authorship is in dispute. E. S. de Beer, I Correspondence of John Locke, 395 n. 2 (1976) (Essential ideas were probably those of Locke's patron Lord Shaftesbury).

15. M. PARKER at 149.

16. M. PARKER at 148.

17. M. PARKER at 148.

18. M. PARKER at 148-49 (emphasis added).

19. M. PARKER at 150.

20. M. PARKER at 150.

21. M. PARKER at 150.

22. M. PARKER at 150.

23. M. PARKER at 150.

24. M. PARKER at 150.

25. 1 THE ANNALS OF AMERICA 88 (1976).

26. M. PARKER at 165.

27. M. PARKER at 181.

28. J. BRINSFIELD, RELIGION AND POLITICS IN COLONIAL SOUTH CAROLINA 7-8 (1983) [hereinafter cited as J. BRINSFIELD].

29. J. BRINSFIELD at 7-8.

30. J. BRINSFIELD at 7-8.

31. M. PARKER at 202.

32. M. PARKER at 227.

CHAPTER ONE—NOTES

33. M. PARKER at 227-28 (emphasis added).

34. M. PARKER at 228.

35. M. PARKER at 23 8. The 1698, version did not contain the prohibition on ministers serving in civil offices that was found in Article 102 of the August, 1682, version.

36. *See* B. ELZAS, THE JEWS OF SOUTH CAROLINA FROM THE EARLIEST TIMES TO THE PRESENT DAY 17-18 (1905) [hereinafter B. ELZAS].

37. B. ELZAS at 17-18.

38. R. ST. JOHN, JEWS, JUSTICE AND JUDAISM 62 (1969) [hereinafter cited as R. ST. JOHN].

39. *See* Act. No. 154 of 1696-97, 2 S.C. STATUTES AT LARGE 131 (Cooper 1837).

40. *See* R. ST. JOHN AT 63; L. LEVINGER, A HISTORY OF THE JEWS IN THE UNITED STATES 93 (1949) [hereinafter cited as LEVINGER].

41. *See* Act No. 154 of 1696-97, 2 S.C. STATUTES AT LARGE 131, 133 para. VI (Cooper 1837).

CHAPTER TWO

ERECTING THE ADMINISTRATIVE MACHINERY OF AN ESTABLISHED CHURCH

The officially sanctioned position of the Church of England and the intimate relationship between civil and ecclesiastical governance were delineated in a voluminous 1704 law.[1] The preamble of the act declared that in ". . . a well grounded Christian commonwealth . . . matters concerning religion and the honour of God . . ." should receive the primary consideration. To achieve these ends, the Book of Common Prayer, as used in the Church of England, the Psalms of David and the Morning and Evening Prayer, were to be read in every church ". . . settled and by law established within this Province."[2] All Church of England congregations whose ministers were supported by public funds were considered established churches. The act prescribed parish boundaries, provided for the creation of new parishes and the construction of churches. Significantly, the ultimate province-wide governing body for the church was not a group of bishops or professional clergymen but a politically prominent group of laymen named in the act.[3] That religious power was to be closely related, but subservient, to civil power, was indicated by the fact that all of the officials certifying the statute were also listed in the act as church commissioners. The commissioners' powers were extensive. For example, although rectors of the churches were to be elected by the inhabitants of the parish who were both members of the church and freeholder-taxpayers, or persons who otherwise, paid taxes, the removal of ministers was to be by the commissioners, who would hold a hearing upon a complaint filed by at least nine reputable members of the parish.[4]

The Governor could veto the dismissal of a minister.[5] The extensive power of the church membership in electing ministers and of the lay commissioners in controlling church policy caused protests by the church hierarchy in London that such ecclesiastical democracy was undermining their authority.[6]

The existence of an established church with an officially prescribed doctrine did not mean that control over religious messages was so pervasive that unorthodox doctrine was successfully suppressed. A notable example of a minister who defied the high priests of church orthodoxy but continued to attract adherents was the Reverend George Whitfield, an ordained priest of the Church of England, who became a leading figure of the Methodist movement, which began as a faction within the Anglican Church before becoming a separate denomination. In 1740 Whitfield was charged by the Reverend Alexander Garden of St. Philip's Church in Charleston with conducting services without using the official book of common prayer. He also was charged with advocating unsanctioned doctrines emphasizing the role of a sudden conversion experience as distinguished from the steady performance of good works as the proper route toward salvation.

Garden charged Whitfield with these departures from orthodoxy and ordered him to stand trial before a tribunal of priests. Because of the established position of the Church of England, the proceeding had the aura of a civil proceeding as well as an ecclesiastical inquisition. Whitfield contested the authority of the tribunal and requested that the judges disqualify themselves, presumably because they were interested parties rather than impartial adjudicators. Eventually, Whitfield decided to ignore the proceedings and go on with his ministry. Despite his absence, the tribunal concluded that Whitfield had breached official doctrine to which he had promised to adhere upon becoming a priest. It ordered Whitfield suspended from his position as a Church of England minister. Despite the order Whitfield continued his evangelizing with considerable success, preaching throughout the colonies for many years, including numerous visits to South Carolina.[7] Even though maverick preachers, such as Whitfield, sometimes had success among the people, the elaborate legal machinery supporting the Church of England remained entrenched.

The 1704 act set the general areas in which new churches were to be established but the commissioners had the authority to pick the precise location in consultation with Church of England adherents in the area.[8] The commissioners were authorized to receive gifts for the erection of new churches. If those were insufficient, the commissioners could draw a draft upon the treasury for the remainder.[9] If the public treasury held insufficient funds to pay Church of England ministers, the commissioners could assess an additional tax for that purpose. In addition to paying taxes, there were other ways in which a citizen could find himself involuntarily supporting the Church of England. For example, supervisors of church building projects could draft bricklayers, carpenters, and "joyners" to work on the project. Those who refused were subject to penalty.[10] Although the economic benefits of being an established church were considerable, these were not without cost. The congregation could not determine its own mode of governance. This was set by statute. Each church was to have a policy-making board, the vestry, which was to consist of nine elected members. To vote for or serve on the vestry, one must be (1) an inhabitant of the parish, (2) an adherent of the Church of England, and (3) a taxpayer.[11] Each parish was also to elect two church wardens who were charged with a variety of practical tasks, such as keeping the church in good repair. Repairs were to be paid for by gifts or charges due the church. If these proved to be insufficient, the vestry could levy an additional tax on ". . . *all* and *every* the inhabitants, owners and occupiers of lands, tenements and hereditaments, or any personal estate . . ." and not just Church of England members.[12] So detailed was government control over the affairs of the church that even the dates of key vestry meetings were statutorily prescribed.[13]

The 1704 establishment statute ushered in a swelling flow of enactments in which a colony-wide legislature dealt with the minutiae of church government that today would be resolved by individual church boards. One of the prices paid for intermixture of church and state is the diversion of enormous amounts of government time away from the problems of the general population to the administrative details of the favored institution. As we shall see, this high tide of ecclesiastical legislation began to recede only with the replacement of the Church of England establishment by a general Protestant establishment in the Constitution of 1778 and finally sputtered to an end following enactment of the broad religious freedom provisions of the Constitution of 1790. We must examine the statutes that flowed in the wake of the 1704 law to fully appreciate the intricate web of legislation an established church entails.

The 1704 act was superseded by a 1706 law that continued the Church of England establishment, the endorsement of the Book of Common Prayer and the ultimate authority of the colony-wide lay commissioners.[14] The 1706 act created additional parishes, placed a ceiling on the amount the commissioners could draw from the public treasury to complete church buildings, set the salaries of the rectors of the various parishes and provided the means by which all parish inhabitants could be taxed upon a levy made by two free-holder assessors appointed by the commissioners. Taxpayer recalcitrance could be met by seizure and sale of his goods.[15] The law permitted rectors in parishes with predominantly French populations to read the services in their native language, but it specified the translation of the Book of Common Prayer that must be used.[16]

The smallest detail of church administration seemed to demand statutory attention. If the church wished to establish an auxiliary ministry, called a Chapel of Ease, for parishioners too far from the main building to attend services conveniently, legislative permission was obtained.[17] Church repairs sometimes required legislative authorization.[18] Church land transactions such as buying, selling, renting, and changing the use to which land was put often required legislation authorizing the specific transaction.[19] If a parish grew too populated and a new church and parish needed to be established in part of the old parish territory, legislation was required.[20] Since secular and religious powers were intimately blended and the parish served as the unit for legislative membership during much of the eighteenth century, an act dividing or rearranging a parish to facilitate church service to members had political consequences concerning control of the legislature. Thus statutes dividing parishes also specified the allocation of legislative representatives between the new parish and remnants of the old.[21]

A church that is supported by public funds finds itself competing with secular uses for sometimes scarce resources. A 1722 act set salaries for Church of England ministers and gave priority to such salaries in drawing upon certain revenue sources, such as the duty upon skins and furs. Only another religious expense, the construction of churches, would take precedence over ministerial salaries in using those revenue sources.[22] A 1757 statute shifted funds from building a beacon near Charleston Harbor to completion of the steeple and spire of St. Michael's, for which the appropriated funds had proven to be insufficient. Ironically, the funds received by the church were what today might be called tainted money. The funds were derived from the tax on the sale and importation of slaves and the importation of liquor and other goods from other British colonies.[23] Funding can sometimes subtly influence moral choices as the recipient consciously or unconsciously conforms to the expectations of the grantor. At the very least, the system gave the church a financial stake in the slavery system.

Government control over church financial transactions was sometimes pervasive. A prime source of church revenue was the sale or rental of church pews and annual assessments that were sometimes levied against the owners of those pews. Legislation controlled the authority to install and dispose of pews, the prices that would be charged and who would have priority in the purchase of the pews.[24] Oddly enough, acts of this sort occasionally continued to be passed long after the demise of the establishment of the Church of England. For example, an 1820 act gave authority to the Episcopal Church at Prince George Winyaw to assess pew owners every year, but it stipulated that such tax should not exceed fifteen percent of the pew's value.[25] The church was granted power to bring suit if the pew holder proved uncooperative.[26]

As time went on and the population became more varied, the competition for government fiscal resources more intense, and the relationship with England more strained, the financial support of the church became less often a free ride. A 1768 law did not provide a government appropriation or ear-mark revenue sources for the building of a new parsonage for St. Michael's. Instead it authorized an interest free, three-year loan repayable out of the rents to be charged for new pews. If the church should fail to make timely repayment, the public treasurer was authorized to conduct a sale of the pews.[27]

Establishment of the Church of England not only meant financial support for the church's programs and official endorsement of its beliefs, it also meant that the church was used as an instrument through which government services were dispensed or public conduct with moral implications was regulated. An omnibus 1712 act that redefined the powers of the church commissioners, vestry and wardens, set ministerial salaries and clarified parish boundary lines also established a provincial library and stipulated that it was to be housed in the parsonage at St. Philip's. Conditions under which these books, as well as those in other parochial libraries, could be borrowed, were set by the act.[28] The education function seemed to be a natural extension of the church's responsibility for moral training. Many early eighteenth century schools were founded by the Society for Propagating the Gospel in Foreign Parts.[29] When the government began to assume the responsibility for educating indigent youth by the creation of a commission to receive and administer gifts for educational purposes, the program was coordinated with the concept of an established church by the requirement that not only should the school master be skilled in Latin and Greek but that he also should be an Anglican.[30] The act required instruction not only in grammar, art and science but in the Christian religion.[31]

Just as the educational function was a logical expansion of the church's responsibility for ethical training, the administration of government aid to the indigent was a natural extension of the church's biblical responsibility for care of the poor. In 1712, not long after the law erecting the elaborate machinery of establishment, a statute gave responsibility for raising funds for and distributing aid to the poor to the parish vestries.[32] The vestries were charged with nominating two overseers of the poor, who together with the church wardens would superintend the dissemination of aid. If gifts and fines earmarked for the care of the poor were not sufficient to the need, the vestry could order three respected members of the community to assess the necessary sum. The assessment was to be made ". . . equally upon the estates real and personal of *all* and every the inhabitants, owners and occupiers of lands tenements and hereditaments, or any personal estate, within the several parishes . . . ."[33] It is significant that the tax was to be levied upon "*all* . . . inhabitants owners and occupiers" of property, since this sweeping language included many non-Anglicans who could not, under the relevant statutes, vote for vestry members or other church officials. As noted above, to be eligible to vote in the election of vestrymen, one must be a parish resident, a taxpayer, and member of the Church of England.[34] The slow demise of the vestry involvement in aid to the poor finally culminated in Act No. 2388 of 1826, which vested in the secular commissioners of the poor the remnants of any power over aid to the poor exercised by church vestries.[35]

Another vital administrative function that was delegated to the church early in the eighteenth century was the conduct of elections in the parishes, which were designated the key political subdivisions for electoral and legislative apportionment purposes.[36] Thus, during much of the eighteenth-century period that it enjoyed the status of established church, the Church of England carried out a variety of pivotal governmental roles including (1) the care of the poor, (2) the conduct of elections, and (3) the housing and administration of libraries and education. The Church of England officials who controlled these vital functions were not subject to electoral control by the general non-Anglican population.

NOTES

1. *See* Act No. 225 of 1704, 2 S.C. STATUTES AT LARGE 236-46 (Cooper 1837).

2. Act No. 225 of 1704, 2 S.C. STATUTES AT LARGE 236 (Cooper 1837).

3. Act No. 225 of 1704, 2 S.C. STATUTES AT LARGE 240-41, para. XVI (Cooper 1837).

4. Act No. 225 of 1704, 2 S.C. STATUTES AT LARGE 239-40, para. XIV and XV (Cooper 1837).

5. Act No. 225 of 1704, 2 S.C. STATUTES AT LARGE 246, para. XXXV (Cooper 1837).

6. G. ROGERS, CHURCH AND STATE IN EIGHTEENTH-CENTURY SOUTH CAROLINA 13-15 (1959).

7. *See* F. DALCHO, AN HISTORICAL ACCOUNT OF THE PROTESTANT EPISCOPAL CHURCH IN SOUTH CAROLINA, FROM THE FIRST SETTLEMENT OF THE PROVENCE, TO THE WAR OF REVOLUTION 128-46 (1820); A. SHIPP, HISTORY OF METHODISM IN SOUTH CAROLINA 118-21 (1883); *and see* A. BETTS, HISTORY OF SOUTH CAROLINA METHODISM 24-25 (1952) (asserting that the proceeding was an attempt by the established church to invoke the civil law against Whitfield).

8. Act No. 225 of 1704, 2 S.C. STATUTES AT LARGE 237, para. VI (Cooper 1837).

9. Act No. 225 of 1704, 2 S.C. STATUTES AT LARGE 238, para. VIII (Cooper 1837).

10. Act No. 225 of 1704, 2 S.C. STATUTES AT LARGE 238, para. IX (Cooper 1837).

11. Act No. 225 of 1704, 2 S.C. STATUTES AT LARGE 242, para. XXI-XXIII (Cooper 1837).

12. Act No. 225 of 1704, 2 S.C. STATUTES AT LARGE 245, para. XXXI (Cooper 1837).

13. Act No. 225 of 1704, 2 S.C. STATUTES AT LARGE 244, para. XXX (Cooper 1837).

14. *See* Act No. 256 of 1706, 2 S.C. STATUTES AT LARGE 282 (Cooper 1837). The 1704 act was repealed by Act No. 255 of 1706, 2 S.C. STATUTES AT LARGE 282 (Cooper 1837). The 1704 establishment act had earlier been supplemented by Act No. 241 of 1704, 2 S.C. STATUTES 259 which dealt with the administrative details of the election of vestrymen and wardens and decreed that dissenting congregation ministers retained the right to conduct marriages, christenings and burials. Act No. 241 of 1704, 2 S.C. STATUTES AT LARGE 259 (Cooper 1837).

15. Act No. 256 of 1706, 2 S.C. STATUTES AT LARGE 287, para. XIX (Cooper 1837).

16. Act No. 256 of 1706, 2 S.C. STATUTES AT LARGE 288, para. XXII (Cooper 1837).

17. *See* Act No. 533 of 1731, 3 S.C. STATUTES AT LARGE 304 (Cooper 1838); *See also* Act No. 505 of 1725, 3 S.C. STATUTES AT LARGE 252-53 (Cooper 1838).

18. Act No. 568 of 1734, 3 S.C. STATUTES AT LARGE 376 (Cooper 1838).

19. For example, *see* Act No. 880 of 1759, 7 S.C. STATUTES AT LARGE 84 (McCord 1840) (authorizing St. Michael's to acquire additional land for a parsonage); Act No. 991 of 1770, 7 S.C. STATUTES AT LARGE 93 (McCord 1840) (authorizing St. Philip's to divide some of its glebe land into rental lots); Act No. 904 of 1761, 4 S.C. STATUTES AT LARGE 152 (Cooper 1838) (authorizing St. Bartholomew's to sell inconveniently located glebe land and to use the proceeds to purchase young female slaves for the rector).

20. For example, *see* Act No. 795 of 1751, 7 S.C. STATUTES AT LARGE 79 (McCord 1840) (dividing St. Philip's to establish St. Michael's).

21. For example, *see* Act No. 795 of 1751, 7 S.C. STATUTES AT LARGE 83, para. XVII (McCord 1840); *and see* Act No. 567 of 1734, 3 S.C. STATUTES AT LARGE 374-75 (Cooper 1838).

22. *See* Act No. 460 of 1722, 3 S.C. STATUTES AT LARGE 174 (Cooper 1838).

23. *See* Act No. 861 of 1757, 4 S.C. STATUTES AT LARGE 38-39, para. II (Cooper 1838).

24. *See* Act No. 811 of 1753, 4 S.C. STATUTES AT LARGE 3 (Cooper 1838).

25. *See* Act No. 2246 of 1820, 8 S.C. STATUTES AT LARGE 815, para. XIV (McCord 1840).

26. Act No. 2246 of 1820, 8 S.C. STATUTES AT LARGE 312, 315 para. XV (McCord 1840).

27. *See* Act No. 977 of 1768, 4 S.C. STATUTES AT LARGE 303 (Cooper 1838).

28. *See* Act No. 307 of 1712, 2 S.C. STATUTES AT LARGE 374-75, para. XXI-XXVI (Cooper 1837).

29. Ramage, *Local Government and Free Schools in South Carolina,* 12 JOHNS HOPKINS STUDIES IN HISTORICAL AND POLITICAL SCIENCE 13 (1883).

30. *See* Act No. 290 of 1710, 2 S.C. STATUTES AT LARGE 342 at 345 (Cooper 1837).

31. For a general discussion of the early history of education in South Carolina, *see,* J. UNDERWOOD, THE CONSTITUTION OF SOUTH CAROLINA VOLUME II, THE JOURNEY TOWARD LOCAL SELF-GOVERNMENT 27-32 (1989) [hereinafter cited as II J. UNDERWOOD].

32. Act No. 325 of 1712, 2 S.C. STATUTES AT LARGE 593 (Cooper 1837).

33. Act No. 325 of 1712, 2 S.C. STATUTES AT LARGE 594, para. III (Cooper 1837) (emphasis added).

CHAPTER TWO—NOTES

34. *See* Act No. 256 of 1706, 2 S.C. STATUTES AT LARGE 290, para. XXX (Cooper 1837); *and see* Vestry of St. Luke's Church v. Matthews, 4 S.C. Eq. (4 Des.) 578 (1815).

35. Act No. 2388 of 1826, 6 S.C. STATUTES AT LARGE 283-84 (McCord 1839).

36. *See* Act No. 394 of 1719, 3 S.C. STATUTES AT LARGE 51 (Cooper 1838); *see also* Sixteenth Assembly List, 1 BIOGRAPHICAL DIRECTORY OF THE SOUTH CAROLINA HOUSE OF REPRESENTATIVES 41 (W. Edgar 1974). Several of the parishes were beginning to become election districts with the election of 1717. For a general discussion of the governmental functions of the parish *see* J. UNDERWOOD VOL. II at 16-20, 30.

CHAPTER THREE

RELIGIOUS QUALIFICATIONS FOR PARTICIPATION IN THE POLITICAL PROCESS

Once the major premise is accepted that a particular church and its doctrines furnish the only religious wisdom, it takes just a short logical leap to conclude that only its adherents possess political and governmental wisdom as well. That conclusion is even easier to reach if it would serve practical political goals to exclude from some key element of the political process those who dissent from the official church. This reasoning was embodied in a 1704 act that effectively excluded Protestant dissenters from the Commons House of Assembly.[1] That statute required that all persons elected to the commons who had not taken the sacrament of the Lord's Supper according to the rites of the Church of England in the year preceding their elections had to participate publicly in that ceremony on a Sunday immediately after divine services. A certificate signed by the presiding minister or two credible witnesses had to be submitted to the Speaker in open Assembly as proof that the would-be commons member participated in the rite. An alternate mode of proving allegiances to the church was provided to any Church of England believer who felt that he was not then fit to receive Communion. He could take an oath that he was loyal to the Church of England, was not opposed to the form of the Lord's Supper sacrament, was a regular attender at church and that he would work diligently for the interest of the Church of England in the legislature. The preamble to the act stated that the reason for excluding Protestant dissenters from the legislative halls was ". . . that the admitting of persons of different persuasions and interest in matters of religion . . . hath often caused great contentions and animosities in this Province, and hath very much obstructed publick business . . . ."[2] The measure was not enacted solely in pursuit of doctrinal purity but to fortify factional political power. John Wesley Brinsfield has described the events leading up to passage of the act excluding dissenters from the Assembly.[3] From 1670 to 1700, a compatible balance of power between Anglicans and dissenters existed. This equilibrium began to dissolve when Queen Anne assumed the throne and began to aggressively support the Church of England. Lord John Granville, the Palentine (the leading proprietor), concluded that the two major centers of power should be brought into a more synchronized relationship.[4] These broader, tidal changes combined with attempts by Governor James Moore to squelch his political opponents in the assembly, who were largely dissenters.[5] Moore and his opponents each launched salvos that the other side was trying to monopolize trade with the Indians. The dissenters balked at bankrolling Moore's expedition to quell the Spanish threat from Florida. Moore's successor, Nathaniel Johnson, continued the quarrel and used a parliamentary sleight-of-hand trick to gain passage in 1704 of the act banning from the commons all those who could not certify that they had taken the Lord's Supper according to the rites of the Church of England. Johnson recalled the Commons House of Assembly for a special session and rushed through a vote on the bill before most dissenter members could arrive.[6] This was a clever but unscrupulous tactical ploy but poor long-term strategy, for it furnished much of the rhetorical fuel by which opponents of the measure lobbied in both the provincial legislature and London for its revocation. The hottest coals of rhetoric were heaped on the heads of the bill's proponents by Daniel Defoe. Prior to the blossoming of his career as a novelist, authoring such books as *Robinson Crusoe*, Defoe was a literary sword-for-hire, a master of sarcasm, hyperbole and political theory. He was retained by opponents of the measure to write a pamphlet against it. Of Defoe's several works relating to the cause of liberty in Carolina, the one displaying the best developed analytical framework for freedom of conscience, as well as the most eloquent advocacy, is the *Case of the Protestant Dissenters in Carolina* (1706). Because of its importance, its contents will be described in detail.

Defoe began by describing the liberty of conscience as:

> . . .the only Security any Government can give us for our safe passage thro this World to another. And Liberty of Conscience being a Liberty for every Man to believe what appears to him to be true, and to act pursuant to his Belief in matters relating to another Life, that don't disturb the Publick Peace; tis no wonder, if Men are generally so much more tender of this Branch of Liberty, than they are of any other: Because both the Interest of another World are infinitely more our Concern to secure than the Ease and Satisfaction of the present. . . ."[7]

Defoe observed that liberty of conscience could only be safeguarded if government acted according to stated and fixed rules that did not fluctuate at the convenience of every faction seeking political power. If man was not left free to define his own relationship with the next world his other freedoms in the world would collapse as well. Liberty of conscience was indefeasible. People could not bargain away their own freedom or that of others. Granting a preference for one religion while pretending to give a measure of liberty to other faiths was illusory. No religion, not even the preferred one, could be secure under such a system. The religion that was then favored could find itself in a vulnerable position when the tide of faction changed. Defoe asserted that the only sure security for any religion was ". . . [u]niversal and [a]bsolute [t]oleration . . ." of all peaceful religions.[8] Establishing one religion inspired a new regime, when it took power, to suppress the previously established religion and persecute its adherents. Such persecution, he argued, was contrary to the teaching of Christ and the philosophy of the Protestant Reformation. He analogized intolerance to the spread of a wildfire. Even if it broke out in a remote corner such as Carolina, it could quickly travel to other parts of the Dominion. Excluding Protestant dissenters from the legislature set a dangerous precedent that could be followed in unexpected ways elsewhere.

The ability to sit in the assembly was akin to a property right which had become vested in the dissenters by previous laws that provided no obstacle to their service. Depriving them of the ability to hold legislative office was an attack on their honor and dignity and left them open to further attacks on other rights. Indeed, shortly prior to the passage of the act, mob violence was instigated against prominent dissenter members of the assembly who had opposed the administration's policies. Law enforcement authorities refused to protect the victims from the mob and refused to prosecute those responsible.[9] Such bully-boy tactics pressured the dissenters to leave the colony. This could be done only by sacrificing their economic well-being. Even if the dissenters were not imprisoned, fined or otherwise punished in the traditional sense, it was still punishment to deprive them of a mark of honor and make them uneasy because of opinions they held.[10] Government-induced uneasiness in matters of conscience was persecution as surely as were the cruder forms of torture. Defoe contended that the exclusion act was equivalent to placing a brand on the dissenters. In essence, it made them symbolically wear a sign saying they were not to be trusted.[11] This brand would be a signal to the mob. Since the assembly would then be composed entirely of their political enemies, the full weight of the legislative power could be expected to fall upon them.

Defoe struck up the band for a parade of horribles. If the dissenters could not be trusted to hold legislative office, then they could not be trusted in executive positions. Their right to vote would soon fall. If they were not worthy of serving in the legislature, then why trust them to select legislators?[12] Because of the intimate link between property rights and political rights, their oppressors would not continue to let them enjoy property rights else that be the vehicle by which they could return to political authority. If these rights fell, then why not rob them of the right to marry and have a family?[13]

Defoe noted that the dissenters had not acted as enemies of the Church of England and did not deserve to be treated as such. In 1698 a dissenter, Governor Blake, had encouraged efforts to persuade Anglican ministers to settle in the colony. Many dissenter-legislators had supported this effort as beneficial to the entire community.[14] The dissenters serving in the legislature prior to the exclusion act made no assault on laws favorable to the Church of England. Defoe asserted that dissenters composed two-thirds of the population. It was impractical and unfair to punish such a large segment of the population when they had done no wrong.[15] The generosity of the dissenters to the Church of England was the product of the system of universal tolerance that previously existed. That system should be revived.[16]

Defoe marshaled pragmatic economic arguments that might appeal to the practical men of affairs who might have the influence to obtain repeal of the law.[17] Suppression of the liberty of conscience depressed all varieties of creative energies, including those that led to the formation and propagation of wealth. Many had left Europe to escape religious oppression. The dissenter population, which then composed about two-thirds of the Carolina colonists, included some of the wealthiest and most enterprising and respectable people in the province. Running them out of the colony by holding them up to ridicule and excluding them from the political arena would cause economic dislocation. Further settlement by religious nonconformists would be discouraged.

Defoe presented collective character sketches of the dissenters and their opponents.[18] Many dissenters were models of probity and civic mindedness. Their opponents did not engineer passage of the exclusion act to achieve doctrinal purity in the counsels of government. They seldom attended the Church of England services, and they gave only a nodding glance to its doctrines. They were simply engaged in a maneuver to defeat their political enemies.

Defoe contended that the political climate that made passage of the act possible was created by Governor James Moore and his successor, Nathaniel Johnson. He asserted that Moore stacked the council with his cronies and manipulated the elections of members of the Commons House to achieve a similar result there. When dissenter members sought an investigation into the election irregularities, means were sought to discredit and intimidate them. A mob was stirred up to attack them. When the authorities failed to prosecute the rioters, the dissenters demanded an investigation into that as well. When dissenter-legislators opposed providing funds for a gubernatorial expedition against the Spanish at St. Augustine, the need to quell the dissenters seemed all the more acute. Defoe even accused the proponents of the exclusion bill of being behind the rejection of the Fundamental Constitutions as the permanent basic law. A nebulous constitutional state presumably made political manipulation easier.[19] He noted that the legislative system of the Fundamental Constitutions contained an intricate system of checks and balances that would have made the stealthy passage of a law like the exclusion act difficult.[20]

Those who thought that the Church of England would benefit from these machinations were mistaken. Here Defoe attacked not just the bill excluding dissenters from the legislature but the general blending of secular and religious power. Creating an established Church appeared to place that entity on a lofty plane, but once secular and religious powers had become entangled, the political power, amplified by church support, someday could be turned against the church. He noted that ministers beholden to the government for their positions and salaries were vulnerable to intimidation and reprisal when they spoke out against government policy. He noted that the church had already lost power as the result of the establishment, since the 1704 establishment act had placed significant power over church affairs in the colony-wide lay commission.[21]

The political guile of the proponents of the act would bring about their own economic destruction. He portrayed a wasteland that would exist if dissenters fled Carolina because of religious oppression. He stated:

> When the Hands are gone, that us'd to manure the Land, Clean the Rice, and graze the Cattle; and when the Merchants are remov'd, that dealt in Furs, Pitch, Tar, Corn, Slaves and Negroes, with other profitable Commodities, what will Proprietorships, Signiorys, Baronys and Colonys be worth? And what will become of the Revenue of Industry, that arises from the very Management of their several Branches of Trade?[22]

Defoe noted that the Fundamental Constitutions contained religious toleration provisions that were designed to avoid such devastating economic consequences.[23] Despite their promulgation of the Fundamental Constitutions, the proprietors were guilty of self-serving duplicity. Defoe contended that the proprietors had supported religious oppression in England to fortify themselves in power but had expressed religious toleration to attract and retain settlers in Carolina.[24] The guarantee of liberty should be permanent rather than an opportunistic contrivance used to achieve political or economic ends. The Charters from the King gave such permanent guarantees of religious liberty. By promulgating the Fundamental Constitutions the proprietors represented to potential settlers that they endorsed such guarantees.

The Charters and the Fundamental Constitutions formed a social contract with the people that could not be contravened by mere legislation, especially that passed by a rump-faction of the assembly. The Charters had granted Carolina to the proprietors subject to the condition that universal religious tolerance be observed. A failure by the proprietors and their agents to observe these conditions could work a revocation of the grant. The settlers were third-party beneficiaries of the Charter agreement between the King and the proprietors. Their legal standing was enhanced further by reliance on the representations made in promises of religious freedom contained in the Fundamental Constitutions. The Constitutions were an express contract between the proprietors and the people. Even though the Fundamental Constitutions had not been accepted by the people *en masse* in a referendum, they had been accepted by each individual colonist as a condition of settlement. This agreement was as binding upon the proprietors as upon the settlers.[25]

The passage of the 1704 act excluding dissenters from the Commons House of Assembly cast doubt on the legitimacy of the government and the laws it enacted. Defoe pointed out that the Charter required popular consent to the passage of the laws. The March 4, 1663, Charter stated that new laws could be made only ". . . with the advice, assent and approbation of the Freemen of the said Provence, or of the greater part of them, or of their Delegates or Deputies . . . ."[26] Since, left to their own unfettered choice, colonists, most of whom were dissenters, might have chosen dissenter representatives, the exclusion of dissenters from the assembly cast doubt on the legitimacy of the legislative work product.[27]

In addition to such concrete legal arguments questioning the validity of the 1704 exclusion law and other legislation passed by assemblies elected under it, the general philosophy of the exclusion act was incompatible with the early drafts of the Fundamental Constitutions and the Charters. Those basic documents were founded on the major premise that civil peace was best achieved by a broad tolerance of a variety of religions, but the 1704 exclusion act sought to achieve tranquility by disqualifying nonconformists from meaningful participation in government.[28]

On March 13, 1705, a merchant from Carolina presented a petition to the House of Lords in London seeking invalidation of the exclusion act.

The petition argued that the law was unconstitutional since it contravened Charter requirements in the following respects:

(1) Laws had to be passed with the advice and consent of the freemen or their delegates. This law was passed by only a fragment of the legislature that met prior to the publicly announced time for reconvening the legislature. In addition, many of those voting for the law had been improperly elected in a 1703 ballot at which unqualified persons, such as slaves, had been permitted to vote.

(2) Laws had to be consistent with good reason and the laws and customs of England. A law disqualifying the majority of the population from office was inherently unreasonable.

(3) By fostering such a law contrary to the Charter, the proprietors assumed the role of the sovereign. Under the Charter, sovereign allegiance was due only to the King.

The petition argued that many colonists had settled in Carolina to escape religious oppression and that they had been induced to do so by the religious freedom provisions of the Charters and the 1669 Fundamental Constitutions. If it were allowed to stand, the 1704 law would amount to a breach of faith.

In response, the House of Lords sent an address to Queen Anne endorsing the petition. The address accepted the petition's contentions that the exclusion act was contrary to the Charter and the customs and laws of England. The House of Lords also listed pragmatic reasons for overturning the exclusion law. The colony would become a commercial leper. No one would want to trade with it. The new settlers necessary for increasing the economic vigor of the state would be discouraged from migrating. On a loftier plane, the address argued that the exclusion law might even encourage atheism. Presumably this meant that using religion in such a cynical political ploy might discredit all religion. Both the petition and the address also criticized the other major 1704 religious statute, that which established the Church of England. They argued that the law undermined ecclesiastical authority by placing crucial power over church affairs in the lay commissioners rather than the bishops.

The Queen responded to the petition and address with majestic ambiguity. She stated:

> I thank the House for laying these matters so plainly before me. I am very sensible of what great consequence the plantations are to England and will do all in my power to relieve my subjects in Carolina, and to protect them in their just rights.[29]

As vague as it was, the Queen's response added to the weight of opinion against the exclusion law. The law was repealed in a 1706 South Carolina statute and the dissenters resumed their role as a vital political force.[30]

If the repeal of the act excluding Protestant dissenters from the Assembly demonstrated growth of a consensus behind broader participation in the political process, that consensus had a decidedly Christian character. A 1759 law went even further and specified that not just Christianity but *Protestant* Christianity was an essential qualification for voting for or serving in the General Assembly.[31] The exclusive, almost private-club nature of the political processes is seen by examining the full list of prerequisites for serving in or voting for members of the General Assembly. A voter had to be (1) free, (2) white, (3) male, (4) a Protestant, (5) twenty-one years of age, (6) a resident of the province for at least a year prior to the issuance of the writ of election, (7) owner of a freeheld estate in a settled plantation, or one hundred acres of unsettled land, or a freehold estate in houses or town lots of at least sixty pounds. The qualifications for serving as a member of the Assembly were similar, including the need to be an adherent of Protestant Christianity. Since it was considered an essential attribute of a political leader that he knew the value of property and was not prone to lavish spending and high taxes, the property qualifications for Assembly membership were even higher than for a voter. The member had to have "a settled plantation or a freehold estate of at least five hundred acres of land and twenty slaves over and above what he shall owe . . ." or have one thousand pounds money in houses, town lots or other land over and above his debts.[32] Earlier laws passed from 1716 to 1759 usually stipulated that a voter had to be Christian, but did not explicitly require acceptance of Protestant doctrine. These earlier laws normally did not contain a concrete religious test for Assembly membership such as that in the 1759 act. However, they usually did contain an oath in which the taker certified himself as qualified for public service by a pledge to God.[33]

A 1745 law required that the oath in which an elected legislator certified to his qualifications prior to assuming his seat be sworn on the "holy evangelist." This apparently caused difficulties to some Protestant dissenters who were conscientiously opposed to swearing on the "holy evangelist." Corrective action was taken in a 1747 statute which limited the fact that the form of the oath apparently kept ". . . many Protestant dissenters in the Province of good estates and sufficient abilities . . ." from service in the assembly.[34] The 1747 law noted that many Protestant dissenters had borne the burdensome and unprofitable tasks of citizenship such as jury service as readily as had persons of other faiths and thus should not be barred from service in the legislature because the form of oath collided with their conscientious scruples. Accordingly, they were permitted to qualify themselves by taking the oath ". . . according to the form of [their] profession . . . ."[35]

Despite this liberalization, the custom of swearing on the "Holy Evangelist" occasionally continued to frustrate the people's choice of representatives when those selected belonged to certain sects, such as the Quakers. In 1766 Samuel Wylly (or Wyly), a respected Quaker duly elected to represent St. Mark's Parish, was denied his seat because of his conscientious objections to taking the oath. The Journals of the Commons House of Assembly for January 25, 1766 contain the following entry:

> Samuel Wylly Esquire, returned a Member to serve for the Parish of Saint Mark, attended at the Door, and being called in, Mr. Speaker acquainted him of his being so returned, and desired to know of him [if] he was willing to qualify himself as a member of this House. He answered in the affirmative.
>
> Ordered that Sir John Colleton, a member of this House, and a Justice of the Peace, do administer the oath appointed by the Election [law] to Mr. Wylly.
>
> But Mr. Wylly being one of the People called Quakers, declared he could not take the Oath on the Holy Evangelists without doing a violence to his conscience.
>
> Upon which the ninth Clause of the Election Act was Read.
>
> Resolved that as Mr. Wylly will not take the Oath appointed by the Election Law to qualify himself upon the Holy Evangelists, he cannot be admitted to take his seat as a Member of this House.

Pursuant to the resolution, the Quaker was denied his seat.[36]

The election laws' insistence upon Christianity as a qualification for service in the assembly obviously would seem to exclude Jews. However, in the 1770's, on the threshold of the Revolution, less attention was paid to such details as colonists attempted to rally a united front behind protest against British rule. Frances Salvador, a young Jew of Portuguese ancestry who had migrated from England, served in the South Carolina legislative body that declared independence from British rule. What appeared to be a promising career of public service was cut short by his death in the Revolutionary War.[37]

Despite such occasional breaches in the religious wall surrounding legislative membership, such public service remained a largely Christian enclave. Religious test oaths long had done damage to harmony in the political community and excluded talented people from public service. The notorious English Test Act of 1677 disqualified Papists from sitting in Parliament. Before taking a seat in Parliament, a member had to take an oath that he did not believe in adoration of the Virgin Mary or transubstantiation of the bread and water in the Lord's Supper into the body and blood of Christ. Failure to take the oath not only resulted in a declaration that the member's seat was vacant but in disqualification from other public offices as well as inability to sue in court, serve as guardian of a child or executor of an estate or to receive a legacy or deed of gift.[38]

Perhaps it was revulsion at the wedge such laws, and their South Carolina equivalents, drove in the political community that prompted Charles Pinckney to make proposals at the Federal Constitutional Convention that no religious requirements be imposed for service as a federal officer. On August 20, 1787, he suggested a section that declared that "[n]o religious test or qualification shall ever be annexed to any oath of office under the authority of the U.S."[39] On August 30, he moved the adoption of refined language which read "but no religious test shall ever be required as a qualification to any office or public trust under the authority of the U. States."[40] With slight modification this is the wording now found in Article VI, section 3 of the United States Constitution.[41] We shall note later, however, that the Constitution of South Carolina retained a religious test in the late twentieth century.

Oddly enough, not only were practitioners of disfavored religions disqualified from legislative service but sometimes so were the paragons of the favored religions. The 21st article of the Constitution of 1778 stated:

> And whereas the Ministers of the Gospel are by their profession dedicated to the Service of God and the Cure of Souls, and ought not be diverted from the great duties of their Function; therefore no Minister of the Gospel, or public preacher, of any religious persuasion, while he continues in the Exercise of his pastoral function, and for two years after, shall be eligible as Governor, Lieutenant Governor, a Member of the Senate, House of Representatives or Privy Council in this State.

When this proposal surfaced in 1776, the Reverend William Tennent, an outspoken critic of the Anglican establishment, assailed it as designed to exclude prophets of change such as himself. However, the publicly announced justification for the measure was that it would serve to remove fractious quarrels based on religious grounds from legislative debate.[42] Later, the Reverend Richard Furman, a noted Baptist pastor and advocate of religious freedom opposed such ministerial disqualification as depriving the state of the legislative services of many of its able and most experienced citizens.[43] Furman opposed the retention in the Constitution of 1790 of the ban against ministers serving in high government positions. However, the disqualification was retained in the 1790 Constitution as Article I, section 23. Oddly enough, the rule did not prevent Furman from serving as a delegate to and taking a leading role in the Constitutional Convention of 1790. The convention records list both Furman and the Reverend Doctor Henry Purcell as delegates from St. Philip's and St. Michael's parishes in Charleston. Several other ministers are also listed among the convention delegates.[44]

Many years later, in 1978, the United States Supreme Court examined the historical origins and modern status of laws disqualifying the clergy from public office holding.[45] In *McDaniel v. Paty,* the Court considered a Tennessee constitutional provision, with strikingly similar wording to the 1778 South Carolina standard, which disqualified ministers from service in the state legislature. This rule had been incorporated by reference in a statute setting qualifications for delegates to the state constitutional convention. McDaniel, a Baptist pastor, was a candidate to be a convention delegate. An opponent, Paty, sued to ban him from the election, and ultimately after his election, to disqualify him from taking his seat. McDaniel contended that the rule disqualifying him was unconstitutional under the First Amendment Free Exercise of Religion Clause since it punished him for practicing his faith by being a minister. The state high court sustained the statute but the United States Supreme Court declared it to be unconstitutional. In doing so the Court examined the history of clergy disqualification. It noted that several of the original states, including South Carolina, followed the English practice of disqualifying ministers from some political offices.[46] Six new states adopted similar provisions as they joined the union. The Court observed that the English disqualification rule was designed to prevent dual office holding and the undue concentration of power that would arise if the same individual served in both the Parliament and a religious convocation. It was further designed to insulate Parliament from undue influence by the King who was thought to control the clergy by virtue of his power to dispense benefits to them.[47]

In this country, the primary reason for clergy disqualification in late eighteenth-century state constitutions was to enhance separation of church and state by reducing the political influence of the clergy. This was especially important in states like South Carolina that moved in 1778 from having the Church of England as the official church to a general Protestant Christian establishment, and moved farther in 1790 to have no established church whatsoever.[48] The Court examined the attitudes of those who were influential nationally in developing the separation of church and state philosophy that undergirds the First Amendment. The Court examined the views of Thomas Jefferson and concluded that while he had initially favored such clergy disqualification as a means of reducing the influence of the clergy on government, which had become greater than he liked under the establishment, that he ultimately concluded that such rules were no longer necessary as the clergy's dominating influence waned. James Madison opposed such disqualification as punishing the ministers for the exercise of one right (religious freedom) by barring them from pursuing another right (seeking public office).[49] At the time of the *McDaniel* case South Carolina no longer had a ministerial disqualification rule and Tennessee was the only state which retained such a standard.[50]

The Court concluded that even if the disqualification rule had at one time been justified as a means of effectuating the separation of church and state, such a need was no longer present. The primary remaining influence of the bar on clergy office holding was to deny ministers their right of free exercise of religion. The Court observed that ". . . the free exercise of religion unquestionably encompasses the right to preach, proselyte, and perform other similar religious functions, or, in other words, to be a minister of the type McDaniel was found to be."[51] Freedom of belief is absolute. Freedom of religious conduct is less sweeping. Being a minister involves conduct as well as belief. However, such conduct should be punished only if it jeopardizes a state interest of the highest order, such as preventing violence. No such interest was present to sustain Tennessee's provision.[52]

Despite the demise of the rule barring ministers from public offices, the other form of religious test, the requirement that certain beliefs be espoused before a person could be a voter or an office holder, has maintained a presence, although a less restrictive one, in the Constitution of South Carolina. Although the Constitution of 1776 was too preoccupied with listing grievances against England to set elaborate voter and officeholder qualifications, the 1778 Constitution focused on religious prerequisites for holding public office as part of its shift from a Church of England to a general Protestant Christian establishment.[53] Article 3 required that the governor, lieutenant governor and members of the privy council be ". . . [a]ll of the Protestant Religion." The 12th Article stipulated that ". . . no person shall be eligible to a seat in the said Senate, unless he be of the Protestant religion . . . ." Similarly, Article 13 required members of the House of Representatives to be Protestants. The standards for being a voter were less denominationally specific. Article 13 required that an elector be one ". . . who acknowledges the Being of a God, and believes in a future State of Rewards and Punishments . . . ." This harkened back to the requirements set by the Fundamental Constitutions for being a free man and holding positions of honor in the colony. The 1778 Constitution did not require the exclusion of Jews and Catholics from the electorate so long as they accepted the beliefs stipulated. However, the state clung to the old belief that no one could be a civilized person, qualified to participate in the political community, who denied the divinity of God and a judgmental afterlife. The 1790 Constitution was more liberal due to the influence of the recently adopted federal constitution which forbade religious test oaths for federal officials in

Article VI, section 3. The Bill of Rights to the United States Constitution was going through the process of ratification by the states at the time the South Carolina Constitution of 1790 was adopted, and the generous spirit of the First Amendment's religious clauses may have influenced formation of the state document. Article VIII of the 1790 Constitution contained a strong guarantee of the free exercise of religion, and the voter and officeholder qualifications did not require acceptance of specific religious beliefs. The oath of office set forth in Article IV did not end with the traditional "so help me God." The first of the post-Civil War Constitutions, the 1865 Constitution adopted during the Presidential Reconstruction era, contained no concrete religious test for either voters or officeholders, but the Article V provision specifying the oath to be taken by officials did return to the customary "so help me God" language.

The 1868 Constitution was adopted during the time of the more radical Congressional Reconstruction by a convention composed primarily of blacks and nonnative whites.[54] The 1868 document contained strong guarantees of religious freedom in Article 1, section 9, and a prohibition of government establishment of religion in Article 1, section 10. No religious test was required of voters. However, Article 3, section 3 decreed that "[n]o person shall be elected Governor who denies the existence of the Supreme Being. . . ." This provision was adopted after a long and bruising debate. The philosophy of the proponents of the provision was well expressed in eloquent hyperbole by R. H. Cain. He stated that:

> I hardly believe even the gentlemen who have argued the question on the other side are prepared to drag God out of the Constitution of the State. I think it highly necessary that persons occupying prominent public positions should certainly have a belief in the existence of an overruling power. If we take away this idea, we snap the foundations of our Government. It seems to me, such a precedent would be dangerous to reason and justice, and dangerous to society at large. Take God out of the Government, and we shall have anarchy, bloodshed, and crime of every class and every kind stalking abroad at noon-day and at midnight. There will be no security for society, no security for the sacred relationship of life, no security of law, no security anywhere. We shall have midnight assassinations. An individual who disbelieves in the existence of a Supreme Being is a dangerous man in the

> community, and into whose hands the people should not intrust their interests. If a man fear not God, he cares little for mankind.
>
> . . . .
>
> I know it has been said by some gentlemen on the floor that this is not necessary. One gentleman from Charleston said it was unconstitutional. *I think this idea of the existence of God was before there ever was any Constitution. The existence of God seems to take priority.*[55]

In other words, the constitution may be the fundamental law, but God's rule is even more fundamental. Any attempt to overrule or ignore it is bound to fail.

Those opposing the measure relied on a variety of arguments including:

(1) The standard would be impossible to enforce unless election officials resorted to mind-reading or highly intrusive tactics. Would a committee have to be formed to question candidates on their beliefs?[56]

(2) The proposal violated religious freedom and constituted a test oath contrary to Article VI, section 3, of the United States Constitution. Even though Article VI, section 3 refers only to offices under the United States, the opponents of the Supreme Being provision apparently believed it expresses a broad principle applicable to the states as well as the federal government.[57]

The advocates of the measure responded that it did not constitute a religious test oath violative of Article VI, section 3. A test oath requires acceptance of specific beliefs or adherence to a particular denomination. This provision does neither.[58]

(3) There are many views of the nature of a Supreme Being. The provision might force conformity to a particular concept of Supreme Being. After making these arguments, R. C. De Large said:

> I am not disposed, however, to have an infidel hold the position of Governor of this State. But whilst this is my individual opinion, I am not prepared to say a religious test should be incorporated into the Constitution of the State.[59]

The difficulty in ascertaining who did and who did not believe in a Supreme Being apparently caused some changes in the wording from that originally proposed. One early draft stated "[n]o person shall be eligible to the office of Governor who does not profess a belief in the existence of the Supreme Being. . . ."[60]

This language could have required either that the candidate affirmatively avow an existence of a Supreme Being or perhaps even that interrogation be conducted to determine his true beliefs that may be contrary to what he claims they are. These concerns apparently led to motions to strike out the words "does not profess" and to substitute "denies."[61] This wording would avoid the necessity of organizing an inquisition into the true beliefs of one who may secretly deny the existence of God. Those openly proclaiming the non-existence of a Supreme Being would be barred from the governorship.[62]

The requirement that no one can be eligible to be governor who denies the existence of a Supreme Being has been retained in the current constitution as Article IV, section 2. This standard has been extended to apply to other offices in Article VI, section 2, of the present Constitution. It states that "[n]o person who denies the existence of the Supreme Being shall hold any office under this Constitution." Similar language was found in Article 14, section 6 of the 1868 Constitution.[63] The phrase "any office" could apply to any public position no matter how low or lofty. Even though Article VI, section 2, does not contain an explicit listing of the offices to which it applies, the overall subject matter of Article VI is suggestive. It deals with office-holding standards for positions running the gamut of state officialdom from the governor and other state-wide constitutional officer the attorney-general and secretary of state, to members of the General Assembly, to local constables. Article VI also contains at section 5 an oath that must be taken by all offices and members of the bar before embarking on their duties. This oath ends with the phrase "[s]o help me God." Thus religious standards survived in the constitution in the late twentieth century. However, they may not survive unchallenged.

In *Torcaso v. Watkins*[64] the United States Supreme Court was confronted with a challenge to a Maryland provision which bore strong resemblance to the South Carolina Supreme Being requirement but which also differed from it somewhat in language and context. Article 37 of the Maryland Declaration of Rights stated that:

> [N]o religious test ought ever to be required as a qualification for any office of profit or trust in this State, other than a declaration of belief in the existence of God. . . .[65]

The Maryland provision's use of the phrase "a declaration of belief" could be interpreted to require an affirmative statement avowing a belief in God, whereas the South Carolina provision might be construed to disqualify the candidate who openly volunteers the information that he does not believe in a Supreme Being. As we shall see, however, the Supreme Court's opinion invalidating the Maryland rule did not focus upon the possibility that the provision affirmatively required an avowal of a belief in God but instead was based on broad reasoning that religious tests for public officeholders deny the free exercise of religion to those who seek to serve the public. Indeed, the South Carolina provision might be even more vulnerable to constitutional attack than the Maryland rule since it demands belief in a Supreme Being, whereas the Maryland rule requires belief in a God who may or may not be considered supreme by the oath taker. At any rate, the Supreme Court used broad reasoning that would seem to be applicable to all forms of religious test oaths as being contrary to the First Amendment of the United States Constitution.

Torcaso was appointed to be a notary public but was denied that position when he refused to avow a belief in God. He brought suit challenging the requirement. The Supreme Court concluded that the provision deviated from the neutral position a government must maintain in matters of religion in that it had the purpose and effect of denying office to those who did not accept a particular religious belief.[66] The Court emphasized the coercive nature of the oath requirement when it said that "[t]he power and authority of the State of Maryland thus is put on the side of one particular sort of believers — those who are willing to say they believe in 'the existence of God.'" The Court acknowledges that there was much historical precedent for religious test oaths, but that many people fled from England and Europe to escape such oppression, and that the test oath had long been an anathema to our constitutional traditions.[67] The Court summarized its conclusions by stating the following:

> We repeat and again reaffirm that neither a State nor the Federal Government can constitutionally force a person "to profess a belief or disbelief in any religion." Neither can constitutionally pass laws or impose requirements

> which aid all religions as against non-believers, and neither can aid those religions based on a belief in the existence of God as against those religions founded on different beliefs.[68]

In reaching these conclusions the Court rejected arguments that the Maryland oath requirement did not punish anyone for his beliefs since it applied only to those who had voluntarily elected to pursue public office. The Court stated that "[t]he fact, however, that a person is not compelled to hold public office cannot possibly be an excuse for barring him from office by state-imposed criteria forbidden by the Constitution."[69] The Court did not specifically rely on this point, but it might also be argued that it is inappropriate to deny a person one right (to seek public office) upon the condition that he compromise another right (freedom of conscience). If the office had been an elective position, it might also have been argued that the oath restricted the range of choice available to the voters.

The reader will recall that in the 1868 convention some delegates had argued that the proposed Supreme Being requirement for the governorship was violative of the anti-test oath provision of Article VI, section 3 of the federal Constitution. He apparently believed that the federal rule applied to the states even though it referred only to offices under the authority of the United States. In the *Torcaso* case, the Supreme Court refused to reach the question of whether Article VI, section 3, applied to state as well as federal positions since it had found the Maryland provision contrary to the First Amendment.

The South Carolina provision would seem to be equally offensive to the First Amendment. As noted above, the Court in *Torcaso* observed that the Maryland provision had the invalid purpose and effect of preferring a particular set of religious beliefs. The South Carolina provision would seem to have a similar purpose and effect. B. F. Randolph, a delegate to the 1868 convention, and one of the most active participants in the debate on the Supreme Being provision, seemed to regard the provision as an endorsement of Christian doctrine. He said:

> I believe we are a Christian People. We all, as a people, believe in the existence of a Supreme Being.[70]

No secular purpose appears to have been offered in justification of the proposal. Many years later, in *Lemon v. Kurtzmen*,[71] the United States Supreme Court announced that an invalid establishment of religion could be found if a state law either had a purpose of advancing religion, or the primary effect of aiding religion, or if it resulted in the entanglement of church and state power structures through such means as the government conducting surveillance of religion. A test oath would seem to be the ultimate form of surveillance.

In the spring of 1990, Herb Silverman, a College of Charleston mathematics professor, announced his intention of running for governor to challenge the validity of the Article IV, section 2, Supreme Being rule.[72] James Ellisor of the State Election Commission commented on the challenge by noting that "[i]f the man hadn't said anything (about being an atheist), he could have run and nobody would have known." In a sense, this observation underscores a criticism of test oaths made by one of the framers of the United States Constitution, Oliver Ellsworth. He said:

> In short, test-laws are utterly ineffectual: they are no security at all; because men of loose principles will, by an external compliance, evade them. If they exclude any persons, it will be honest men, men of principle, who will rather suffer an injury, than act contrary to the dictates of their consciences . . .[73]

Later, the State Election Commission concluded that the Supreme Being rule would not disqualify a properly nominated candidate from running for office but would become applicable only if he were elected. Commissioner William De Pass said:

> His lack of a belief in a supreme being at this moment does not disqualify him from running if he is properly nominated.[74]

Commission Executive Director James Ellisor added that "[t]he requirement does not come into play until he is elected and inaugurated."[75] At the very least, however, the mere existence of the provision would seem to chill the candidacy of those who are not believers in God as a Supreme Being. In addition, it would send a partisan message to voters that such persons are not to be trusted.[76]

The Constitution of 1895 in its current form contains no religious qualifications for voters as distinguished from officeholders. However, in its original form the Constitution of 1895 contained a provision in Article II, the Right of Suffrage, which granted ministers a preference, in the form of accelerated satisfaction of the durational residency requirement that must be met to qualify as a voter. The normal durational residency standard found in Article II, section 4, was two years. A proviso to section 4 stated:

> That ministers in charge of an organized church and teachers of public schools shall be entitled to vote after six months residence in the State, otherwise qualified.

There is no reason to believe that ministers would become knowledgeable about local issues and candidates at any faster rate than the average person. In addition, such vague language as "organized church" gave plenty of maneuver room for subjective, prejudicial interpretation by registration officials. The provision is no longer present in the constitution.

Religious qualifications for voters and public officials were hallmarks of the era of the established church, but the test oath in the diluted form of the required belief in a Supreme Being survived long after the death of the establishment. As injurious as such requirements could be to harmony in the political community, other elements of the establishment, such as taxing the public at large for the benefit of one religion, the inability of non-Anglican congregations to incorporate and own property except indirectly through trustees, and doubt cast on the legitimacy of marriages performed by dissenter clergymen, affected the daily lives of the majority of the population more directly. Some Anglicans began to chaff at the heavy hand of government controlling the fate of the church. It was resentment of these conditions, and the need to unify the population for the Revolutionary struggle with England, that led to the decline of the establishment.

We must now trace the influence of these factors fueling the opposition to the establishment and bringing about its eventual death. Disestablishment proceeded in two phases: (1) the replacement in the Constitution of 1778 of the Church of England establishment by a general Protestant establishment, and (2) the removal of any formal establishment and the adoption of broad religious freedom provisions in the Constitution of 1790. The first phase achieved equality among Protestant denominations. The second phase gained legal parity for the Catholic and Jewish faiths and others outside the dominant Protestant tradition.

NOTES

1. *See* Act No. 222 of 1704, 2 S.C. STATUTES AT LARGE 232 (Cooper 1837).

2. Act No. 222 of 1704, 2 STATUTES AT LARGE 232 (Cooper 1837).

3. *See* J. BRINSFIELD at 14-37. An earlier law, Act No. 202 of 1703, 2 S.C. STATUTES AT LARGE 196-97 (Cooper 1837), had chilled political and religious discourse by disqualifying from "...employments, ecclesiastical, civil or military..." anyone who had made a profession of the Christian religion but had denied the existence of the Holy Trinity or denied that there is only one God or that Christianity is the true religion and that the Bible is divinely inspired.

4. J. BRINSFIELD at 18-19; *see also* M. SIRMANS, COLONIAL SOUTH CAROLINA, A POLITICAL HISTORY 1663-1763 76-89 (1966).

5. J. BRINSFIELD at 19-24.

6. J. BRINSFIELD at 19-24.

7. D. DEFOE, THE CASE OF THE PROTESTANT DISSENTERS IN CAROLINA 3-4 (1706) [hereinafter cited as D. DEFOE].

8. D. DEFOE at 4.

9. D. DEFOE at 8.

10. D. DEFOE 8-9.

11. D. DEFOE at 9.

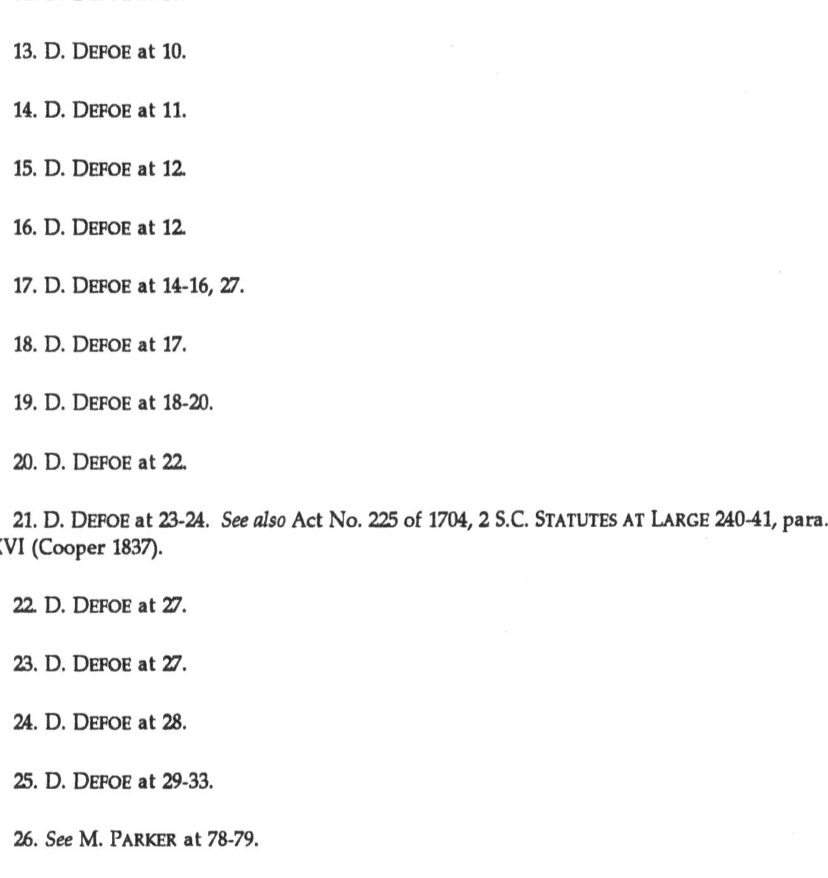

12. D. DEFOE at 10.

13. D. DEFOE at 10.

14. D. DEFOE at 11.

15. D. DEFOE at 12.

16. D. DEFOE at 12.

17. D. DEFOE at 14-16, 27.

18. D. DEFOE at 17.

19. D. DEFOE at 18-20.

20. D. DEFOE at 22.

21. D. DEFOE at 23-24. *See also* Act No. 225 of 1704, 2 S.C. STATUTES AT LARGE 240-41, para. XVI (Cooper 1837).

22. D. DEFOE at 27.

23. D. DEFOE at 27.

24. D. DEFOE at 28.

25. D. DEFOE at 29-33.

26. *See* M. PARKER at 78-79.

27. D. DEFOE at 33-35.

28. D. DEFOE at 37.

29. The petition, address and the Queen's response are available at the South Carolina Department of Archives and History on microfilm in Governor Archdale's Papers, 1690-1706. *See also* J. BRINSFIELD at 22-32.

30. *See* Act No. 255 of 1706, 2 S.C. STATUTES AT LARGE 281 (Cooper 1837).

CHAPTER THREE—NOTES

31. *See* Act No. 885 of 1759, 4 S.C. STATUTES AT LARGE 99, para. I-III (Cooper 1837).

32. Act No. 885 of 1759, 4 S.C. STATUTES AT LARGE 99, para. III (Cooper 1837).

33. *See* Act No. 365 of 1716, 2 S.C. STATUTES AT LARGE 683, 688, para. XX (Cooper 1837) (Assembly membership qualifications did not specifically require acceptance of Christianity, but voter qualifications did stipulate Christianity, and Assembly members had to swear on the holy evangelist that they met the property ownership standards); *and see* Act No. 373 of 1717, 3 S.C. STATUTES AT LARGE 4, para. V (Cooper 1838) (requirement that each member prior to taking his seat must take an oath "on the holy evangelists or according to the form of his profession..." ending with the pledge "[s]o help me God"). *See also* Act No. 394 of 1718-19, 3 S.C. STATUTES AT LARGE 52, para. X (Cooper 1838); Act No. 446 of 1721, 3 S.C. STATUTES AT LARGE 137, para. IX (Cooper 1838).

34. *See* Act No. 746 of 1747, 3 S.C. STATUTES AT LARGE 692 (Cooper 1838) and Act No. 730 of 1745, 3 S.C. STATUTES AT LARGE 657, para. III (Cooper 657).

35. Act No. 746 of 1747, 3 S.C. STATUTES AT LARGE 693 (Cooper 1838).

36. *See* JOURNALS OF THE COMMONS HOUSE OF ASSEMBLY 1766, 50, entry for Saturday the 25th day of January 1766; *see also* C. WOODMASON, THE CAROLINA BACKCOUNTRY ON THE EVE OF THE REVOLUTION 7 n.7 (Hooker ed. 1953).

37. The commentators are in disagreement as to the precise time of his legislative service and how much of that was in the Commons House, The Provincial (Revolutionary) Assembly and the first State Assembly. He appears to have served between 1774-1776. *See* I. SLOAN, THE JEWS IN AMERICA 1621-1970 3-4 (1971) [hereinafter I. SLOAN]; R. ST. JOHN at 75; I. GOLDBERG, (pseud. R. LEARSI), THE JEWS IN AMERICA, A HISTORY 33-34 (1954) [hereinafter R. LEARSI]; L. LEVINGER, HISTORY OF THE JEWS IN THE UNITED STATES at 94 (1952); B. ELZAS, THE JEWS OF SOUTH CAROLINA FROM THE EARLIEST TIMES TO THE PRESENT 68-67 at 84 n. 21 (1905); and C. REZNIKOFF, THE JEWS OF CHARLESTON 34-40 (1950) [hereinafter cited as C. REZNIKOFF].

38. 30 Charles II St. 2, VIII STATUTES AT LARGE (English) 427 (1677) (Pickering).

39. *See* II M. FARRAND, RECORDS OF THE FEDERAL CONVENTION OF 1787 342 (1911) [hereinafter cited as II M. FARRAND].

40. II M. FARRAND at 468.

41. *See*, Ulmer, *Charles Pinckney: Father of the Constitution?* 10 S.C.L.Q. 225, 243 (1958).

42. *See* J. BRINSFIELD at 114.

43. *See* J. ROGERS, RICHARD FURMAN, LIFE AND LEGACY 70 (1985) and A BIOGRAPHY OF RICHARD FURMAN 20 (H. Cook, ed. 1913) (based on a manuscript by Wood Furman).

44. JOURNAL OF THE CONSTITUTIONAL CONVENTION OF SOUTH CAROLINA, May 10, 1790 - June 3, 1790, 1-6.

45. McDaniel v. Paty, 435 U.S. 618, 98 S. Ct. 1322, 55 L. Ed. 2d 593 (1978).

46. *McDaniel*, 435 U.S. 622-23 citing I A. STOKES, CHURCH AND STATE IN THE UNITED STATES 622-23 (1950).

47. *McDaniel*, 435 U.S. at 622.

48. *See* S.C. CONST. OF 1778, art. 38 and S.C. CONST. OF 1790, art. VIII.

49. *McDaniel*, 435 U.S. at 623-24.

50. *McDaniel*, 435 U.S. at 625.

51. *McDaniel*, 435 U.S. at 626.

52. *McDaniel*, 435 U.S. at 627-28.

53. *See* S.C. CONST. of 1778 art. 38 (prescribes the system of Protestant establishment). *See also* Article 3 of that Constitution which requires that certain key office-holders be Protestants.

54. *See* F. SIMKINS AND R. WOODY, SOUTH CAROLINA DURING RECONSTRUCTION 90-95 (1966); *and see* II J. UNDERWOOD at 46-47.

55. Proceedings of the Constitutional Convention of South Carolina 568-69 (1868) (emphasis added).

56. Proceedings of the Constitutional Convention of South Carolina at 547, the remarks of E. W. M. Mackey; and at 563, the remarks of R. C. DeLarge (1868).

57. *See* Proceedings of the Constitutional Convention of South Carolina at 560-62, the remarks of J. J. Wright and R. C. DeLarge (1868).

58. Proceedings of the Constitutional Convention of South Carolina at 561, the remarks of B. F. Randolph (1868).

CHAPTER THREE—NOTES

59. Proceedings of the Constitutional Convention of South Carolina at 562, the remarks of R. C. DeLarge (1868).

60. Proceedings of the Constitutional Convention of South Carolina at 525 (1868).

61. Proceedings of the Constitutional Convention of South Carolina at 548, the motion of N. G. Parker, and at 559, the motion of B. F. Whittemore (1868).

62. Proceedings of the Constitutional Convention of South Carolina at 563, the remarks of B. F. Randolph (1868).

63. Proceedings of the Constitutional Convention at 547, the remarks of L. S. Langley (1868).

64. Torcaso v. Watkins, 367 U.S. 488, 81 S. Ct. 1680, 6 L. Ed. 2d 982 (1961).

65. 367 U.S. at 489.

66. 367 U.S. at 489-90.

67. 367 U.S. at 490-91.

68. 367 U.S. at 495.

69. 367 U.S. at 495-96.

70. Proceedings of the Constitutional Convention of South Carolina at 526 (1868).

71. 403 U.S. 602, 91 S. Ct. 2135, 29 L. Ed. 2d 745 (1971).

72. The State, April 26, 1990, at 2-B cols. 2-5.

73. 367 U.S. at 488, 494 n.9.

74. The State, May 16, 1990, at 6B, col. 2.

75. The State, May 16, 1990, at 6B, col. 2.

76. For other federal courts that have commented on religious belief requirements for office-holders *see* Tirmenstein v. Allain, 607 F. Supp. 1145 (S. D. Miss. 1985) (striking down a Mississippi provision with wording strikingly similar to that of South Carolina); *and see* O'Hair v. Hill, 641 F.2d 307 (5th Cir. 1981) and 675 F.2d 680 (5th Cir. 1982) (avoiding rulings

on the merits). Silverman brought suit in federal court against members of the State Election Commission alleging that the rule that anyone who denies the existence of a Supreme Being can not serve as governor violates provisions in the U.S. Constitution forbidding test oaths and the establishment of religion. In an unpublished order dated October 31, 1990, Judge David Norton dismissed the case on grounds that it would not be ripe for adjudication until Silverman was elected governor and the commission attempted to bar him from office. The ruling is on appeal.

CHAPTER FOUR

THE DEMISE OF THE ESTABLISHED CHURCH

The slow decline of the established church quickened with the convulsions produced by two seminal events: the Revolutionary War and the flurry of constitution making that swept the national and state governments after the Revolution. The first of the South Carolina state constitutions, that of 1776, was basically an emergency document in the mode of the Declaration of Independence that listed grievances against England and erected only the most skeletal form of temporary government. The document did not deal with civil rights in a section guaranteeing freedoms. Instead, it used abuses of civil rights as the basis of complaints against British rule. One such complaint involved establishment of religion but oddly enough it did not involve the Church of England directly, or even South Carolina laws on religion. It involved charges of a British-sponsored Catholic establishment in a far-off province of Canada.

The Quebec Act of 1774 was widely regarded as an establishment of the Catholic religion in that Canadian province. In actuality it came closer to being a dual establishment of the Protestant and Catholic religions and a recognition of the right of Catholics to practice their faith.[1] The act yielded to the reality that there was a high concentration of French Catholics in Quebec and, accordingly, granted them the right to practice their religion subject to the supremacy of the sovereign. It further granted the Catholic priests the right to ". . . hold, receive, and enjoy, their accustomed dues and rights with respect to such persons only as shall profess the said religion."[2] Thus it did not subject the non-Catholic population to taxation to aid that church. It further provided for provision to be made ". . . for the encouragement of the protestant religion, and for the maintenance and support of a protestant clergy . . . ."[3] Thus rather than providing for the suppression of the faith it provided for its support. Despite this fact, it raised the specter of the spread of a Catholic establishment throughout the North American colonies and the use of Catholic troops to quell dissent from British policies. The South Carolina Constitution of 1776 stated:

> . . . the Roman Catholic Religion (although before tolerated and freely exercised there [Quebec]) and an absolute government are established in that province, and its limits extended through a vast tract of country so as to border on the free Protestant English settlements, with design of using a whole people differing in religious principles from neighboring colonies, and subject to arbitrary power, as fit instruments to overawe and subdue the colonies.[4]

Judge John Drayton graphically described the South Carolina reaction to the Quebec Act by saying that it ". . . sunk deep into the minds of the people."[5] The shock waves were felt by the clergy as well as by the politicians. In his influential *Address On Liberty*, Richard Furman, a prominent Baptist minister declared that:

> They [the English] have enlarged the government of Canada, and extended it all along the back of the other Provinces, and established the Roman Catholic religion, and made it a Military, Arbitrary and Tyrannical government, intending as the Ministers declared in the House of Commons, to have Canadians as a force always ready to bring down on the back of the other colonies (should they oppose the designs of Parliament) to subdue them. And should they succeed, we have nothing to assure us, but that the Popish religion may be established in all the colonies.[6]

In view of such deep suspicion directed at the Catholic faith, it is easier to understand why the grant of religious freedom to Catholics lagged behind the extension of freedom to other denominations. This Catholic "establishment" in Canada must have been an eye-opener to Anglican proponents of a system of government-endorsed churches. To see some other church besides the Church of England receive statutory sanction may have forced a reassessment of the desirability of a regime of established churches. If such a system can be used for you, it can be used against you. If it had its benefits, it had its costs.

Indeed, Church of England officials began to speak more often of the drawbacks of establishment which were increasing as the non-Anglican population increased in power. Charles Woodmason, the itinerant Anglican missionary in the Carolina back-country during the 1760's, has left a graphic record of the daily trials of a representative of the established church.[7] Woodmason complained that the church was not able to spread more rapidly in the backcountry because this would have required establishing new parishes, and since parishes were also the units of legislative representation, such ecclesiastical changes would have led also to an alteration in the political-geographical balance of power.[8] He lamented the fact that dissenter legislators, described as crafty lawyers, bottled up legislation that would have been favorable to the Church of England.[9] He muttered in his diary that the legislature had failed to make the appropriations necessary to add additional ministries. To a bishop, he complained that an unfair disparity existed between the salaries of the town and rural clergy and that legislation to correct the imbalance had been shunted aside by the Stamp Act controversy.[10] Expanded emphasis on Church of England instruction in schools was being thwarted by dissenters who had reached positions of power.[11] The Anglican church was used by the government as an instrument of social control. Accordingly, on at least one occasion, Woodmason was directed by Lieutenant Governor William Bull as to sermon topics.[12] Pursuant to instructions, he drafted a sermon taking as its text I Thessalonians 4:11 which began with the phrase "[a]nd ye study to be quiet . . . ."[13] Apparently, this was intended to quell discontent in the backcountry. In his notes accompanying a sermon entitled *The Plight of Anglicans,* he complained that a Church of England clergyman could not even leave the province without obtaining legislative permission.[14] Government support was paid for by a loss of freedom.

Although Protestant dissenters enjoyed general freedom of worship, they occupied a shaky position with regard to the performance of certain significant rites, such as marriage. In a January 25, 1767 diary entry, Woodmason noted that Church of England ministers enjoyed a monopoly over the legal performance of marriage ceremonies.[15] The lack of the regular presence of Anglican ministers in the backcountry resulted in many couples living together without benefit of a marriage ceremony. Others were married by ministers of other denominations. Since their authority to conduct such ceremonies was questioned, not only was the validity of the marriages placed in doubt but so was the legitimacy of the children of such unions. Thus, another price of the establishment was family stability. We shall note presently that dissenter ministers, such as the Reverend William Tennent, deeply resented not being able to offer such basic rites to their members. As rankling as this was, even more irritating was the onerous tax system under which the faithful non-Anglican Protestant had to do double fiscal duty: pay taxes to support the Church of England, and obey the dictates of his conscience and lay aside additional sums for his own church.

Concerted action began to form around these grievances. In March, 1776, the Reverend Richard Furman and Oliver Hart, a leading Charleston Baptist pastor, gathered ministers of many denominations at the Baptist Church in the High Hills of Santee to formulate their grievances.[16] A secular group with official clout, the Grand Jury of Ninety-Six District, in its 1776 presentments pointedly declared that "[w]e recommend that the Legislature may put all Sects and Denominations of true Protestants in this State on equal Footings."[17] The Grand Jury's most salient complaint was the tax burden non-Anglicans bore in supporting the clergy and the building program of the Anglican church, while other Protestant churches that were just as worthy morally had to struggle to get donations from what was left after taxes.[18]

The Reverend William Tennent of the Independent or Congregational Church in Charleston served as spokesman for a dissenter petition presented to the Commons House of Assembly on January 11, 1777.[19] As a skilled political tactician Tennent knew that to achieve constitutional abolition of the preferred position of the Anglican church he would need to avoid antagonizing influential Church of England members. Accordingly, he opened his speech by noting that he did not oppose the Church of England as an institution. He respected it. He only opposed the preferred position given it.[20] Later in his address he sought to further lessen the blow of disestablishment on the Church of England by saying that the petitioners did not seek to dispossess that church of property it had already acquired with government funds.[21] They only sought to prevent additional acquisitions.

The petitioners were opposed to the establishment of any particular denomination no matter how worthy that church was. An establishment was an infringement on the liberty of conscience. Establishments ". . . amount to nothing less, than the legislature's taking the consciences of men into their own hands, and taxing them at discretion."[22] He contended that no government had a right to interfere with any man's search for the proper relationship with God so long as that search does no palpable injury to the state or others. Such matters of conscience are not subject to the state but only to a "higher tribunal."[23] The proper relation of the state to religion is for the government to protect the right to worship but not to impose any religion upon the people.[24] The state could also enact legislation embodying the general moral standards necessary for a civilized society. In this regard he noted that:

> The state may enact good laws for the punishment of vice, and the encouragement of virtue. The state may do anything for the support of religion, without partiality to particular societies, or imposition upon the rights of private judgment.[25]

After sketching this broad philosophical framework, Reverend Tennent turned his fire directly on the problems presented by the South Carolina establishment. He noted that:

> Its chief characteristics are, that it makes a legal distinction between people of different denominations, equally inoffensive; it taxes all denominations, for the support of the religion of one; it only tolerates those that dissent from it, while it deprives them of sundry privileges which the people of the establishment enjoy.

> I say it makes a legal and odious distinction between subjects equally good. The law knows and acknowledges the society of the one, as a Christian Church; the law knows not the other Churches. The law knows the Clergy of the one, as ministers of the gospel; the law knows not the Clergy of the other Churches, nor will it give them a license to marry their own people. Under this reputedly free government, licenses for marriage are even now refused by the ordinary, to any but the established clergy. The law makes provision for the support of one Church, - it makes no provision for the others. The law builds superb Churches for the one, - it leaves the others to build their own Churches: the law, by incorporating the one Church, enables it to hold estates, and to sue for rights; the law does not enable the others to hold any religious property, not even the pittances which are bestowed by the hand of charity for their support. No dissenting Church can hold or sue for their own property at common law. They are obliged therefore to deposit it in the hands of trustees, to be held by them as their own private property, and to lie at their mercy. The consequence of this is, that too often their funds for the support of religious worship, get into bad hands, and become either alienated from their proper use, or must be recovered at the expense of a suit in chancery.[26]

Tennent next focused on the political power wielded by the established church. It could tax the entire polity to fund the aid to the poor administered by the Church of England. Such a vital public service, affecting the society in which everyone lived, should have a more widely dispersed power base. Particularly galling was granting ". . . the whole management of elections, that most inestimable of all rights of freemen! into the hands of Church officers exclusively."[27] It is dangerous to permit any minority of the population, whether religious or otherwise, to have the opportunity to manipulate the electoral process even if such manipulation never occurs.

He charged that the tax burden of the establishment was high, and the burden fell most heavily upon Protestant dissenters. He estimated the funds allocated to the established church from 1765 to 1775 at 164,027 pounds 16 shillings, of which the dissenters, a majority of the population had paid 82,013 pounds. Contributions to their own religions were made from what funds they had left after taxes.[28]

Tennent then made an important legal and philosophical distinction: that between *toleration* and *rights*. He noted that the keepers of the flame of the establishment asked: has it not been enough that your freedom to worship as you please has been tolerated by the government? No! Under those conditions freedom of worship existed at the discretion of the government. Such a privilege had to be exercised so as not to offend. Instead, freedom of religion should be a guaranteed right protected against government intrusion.[29]

Reverend Tennent then attacked compromise proposals that would salvage some vestiges of the establishment. First he considered suggestions that the right to tax the general population for the support of the Anglican church be abolished but that the Church of England remain as the one that received the ideological imprimatur of support from the state. To this proposal he replied:

> But they seem to forget, that every reason for which they desire the superiority by establishment, operates as an abridgement of religious liberty. For when a man presumes to follow his own judgment in religious matters, and refuses to *conform*, he must at least submit to this inferiority, or rather bear the reproach of the law, as not being on a level with those that are Christians in its esteem.[30]

Such ideological endorsement of one religion by the state, even if it does not involve overt coercion, creates psychological pressure to conform to the preferred religion.

Tennent argued that giving the Church of England the ". . . mere empty name . . ." of an established church would create ". . . a bone of endless contention in the state."[31] The political community would still be split in fractious quarrels.

He then confronted suggestions that all Protestant denominations receive equal financial establishments. He labeled such an "establishment" as a contradiction in terms. The establishment of all is the establishment of none. As a practical matter, such a proposal would lead to the local establishment of the denomination that was the majority in a particular precinct. This would be another ". . . means of everlasting strife . . ." as each sect jealously fought to contain the most adherents.[32] Instead, the desirable course was to "[l]eave each Church to be supported by its own members, and let its real merit be all its pre-eminence."[33] Reaching his oratorical peroration, he demanded "Equality or Nothing."[34]

His speech ended on a pragmatic note. The dissenter majority would provide more enthusiastic support for the Revolution if they had an equal stake in the freedoms it would produce. Continuation of religious preferences would discourage the migration of new settlers and create resentment and divisions in the community.[35] "That state in America which adopts the freest and most liberal plan will be the most opulent and powerful, and will well deserve it."[36] This last point is one that should be pondered even today by those who fear that the spread of freedom throughout the population will somehow diminish the strength of the state.

John Wesley Brinsfield has noted that the assembly considered several alternatives in realigning the relationship of church and state.[37] Among these were the following: (1) that there be no establishment either in the form of ideological endorsement or financial support from the government; (2) that the Church of England retain its authority to administer aid to the poor and conduct elections but that no taxes be extracted from practitioners of other faiths to support Anglican worship activities; (3) that all Protestant denominations meeting certain general standards become established and receive equal state financial support as well as ideological endorsement; (4) that all Protestant denominations would become established churches in the sense of receiving ideological endorsement and certain legal rights, such as the right to incorporate.[38] The last-mentioned alternative formed a compromise between those wanting no establishment and those wanting the state to retain an active role in monitoring religious conduct. This compromise position is sometimes attributed to Charles Coatesworth Pinckney.[39] The second option, that would retain Anglican administrative control over aid to the poor and the conduct of elections but without tax-supported worship, was narrowly defeated.[40] The final option, an establishment of all Protestant denominations meeting certain broad-belief standards but without tax support, ultimately became Article 38 of the Constitution of 1778 after that document was at first vetoed by the chief executive, John Rutledge, but finally signed by his successor.[41] Article 38 had the detailed complexity of a code provision rather than the broad majestic phrases of a modern constitution. This remarkable provision must now be set forth in full:

> That all Persons and religious Societies, who acknowledge that there is one God, and a future State of Rewards and Punishments, and that God is publicly to be worshipped, shall be freely tolerated. The Christian Protestant Religion shall be deemed, and is hereby constituted and declared to be, the

established Religion of this State. That all Denominations of Christian Protestants in this State, demeaning themselves peaceably and faithfully, shall enjoy equal religious and civil Privileges. - To accomplish this desirable Purpose, without Injury to the religious Property of those Societies of Christians, which are by Law already incorporated, for the Purpose of religious Worship; and to put it fully into the Power of every other Society of Christian Protestants, either already formed, or hereafter to be formed, to obtain the like Incorporations, It is hereby constituted, appointed, and declared, That the respective Societies of the Church of England, that are already formed in this State, for the Purposes of religious Worship, shall still continue incorporate, and hold the religious Property now in their Possession. And that, whenever fifteen or more male Persons, not under twenty-one Years of Age, professing the Christian Protestant Religion, and agreeing to unite themselves in a Society, for the Purposes of a religious Worship, they shall (on complying with the Terms hereinafter mentioned) be, and be constituted, a Church, and be esteemed and regarded in Law as of the established Religion of the State, and on a Petition to the Legislature, shall be entitled to be incorporated, and to enjoy equal Privileges. That every Society of Christians, so formed shall give themselves a Name or Denomination, by which they shall be called and known in Law; and all that associate with them for the Purposes of Worship, shall be esteemed as belonging to the Society so called: But that, previous to the Establishment and Incorporation of the respective Societies of every Denomination as aforesaid, and in order to entitle them thereto, each Society so petitioning, shall have agreed to, and subscribed, in a Book, the following Five Articles, without which, no Agreement or Union of men, upon Pretence of Religion, shall entitle them to be incorporated, and esteemed as a Church of the established Religion of this State:

First, That there is one eternal God, and a future State of Rewards and Punishments.

Second, That God is publicly to be worshipped.

Third, That the Christian Religion is the true Religion.

Fourth, That the Holy Scriptures of the Old and New Testament, are of Divine Inspiration, and are the Rule of Faith and Practice.

Fifth, That it is lawful, and the Duty of every Man, being thereunto called by those that govern, to bear witness to Truth.

That every Inhabitant of this State, when called to make an Appeal to God, as a witness to Truth, shall be permitted to do it in that Way which is most agreeable to the Dictates of his own Conscience. And, that the People of this State may forever enjoy the Right of electing their own Pastors or Clergy; and, at the same Time, that the State may have sufficient Security, for the due Discharge of the Pastoral Office, by those who shall be admitted to be Clergymen, no Person shall officiate as Minister of any established Church, who shall not have been chosen by a Majority of the Society to which he shall minister, or by Persons appointed by the said Majority to chose and procure a Minister for them, nor until the Minister so chosen and appointed, shall have made and subscribed to the following Declaration, over and above the aforesaid five Articles, viz:

That he is determined, by God's Grace, out of the Holy Scriptures, to instruct the People committed to his Charge, and to teach nothing (as required of Necessity to Eternal Salvation) but that which he shall be persuaded may be concluded and proved from the Scripture; that he will use both public and private Admonitions, as well to the Sick as to the Whole, within his Cure, as Need shall require and Occasion shall be given; and that he will be diligent in Prayers, and in reading of the Holy Scriptures, and in such Studies as help to the Knowledge of the same; and he will be diligent to frame and fashion his own self, and his Family, according to the doctrine of Christ, and to make both himself and them, as much as in him lieth, wholesome Examples and Patterns to the Flock of Christ; that he will maintain and set forwards, as much as he can, Quietness, Peace, and Love among all People; and especially among those that are or shall be committed to his Charge.

No person shall disturb or molest any religious Assembly; nor shall use any reproachful, reviling, or abusive Language, against any Church; that being the certain Way of disturbing the Peace, and of hindering the Conversion of any to the Truth, by engaging them in Quarrels and Animosities, to the Hatred of the Professors, and that Profession which otherwise they might be brought to assent to. No person whatsoever shall speak any Thing, in their religious Assembly, irreverently, or seditiously, of the Government of this State. No Person shall, by Law, be obliged to pay towards the Maintenance and Support of a religious Worship that he does not freely join in, or has not voluntarily engaged to Support: But, the Churches, Chapels, Parsonages, Glebes, and all other Property, now belonging to any Societies of the Church of England, or any other religious Societies, shall remain, and be secured, to them for ever. The Poor shall be supported, and Elections managed, in the accustomed Manner, until Laws shall be provided to adjust those Matters in the Matters in the most equitable Way.[42]

If someone were to look at this provision in the abstract, or with the point of view of a modern civil libertarian, without considering the historical context, it would appear to establish a theocratic state in which the government even prescribes the details of the beliefs a citizen must have in order to be part of the most favored group. Viewed in a historical context, however, it significantly liberalizes the grant of religious freedom and greatly expands the range of denominations acceptable to the government. In the final analysis, however, its attempt to both expand religious freedom and regulate it in detail is self-contradictory and self-defeating. Let us consider some of its pivotal characteristics:

(1) It replaced the Church of England establishment with a general endorsement of all Protestant denominations that met some widely shared standards of belief. This document did *not* replace the extensive tax support of the Church of England with a system supporting from public funds all Protestant denominations, or even some of them. The provision specifically stated that ". . . [n]o Person shall, by Law, be obliged to pay towards the Maintenance and Support of a religious Worship that he does not freely join in, or has not voluntarily engaged to Support . . . ."[43] When we later examine church incorporation statutes passed by the legislature under the Constitution of 1778, we shall note that a church could assess its own pewholders and could enforce the assessment through court action against the recalcitrant member with the ultimate sanction being denial of membership or forfeiture of the pew. This was a long way from taxing the general population for the support of churches. David Ramsay, who was not only a historian but a person deeply involved in public service in the late eighteenth and early nineteenth centuries, described the new system as one that ". . . comprehended every denomination of Protestant Christians, giving to each of them equal rights and capacities, but withholding public pecuniary support from all."[44]

(2) Other Protestant denominations, in addition to the Church of England, could become incorporated and exercise the rights of a legal entity, such as directly owning their own property rather than having it

held in their behalf by trustees. However, Article 38 dictated five major doctrines that had to be subscribed to by any group seeking incorporation as an established church. Thus the document reflected the belief that the search for religious truth was not a dynamic process but a completed one in which truth was known and set in theological concrete. Even if an individual could have believed what he wanted, his ability to practice those beliefs as part of an incorporated entity was sharply curbed. One church objected that the list of beliefs that had to be adhered to in order to qualify for incorporation was incomplete. The Independent or Congregational Church in Charleston signed the official book of beliefs but insisted on adding doctrines, such as the trinitarian nature of God, that it considered to be essential but missing from the list.[45]

It is also notable that even though the list of churches that could become incorporated was becoming less exclusive, it was still limited. Catholic churches and Jewish synagogues still could not enjoy the convenience of incorporation.

(3) Even though their churches and synagogues could not yet become incorporated entities, Catholics and Jews could enjoy freedom of worship so long as they subscribed to the general core beliefs that ". . . there is one God, and a future state of Rewards and Punishments, and that God is publicly to be worshipped. . . ."[46] Of course, any requirement that one must meet certain belief standards before enjoying freedom of conscience is inherently contradictory to the modern concept of religious freedom. In fact, the list of basic beliefs is reminiscent of the itemization of beliefs necessary to be a freeman in Carolina that was inserted a century earlier in the Fundamental Constitutions.[47]

(4) The free exercise of religion of ministers was restricted by the portions of Article 38 that, in effect, told them how to interpret the Bible and what to preach. A literal interpretation of the Bible was embodied in constitutional form. A minister could preach only what he could prove from the Bible. He could not say anything seditious about the government. He had to be cautious about engaging in theological debate with other denominations because that might be interpreted as saying something "reproachful, riling, or abusive" against another church.

(5) A form of congregational democracy was decreed concerning the selection of ministers. This was in accord with the tradition that had earlier frustrated the English bishops who wanted to curb lay control of

the selection of ministers in South Carolina.[48] Such a rule would seem to be a positive features; it struck a blow for democracy. Ironically, however, it was a curb on freedom in the area of church administration. The provisions seemed to forbid the adoption of a system such as that used by the modern-day Methodist Church in which bishops, rather than congregational vote, determine the selection of ministers.

Adoption of the 1778 Constitution made possible a wave of incorporation of dissenter congregations. These incorporations took the form of special acts of the legislature. One act often incorporated several congregations giving each the same or similar powers. For example, one 1778 act incorporated the Independent or Congregational Church in Charlestown, the Reverend Oliver Hart's Baptist church in Charlestown, The Presbyterian Church of Bethel in Saint Bartholomew's parish, The Presbyterian Church of Cainhoy in Saint Thomas parish and the Presbyterian Church of Salem in Saint Mark's parish.[49] The preamble of the statute announced that all of the listed churches had complied with the constitutional standards for incorporation of an established church. The remainder of the act granted corporate powers to the churches. These included existence as a body corporate and politic, the right to adopt a seal, to hold property, receive contributions, have perpetual succession of the entity, the right to sue and be sued, make by-laws consistent with state law, elect ministers, and hire other employees and set their salaries. Expenses were to be defrayed out of funds belonging to the corporation and from pew rents assessed against its members.

A 1783 act incorporating a Calvinist church of French Protestants began by noting that the church had subscribed to the five articles of faith which the constitution required for incorporation.[50] The act recited as a key reason for seeking the status of an established, incorporated church the desire to be placed on a ". . . more solid and lasting foundation than they could be by their voluntary subscriptions."[51] At first, one might assume that the alternative to voluntary subscriptions for the church was seeking tax-raised funds from the state. However, later in the act it appeared that the financing was not involuntary in the sense of funds raised by a tax on the general population. It was involuntary in the sense that once a person elected to become a member of the church, a necessary incident of that membership was paying the pew rent. A failure to make timely payment could result in a lawsuit and forfeiture of membership.

The state did not assess the charge. The church made the assessment by vote of the members. The assessment was not on the general population but only on those who elected to become members. This was state-financed religion only in the most indirect sense. The state provided a legal mechanism for enforcement of membership obligations.[52] It did, however, have the potential for entangling the state in internal church squabbles. The statute limited the amount of property the church could receive in one year to 500 pounds.[53]

The older churches that had been the jewels of the establishment system obtained incorporation legislation adapting their governance and finances to the realities of the new constitution. A 1785 act incorporated the vestries and church wardens of Saint Michael's and Saint Philip's in Charleston.[54] The preamble to the act noted that the petition of the two churches stated ". . . that since the passing of the Constitution of this State, the support which was formerly provided by the Legislature for the clergy and other offices of the church is withdrawn . . ." but that many voluntary contributions have been received, and that such contributions would be best managed by adopting a corporate form.[55] The statute granted the vestries the usual corporate powers given churches including the ability to hire and fire ministers.[56] The reader will recall the previous discussion of the early eighteenth-century church laws in which a province-wide body of lay commissioners was able to review church decisions to discharge ministers. Thus, ironically, the lessening of the grip of the establishment actually gave individual local Episcopal churches more control over their own destiny. The 1785 act gave the vestries the right ". . . annually to rate and assess each and every of the pews in the said churches, at such sum or sums of money as they, or a majority of them, shall think proper. . . ."[57] If any member fails to pay within one month the amount at which his pew is assessed, the church is authorized ". . . to let to hire the said pew or pews, for any term not exceeding one year, to any person or persons who may be willing to hire the same."[58] The pew rental system was the heart of the new system of church finance after demise of the system of legislative appropriations.[59] Although the general thrust of such statutes was to give more control over their affairs to the churches themselves, the intrusive hand of government still is seen in the regulation of such matters as the disposition of pews.

Some influential people regarded the pew assessment as a slightly disguised form of taxation for religious purposes, even if in theory under Article 38 of the 1778 Constitution, such assessments could only be imposed on those willing to become affiliates of the assessing church. As long as Protestant Churches meeting the doctrinal standards of Article 38 were labeled by the government as established, state-sanctioned bodies, such assessment produced the odor, if not the reality, of taxation for religious purposes. This attitude was displayed by a petition presented by Samuel Beach of Charleston to the General Assembly on February 19, 1787. Mr. Beach was a member of St. Philip's church in Charleston. He complained that the 1785 act incorporating St. Philip's and St. Michael's, as well as many other church incorporation laws, endorsed a pew assessment system that amounted to a tax for religious purposes in violation of Article 38.[60] He noted that the pew had been sold, not merely rented, to him. It was now his private property in as full a sense as was his house. The Constitution of 1778, Article 38, guaranteed that no person would be forced to contribute to the support of any religion. Under this provision, he was obligated to pay only the amount he had voluntarily agreed to incur. He had contracted to purchase a pew outright. Once he had paid the agreed upon amount in full, any further assessment would amount to taxation of private property.

Even though the government did not impose the tax directly itself, it, in essence, delegated taxing authority to the incorporated, established churches when it permitted, and made enforceable at law, assessments going beyond the terms of the pewholder agreement with the church. It is true that no particular Protestant denomination had been given exclusive power to impose such taxes, but by creating a general Protestant establishment, endorsing certain churches as meeting the doctrinal requirements for becoming an established body, and granting such entities pew assessment authority in incorporation acts, the state had created a precedent that could lead to a return to an establishment of a favored group of churches. The implication of the Beach petition was that some churches had pew assessment power and others did not, and that this violated the spirit of Article 38 that required that all Protestant denominations should be placed on an equal footing. The legislative committee assigned to study the petition cited a series of church incorporation laws and concluded that such pew assessment authority was so widely granted to such a great variety of Protestant denominations that all Protestant sects were, in fact, on an equal footing. The committee never squarely met Beach's other argument that when the assessment went beyond the amount agreed to in the pew purchase contract, it was a coerced contribution that could be enforced by legal process. Beach had also argued that since some pew owners in the church were actually adherents of other denominations, the assessments amounted to taking one man's money for another man's religion. The committee merely flippantly replied that if Beach did not like the system, he could always sell his pew.[61] Even though the Beach petition was not formally granted, one commentator has concluded that the petition may have prompted the legislature, in passing later incorporation acts, to make the church choose between selling or renting the pews. If the first option was selected, further assessment, after an absolute sale, was invalid.[62]

The petition came the same year as the federal constitutional convention. The air was charged with desire for constitutional change. Perhaps the resentment revealed by the petition added to the momentum for jettisoning the remaining vestiges of establishment. The remnants of establishment had crossed swords with even more lofty icons in the South Carolina pantheon: the respect for private property and the desire to avoid taxes. This stirs the blood for constitutional reform as nothing else will. Among the other conditions driving the state toward the greater religious freedom provisions that emerged in the Constitution of 1790 was the still second-class status of minority religions such as the Catholic and Jewish faiths.

The Constitution of 1778 represented significant advances in religious freedom in the form of the replacement of the Anglican establishment by a general Protestant establishment and the grant of freedom of worship to anyone who adhered to the broad standards of belief in God, that God is publicly to be worshipped and that there is a future state of rewards and punishments. Important restrictions on religious freedom remained, however. Even though the Constitution of 1778 did not direct that a religious test be attached to the right to vote, key state officeholders still had to be Protestants. No provision had been made for the incorporation of Catholic churches or Jewish synagogues. This would be done in the Constitution of 1790. Why was the grant of important elements of religious freedom, such as the ability to incorporate, delayed for Catholics and Jews, and why was the time of the adoption of the 1790 Constitution a ripe one for finally extending those rights to them?

In a 1768 journal entry Charles Woodmason, Anglican missionary to the backcountry, reported that hostility to Catholics was so great that some practitioners of that faith felt it necessary to disguise themselves as adherents of other religions. He stated:

> Among these Quakers and Presbyterians are many concealed Papists. They are not tolerated in this Government -- and in the shape of New Light Preachers, I've met many Jesuits.[63]

The earlier discussion of the Quebec Act which allegedly "established" Catholic religion in that Canadian province in 1774 noted that this statute was so provocative that it was listed in the Constitution of 1776 as one of the chief grievances against Britain that led to the Revolution. The Canadian Catholics were viewed as agents of Britain who would be used to keep the other North American colonists in check. Earlier, in 1749, rumors abounded that the Jesuits were conspiring with the French in Mobile to send an expedition against South Carolina.[64] In 1775 the Committee of Public Safety of the Provincial Congress ordered that Catholics, along with Negroes and Indians, be disarmed.[65] Whether considered agents of the British, the French, or the Papal state, the loyalty of Catholics was viewed with deep suspicion.

Unfortunately, this biased perception has recurred from time to time even after adoption of the federal Bill of Rights and the South Carolina Constitution of 1790. In an 1826 address to Congress, Bishop John England of Charleston felt it necessary to rebut allegations that Catholics owed their primary allegiance to the Papal state rather than the United States. In addition, he also considered it necessary that he respond to charges that Catholicism, with its hierarchical structure of church governance, was inherently incompatible with a democratic civil government.[66] In 1960, Democratic Presidential candidate John F. Kennedy felt it necessary to appear before a group of Protestant ministers in Houston to convince them that he believed in the separation of church and state and that he would make up his own mind with regard to issues of public policy, and that he would not take dictation from foreign powers or ecclesiastical authorities.[67]

Even though suspicions about the loyalty of Catholics flared after passage of the Quebec Act and probably contributed to the delay in granting equal religious freedom to Catholics, the Revolutionary War provided them with an opportunity to demonstrate patriotism and thus paved the way for the grant of broader liberty to them. David Ramsay observed that:

> The orderly conduct and active cooperation of its [Catholic Church] members in all measures for the defense and good government of the country, proves that the apologies offered in justification of the restrictions imposed on them by the protestant governments of Europe are without foundation, or do not apply to the state of things in Carolina.[68]

Thus the Revolutionary War proved to be pivotal in the expansion of religious freedoms by (1) providing the impetus for replacing the Church of England establishment with a general Protestant Establishment as a means of increasing dissenter support of the war, and (2) by giving Catholics and Jews an opportunity to demonstrate loyalty deserving of greater religious freedom. With regard to granting dissenter demands for equal freedom in order to encourage their support of the independence movement, Ramsay said "[t]he dissenters felt their weight, and though zealous in the cause of independence, could not brook the idea of risking their lives for anything short of equal rights. . . ." The prize contended for being made equally interesting to all, equal exertions were made by all for obtaining it."[69]

Commentators have placed the presence of Jewish settlers in South Carolina at least as far back as 1695 when Governor John Archdale used a Jewish interpreter for negotiations with Indians.[70] Disputed accounts have Jews voting in an election in Charleston as early as 1702-03.[71] Even if accounts of Jews voting at that early date are accurate, such participation was soon supplanted by the statutes discussed above which limited the electorate to Christians. As noted previously, the 1778 Constitution contained no language directing the exclusion of non-Christians from voting but did limit key offices to Protestant Christians. Despite these limitations on the political rights of Jews prior to the adoption of the 1790 Constitution, one commentator has described Charleston Jews in that period as enjoying broad economic and social freedom. Robert St. John has said that:

> In Charleston, Jews had the right to worship as they pleased and to work at any occupation they chose, or to conduct any type of business, or to engage in any form of trade, without restriction. This was the sort of freedom that persecution-weary Old World Jews were seeking.[72]

As the Revolution approached, Jewish participation in political life increased. As noted earlier, Francis Salvador participated in the legislative body asserting independence.[73] A military unit, colloquially known as the Jewish Company, fought actively on the American side during the Revolutionary War. A vigorous dispute has taken place concerning whether the company was entirely, or largely, or only somewhat composed of Jews.[74] Despite this debate over the percentage of the company that was Jewish, it does appear that their participation was significant and conspicuous. Participation in the birth and defense of a country naturally would lead to a desire to share more broadly in its freedoms. Learsi, in his history of Jews in America, noted that since the Jews had contributed much to the Revolutionary cause they were no longer content with second-rate versions of the civil and political rights enjoyed by other South Carolinians.[75]

The congregation of Beth Eloihim (now spelled Beth Elohim) in Charleston, one of the oldest synagogues in America, its earliest surviving records going back to 1750, still could not incorporate under the Constitution of 1778.[76] David Ramsay described the Jews of South Carolina as "[e]qually interested in the welfare of the country, they are equally zealous for its defense and good government."[77]

Not only was the time ripe for expanding the freedom for Catholics and Jews because they had proved their loyalty in the Revolutionary War but also because the national climate was moving toward expanded freedom. In July 13, 1787, the Congress passed the Northwest Ordinance which set the government framework for the territories and the conditions under which they might become states. Article I of the ordinance stated that:

> No person demeaning himself in a peaceable and orderly manner shall ever be molested on account of his mode of worship or religious sentiments in the said territory.[78]

The ordinance tried to combine religious freedom with a mild endorsement of religion. Article III stated:

> Religion, morality, and knowledge being necessary to good government and the happiness of mankind, schools and the means of education shall forever be encouraged.[79]

Religion was considered a key balance wheel of society, but the individual should be left free to find his own faith.

Not only was the time ripe for expansion of greater religious freedom beyond the dominant Protestant Christian segment of the population but leaders were gaining ascendancy who had a special interest in freedom of conscience. Charles Pinckney was governor in 1790 and became president of the state constitutional convention that year.[80] Earlier, while a delegate to the federal constitutional convention of 1787, Charles Pinckney had presented a plan for the national government which included the following provision as part of the sixth article:

> The Legislature of the United States shall pass no Law on the subject of Religion, nor touching or abridging the Liberty of the Press nor shall the Privilege of the Writ of Habeas Corpus ever be suspended except in case of Rebellion or Invasion.[81]

On August 20, 1787, Charles Pinckney proposed to the federal convention that "[n]o religious test or qualification shall ever be annexed to any oath of office under the authority of the U.S."[82] Similar language forbidding religious test oaths for federal officials ultimately was embodied in Article VI, section 3, of the Constitution of the United States.[83]

The First Amendment to the United States Constitution and the South Carolina Constitution of 1790, with its expanded religious freedom in Article VIII, are part of the same current in the same constitutional stream. The First Amendment states that:

> Congress shall make no law respecting an establishment of religion, or prohibiting the free exercise thereof; or abridging the freedom of speech, or of the press; or the right of the people peaceably to assemble, and to petition the government for a redress of grievances.

Congress completed passage of the First Amendment when the Senate adopted it along with the rest of the Bill of Rights, on September 25,

1789.[84] During the debates in the House of Representatives, James Madison unsuccessfully urged inclusion of a provision prohibiting the states, not just the federal government, from harming basic rights such as the ". . . right of conscience . . . or . . . trial by jury in criminal cases. . . ."[85] Madison noted that several state constitutions protected those rights, but others did not. Even for those states that already guaranteed such freedoms, federal constitutional protection against state abuse was still desirable to provide a "double security."[86] Even though Madison was advocating inclusion of religious freedom guarantees in the federal Constitution, his words also served as a reminder to states to provide protection to freedom of conscience in their own fundamental law.

Adoption of the Bill of Rights to the United Sates Constitution was part of the same procession of watershed changes as the South Carolina Constitution of 1790. On April 3, 1790, the Congress received a message from the President of the United States informing it that the South Carolina legislature had adopted the amendments to the federal Constitution, and a bit over a month later, on May 10, 1790, the South Carolina Constitutional Convention began.[87] The federal Bill of Rights became effective on December 15, 1791. Sandwiched in the middle of this sequence of events is the South Carolina Constitutional Convention of 1790. The formation of a new federal union of which South Carolina was a constituent part made it necessary that the state realign its government structure to mesh more readily with that of the federal union. The development of the Bill of Rights did not require that states precisely emulate the federal example in the civil rights field. It did create a climate in which states wanted a system philosophically compatible with the federal system. Thus Judge Brevard in his commentary on the Constitution of 1790 in his statutory compilation stated:

> The delegates of the people met in general convention at Columbia, in June 1790, established a constitution for the government of the state, conformably to principles of the constitution of the United States.[88]

Judge Brevard's observations were made with regard to the 1790 Constitution in general. David Ramsay made similar comments in a discussion more precisely directed at the freedom of religion provisions of the new state fundamental law. He noted that the 1790 Constitution was the product of a convention called to draft a state constitution ". . . adapted to the new order of things" created by the new Constitution of the United States.[89]

The South Carolina Constitutional Convention of 1790 was a departure from the state's previous custom of constitution making. Rather than having the legislature simply switch hats from its usual statute-enacting mode to that of fundamental law draftsmen, this convention was to consist of delegates elected specifically for the purpose of drafting a new constitution. This gave Jewish citizens an opportunity to affect the electoral process by working for the selection of candidates favorable to expanded religious freedom.[90] However, they did not sacrifice their high ethical standards in the process. Several commentators on the history of Jews in South Carolina have recounted an incident in which members of Beth Elohim had worked for the election of a candidate, and the grateful candidate later offered a fifty guinea contribution to the synagogue to be used as aid to the poor. The congregation, in a letter signed by its president Jacob Cohen, refused the donation. The letter politely said that even though the offer doubtless was made out of good motives, the contribution had to be refused because acceptance might create the impression that the congregation could be bought by political candidates.[91]

What sort of constitution did this convention produce with regard to the subject of religious freedom? Section 4 of the 1790 Constitution listed the qualifications necessary to be a voter. The 1778 Constitution, in Article 13, did not require that a voter be a Christian as had several earlier statutes, but it set as a voter qualification belief in God and a future state of rewards and punishments. Section 4 of the 1790 Constitution did not retain those requirements. The 1778 Constitution required that key officeholders be Protestants. Article 3 of that Constitution required that the governor, lieutenant governor and members of the privy council be Protestants. Articles 12 and 13 required that members of the Senate and House of Representatives respectively be Protestants. The 1790 Constitution did not retain religious tests for officeholders. Article IV sets forth the oath to be taken by officeholders. It did not end with the phrase "so help me God." This absence of religious test oaths is consistent with the fact that Charles Pinckney was governor and president of the state convention, and he had been a leading proponent of the Article VI, section 3, prohibition of religious test oaths in the federal Constitution. The reader is reminded, however, of the reintroduction of the test oath in the form of the Supreme Being belief requirement in the Reconstruction Era Constitution of 1868 in Article 3, section 3 (governor's qualifications), and Article 14, section 6 (qualifications for other offices). The phrase "so help me God" was reintroduced as part of the oath for officeholders in an 1834 amendment to the 1790 document.[92] The 1790 Constitution, in Article 1, section 23, continued the prohibition against ministers being able to serve as governor, lieutenant governor or as members of the Senate or House of Representatives.

The centerpiece religious freedom provision of the Constitution of 1790 was Article VIII. It stated:

> Sec. 1. The free exercise and enjoyment of religious profession and worship, without discrimination or preference, shall, forever hereafter, be allowed within this State to all mankind; provided that the liberty of conscience hereby declared shall not be so construed as to excuse acts of licentiousness, or justify practices inconsistent with the peace or safety of this State.
>
> Sec. 2. The rights, privileges, immunities, and estates of both civil and religious societies and of corporate bodies shall remain as if the constitution of this State had not been altered or amended.

The most notable achievement of this document is that it does not provide for any religious establishment. Thus there has been a progression from (1) the Church of England establishment which held sway prior to the Constitution of 1778, to (2) the general Protestant Christian establishment of the Constitution of 1778, to (3) total disestablishment under the Constitution of 1790. The form of this disestablishment is worthy of note. The First Amendment to the United States Constitution contains two religious clauses: (1) the free exercise clause, guaranteeing religious freedom, and (2) the establishment clause, precluding Congress from passing laws respecting the establishment of religion. The South Carolina Constitution of 1790 contains a provision insuring free exercise of religion, but it does not contain the equivalent of the establishment clause. Establishment clause language did not appear in a South Carolina constitution until it was embodied in Article I, section 10, of the Radical Reconstruction Era Constitution of 1868. Instead, the 1790 Constitution spoke by eloquent omission. Gone was the intricate code of beliefs specified in Article 38 of the 1778 Constitution which was even so bold as to tell ministers their duty. In addition, the portion of Article VIII, section 1, that guarantees freedom of worship ". . . without discrimination or preference" has anti-establishment implications since a major thrust of the establishment was to discriminate and prefer first the Church of England by ideological endorsement and financial sponsorship, and later Protestantism by ideological endorsement and the grant of the exclusive advantage of incorporation in the 1778 Constitution.

Thus David Ramsay described its philosophical essence in the following terms:

> That it is the true policy of States to afford equal protection to the civil rights of all individuals and of all sects of religionists without discrimination or preference and without interference on the part of the State in all matters that relate only to the intercourse between man and his maker.[93]

Thomas Cooper, the great codifier of South Carolina statutes, in defending himself against charges of heresy as President of South Carolina College, gave such a broad interpretation to the "without discrimination or preference" language that it would satisfy even the most expansive modern-day interpreter of the federal constitution's anti-establishment provisions. He argued that the legislature could pass no law that in any way touched upon the subject of religion because in doing so a preference for some religious beliefs over others would be the invariable result.[94] In a more objective mood in his commentaries to his compilation of statutes, he observed that the 1790 Constitution did not prevent the legislature from incorporating religious organizations to achieve civil ends, nor did he believe that it prevented the enactment of laws observing Sunday as a secular day of rest.[95]

Despite Article VIII's decree that freedom of religion was guaranteed without discrimination or preference, it is unlikely that the drafters of the Constitution of 1790 thought that they were banishing any recognition of God from the halls of government, since it was their custom to meet as a body on Sundays for a prayer or religious discourse, usually led by one of the ministers who served as a delegate. Among those leading such services was the Reverend Richard Furman, prominent Baptist minister and advocate of religious freedom.[96] Many years later in the 1983 case of *Marsh v. Chambers*[97] the United States Supreme Court relied upon the fact that the same Congress that adopted the First Amendment also hired a chaplain at public expense to begin daily sessions with prayer as the basis of upholding the Nebraska legislature's use of government funds to retain a chaplain to start the legislative day with an invocation. The original intent of the framers as revealed in their conduct at the time of the First Amendment's passage provided persuasive evidence of the amendment's scope.

One prominent early nineteenth-century South Carolina clergyman concluded that the framers of the 1790 Constitution had no intention of completely removing all traces of the establishment. In scholarly annotations to a sermon he had delivered to the convention of the Episcopal diocese of South Carolina in 1833, the Reverend Doctor J. Adams, President of the College of Charleston, argued that the 1790 document was a mere alteration or amendment to the 1778 fundamental law and left intact its religious establishment provisions. The result was not disestablishment but a broadening of the establishment from a state endorsement of Protestant Christianity to establishment of Christianity in general, presumably including principles shared by Protestants and Catholics. Doctor Adams described the 1790 document as changing its 1778 predecessor in the following respects:

> The Constitution of 1790 then 'alters and amends' the former Constitution [1778], so far as religion is concerned, chiefly in these particulars - 1st It discontinues all preference for Protestantism over any other form of Christianity. 2d. It 'allows' the 'free exercise, of their religion,' whatever this may be, to all mankind. It is too manifest to require argument, that these 'alterations and amendments' made by the Constitution of 1790, leave Christianity, that is Christianity without distinction of sects, precisely as they found it established by the constitution of 1778.[98]

One of the practical impacts of the adoption of the Constitution of 1790 was that it permitted the incorporation of Catholic churches and Jewish synagogues as well as Protestant churches. A 1791 act incorporated the Catholic Church in Charleston giving it the standard powers to sue and be sued, adopt a seal, have "perpetual succession of officers and members," to adopt by-laws consistent with the "laws of the land," to select ministers and pay them out of corporate funds, and to buy and sell property and to "have, hold, receive, enjoy, possess and retain, to itself and to its successors . . ." property not to exceed 5000 pounds in value.[99] An upper limit on the amount of property that could be held was not found in all church incorporations, but it was not unusual either. It does not seem to represent an anti-Catholic form of discrimination.[100] On the same day that the Catholic Church Incorporation Act was passed, the legislature enacted a statute incorporating Beth Elohim (House of God).[101] The preamble of the act quoted Article 8, section 1, of the 1790 Constitution noting that it granted free exercise of religion without discrimination or preference. The act then proceeded to grant the standard corporate powers to the congregation. The powers granted were substantially the same as those given to the Catholic Church including the 5,000 pound limit on property holdings. A few minor differences between the two acts are attributable perhaps to the different traditional forms of governance of the two religions. The Beth Elohim Act stressed the role of the elders in property management. Beth Elohim had the power to fire as well as hire its ministers or rabbis. No mention of a congregational right to fire ministers was made in the Catholic Act.

A few years after the Act of Incorporation, another piece of special legislation was passed with regard to the Catholic Church in Charleston. This act noted that land had escheated to the state from the estate of Joseph Mincon. The statute noted that Mincon was a member of the Church and had expressed a desire to leave the land to the church, but that his death intervened before formalities could be completed. The act carried out the deceased's intention by transferring the property from the state to the church authorities.[102] This bespeaks fair treatment by the state to the church rather than the fiscally stingy measures that could have been taken toward a minority religion. In addition to the greater ease in property management wrought by the Constitution of 1790, it also facilitated open celebration of the Mass.[103]

The established church had been a strong gravitational force that had kept the concept of church-state relations in South Carolina mired in a bog of discrimination among religions. The 1790 Constitution with its abolition of the established church, protection of free exercise without discrimination or preference, and its abolition of religious tests for voting or office holding, permitted the South Carolina concept of church-state relations to break free of that gravitational pull of officially-endorsed religion to join the more liberal orbit influenced by the federal Bill of Rights, and local leaders such as Charles Pinckney, who embraced its concept that the search for faith was a matter for personal rather than government decision. However, the 1790 Constitution did not usher in a golden age of freedom. Prejudice and discriminatory practices were far from extinct. Sometimes prejudice became inextricably entwined with good motives, with reforms that achieved beneficial results along with the baser metal it also produced. Such an anomalous mixture is found in the Sunday Laws, or Blue Laws, which afforded the benefit of a day of rest but sometimes at the expense of adopting the customs of one religion in preference to others. The nature of these laws in early colonial times, their fate under the 1790 Constitution and later fundamental laws, and their legislative revision to accommodate the realities of the market place form our next focal point.

NOTES

1. Quebec Act, 14 George III C. 83, XXX STATUTES AT LARGE (English) 551, para. V and VI (1774) (Pickering edition) [hereinafter Quebec Act].

2. Quebec Act at 551, para. V.

3. Quebec Act at 551, para. VI.

4. Preamble, S.C. CONST. OF 1776.

5. J. DRAYTON, MEMOIRS OF THE AMERICAN REVOLUTION, VOL. I at 136, VOL. II at 186 (1821); *and see* J. BRINSFIELD at 81.

6. Richard Furman, *Address on Liberty, Nov. 1775,* at 5, Richard Furman Collection, Furman University.

7. C. WOODMASON, THE CAROLINA BACK COUNTRY ON THE EVE OF THE REVOLUTION (R. Hooker ed. 1953)[hereinafter cited C. WOODMASON].

8. C. WOODMASON at 27-28, 72, 86.

9. C. WOODMASON at 43.

10. C. WOODMASON at 86.

11. C. WOODMASON at 119.

12. C. WOODMASON at 57.

13. C. WOODMASON at 57 n. 48.

14. C. WOODMASON at 90.

15. C. WOODMASON at 15.

16. J. BRINSFIELD at 64.

17. South Carolina and American General Gazette, Dec. 5-12, 1776, 129, Col. 3.

18. South Carolina and American General Gazette Dec. 5-12, 1776, 129.

19. *See* the text of the speech reproduced in full in the appendix to D. RAMSAY, THE HISTORY OF THE INDEPENDENT OR CONGREGATIONAL CHURCH IN CHARLESTON, SOUTH CAROLINA, FROM ITS ORIGIN TILL THE YEAR 1814, 53-71 (1815) [hereinafter cited as INDEPENDENT HISTORY].

20. INDEPENDENT HISTORY at 53-54.

21. INDEPENDENT HISTORY at 65.

22. INDEPENDENT HISTORY at 54.

CHAPTER FOUR—NOTES

23. INDEPENDENT HISTORY at 54.

24. INDEPENDENT HISTORY at 54-55.

25. INDEPENDENT HISTORY at 55.

26. INDEPENDENT HISTORY at 57-58.

27. INDEPENDENT HISTORY at 58.

28. INDEPENDENT HISTORY at 59.

29. INDEPENDENT HISTORY at 60.

30. INDEPENDENT HISTORY at 60-61 (emphasis in original).

31. INDEPENDENT HISTORY at 61.

32. INDEPENDENT HISTORY at 61-62.

33. INDEPENDENT HISTORY at 62.

34. INDEPENDENT HISTORY at 62.

35. INDEPENDENT HISTORY at 63-64.

36. INDEPENDENT HISTORY at 63.

37. J. BRINSFIELD at 120-23.

38. J. BRINSFIELD at 120; *and see* H. COOK, A BIOGRAPHY OF RICHARD FURMAN 55 (1913) (based on notes by Wood Furman).

39. J. BRINSFIELD at 120.

40. E. MCCRADY, THE HISTORY OF SOUTH CAROLINA IN THE REVOLUTION 1775-1780 212-13 (1901) [hereinafter cited as E. MCCRADY]; *and see* J. BRINSFIELD at 120.

41. J. BRINSFIELD at 126.

42. S.C. CONST. OF 1778 art. 38.

43. *See* MERIWETHER, BASIC DOCUMENTS OF SOUTH CAROLINA HISTORY, THE CONSTITUTION OF 1778, INTRO. TO THE S.C. CONST. OF 1778, (S.C. Historical Society) (J.H. Easterby ed. 1953).

44. INDEPENDENT HISTORY at 33.

45. INDEPENDENT HISTORY at 33-34.

46. J. BRINSFIELD at 123-24.

47. J. BRINSFIELD at 123-124.

48. *See* G. ROGERS, CHURCH AND STATE IN EIGHTEENTH CENTURY SOUTH CAROLINA at 13.

49. *See* Act No. 1102 of 1778, 8 S.C. STATUTES AT LARGE 119 (McCord 1840).

50. Act No. 1166 of 1783, 8 S.C. STATUTES AT LARGE 122 (McCord 1840).

51. Act No. 1166 of 1783, 8 S.C. STATUTES AT LARGE at 122, preamble (McCord 1840).

52. Act No. 1166 of 1783, 8 S.C. STATUTES AT LARGE at 123-24, para. IX (McCord 1840).

53. Act No. 1166 of 1783, 8 S.C. STATUTES AT LARGE at 122-23, para. IV (McCord 1840).

54. Act No. 1278 of 1785, 8 S.C. STATUTES AT LARGE 130 (McCord 1840).

55. Act No. 1278 of 1785, 8 S.C. STATUTES AT LARGE 130, preamble (McCord 1840).

56. Act No. 1278 of 1785, 8 S.C. STATUTES AT LARGE 131, para. III (McCord 1840).

57. Act No. 1278 of 1785, 8 S.C. STATUTES AT LARGE 131, para. IV (McCord 1840).

58. Act No. 1278 of 1785, 8 S.C. STATUTES AT LARGE 131, para. IV (McCord 1840).

59. For another statute describing the shift of Episcopal churches from a government support to a membership support system *see* Act No. 1289 of 1785, 4 S.C. STATUTES AT LARGE 703 (Cooper 1838).

60. *See* Petition of Samuel Beach With Regard to Pew Assessments for St. Philip's and St. Michael's Churches to the General Assembly February 19, 1787 (available S.C. Department of Archives and History, Document number 0010 003 1787 00040 00).

CHAPTER FOUR—NOTES

61. *See* Reports of the Committee To Review the Petition of Samuel Beach on Pew Assessments at St. Philip's and St. Michael's Churches, February 24 and 26, 1787 (available at S.C. Department of Archives and History Document Numbers 0010 004 1787 000 58 [and 62] 00); *see also* M. Chandler, Church Incorporation in South Carolina under the Constitution of 1778 56-58 (1969) (unpublished master's thesis available University of South Carolina, Columbia, South Carolina) (contains an account of the reasoning of the committee Reports. Chandler notes that one of the "laws" upon which the committee based its conclusion that the various denominations had been given equal pew assessment authority had never been enacted).

62. *See* Chandler *supra* at 58-59 *but see* Act No. 1415 of 1788 of 8 S.C. STATUTES 145 at 147 para. IV (McCord 1840).

63. C. WOODMASON at 42.

64. *See* J. BRINSFIELD at 47.

65. J. BRINSFIELD at 47, 90; *see also* I J. DRAYTON, MEMOIRS OF THE AMERICAN REVOLUTION 300-302 (1821).

66. Bishop England's Discourse Preached in the Hall of the House of Representatives of the Congress of the United States in the City of Washington, January 8, 1826 (available South Caroliniana Library, Columbia, S.C.).

67. TIME MAGAZINE, February 19, 1990 at 75; *see* the discussion of the difficulties encountered by twentieth-century Catholic governors Alfred E. Smith and Mario Cuomo of New York in resisting the pressure of church officials that they follow Catholic policy with regard to child labor laws and abortion restrictions respectively. N.Y. Times, February 22, 1990 15-A, col. 1 (National Edition).

68. II D. RAMSAY at 22.

69. II D. RAMSAY at 22.

70. B. ELZAS, THE JEWS OF SOUTH CAROLINA, *supra* at 19; *and see* L. LEVINGER at 92.

71. R. ST. JOHN at 62; *and see* R. LEARSI at 33; *but see* Comments of A.S. Salley Jr. described in Elzas v. Huhner reprinted in The News and Courier, February, 1903 at 2. Salley contends that Jewish votes in the 1702 election were considered by many to be illegal and thus not eligible to be counted. He further argues that there were not enough Jewish settlers in the colony at that time to have an appreciable impact on the outcome of the election.

72. R. ST. JOHN at 63.

73. I SLOAN, THE JEWS IN AMERICA 1621-1970 at 4 (1971); R. ST. JOHN at 75; R. LEARSI at 33; L. LEVINGER at 94; Elzas v. Huhner, reprinted in the News and Courier, February, 1903 at 2; and C. REZNIKOFF at 7-8.

74. R. ST. JOHN at 75 (Jews composed about fifty percent of the company); *see also* L. HUHNER, SOME ADDITIONAL NOTES ON THE HISTORY OF JEWS IN SOUTH CAROLINA (1910) (Publication of the American Jewish Historical Society No. 19; available in the South Caroliniana Library); *but see*, Elzas v. Huhner reprinted in The News and Courier, Feb., 1903 at 3 (Rabbi Dr. Barnett Elzas states that the company, commanded by Captain Richard Lushington was not made up exclusively or even predominantly of Jews).

75. R. LEARSI at 48.

76. *See, The Congregation 'Beth Elohim,' Charleston SC*, 1750-1883, reprint from YEAR BOOK OF CITY OF CHARLESTON SC, 301 (1883) (spelled Beth Eloihim in incorporation act but now known as Kahal Kadosh Beth Elohim or Beth Elohim); L. LEVINGER at 93 (Levinger considers Beth Elohim to be the third oldest Jewish congregation in the United States after those in New York and Newport, with Savannah, Philadelphia and Richmond having the fourth, fifth, and sixth oldest respectively); *see also* S.C. CONST. OF 1778 art. 38 (provides only for incorporation of Protestant churches).

77. II D. RAMSAY, HISTORY OF SOUTH CAROLINA FROM ITS FIRST SETTLEMENT IN 1670 TO THE YEAR 1808 23 (1809, reprinted 1858) [hereinafter II D. RAMSEY].

78. 3 THE ANNALS OF AMERICA 1784-1796 194 (1976).

79. 3 THE ANNALS OF AMERICA at 194-95; *see also* R. LEARSI at 48.

80. Journal of the Constitutional Convention of South Carolina, May 10, 1790-June 3, 1790 11 (1946).

81. Ulmer, *James Madison and The Pinckney Plan*, 9 S.C.L.Q. 415, 442 (1957).

82. *See* II M. FARRAND, RECORDS OF THE FEDERAL CONVENTION OF 1787 342 (1911).

83. For a Jewish commentator who credits Charles Pinckney as being a major force in broadening religious freedom in the Constitution of 1790, *see* H. GOLDEN, JEWISH ROOTS IN THE CAROLINAS — A PATTERN OF AMERICAN PHILO-SEMITISM 14-15 (1955).

84. I ANNALS OF CONGRESS, FIRST CONGRESS 88 (1789). Apparently the printer mislabeled the date as February 25th even though the passage appears in the September sequence.

85. 1 ANNALS OF CONGRESS, FIRST CONGRESS 440-41 (1789).

CHAPTER FOUR—NOTES

86. 1 ANNALS OF CONGRESS, FIRST CONGRESS 440-41 (1789).

87. 1 ANNALS OF CONGRESS, FIRST CONGRESS 961 (1790); *and see* Journal of Constitutional Convention of South Carolina, May 10, 1790 - June 3, 1790 (1946).

88. Brevard's Observations, 1 S.C. STATUTES AT LARGE 436 (Cooper 1836).

89. II D. RAMSAY at 78-79.

90. C. REZNIKOFF at 59.

91. *See* B. ELZAS at 126-27; *and see* C. REZNIKOFF at 59-60. Both accounts list the candidate's name as Christopher Knight and give the impression that his candidacy was successful. However, an examination of convention records does not find him listed among the delegates. *See* Journal of the Constitutional Convention of South Carolina, May 10, 1790-June 3, 1790 3-7 (1946).

92. *See* S.C. CONST. OF 1790, Dec. 19, 1833 Amendment, Ratified Dec. 6, 1834, BASIC DOCUMENTS OF SOUTH CAROLINA HISTORY, HISTORICAL COMMISSION OF SOUTH CAROLINA (Lesesne ed. 1952).

93. II D. RAMSAY at 79.

94. *See* The Case of Thomas Cooper M.D. President of the South Carolina College, submitted to the Legislature and the People of South Carolina, Dec. 1831 at 3-6 (1839) (Available in South Caroliniana Library).

95. 2 S.C. STATUTES AT LARGE 707 (Cooper 1837).

96. *See* Journal of The Constitutional Convention of South Carolina (1790) May 24 at 20, May 15 at 14 (1946) (referring to services conducted by the Reverend Doctor Henry Purcell and Reverend Richard Furman).

97. Marsh v. Chambers, 463 U.S. 783, 103 S. Ct. 3330, 77 L. Ed. 2d 1019 (1983).

98. A Sermon, Preached in St. Michael's Church, Charleston, February 13, 1833, Before the Convention of the Protestant Episcopal Church of the Diocese of South Carolina by Rev. J. Adams, DD, President of the College of Charleston at 38, 44. *See* especially p. 38, available at the South Caroliniana Library, University of South Carolina, Columbia, South Carolina.

99. *See* Act No. 1515 of 1791, 8 S.C. STATUTES AT LARGE 161-162 (McCord 1840).

100. *See* Act No. 1166 of 1783, 8 S.C. STATUTES AT LARGE, 122-23, para. IV (McCord 1840) (500 pound limit on the holdings of a Calvinist church).

101. *See* Act No. 1516 of 1791, 8 S.C. STATUTES AT LARGE 162 (McCord 1840).

102. *See* Act No. 1723 of 1799, 5 S.C. STATUTES AT LARGE 357 (Cooper 1839).

103. *See* J. BRINSFIELD at 47 (places the time of the first legal Mass in Charleston as 1790).

CHAPTER FIVE

SUNDAY: THE LORD'S DAY

A. THE EARLY SUNDAY STATUTES

Modern Sunday laws have taken on a secular cast by serving the purpose of providing a day of rest and quiet that permits the worker and the economy to recharge batteries for another day of maximum effort. Earlier Sunday laws had an undeniably religious flavor, and atavistic traces of a religious purpose are seen by some to be lurking just beneath the thin patina of secular justification that covers such laws. South Carolina Sunday laws trace their language and approach to a 1677 English statute.[1] A key portion of that statute states:

> And that all and every person and persons whatsoever shall on every Lords day apply themselves to the observation of the same by exercising themselves thereon in the dutyes of piety and true religion publiquely and privately and that noe tradesman, artificer workeman labourer or other person whatsoever shall doe or exercise any worldly labour, busines or worke of their ordinary callings upon the Lords day or any part thereof (workes of necessity and charity onely excepted) and that every person being of the age of fourteene

> yeares or upwards offending in the premisses shall for every such offence forfeit the summe of five shillings, and that noe person or persons whatsoever shall publickly cry shew forth or expose to sale wares merchandizes, fruit, herbs goods or chattells whatsoever upon the Lords day or any part thereof upon paine that every person soe offending shall forfeite the same goods soe cryed or shewed forth or exposed to sale.[2]

Another section of the act forbade travel on Sunday except when ". . . upon extraordinary occasion . . ." permission was given by a justice of the peace or head officer of the county or city in which such travel was to occur.[3] The intermixture of church and state authority is signaled by the fact that enforcement of key features of the act, such as seizure of goods sold on Sunday, could be enforced by church wardens as well as civil constables.[4] Even in this early statute, the law-makers had to bow to reality and insert practical exceptions. Families were permitted to dress their own meat on Sundays, ". . . inns, cookeshops or victualling houses . . ." could prepare and sell food ". . . for such as otherwise cannot be provided . . ." and milk, an item that spoiled quickly in the days before refrigeration, could be sold before nine in the morning and after four in the afternoon.[5]

Legal process could not be served on Sunday except with regard to treason, felony or breach of peace, all matters requiring immediate action else the perpetrator flee or additional offenses be committed.[6]

The religious goals underlying this act are seen not only in its directive to cease "worldly labour" but also in the affirmative obligation of all ". . . to apply themselves to the observation of the same . . ." by acting according to ". . . the dutyes of piety and true religion. . . ." The religious nature of the statute is further underscored by the enforcement authority given to church wardens. Most of the major features of the act and much of its language eventually found their way into South Carolina law. Among these are the prohibition of worldly labor and the sale of goods on Sunday as well as the curbs on Sunday travel and the service of legal process.

The paucity of early records makes it impossible to pinpoint the first Sunday law in South Carolina. A 1685 act revived a 1682 act for the observation of the Lord's Day, but it contains no description of the 1682 law and no copy of the earlier act is available.[7] A 1691 act has survived intact.[8] The preamble of the law reveals that it was enacted to seek God's favor and avoid his harsh judgment. It said:

> Forasmuch as there is nothing more acceptable to Almighty God than the true sincere performance of and obedience to the most divine service and worship, which although at all times, yet chiefly upon the Lord's Day, commonly called Sunday, ought soe to be done, but instead thereof many idle, loose and disorderly people doe wilfully profane the same in tipling, shooteing, gameing, and many other vicious exercises, pastimes and meetings, whereby ignorance prevails and the just judgement of Almighty God may reasonably be expected to fall upon this land if the same by some good orders be not prevented.[9]

The law sought God's bounty for the province by legally enforced standards of morality. In language similar to the 1677 English Act, the statute enjoined all people to observe the Lord's Day by ". . . exercising themselves of piety and true religion."[10] All "worldly labour," except works of "necessity or charity," was to cease on Sunday.[11] The sale of goods on Sunday was forbidden.[12] Travel on the Lord's Day was forbidden except that which was necessary or connected to public worship.[13] To adapt the act to the conditions of the colony, travel was forbidden by canoe as well as by conventional means. Slaves as well as masters were stopped from venturing forth on Sunday. Taverns and public houses could not sell intoxicating beverages on Sunday ". . . unless it be for necessary occasions, for lodgers or sojourners. . . ."[14] In addition to the provisions with a specific focus on Sundays, the act also contained rules applicable every day in order to raise the moral tone of the colony. The statute stated that ". . . whereas the odious and loathsome sin of drunkenness hath of late growne into common use within this province, being the roote and foundation of many other enormous sins . . ." any person found to be drunk would be fined five shillings.[15] In addition ". . . forasmuch as profane sweareing and curseing is forbidden by the word of God . . ." those convicted of uttering profanity would be fined ". . . seaven pence halfepenny . . ." for each "oath or curse."[16] Goods offered for sale on Sunday could be seized and sold. Offenders unable to pay their fines could be placed in the public stocks for two hours.[17] At the discretion of the justices, one-third of the fines or forfeiture sale's price could be given to those who informed on the offender.[18] What a swarm of pious busybodies this must have produced, scurrying about to please God and pad their bank accounts. Like its English predecessor, the act contained practical exceptions permitting taverns and victualling houses to prepare and serve meals to those for whom provision could not otherwise be made as well as an exception for preparing family meals on Sunday. Milk could be sold before nine in the morning or after four in the afternoon.[19]

The law grew increasingly more intricate and precise in directing the manner in which the Lord's Day was to be observed. A 1712 statute not only directed everyone to refrain from worldly work and engage in the worship of the "true religion, publickly and privately . . ." but also mandated that they ". . . shall resort to their parish church, or some other parish church, or some meeting or assembly of religious worship, tolerated and allowed by the laws of this Province, and shall there abide orderly and soberly during the time of prayer and preaching, on pain and forfeiture for every neglect the sum of five shillings current money of this Province."[20] The act continued to permit work of necessity or charity to be performed on Sunday and forbade the sale or display of goods on Sunday.[21] The act continued to restrict travel on Sunday but not only permitted travel to attend worship but also to visit the sick. Those who were on the road when Sunday arrived could proceed no further than necessary to find a suitable resting place. Emergency travel was permitted upon approval by officials.[22]

To assure that people devoted their Sundays to worship instead of idle pursuits that might loosen their moral fiber, the law decreed:

> [T]hat no publick sports or pastimes, as bear-baiting, bull-baiting, foot-ball playing, horse-raceing, enterludes or common plays, or other unlawful games, exercises, sports or pastimes whatsoever, shall be used on the Lord's Day by any person or persons whatsoever, and that every person or persons offending in any of the premises, shall forfeit for every offence the sum of five shillings current money.[23]

This passage demonstrates that the original purpose of Sunday laws was not to provide a day of rest and recreation but was instead to mandate a day of worship. Most forms of recreation were systematically precluded; travel was forbidden and church attendance required. Forbidding such pastimes as "bear-baiting" and "bull-baiting" has a bizarre ring to the modern ear. Oddly enough such archaic language survived into the late twentieth century as if bear-baiting vied with stockcar racing as a means of spending Sunday.[24]

Not only did the 1712 act forbid those who kept inns or "publick houses" from permitting anyone other than transients from remaining on the premises on Sunday and ". . . drinking or idly spending their time on the Lord's Day . . .", it also granted extensive police powers to church-wardens and constables in Charleston to search the "publick houses," and if they found the premises locked, they were empowered to ". . . break open . . ." the doors.[25] In modern jargon, this would be considered a pro-active ordinance. Don't just arrest the lawbreakers who float across your path. Track them down in their lair.

On a more benign note, the act forbade slave owners and masters from forcing their charges to work on Sunday.[26] The proceeds of fines extracted from those who violated the act went to the poor except that informers could be given a portion.[27] The service of legal process except for treason, felony or breach of peace continued to be forbidden.[28]

The more detailed, complex and intrusive laws become, the more difficult they are to enforce because of the difficulty of policing so many aspects of the lives of so many people. Some people assume an air of deliberate defiance born of resentment of the pervasive regulation of highly personal activities. Others simply assume they will not be caught. Charles Woodmason, the Anglican backcountry missionary, complained in a 1768 entry in his journal that:

> The open profanation of the Lords Day in this Povince [sic] is one of the most crying Sins in it - and is carried to great height - Among the low Class, it is abus'd by Hunting fishing fowling, and Racing - By the Women in frolicing and Wantonness. By others in Drinking Bouts and Card Playing--Even in and about Charlestown, the Taverns have more Visitants than the Churches.[29]

A New England visitor to the colony, Josiah Quincy of Massachusetts, wrote perceptively about social and political conditions of South Carolina in 1773. Sunday was indeed a day set aside, but not necessarily for worship as those passing the law intended. He noted that:

> The Sabbath is a day of visiting and mirth with the rich, and of licence, pastime and frolic for the negroes. The blacks I saw in great numbers playing pawpaw, huzzle-cap, pitch penny, and quarrelling round the doors of the Churches in service-time; and as to their priests — Voltaire says "always speak well of the prior." The slaves who don't frolic on the Sabbath, do all kinds of work for themselves on hire.[30]

Woodmason was so irritated by the lack of observance of the Sabbath as a day of worship that he would have extended the laws so that Saturday activities that left the potential worshippers in no condition to attend Sunday services would be banned or rescheduled. He noted that crowds of people descended on the town on Saturdays. Magistrates conducted court on Saturday, planters and merchants conducted sales, and the militia called musters. Many of these activities took place in taverns that were the social focal points. After business was concluded the tendency was to linger in the tavern and drink. Dances and celebrations were held on Saturday. The result of such intense trading, litigating, partying and drinking was that many people were too tired to get up and go to church on Sunday.[31] Of course, expanding the regulations in the manner sought by the frustrated Woodmason would have been impractical because it would have made much of the economic and governmental business impossible to transact if Saturday, as well as Sunday, were placed off bounds for anything but worship and emergency activities.

Certainly such an expansion of the sweep of the Sunday laws would have earned even greater resentment of the general population toward the Anglican establishment. Distaste for the enforcement powers granted to church wardens helped build up popular support for the movement in the mid 1770's to replace the Church of England establishment with a general Protestant establishment as was done in the Constitution of 1778.[32] A noted historian has painted a scene of officious Charleston church wardens stopping butchers, drovers and servants from transporting their goods in carts.[33] Such measures, together with searches of the taverns to ferret out idlers and drunks, may have struck some as exercising too much control over the commercial and social minutiae of life.

B. THE SUNDAY LAWS IN COURT

Sunday closing laws that prohibit the doing of worldly work, the sale of goods, and the pursuit of many recreational activities on a day viewed by many proponents of such laws as a time for worship have raised many constitutional questions beginning with challenges to such provisions brought under the liberal religious freedom standards of the Constitution of 1790 and continuing into the late twentieth century. Many of these challenges were launched by merchants who wanted to operate their stores on Sunday. Most often these suits argued that the Sunday laws forced them to observe the religion of those who choose to worship on Sunday. They further contended that the laws deprived them of their property rights by reducing the profitability of their stores. The attackers also argued that such laws created a preference for, or establishment of, the religions of those who had chosen Sunday as a day of worship. Generally, the Sunday laws have survived such assaults whether launched under the state or federal constitutions. In addition to the fundamental questions raised about the constitutional validity of the Sunday laws, scores of questions concerning the scope and meaning of such laws have arisen.

An early case that significantly influenced the tone and direction of later cases was the 1833 case of *Ex Parte Duke.*[34] That case involved an attack on a Columbia city ordinance that forbade merchants from offering their wares for sale on Sunday. Two shopkeepers brought suit to prohibit enforcement of the provision. They argued that the law violated Article VIII, section 1, of the Constitution of 1790 which guaranteed the free exercise of religion without discrimination or preference for any religion by the government. They also contended that the provision violated the First Amendment of the United States Constitution by creating an establishment of religion and interfering with freedom of conscience. Judge Martin quickly disposed of the allegations of invalidity under the federal Constitution by noting that the First Amendment did not apply to state legislation. The reader should recall that this decision was rendered before passage of the Fourteenth Amendment which applied national standards of justice to the states.[35]

With regard to the challenges brought under the state Constitution of 1790, Judge Martin concluded that the ordinance created no invalid preference since ". . . every class of citizens is embraced . . ." by its prohibition against Sunday commerce. The law did not force some to close while others were allowed to remain open.[36] In a sense the judge was missing the point: the preference lay in choosing the worship day of one segment of the population as the day on which all trade must cease. Did this not encourage the observance of the favored religion and discourage the observance of others? The general thrust of the judge's reasoning went only part of the way toward answering such contentions. A religion is not preferred merely because it is guaranteed a day of quiet for its worship. However, the fact remained that the ordinance singled out the Sunday worshipper for the greatest protection. Even though he does not explicitly say so, the judge seems to be assuming that the only preference or discrimination that violates the religious clauses of the 1790 Constitution are those that force a person to adopt a religion other than his own. Preferences that are more ideological, and less directly coercive, pass muster. It is theoretically possible that if the 1790 Constitution contained an explicit provision prohibiting establishment of religion rather than just having whatever anti-establishment meaning a judge was willing to read into the rule against preferences, that the result would have been different. However, as we shall see, later cases decided under constitutions having explicit anti-establishment provisions upheld similar laws.[37]

The essence of Article VIII, section 1, of the 1790 Constitution was not in forbidding subtle endorsements of certain religious beliefs in preference to others, but in preventing coercion. The judge concluded that the force necessary to violate such a provision was not present. The judge does note that although one of the plaintiffs does not complain about infringement on his religious freedom, that the other, an "Israelite," does contend that there is a discrimination ". . . in favor of all who conceive it to be a duty to keep this day holy. . . ."[38] The implication of the plaintiff's argument was that this preference pressured him toward accepting the dominant religion. The court rejected arguments that coercion was present by noting that the law ". . . enjoins no profession of faith, demands no religious test, extorts no religious ceremony, confers no religious privilege or 'preference.'"[39] Later in the opinion, the judge elaborates on these points by noting that the law ". . . neither compels the relators nor any other to observe or perform devotional exercises on that or any other day, nor forbids or interferes with their doing so, on any other day which their creed may suggest as more sacred."[40] The economic loss arising from inability to open a store on Sunday does not directly forbid the practice of plaintiff's religion and is thus not coercion. The legislature has the power to decide upon what conditions businesses shall be licensed to operate. This includes the power to close the business entirely. Merely requiring the closure of the business on Sunday is merely a less extreme exercise of that same power.[41] It is significant that the Columbia ordinance did not contain provisions like those in the 1677 English act, or the 1712 South Carolina colonial statute, which placed affirmative worship requirements on all citizens such as the provision in the 1712 act requiring church attendance.[42] Such rules clearly would have fit Judge Martin's definition of coercion.

Even though it was apparently a trial court decision rendered by a single judge, the *Duke* case proved to be influential in an 1846 high court decision, *City Council of Charleston v. Benjamin*.[43] The basic skeletal structure of the court's reasoning in *Benjamin* tracked that in the *Duke* decision. However, the *Benjamin* opinion had an aggressive evangelical Christian fervor that had been absent from the dry, unemotional style used in the *Duke* decision. The *Benjamin* case involved a Charleston ordinance that forbade the public sale or display of goods for sale on Sunday. Mr. Benjamin was charged with violating the ordinance by selling gloves in his East Bay Street shop on Sunday, and exposing for sale other merchandise including pantaloons and other clothing. A twenty-dollar fine for each of two alleged offenses was sought from Benjamin in a summary process action brought by the City. The defendant admitted selling the gloves but denied exposing the other goods for sale. The main thrust of his defense was that the city ordinance violated Article VIII, section 1, of the Constitution of 1790 by violating his right to free exercise of religion. These contentions were first considered in the City Recorder's Court. The recorder declared a non-suit because the city ordinance was contrary to Article VIII, section 1, of the Constitution of 1790.

The recorder concluded that the city lacked authority to enact a sweeping ban of all worldly work on Sunday. The only acts that could be banned consistently with the broad free exercise of religion grant of the 1790 Constitution are those that fit under the narrow exceptions to that grant of freedom which is mentioned in Article VIII, section 1 itself, i.e., acts that are "licentious" or inconsistent with "peace or safety." Mr. Benjamin's actions were innocuous and peaceful. The city argued that no damage was done to Benjamin's free exercise rights if he remained free to worship on Saturday as was required by his religion. The act did not interfere with his worship. It only called for the cessation of worldly labor, including the sale of goods, on Sunday. The recorder rejected these contentions and concluded that the law forced the Jewish merchant ". . . to unite, externally, at least, in its [Christian Sunday] observance. . . ."[44]

A discrimination in favor of Christian Sunday worshippers is created by passing laws ". . . to protect from possible disturbance those who worship on that day, by requiring all others to abstain from every species of labor and employment, while the Jewish Sabbath is protected by no similar regulation."[45] The recorder urged Christian advocates of such laws to imagine how they would feel if they were in the minority and a Jewish majority required everyone to cease commercial activity on their day of worship. Religious freedom should be constant and even-handed and not depend upon ". . . the fluctuations of party . . ." brought about by fickle shifts in the majority's view.[46]

The recorder traced the ordinance's philosophy back to the 1712 provincial Sunday law. This theocratic view had been superseded by the broad grant of liberty found in the Constitution of 1790. The city argued that the ordinance was merely a police provision, designed to maintain peace and order, and that it was not enacted with the view of favoring any religious faith. In response, the recorder observed that even if the law had no purpose of favoring a particular religion, it had that effect.[47]

The recorder hastened to note that he was not suggesting that no police measures could be adopted regarding Sunday. Neutral health-safety rules could be adopted. Among the measures that he believed would meet the neutrality test would be laws regulating or forbidding the sale of liquor on Sunday and laws forbidding the service of process on that day. These rules served the neutral purpose of providing a day of rest and quiet on Sunday. He also observed that laws prohibiting slave labor on Sunday were humane measures serving a neutral purpose of preserving the slaves' health.[48] Laws against the disturbance of religious worship service also were valid because they sought to provide ". . . equal security . . ." to all sects.[49] All of these conclusions reflected the recorder's philosophy that the 1790 Constitution resulted in a ". . . complete severance between Church and State. . . ."[50]

The city moved in the high court to set aside the non-suit. Mr. Porter, the city attorney, aided by Mr. Petigru, argued that the 1790 Constitution did not change the historic fact that Christianity was a basic premise on which the common law was founded. All the 1790 Constitution did was to remove civil disabilities, such as inability to incorporate. The Constitution tolerated other religions but Christianity was still the foundation of society.[51] Benjamin's attorney, Mr. Philips, pointed to the extreme economic disadvantage which the law caused to his client as it interacted with the dictates of his religion. The result was that he was deprived of two days of livelihood — one because he obeyed the command of his religion not to work on Saturday, and the other day as a result of the Sunday closing law. Thus he was forced to pay a high price for his faith.[52]

Judge O'Neall delivered the court's opinion reversing the recorder. After perfunctory expression of respect for the Jewish religion he adopted a rationale that was based as much on Christian doctrine as civil law. If a traveler had wandered into the proceedings he would have been confused as to whether he was in church or court. With regard to the Sabbath and the influence of Christianity on constitutional law, O'Neall said:

> On that day we rest, and to us it is the Sabbath of the Lord - its decent observance in a Christian community, is that which ought to be expected. It is not perhaps necessary, to the purpose of this case, to rule and hold that Christian religion is part of the common law of South Carolina! Still it may be useful to show that it lies at the foundation of even the Article of the Constitution under consideration, and that upon it rests many of the principles and usages, constantly acknowledged and enforced, in the Courts of justice![53]

Judge O'Neall decided that Article 1, section 8, should receive a "Christian construction."[54] The religious freedom provisions of Article VIII are based on Christ's teaching that his followers should love their enemies. The religious freedom provisions demonstrate a tolerance on the part of Christians for the practices and beliefs of other religions. "But this toleration, thus granted, is a religious toleration. . . ."[55] Article VIII prohibits religious practices that are "licentious." Licentious acts are those which are ". . . calculated to shock the moral sense of the community, where they take place."[56] Standards of morality were community-oriented in O'Neall's view. He noted that the "orgies of Bacchus" and the "Carnivals of Venice" were acceptable in their day and time, but in 1846 Charleston, an open playhouse or circus on Sunday would violate community standards.[57] The people of Charleston loved the "'house of God' more than the 'tents of wickedness'."[58] Not only was constitutional law based on Christian principles but so were such staples of the common law as contract laws which were based on the integrity of a person's word. The common law was based on general Christianity not the Christianity of a particular sect but the doctrines on which all Christians agreed. These principles undergirded the constitution.[59]

O'Neall was rewriting the Constitution of 1790 to recapture an idyllic earlier time. Religious freedom was a matter of tolerance to him rather than guaranteed rights. The reader will recall that the discussion above of the adoption of the 1778 Constitution noted the distinction made by the Reverend William Tennent between mere toleration and guaranteed rights. It was not enough that Protestant dissenters were tolerated in a system that established the Church of England. Such a tolerance was subject to revocation by the dominant sect. Minority rights had to be guaranteed against the possibly fickle attitude of the majority. Jewish citizens also might prefer to anchor their religion in the firm ground of guaranteed rights rather than the quicksand of tolerance. O'Neall did not seem to recognize these distinctions. His insistence that the common law was based on a consensus among Christians virtually read out of Article VIII the words extending religious freedom "to all mankind" except to the limited extent of recognizing the removal of civil disabilities, such as inability to incorporate and sue and be sued as an entity, that had previously handicapped non-Christian religions. In sustaining the Sunday closing laws, the *Benjamin* case did nothing unusual. This was a mainstream outcome which, as we shall later see, would fit comfortably among modern case law. What was significant was the recasting of the Constitution of 1790 as an essentially Christian document.

Oddly enough, after arguing that Christianity formed the basis of constitutional law and that thus statutes could be enacted to preserve its principles, he found it necessary to conclude that the Sunday laws were not designed to serve religious purposes, but merely to achieve the secular goal of a day of rest and quiet.[60] No preference was given to Christianity, he argued, since adherents of all sects were equally required to close on Sunday.[61] This reasoning proves too much. Following it, you could just as easily conclude that a law requiring the recitation of a Mohammedan prayer is valid because all sects, Mohammedan and non-Mohammedan, are equally subject to the requirement to say the prayer.

O'Neall observed that the free exercise of religious rights of the Jewish merchant was not violated since he was not required to work on his Sabbath. He could still worship. Thus the law, by requiring Sunday rest, did not directly harm his Saturday worship. This reasoning anticipated part of the rationale underlying twentieth-century United States Supreme Court cases, such as *Braunfeld v. Brown*, which sustained Sunday closing laws.[62] In other words, the same result could have been reached in the *Benjamin* case without the use of such divisive rhetoric that watered down the religious freedom guarantees of the Constitution of 1790 to mere favors granted by the tolerance of the Christian majority.

Judge Wardlaw filed a brief concurring opinion in *Benjamin*. He concluded that it was a legitimate police measure to set aside a day of rest to preserve health and safety. It was only logical that the day set aside be one on which the majority of the population would be taking the day off anyway.[63]

Morton Borden has collected contemporary Jewish reactions to the *Benjamin* decision.[64] One commentator called O'Neall "unquestionably a fanatic" and "an unsafe judge on all questions bearing upon his own bigoted notions."[65] This commentator thought that the opinion treated Jews as less then full members of the political community. He stated that:

> The Judge, throughout, treats Jews as though they were not his equals -his fellow-citizens . . . I protest against these terms, "*you*", "*us*", "*our laws*". Such language is unworthy of an American judge.[66]

Other Jewish critics of the opinion focused upon what they believed to be O'Neall's contention that Christianity could be the only true basis of morality.[67] O'Neall responded to these criticisms, but in terms that only served to reinforce the view that he had written his personal opinions as if they were law. He stated ". . . how I, *not born a Jew*, could say otherwise, than that Christianity was the only standard *known* to me of good morals, is hard for me to conceive."[68] By contrast, another contemporary Jewish observer described the decision as "a very able opinion" with which he was in complete agreement.[69] He concluded that the Sunday laws were reasonable exercises of the police power which did not interfere with the Jewish day of worship but which only insured a day of quiet on Sunday for Christian worship.[70]

That the *Benjamin* opinion was not an aberration but a creature of its time is seen by another event nearly contemporaneous with it. In 1844 Governor James H. Hammond of South Carolina issued a Thanksgiving Day Proclamation which announced that America was a Christian nation. He urged "our citizens of all denominations to assemble at their respective places of worship, to offer up their devotions to God their Creator, and his Son Jesus Christ, the Redeemer of the World."[71] Upon receiving a protest from Charleston Jews, Hammond stood his ground when he stated:

> I have always thought it a settled matter that I lived in a Christian land! And that I was the temporary chief magistrate of a Christian people. That in such a country and among such a people I should be, publicly called to an account, reprimanded and required to make amends for acknowledging Jesus Christ as the Redeemer of the world, I would not have believed possible, if it had not come to pass.[72]

The Thanksgiving Day Proclamation was rhetoric, an exhortation to give thanks rather than overt coercion. It created psychological pressure to conform. It did not compel it. Perhaps such a proclamation could pass muster under the free exercise-oriented Constitution of 1790, even though it could be argued that it declared a preference for Christianity. However, many years later, a United States Supreme Court Justice would use the incident as an example of the kind of divisive, biased statement that violated the standard of neutrality underlying the First Amendment of the federal Constitution which prohibits laws respecting the establishment of religion as well as interferences with free exercise of religion. In *County of Allegheny v. A.C.L.U.*[73] Justice Blackmun in his lead opinion stated that such proclamations ". . . demonstrate an official *preference* for Christianity and a corresponding official *discrimination* against all non-Christians, amounting to an exclusion of a portion of the political community."[74]

Hammond complained to his diaries that his successors in the governorship had not continued in their Thanksgiving proclamations the precedent he had set in his decree of making a reference to the Redeemer and thus make a "point" to the Jews.[75] Governor Hammond's reaction to the protest of the Charleston Jews stands in contrast to the response of one of his predecessors in a similar controversy. In 1812 Governor Henry Middleton inadvertently omitted Jews from a proclamation calling upon Christian denominations to have Thanksgiving services. When this omission was called to his attention Governor Middleton sent an apology to Beth Elohim Synagogue. He announced that he intended no slight against his Jewish fellow citizens. After receipt of this apology Beth Elohim held Thanksgiving services according to its own mode.[76] However, in the 1840's, the court's reasoning in the *Benjamin* case and Governor Hammond's Christian-oriented Thanksgiving Day Proclamation seemed to express the same core idea: law, morality and freedom were all founded upon Christian principles and should be interpreted in a manner that would vindicate Christian beliefs if this could be done in a way that did not directly coerce adherents of other religions into adopting Christian modes of worship or into abandoning their own. Psychological pressure and indirect economic pressure arising from the arrangement of society's schedule around Sunday as a day of worship were permissible even if direct coercion was not.

The practice of the early Presidents of the United States with regard to Thanksgiving proclamations varied. Washington issued proclamations urging the citizens to give thanks for the formation of the *new* Constitution, and on two occasions he issued proclamations advocating that the people give thanks for the cessation of the threat of war.[77] Thomas Jefferson and Andrew Jackson opposed issuing such proclamations, and James Madison was described as having "misgivings" about such proclamations.[78]

After the *Duke* and *Benjamin* cases, most South Carolina cases dealing with Sunday closing laws dealt with statutory interpretation. What did the statutes permit to be done and what did they prohibit being done on Sunday? Most of these cases did not confront constitutional issues but implicitly assumed the validity of Sunday closing laws. A few early twentieth-century cases gave the constitutional issues a quick glance and upheld the statutes in an automatic, reflexive way, unaccompanied by much reasoning. In a 1915 case, *State v. Hondros,*[79] the defendant was charged with violating section 699 of Vol II, Criminal Code of South Carolina, by selling two after-dinner cigars to a guest in his boarding house on a Sunday. He was convicted and ordered to forfeit twelve boxes of cigars. The court summarily rejected defense allegations that the conviction violated the South Carolina Constitution of 1895 and the United States Constitution. Among the contentions of unconstitutionality rejected virtually without any explanation by the court were the following: (1) the confiscation of the cigars constituted an illegal forfeiture of an estate in violation of Article I, section 8, of the original Constitution of 1895; (2) the magistrate exceeded his jurisdiction in violation of Article V, section 21, of the Constitution of the state; (3) the fine assessed was excessive, contrary to South Carolina Constitution Article I, section 19; (4) the defendant was not afforded due process of law as required by Article I, section 5, of the state Constitution and the Fifth Amendment of the federal Constitution; (5) the confiscation was an unreasonable seizure under the federal Fourth Amendment and (6) the Sunday closing laws were an invalid establishment of religion contrary to Article I, section 4, of the original Constitution of 1895 as well as the First Amendment to the federal Constitution. It should be noted that the Constitution of 1895 in Article I, section 4 (now section 2), had an explicit clause prohibiting laws respecting the establishment of religion as well as guaranteeing free exercise of religion. The 1790 Constitution under which *Benjamin* was decided focused primarily on protecting freedom of worship and dealt with the problem of the establishment of religion by the omission of any provision creating an officially-sanctioned church. However, the presence of an explicit prohibition of the establishment of religion in the 1895 Constitution did not change the result.

The court justified its conclusion that the Sunday laws did not constitute an establishment of religion by flatly saying that the contention has ". . . over and again been construed against the appellant." This assertion is fortified only by the citation of three cases: the *Benjamin* case; *Cain v. Daly,*[80] and *State v. James.*[81] None of these cases fully justifies the *Hondros* outcome. *Benjamin* was decided under the 1790 Constitution which contained no explicit establishment clause as does the Constitution of 1895. *Cain* and *James* were basically statutory construction cases rather than cases determining the statute's validity under the religion clauses.

Cain determined that the rule against Sunday sales applied to sales made by automatic vending machines as well as those made by human labor. The court did confront the contention that the statute was void as a result of obsolescence or desuetude (non-use) but concluded that courts should be hesitant to declare a statute inoperative unless it clearly was superseded by later statutes. A declaration of obsolescence might constitute court intrusion on a legislative role.[82] However, in reaching this conclusion, the court did not consider the statute's validity under the religious clauses. In *James*, the court concluded that the sale of ice and fresh meat on Sunday did not amount to acts of necessity permitted to be done on Sunday under the statute. The court does not explicitly address the constitutionality of the statute. Thus the court in *Hondros* essentially issued a flat decree that the statute was constitutional. A similar approach was followed in *Charleston Oil Co. v. Poulnot*,[83] which simply stated that the Sunday closing laws had been consistently held to be constitutional. The case was largely concerned with holding that the statutes prohibited the routine sale of gasoline on Sunday. Gasoline was not then considered a necessity exempt from the prohibition on Sunday sales. In *Palmetto Golf Club v. Robinson*[84] the court held that section 715 of the 1922 Criminal Code, Volume 2, which prohibited certain sports considered disruptive of the Sunday quiet and work-free environment, did not prohibit amateur golf but did prohibit compensated labor associated with golf. Applied in this fashion, the law was constitutional. Here again, the court simply issued a constitutional clean bill of health without explanation.

In a 1928 case, *Xepapas v. Richardson*,[85] the plaintiffs, Columbia merchants, stated that some of them were Jewish and others Christians but all had for many years operated their stores on Sunday. Recently, however, Columbia police officers had threatened to confiscate and sell the goods which the plaintiffs had exposed for sale on Sunday. The plaintiffs contended that the Sunday closing statutes upon which the officers based their warnings, sections 713, 714 and 717 of the Criminal Code of 1922, Vol. 2 c. 16, were unconstitutional in that they were laws respecting the establishment of religion, would subject them to a trial without a jury, granted a magistrate power in excess of that permitted by the state constitution and violated their rights to equal protection and due process of law. Thus they asked the court to enjoin enforcement of the law.

The court rejected the attack on the Sunday closing laws as being provisions respecting an establishment of religion. The court considered the question to have been settled long ago in the *Benjamin* case which had been cited repeatedly with approval by more recent cases such as *Charleston Oil v. Poulnot.* The *Benjamin* precedent furnished a ready vehicle for disposing of the plaintiffs' free exercise clause contentions that Jews and Seventh Day Adventists, who did not recognize Sunday as their day of worship, were forced to hold that day sacred by having to cease business to preserve a day of quiet. However, as noted earlier, *Benjamin* is a less useful precedent for deflecting arguments that the Sunday laws violated the establishment clause since the 1790 Constitution under which it was decided had no such clause.

The court ruled against the plaintiffs on their contention that the statutes violated their rights to a jury trial and due process of law as guaranteed by sections 18, 25 and 5 of Article I of the Constitution of 1895 as it was then numbered. The court concluded that when the Sunday laws were viewed not in isolation, but together with other provisions governing magisterial proceedings, the plaintiffs were guaranteed a jury trial and an adequate opportunity to present their case. The court used a similar technique to jettison the plaintiffs' contentions that Sunday laws granted magistrates power in excess of their constitutional maximum as defined by Article V, section 21, of the original 1895 Constitution which prohibited magistrates from exercising jurisdiction in cases in which the amount claimed exceeded $100. The court concluded that any implication found in the Sunday laws that magistrates could preside over forfeiture proceedings involving goods valued at more than $100 was removed when the Sunday statutes were considered together with other laws controlling magistrates' courts which clearly made such an interpretation impossible.

Only on the allegations of equal protection clause violations did the Sunday closing laws stumble. The plaintiffs argued that the Sunday laws violated the equal protection clauses found in Article I, section 5, of the state constitution and the Fourteenth Amendment to the United States Constitution because the provisions providing for forfeiture of goods exposed for sale on Sunday applied only to individual proprietorships and partnerships such as the plaintiffs and left their corporate competitors unscathed. The court agreed that in *Charleston Oil v. Poulnot* it had held that the forfeiture provisions did not apply to corporations. The court concluded that the statutes violated the equal protection clauses by treating similarly situated businesses differently. The plaintiffs were less successful in arguing that another provision of the Sunday laws, section 713, prohibiting worldly work on Sunday, also violated the equal protection clauses by treating the plaintiffs unfairly in comparison with corporations. Since work is performed by individuals, not abstract entities, section 713 could not be applied directly to corporations except when they illegally forced employees to work on Sunday. However, individual employees of corporations could be fined for doing worldly labor on Sunday. This was enough to discourage corporate competitors from stealing a march on the plaintiffs. However, the court did agree to enjoin enforcement of the forfeiture provision as violative of the equal protection clauses. Normally, courts are reluctant to enjoin enforcement of the criminal laws, but when application of those laws would inflict irreparable harm on property rights, an exception to the usual rule can be made.

Justice Carter dissented without opinion. Justice Cothran concurred in the result but expressed serious misgivings about the validity of the Sunday closing laws under the religious clauses of the constitution. The statutes seemed to him to enshrine the beliefs of one religion concerning the appropriate day of worship thus discriminating against religions choosing a different day. However, he was not yet sure enough of these arguments that he would vote to strike down the laws.

As the economic stakes involved in Sunday closing grew, so did the energy with which those statutes were challenged. As a result, court decisions disposing of those attacks could no longer afford summarily to brush aside such controversies as dealing with issues that had long been settled. The most complete discussion of the validity of Sunday laws since the 1846 *Benjamin* decision came in the 1960 case of *Carolina Amusement Co. v. Martin.*[86] That case involved a suit brought by motion picture exhibitors and patrons seeking an injunction against enforcement of section 64-1 of the 1952 code by the sheriffs of Greenville and Spartanburg counties. Section 64-1 stated that:

> No public sports or pastimes, such as bear-baiting, bull-baiting, football playing, horse-racing, interludes or common plays, or other games, exercises,

sports or pastimes, such as hunting, shooting, chasing game or fishing, shall be used on Sunday by any person whatsoever. Every person offending in any of the premises shall, upon conviction, be guilty of a misdemeanor and be subject to a fine not to exceed fifty dollars or imprisonment not to exceed thirty days.[87]

The court quickly disposed of the contention that the statute did not apply to motion pictures since that form of entertainment was not specifically mentioned in the statute, and the language originally was drafted long before the invention of the cinema, thus the framers could not have contemplated applying it to such a pastime. The court decided that motion pictures were included in the statutory phrase ". . . interludes or common plays. . . ." The court also rejected plaintiff's argument that the statute should only be construed as prohibiting noisy and disorderly Sunday pastimes. The court observed that the purpose of the statute was to provide a day of rest and that the legislature could reasonably have concluded that motion pictures, even if not noisy, could interfere with the tranquility needed for a day of rest.

As a prelude to addressing the question of whether or not the Sunday laws violated the religious clauses, the court quoted an annotation written in 1837 by the famous editor of South Carolina statutes, Dr. Thomas Cooper, who was by no means a slavish adherent to religious orthodoxy. Dr. Cooper wrote:

For all the laws of morality arise from and are founded upon the duties of man towards man in a state of society. The affairs of the next world, are matters of private belief, not of public cognizance; and the business of society can go on without reference to any religious creed whatever. This principle seems to have suggested the 8th article of our Constitution [of 1790], which enacts that "the free exercise of religious profession and worship, without discrimination or preference, shall forever after be allowed in this State to all mankind." Constitutional law is the paramount law of the land, and every legislative Act contravening it, is ipso facto void.

This does not interfere with the right of the legislature to incorporate religious societies for civil purposes. Nor with the right of appointing a Sabbath or day of rest from labour, as a municipal institution, conducive to civil expedience.[88]

The court then addressed the question of whether the law forbidding motion pictures and other specified forms of entertainment on Sunday violated the provisions in Article I, section 4 (now section 2), of the state Constitution of 1895 and the First Amendment to the United States Constitution which prohibit, in identical terms, government interference with the free exercise of religion and the passage of laws respecting the establishment of religion. The court first considered the question of whether or not the Sunday laws served the purpose of establishing as official doctrine a belief in Sunday worship. In concluding that there was no violation, the courts used a distinction between motive and purpose adopted by the United States Supreme Court in *Hennington v. Georgia,* [89] a case which upheld a Georgia law forbidding the running of freight trains on Sunday. *Motive* concerned the subjective intent of individual legislators. A legislator's motives were no business of the courts. By contrast, in seeking to determine the purpose of the law, the court was not concerned with motive but whether or not a reasonable justification for the act could be found even if the motives of some legislators were not appropriate. According to this analysis, even if legislators originally enacting the Sunday laws had a purpose of advancing religion in mind, if a reasonable secular purpose now could be found to justify continuance of the law, it would withstand constitutional scrutiny. Thus, even though the original motive in adopting the Sunday closing laws was to foster religious worship, an independent, secular purpose now justified their continuance. The laws were legitimate exercises of the police power designed to increase health and safety by providing a day of rest.

Another United States Supreme Court decision cited by the state court as supporting health and safety as valid secular goals for Sunday closing legislation was *Soon Hing v. Crowley.*[90] In that case, the Court emphasized the humane nature of the Sunday laws in providing an opportunity for the urban poor to obtain temporary relief from the monotony and unsanitary conditions of many factory jobs. The South Carolina court in *Carolina Amusement* said that the neutral, secular, health-safety purpose that justified modern Sunday closing laws was not spoiled by the fact that the day chosen by the legislature as one of universal rest happened to coincide with the Christian Sabbath. In fact, that made the choice logical even when viewed through secular glasses since many people would be voluntarily taking that day off anyway. An alternative approach might be to serve the health goal of a day of rest by letting individuals choose their own day of rest. However, the court was quick to point out that this alternative would be much more difficult to enforce than a single day of rest. The choice of a day convenient to the majority who consider Sunday the appropriate rest time because of their religious beliefs does not result in the establishment of those beliefs by the government but is a mere "accommodation" of state health-safety regulations to the customs of the population. This approach follows the lead of the United States Supreme Court in *Zorach v. Clauson*[91] in which the Court approved a voluntary religious study program in a public school system which released students, whose parents so desired, for a period during the school day during which they could go to off-campus religious study centers run by churches. Since the school did not instruct the students in religion, force them to attend or use public facilities for religious instruction, it was merely rearranging its schedule in a way that facilitated (accommodated) religion but did not endorse or sponsor it. Similarly, the laws may have facilitated attendance at Sunday services by affording that day off, but they did not require it nor endorse it as the proper way to spend the day off.

In addition to the religious clause challenges to the ban on Sunday motion pictures, the court considered a grab-bag of equal protection arguments. The plaintiffs argued that by stopping the Sunday exhibition of motion pictures while permitting other commercial leisure activities, the court was discriminating against the plaintiffs in violation of the equal protection clauses in Article I, section 5 of the original state Constitution of 1895 and the Fourteenth Amendment to the federal Constitution. The court rejected these assertions. Governments have limited resources. They cannot always stop all forms of undesirable behavior. Reasonable classifications can be made, but, of course, those within the class must be treated equally. The legislature's classifications are presumed valid. The challenger has the burden of demonstrating that the classification is unreasonable. This is done by showing that there is no permissible hypothesis on which the classification can be based. The legislature is not required to treat all forms of worldly amusement precisely the same. It may ban those which it considers to be most disruptive of the day of rest and permit others. The court will not substitute its judgment for that of the legislature just because members of the court might have made different classifications if they had been in the legislature formulating the system.

Another equal protection clause attack made by the plaintiffs on the Sunday motion picture ban was that the legislature created so many exceptions to the rule by special local legislation permitting the exhibition of motion pictures in certain towns on Sunday, that geographical discrimination was the result. The court spurned this argument by noting that it had not been properly raised in the court below.

Finally, the court tackled the contentions that the plaintiff's free speech rights had been circumscribed in violation of Article I, section 4 (now 2), of the state Constitution of 1895.[92] The state supreme court recognized that the United States Supreme Court in *Joseph Burstyn, Inc. v. Wilson*[93] had ruled that motion pictures were a protected form of speech and that a picture cannot be banned because its content is considered sacreligious. The state court agreed with the conclusion but decided that the rule stopping the exhibition of motion pictures on Sunday did not amount to censorship. It was not a content-based ban reflecting a view that the pictures were sacreligious. The pictures still could be seen on days other than Sunday. Thus the regulation did not fit under the hard-to-justify category of content-based censorship but fell under the more easily sustainable category of time-place-manner regulations. A reasonable time limit in pursuit of the valid health-safety goal of providing a day of rest is permissible.

The court then announced a philosophy that preferred majority rule over minority rights even when it came to such basic rights as freedom of speech. This philosophy was especially appropriate when the speech was profit-motivated. In this vein the court observed:

> With reference to the First Amendment, it seems to us that the court overlooked the fact that the plaintiffs in the case were representatives of a small minority and that the law imposed by the majority cannot be shaped or bent to accommodate their convenience or serve their financial ends.[94]

Several significant United States Supreme Court cases entered the stage at this point and influenced significantly the next round of South Carolina cases. These federal cases, however, signaled no major change in direction. They sustained Sunday closing laws on the basis of reasoning strikingly similar to South Carolina cases stretching all the way back to *Duke* and *Benjamin, supra.*

In *Braunfeld v. Brown*[95] the Supreme Court considered an attack by Orthodox Jews on a Pennsylvania Sunday closing law. The plaintiffs noted that their religion required them to cease all commercial activity on Saturday. When this religious dictate interacted with the state's Sunday closing rule, the result was a devastating economic blow that jeopardized the ability of one of the plaintiffs to remain in business. Not only did the Pennsylvania law place them at a competitive disadvantage vis-a-vis Sunday-worshipping competitors who would be open on Saturday, it placed the Orthodox Jewish religion in an unfavorable position for attracting new adherents. They alleged that this combination of disadvantages wrought by the Pennsylvania law constituted a significant interference with their free exercise of religion.

The Supreme Court rejected these contentions. It noted that although freedom of belief was absolute, freedom of religious practice was subject to regulation to maintain peace and accomplish social goals. However, religious action cannot be regulated by directly compelling one to engage in a practice obnoxious to his religion or to cease a practice required by it. The Pennsylvania law does not directly compel Orthodox Jews to cease worshipping on Saturday or to start worshipping on Sunday. The law's direct impact falls entirely on the secular practice of Sunday commercial activity. It is true that the law has the indirect effect of making the practice of plaintiffs' religion more expensive. However, this indirect economic impact is as much the result of the plaintiffs' own religious choices as of government regulation. The plaintiffs' arguments that they were confronted by the law with unpalatable choices among (1) adhering to both the law and their religion, and thus incurring the economic loss of two days' closure; (2) adhering to their religion and closing on Saturday but flouting the law and opening on Sunday and risking legal penalties; (3) abandoning their religion and adopting a new one that does not require a Saturday day of rest; (4) abandoning their business for one that would not require Sunday opening to make up for the loss required by Saturday closing. Being placed in the position of having to make these difficult choices still fell into the category of indirect disadvantages rather than direct compulsion.

The Court was quick to acknowledge that not all indirect burdens were constitutionally innocuous. It stated that:

> If the purpose or effect of a law is to impede the observance of one or all religions or is to discriminate invidiously between religions, that law is constitutionally invalid even though the burden may be characterized as being only indirect. But if the state regulates conduct by enacting a general law within its power, the purpose and effect of which is to advance the State's secular goals, the statute is valid despite its indirect burden on religious observance unless the state may accomplish its purpose by means which do not impose such a burden.[96]

The plaintiffs asserted that there were indeed less intrusive means by which the state could achieve its secular health-safety goal of providing a day of rest: citizens could choose their own day of rest. The Court concluded that this alternative would not really achieve the state's purpose and would create constitutional problems equally as severe as those about which the plaintiffs complained. It would not provide a universal day of rest on which quiet was the prevailing rule. Rather than policing one day, the government would have to tailor the administration of the day of rest law to each individual's choice. Such individualized policing would entangle the government more deeply in religious affairs. If a person claims the right to open on Sunday because his religion dictated that Saturday would be his day of rest, the state might have to test the sincerity of his beliefs. Permitting each person to choose his own day of rest might result in more religious discrimination in employment practices since it would be more convenient for the employer to select personnel who preferred the same day of rest that he did. In addition, one religiously-based competitive disadvantage would be replaced with another just as obnoxious. If the merchant whose religion decrees Saturday as a day of rest is allowed to open on Sunday when others are not, he will walk away with all of the business. It is less trouble to stick with Sunday as the day of rest. Perhaps that day had been chosen originally to advance the Christian religion, but that reason had long since been overtaken by secular reasons. People were just used to that as the day of rest. Thus it afforded the best route to achieve the government's health-safety goals.

Justices Brennan and Stewart dissented. In their view the plaintiffs were forced to choose between their religion and their livelihood. Such a cruel choice, even though it does not result from a direct compulsion to engage in or cease a religious practice, is a significant free exercise clause violation. Such violations can be justified only by state interests of the highest order such as the prevention of serious and immediate danger. It is not sufficient that such a harsh regulation is merely rationally related to a valid state purpose. The state's purpose of granting everyone a day of rest could be achieved by permitting each individual to select his own day of rest. The administrative convenience of having everyone rest on the same day should not be exalted over one of our most revered rights.[97]

Oddly enough, two years later in *Sherbert v. Verner*[98] the Supreme Court struck down a South Carolina unemployment compensation policy which denied benefits to a Seventh Day Adventist who had been discharged from her position and was unable to find a new job because of her unwillingness to work on Saturday. The state commission which denied her benefits reasoned that she was disqualified because the Saturday worship tradition of her faith did not constitute good cause for turning down jobs that involved Saturday labor. The United States Supreme Court concluded that it constituted an invalid intrusion on her free exercise of religion to make her choose between benefits that might be essential to her livelihood and beliefs vital to her faith. This is much the same kind of cruel choice that left the court unmoved in *Braunfeld*. South Carolina attempted to justify its benefit-denial policy as a measure crucial to avoiding fraudulent claims based on spurious arguments that the claimant's religion necessitated the refusal of proffered work. This justification was rejected by the Court as not properly raised in the court below and unsupported by proof that such malingering was common. However, the Court's conclusion in *Braunfeld* that putting Orthodox Jews to a similar no-win choice was justified because of the administrative convenience of a universal day of rest, as distinguished from individually chosen days, is no more compelling than the state's argument in *Sherbert* that the benefit denial was useful in avoiding fraud.

On the same day that the federal Supreme Court decided *Braunfeld*, it rendered a decision in *McGowan v. Maryland*.[99] In that case, seven employees of a large Maryland discount store were indicted for selling prohibited goods on Sunday. The defendants attacked the Maryland Sunday closing law as violating the equal protection and due process clauses of the Fourteenth Amendment as well as the First Amendment prohibition of an establishment of religion. The defendants contended that the laws violated the equal protection clause by permitting some goods to be sold on Sunday while blocking the sale of other items, including those the defendants were accused of marketing on Sunday. The Court determined that a legitimate distinction could be made between the items permitted to be sold on Sunday and those that were prohibited, since the former were primarily necessities or items that would aid the recreational purpose of Sunday closing, whereas the latter items were goods the purchase of which could easily be postponed to another day.[100] The Court also rejected two charges of geographical discrimination. The first involved an allegation that some sales and forms of entertainment were permitted in some parts of the state but not in others. The Court rejected this argument because the equal protection clause protects persons, not geographical areas.[101] In addition, the Court rejected allegations that the equal protection clause was violated by permitting beach vendors to sell certain items on Sunday but prohibiting sale by stores farther from the beach. The Court concluded that the distinction between the two categories of stores was justified because it made sense to let stores located at recreation sites sell recreation items related to those sites but to deny the right to make similar sales to stores in other areas.[102] The Court also disagreed with the plaintiff's arguments that the laws were too vague to be understood by reasonably intelligent laymen.

The core issue in the case dealt with charges that the Sunday closing laws constituted an establishment of religion in violation of the First Amendment. The Court concluded that the plaintiffs had no standing to raise free exercise clause issues since they had not declared what their religious beliefs were or how the law interfered with their free exercise.[103] On the establishment clause issue, they had standing because they claimed economic injury resulting from establishment of the Christian day of worship.[104]

The Court gave the Sunday laws close scrutiny to determine whether or not they that had the purpose or effect of advancing religion.[105] The plaintiffs argued that the laws were designed to nudge those with "marginal religious beliefs" in the direction of joining the "predominant

Christian sects."[106] They also contended that the day of quiet was intended to create an atmosphere of worship rather than a day of rest to preserve health. In support of this assertion, they noted that forms of activity that were exempt from the Sunday closing laws were not permitted within a certain distance of worship services or were not allowed to begin until the close of normal worship hours. The Court implicitly seemed to regard these schedule regulations as reasonable accommodations to, rather than endorsement of, religion. Picking Sunday as the day of general rest was not intended to advance the predominant Christian sects that worshipped on that day. This was simply the easiest time to administer a day of rest statute since it was the traditional time most people took off anyway. The mere fact that the day chosen by the state as a day of rest happened to coincide with the worship day of some religions was not an endorsement of the doctrines of those religions.[107]

The Court acknowledged that the early Sunday laws were intended to channel the population toward worship.[108] However, such a purpose is not cast in concrete. It can be replaced by another goal. In modern times, the Sunday closing laws have the neutral, secular, health-safety purpose of providing a day of rest and recreation. This modern secular purpose is seen not only in the support given Sunday closing laws by labor leaders and social engineers but by the spate of exemptions from the general closing requirement that permit a wide variety of recreational activities unrelated to worship.[109] The justices also reasoned that there was no effect of advancing religion by nudging citizens in the direction of worship on Sunday since there were too many competing alternative activities, from golf to fishing to late sleeping, in which people could engage.[110] Having determined that the statutes were sufficiently related to a neutral secular goal within traditional police powers, the Court had to confront the question of whether or not these goals could be achieved by means less likely to put pressure toward religious conformity on people. As in *Braunfeld,* one suggested alternative was to let everyone choose his own day of rest. Here again the Court concluded that this technique would not achieve a general day of quiet and would be more difficult to police than a uniform day.

Also decided on the same day as *Braunfeld* and *McGowan* was another attack on Pennsylvania Sunday closing laws in *Two Guys from Harrison - Allentown, Inc. v. McGinley.*[111] The Court rejected contentions that the laws violated the equal protection and establishment clauses. In *Gallagher v. Crown Kosher Super Market*,[112] another companion case to *McGowan* and *Braunfeld*, the Court faced challenges by Orthodox Jewish rabbis, members of their congregations, and Kosher food merchants that the Massachusetts Sunday closing laws violated the equal protection, free exercise and establishment clauses. Based on reasoning similar to *McGowan* and *Braunfeld*, the Court disallowed all challenges.

The cases discussed above loomed large in the reasoning of the South Carolina Supreme Court when it decided *State v. Solomon*.[113] The court described the laws prohibiting Sunday sales in the following terms:

> Three separate offenses are created: (1) engaging in worldly work, labor, or business of one's ordinary calling on Sunday; (2) selling or offering to sell, publicly or privately or by telephone, at retail or wholesale to the consumer any goods, wares or merchandise on Sunday; (3) employing others to engage in work, labor, business or selling or offering to sell any goods, wares or merchandise on Sunday. This section excepts "work of necessity or charity" from the foregoing prohibitions, and is followed by . . . a list of permitted activities and sales and a list of merchandise specifically prohibited from sale on Sunday.[114]

Aaron Soloman was charged with selling and offering to sell at the Sam Solomon Company on Sunday various items including two baby chairs and clothing. The court first disposed of allegations of defective pleading. The defendant contended that the indictment should have alleged that none of the goods sold fit under exemptions to the ban on Sunday sales. The court concluded that the burden was on a defendant claiming to fit under an exception to the ban to plead the exemption.[115]

Much of the court's reasoning with regard to religious clause issues revisited terrain made familiar in *Braunfeld* and *McGowan*. The defendant asserted that the rule against Sunday sales violated Article I, section 4 (now 2), of the state constitution and the First Amendment of the federal Constitution by seeking to create a climate favorable to worship on Sunday. In accordance with the federal Supreme Court decision in *Braunfeld* and *McGowan*, and the earlier state court decision in *Carolina Amusement*, the South Carolina court held that even if the purpose of the early Sunday laws had been to foster worship, the modern purpose was the secular goal of insuring a day of rest. Such a state interest is compelling enough to justify any indirect harm to the defendant's freedom of religion. Such health-safety measures are a valid exercise of the state's police power.[116]

Difficult questions were raised with regard to the provision admonishing those employers who were permitted to be open on Sunday to grant their employees time off to attend church. The court observed that since this measure did not compel the employee to attend services, and attached no penalty to an employer's failure to comply with the admonition, then the statute did not violate the religious freedom of the employer or employee.[117]

The court quickly confronted and disposed of the defendant's allegations of free exercise clause violations by invocation of the United States Supreme Court decision in *Braunfeld,* in which the Court pointed out that since the Sunday closing laws did not directly forbid Saturday worship or compel Jews to observe Sunday as a sacred day, it created only indirect economic burdens on the Orthodox Jews that did not amount to the degree of coercion necessary to violate the free exercise clause. It made the Orthodox Jewish religion more expensive to pursue but it did not block its adherents from remaining loyal to it. The defendant pointed out, however, that in *Sherbert v. Verner,* in which the United States Supreme Court had struck down the South Carolina unemployment compensation policy of denying benefits to those who refused for religious reasons to accept Saturday employment, the Court had based its reasoning on the premise that the free exercise clause prohibited a state from making a person choose between his livelihood and his religion. The South Carolina court in *Solomon* quickly disposed of these contentions by noting that the United States Supreme Court in *Sherbert* had distinguished and left intact its *Braunfeld* approval of Sunday closing laws by noting that the health-safety goal achieved by a universal day of rest was stronger justification for indirect economic burdens on religion than were the state's flimsy attempts in *Sherbert* to rationalize its benefits-denial policy by the need to avoid fraudulent claims. It is interesting to note that more than two decades later in *Lyng v. Northwest Indian Cemetery Protective Association,*[118] the Supreme Court returned to this distinction between direct and indirect burdens on free exercise. In that case, the Court rejected challenges to a federal policy that would permit the completion of a logging road through a portion of a national forest that skirted the periphery of an area that had been used for centuries by Indians as a sacred location in which they could seek the highest levels of spiritual fulfillment. Even though these spiritual exercises were designed for that specific site, and the Court admitted that the intrusion of the road could make it significantly more difficult for the Indians to reach the desired levels of spiritual fulfillment, the Court concluded that the burden on the free exercise of the Indians' religion was not even significant enough to trigger the free exercise clause analytical process of balancing the strength of the government's goals against the degree of intrusion on religion. The burdens on free exercise were too indirect and intangible. The Indians still had complete access to the sacred areas and it was highly speculative as to whether or not their religion would really suffer. Similarly, the courts regarded the impact of Sunday closing laws on Saturday worshippers as too indirect to justify finding an establishment clause violation.

The *Solomon* court then turned to due process and equal protection clause issues. At least since the time of the 1677 English statute with which we began this discussion, the prohibition on worldly labor on Sunday had included an exemption for work of necessity.[119] The defendant in *Solomon*, contended that this exemption was so vague that it violated his due process right to have clear notice under the criminal laws of what he could and could not do. For all he knew, the selling of a baby carriage on Sunday might supply a necessity to a family with children. The court admitted that the term "necessity" was a flexible one that varied as society changed and as circumstances surrounding a particular sale differed from those leading to other transactions. However, "[u]nder the statute, one is not left to guess as to the prohibited conduct."[120] The court noted that a long line of cases interpreting its meaning had added to the specificity of the term.[121] These decisions have developed a definition of necessity that furnished clear guidance to the practical businessman. The court stated that:

> Our decisions have held that a work of necessity means labor reasonably necessary for the worker to perform to save himself from some unforeseen or irreparable injury or loss, or necessary for the welfare of the community in which he resides, viewed in light of the facts and circumstances existing at the time. It does not mean that which is indispensable, but it means something more than that which is merely needful or desirable.[122]

The court concluded without further explanation that the defendant's sales did not fit the definition. Perhaps a baby chair sale, although it was "needful" from a parent's perspective, was not needed to prevent an irreparable harm or to perform a community service. The defendant leveled a similar charge of vagueness at the language exempting "novelties" and "souvenirs" from the ban on Sunday sales. The court summarily dealt with these allegations by noting the exemption employed ". . . terms of common usage in the business world and business people of ordinary intelligence in the position of the defendant would be able to know what exceptions are meant by the terms, either as a matter of ordinary commercial knowledge or upon reasonable investigation."[123]

The court then faced a cluster of equal protection clause challenges to the act. The first of these bore a distinct resemblance to the contention rejected by the United States Supreme Court in *McGowan*, that the lists of goods permitted to be sold on Sunday and those banned bore no rational relationship to the day of rest purpose and amounted to arbitrary and capricious classifications that discriminated against the sellers of the blacklisted items. In denying this challenge, the court employed a more relaxed standard of scrutiny than it had used with regard to the religious clause attacks on the act. Classifications made in business regulations should be struck down only if they are "wholly irrelevant" to accomplishing the state's goal.[124] Legislatures are given broad discretion in superintending the local business climate. The legislature was confronted with a difficult balancing act: prohibiting most sales in order to preserve a day of quiet but allowing transactions that were necessary or contributed to the recreational purpose. The court should not disturb the manner in which the legislature has struck this balance just because the court might have resolved the dilemma differently. Even though it was rejected by the court, it does appear that the defendant had a point. How logical is it to forbid the sale of cameras but permit the sale of films, to permit the sale of swimwear but not the sale of sporting goods except at localities at which athletics were permitted to take place? Both the prohibited and permitted sales would be roughly equal in their contribution to the recreational purpose of the day and similar in their potential for disruptiveness.[125] However, correction of these inconsistencies often can be left to the legislative process. For example, a later version of the Sunday law permitted sale not only of film but cameras and flash bulbs.[126]

An additional equal protection clause challenge dealt with the differential impact of the law on persons and corporations. The defendant argued that since the fines for Sunday sales were assessed only against natural persons and not against corporations that sales personnel were the victims of discrimination. The court observed that all the equal protection clause demanded was similar treatment of those within the same class. Here, all within the class of sales personnel were subject to the same range of fines whether they were employed by individual proprietorships, partnerships or corporations. Since the corporations would not want to expose their employees to fines, they would be deterred from violating the law just as would companies using other business forms. Corporations, as abstract entities, operate through individuals, and it is against the individuals that the onus of the violation must be placed.[127] This reasoning is not entirely convincing since the abstract nature of corporations did not prevent them from being fined. The court was retracing the slippery path it had taken in *Xepapas v. Richardson*. In that case, the court had approved an injunction against the portion of the Sunday closing laws which subjected individuals but not corporations to fines and forfeiture of goods sold on Sunday on the ground that the differential treatment violated the equal protection clause. However, it refused to enjoin enforcement of another section that prohibited the performance of worldly labor on Sunday. The court observed that worldly labor could be carried out only by individuals and not by abstract entities. It makes little sense that the sales prohibition provision must apply to both corporations and individuals, but the worldly work provision does not have to, when the nature of the worldly work is conducting sales on behalf of corporations. At any rate, the court in *Xepapas* enjoined the application of the fines and penalties provisions of the Sunday closing laws because it was applicable only against individuals, but in *Solomon* it refused to enjoin a law with similar discriminatory impact. Yet, despite this inconsistency, the court cited *Xepapas* in support of its conclusion that there was no equal protection violation in *Solomon*.[128] In a final attempt to find an equal protection flaw in the statute, the defendant asserted that the prosecutor had pursued a discriminatory enforcement policy. Others equally guilty had not been charged. The court thought little of this argument, concluding that so long as such differential enforcement did not result from purposeful discrimination, it was permissible.[129]

In a last desperate attempt to escape the web of the Sunday closing laws, the defendant sought to invoke a "higher law," a Charleston city ordinance enacted prior to the State Sunday law under adjudication. That ordinance permitted those who observed a day other than Sunday as their day of worship to open their stores on Sunday. However, the court concluded that the state law prevailed over an inconsistent local ordinance.[130] The matter did not rest there, however. The legislature later enacted a proviso to the prohibition against worldly work on Sunday that stated:

> . . . .that in Charleston County the foregoing shall not apply to any person who conscientiously believes, because of his religion, that the seventh day of the week ought to be observed as the Sabbath and who actually refrains from secular business or labor on that day.[131]

This legislative "solution" to the outcome in the *Solomon* case has some troubling aspects. Since its benefits were limited to a particular group in a particular locality, did it violate the Article III, section 34 prohibition of special and local laws?[132] In addition, it seems to invite the kind of inquiry by the state into the sincerity of one's beliefs that lends itself to highly subjective judgments by those applying the law.

After the *Solomon* case came the first of a flurry of cases involving Whitney Stores, a company repeatedly charged with violating the Sunday closing laws. In *Whitney Stores, Inc. v. Summerford*[133] a three-judge federal district court upheld the Sunday closing laws against the plaintiff store's request for a declaratory judgment that the laws violated the equal protection and due process clauses of the federal Fourteenth Amendment and against a novel allegation that the statute transgressed the federal Constitution's Eighth Amendment provision against excessive fines and cruel and unusual punishments. The court rejected the plaintiff's due process and equal protection contentions largely because they were substantially the same arguments turned down by the United States Supreme Court when it refused to review the *Solomon* case because of a lack of a substantial federal question.[134] The three-judge panel considered the Supreme Court's disposition of the case to be a decision on the merits that was binding on the lower federal court.

The plaintiff's fanciful arguments that the statutes, and the manner in which they had been applied to it, violated the Eighth Amendment took the form of allegations that the repeated assessment of progressively higher fines against it had resulted in the cumulative amount becoming excessively high. The court saw no merit to these contentions and observed that the frequency of the fines was the result of the plaintiff's frequent violations and not a defect in the statute.[135] The court also found no evidence to sustain the plaintiff's contentions that it had been the victim of discriminatory prosecutions, an argument that could be sustained only if purposeful discrimination were found.[136] The court further decided that due process clause attacks on the statutory exemptions permitting works of "necessity" and the sale of "novelties" and "souvenirs" on Sunday already had been determined to be meritless in *Solomon* which had concluded that the terms were not too vague to give reasonable notice to potential violators of the scope of the exemptions. In applying the terms "novelties" and "souvenirs," the court concluded that the wide range of standard clothing sold by plaintiffs could not be considered to be novelties.

Whitney, or its agents, raised virtually the same contentions that the Sunday closing laws were violative of the equal protection and due process clauses as it had raised in *Summerford*, in *Whitney Trading Corp. v. McNair*[137] and in *State v. Johnson*[138] and for its monotonous persistence received a similarly unfavorable decision. The cases did afford variety in the form of clever but unsuccessful ploys by the company, or its manager, to evade the sanctions. In one of the cases consolidated with *McNair, supra*, an injunction had been issued directing the store to halt Sunday operations. The company claimed that the injunction was improperly directed at it since the sales were made by independent contractors who rented various parts of its store. Even if the contention that the vendors were genuine independent contractors rather than employees was accepted, the company was still a proper target for the injunction since it directly operated the clothing, magazine, and alcoholic beverage departments and also set the schedule and operating standards for the entire operation. An earlier case, *McLeod v. Whitney*,[139] had ruled that a sheriff had the authority to seek an injunction against a repeat Sunday law violator for being a public nuisance. Thus, in a way, a rough form of parity was ultimately achieved with regard to an equal protection argument raised in the *Solomon*, *Xepapas* and *Charleston Oil* cases.

Corporations, not just individuals, were indeed subject to the strictures of the Sunday laws by means of this equitable remedy.

In *State v. Johnson*, the manager of one of the stores tried to pass responsibility down the line to the sales force. This maneuver did not work and the defendant manager was held responsible as the official who set sales policy and directed the sales force. The defendant was no more successful with an entrapment defense which he had raised based on the fact that the purchases that formed the basis of the charges against him were made by an undercover officer. Since the officer did not instigate the sales but only purchased items offered for sale by the store, the police action did not constitute entrapment.[140]

Other cases confronted additional equal protection arguments that were based on distinctly different factual predicates than those rejected in *Solomon* and the *Whitney* line of cases. However, they were no more successful. In *State v. Smith*[141] the defendant store manager asserted that the Sunday closing laws discriminated against large stores because an exemption had been granted to food stores that employed no more than three people on Sunday.[142] Large stores were placed at a competitive disadvantage since it was impracticable to operate many of them with such scant personnel. The court subjected the law to the most easily satisfied standard of review (i.e., is the discrimination not wholly irrelevant to the achievement of a valid state purpose?). The classification was conducive to achieving the state's health-safety goal of a universal day of rest while still making needed items available. Allowing food stores employing no more than three persons would permit the purchase of food items by those who found it difficult to shop on other days but did so in a way that diverted as few employees as possible from a day of rest and which kept the bustle and noise to a minimum. Justice Ness filed a vigorous dissent charging that the law grossly discriminated among members of the same class (i.e., food store operations).[143]

The religious zeal that originally inspired vigorous Sunday closing laws forbidding virtually all varieties of worldly work on Sunday has given ground to economic pressures and technological imperatives. *Mullis v. Celanese Corp. of Am.*[144] involved an amendment to the Sunday closing laws that permitted plants utilizing chemical processes requiring continuous operation to run on Sundays.[145] A group of employees brought suit to enjoin Celanese from requiring Sunday work as a condition of employment on the grounds that the amendment violated equal protection standards by treating some manufacturers more favorably than others. The court upheld the law as making a logical distinction between plants using processes requiring constant attendance and those that did not.[146]

Despite the logic underlying individual exemptions such as that for food stores employing three or less people and plants using processes requiring continuous operation, the cumulative weight of the dense web of exemptions made for certain types of businesses, or certain geographic localities or for the sale of certain types of goods, created the appearance of an arbitrary and unfair law that revealed its meaning only to the most persistent expert. By 1967, the head of the State Law Enforcement Division found it necessary to obtain an attorney general's opinion clarifying the numerous permutations on the basic Sunday law prohibition of certain sports and other forms of public entertainment. The opinion listed counties in which stock car and drag racing were prohibited on Sunday, and counties in which it was permitted after a specified time. An even more bewildering mixture of total prohibition and hour limitations existed with regard to exhibiting motion pictures on Sunday, but the opinion managed to bring a measure of order out of this chaos.[147] Some exemptions appear to have been designed to accommodate particular sports events or a narrow range of events. For example, the original 1976 code contained an exemption for the ". . . holding of nationally recognized golf tournaments sponsored by nonprofit organizations held at times other than hours of regular church worship."[148] The more the basic law became pockmarked with exceptions, the more confusing it became to law enforcement authorities, the more the law assumed an aura of favoritism for special interest groups, and the more diluted became the purpose of a universal day of quiet.

The above discussion has focused on the constitutional attacks made on Sunday closing laws and the exemptions that signaled a disenchantment with rigid laws that frustrated modern economic, technological and recreational needs. Disenchantment long had been building up for another reason as well: the esoteric and voluminous case law that was necessary to clarify the ever-shifting scope of the Sunday closing laws. Before noting the watershed changes that recently have occurred in the Sunday laws, let us examine the history of the case law dealing with problems of statutory interpretation. Since several statutory interpretation issues were integral parts of the earlier discussion of constitutional problems, cases dealing with those matters will be omitted from the following account.

Several cases have involved people trying to use statutes prohibiting certain activities from taking place on Sunday as a means of avoiding obligations they otherwise would have under contract and tort law. These maneuvers were generally unsuccessful since they were obvious attempts to distort, for a personal litigation advantage, laws that were enacted for the health and safety of the entire community. In *Eason v. Witcofskty*,[149] a purchaser of land sold by the state at public auction after the property had escheated to the state after heirs to an estate had failed to claim it, tried to escape consummation of the sale by claiming that the sale was invalid since the notice to the heirs had been published in a Sunday paper in violation of a provision prohibiting the service of most forms of legal process on Sunday. The court concluded that the prohibition did not apply to something so minimally disruptive as Sunday newspaper legal ads. In *Trakas v. Charleston & Western Carolina Railway Company*,[150] a railroad tried to escape liability for spoilage of fruit that had occurred during transit on the grounds that the prohibition of Sunday train operations had caused the delay that had led to spoilage. The court rejected this contention, noting that an exception to the prohibition of train operations on Sunday permitted carriage of fresh fruit. In *Rosamond v. Lucas Kidd Motor Co.*,[151] the court was unimpressed with the motor company's attempt to avoid tort liability incurred by its sales agent while operating and attempting to sell a car on Sunday. The court noted that even though the Sunday law forbade automobile sales on Sunday that the salesman had been acting within the scope of his employment as defined by the company.

Emergencies, such as war, have given rise to exemptions that have raised fine points of interpretation. In *Greenville Baseball, Inc. v. Bearden*,[152] the court interpreted a World War II vintage exception to the ban on Sunday professional baseball that permitted games after 2 p.m. on Sunday, when the games would not conflict with evening church services, if the county were one in which the United States had established an army fort or a naval or marine base. The Greenville County Sheriff stopped a Sunday game between Greenville and Macon and (living out the ultimate fantasy of baseball fans) arrested the umpire. The court concluded that the reference to army forts could be interpreted to include army airbases as well as installations for ground forces since that view was conclusive to the act's purpose of affording recreation for troops on what might be the only day off for many of them.[153] However, having exhausted its store of liberality, the court concluded that since the airbase was under construction and large numbers of troops were not yet in place, the exemption had not been activated at the time of the arrest. The court was more likely to depart from the literal language of the act to expand rather than contract the coverage of the Sunday prohibitions. For example, in *Bishop v. Hanna*[154] the court had no trouble in extending the ban against public sports on Sunday to stock car racing despite the fact that this form of entertainment was not specifically mentioned in the statute even though other sports were. The list was not meant to be exhaustive. The prohibition against public sports extended to other athletic contests equally disruptive to Sunday tranquility as those on the list.[155] The same technique was used to apply the Sunday sports prohibition to professional golf and baseball in *Palmetto Golf* and *Greenville Baseball.* The court in *Hanna* suggested that those not agreeing with these restrictions on popular and lucrative pastimes should resort to the legislative process for the passage of more indulgent language.[156] This is in fact what happened in the passage of the exemption for nationally recognized golf tournaments discussed earlier and the enactment of legislation to accommodate stock car race enthusiasts, such as the broad exception passed for ". . . automobile races which are scheduled to be two hundred fifty miles or more in length."[157] The enactment of such an exemption would seem to belie any pretense that the Sunday laws were designed to provide a day of quiet — a day of recreation perhaps — but quiet — no! It became less and less logical to justify the general rule banning public sports on Sunday when an exception favoring such a noisy and highly commercialized pastime was enacted. An exemption was also enacted for ". . . a steeplechase event held between the hours of one o'clock and six o'clock p.m. that is sanctioned by the national Steeplechase and Hunt Association and held under the auspices of the Department of Parks, Recreation and Tourism."[158] An additional exception was created for harness or boat races not conflicting with church services.[159]

However, in the absence of such concrete exemptions even non-profit sports were banned. In *State v. Galloway*[160] the president of a motorcycle club was arrested for conducting a race on Sunday. The defendant contended that "public" meant "commercial" and since the club did not charge admission to the race, though donations were welcome, the event did not fall under the Sunday sports ban. The court tossed this argument aside in concluding that the essence of the term "public" was in advertising directed to encourage attendance by the general public. Money changing hands was not essential for a sport to be public even though that seems to have influenced the court in the earlier *Palmetto Golf* case, distinguishing between amateur golf, which was permitted, and professional golf, which was not permitted absent a statutory exemption.

The maze of exemptions from the prohibition of Sunday sales and public sports was not only confusing and arbitrary to the layman who often was unfamiliar with the subtle policy distinctions that justified permitting some activities on Sunday and banning others, it became increasingly clear that the laws caused substantial economic loss to some parts of the state — especially those areas bordering on other states with more lax standards and those competing with other states for the tourist dollars, many of which are spent on Sunday. Legislators from these areas began to call for major changes in the Sunday closing laws in the 1980's. Senator J. M. "Bud" Long, who represented the coastal tourist area known as the Grand Strand, argued that the laws were unenforceable. Many merchants stayed open on Sunday in defiance of the law to ensure competitiveness or economic survival.[161] In the Piedmont area, Waccamaw Pottery of Spartanburg blatantly opened on Sunday to test the dedication of police officers in enforcing the law. The exemptions from the law's general prohibition against Sunday sales and public sports were not only chipping away at the structural integrity of the rule, they were often producing results clearly at odds with an unarticulated major premise of the Sunday laws; the encouragement of worthy forms of recreation and the discouragement of those less worthy. Senator Long dramatically demonstrated this by displaying an "obscene" t-shirt which he alleged could be purchased on Sunday under the exemption for "novelties," even though a dress shirt that could be worn to church could not be bought on Sunday in most areas. The original day of worship purpose still lurked not far beneath the thin gloss of secular, health-safety, day of rest purposes spread over the laws in *Braunfeld.*[162] However, even those dedicated to making Sunday "a day apart" whether for secular or religious purposes sometimes give ground in the face of economic imperatives, changing recreational styles, and modern technology requiring Sunday operations.

The long-anticipated major revamping of the Sunday laws occurred in 1985 after minor tinkering with the list of what could and what could not be sold on Sunday had failed to stanch the mounting pressure for change. New section 53-1-5 was enacted in 1985 and stated:

> The provisions of this chapter [prohibition of Sunday sales, worldly work and public sports] do not apply after the hour of 1:30 p.m. on Sunday. Any employee of any business which operates on Sunday under the provisions of this section has the option of refusing to work in accordance with the provisions of 53-1-100 [protecting machine shop employees who object to Sunday work on conscientious or physical grounds]. Any employer who dismisses or demotes an employee because he is a conscientious objector to Sunday work is subject to a civil penalty of triple the damages found by the court or the jury plus court costs and the employee's attorney's fees. The court may order the employer to rehire or reinstate the employee in the same position he was in before the dismissal or demotion without forfeiture of compensation, rank, or grade.
>
> No proprietor of a retail establishment who is opposed to working on Sunday may be forced by his lessor or franchisor to open his establishment on Sunday nor may there be discrimination against persons whose regular day of worship is Saturday.[163]

Professional ". . . athletic events, public exhibitions, historic or musical entertainment, or concerts . . ." could be conducted on Sunday if a permit were obtained from the appropriate local government.[164] Automobile races of two hundred fifty miles or more were exempt even from the permit requirement.[165] Prior to 1:30 p.m. on Sunday, most sales were still prohibited except items on a modernized exempt list. The updated list of exemptions permitted sales, even before 1:30 p.m. of a long list of items including non-commercial real estate and mobile homes. It also permitted the rental of ". . . swimming, fishing, and boating equipment."[166]

Even the liberal provisions of new section 53-1-5, which permitted after 1:30 p.m. most sales, sports, and entertainment activities that previously had been prohibited on Sunday, did not apply to stop pre-1:30 p.m. sales in areas heavily reliant on the tourist dollar which seemingly demands non-stop merry-making. Also passed in 1985 was new section 53-1-150 which stated:

> (A) The General Assembly finds that certain areas of the State would benefit greatly from a complete exemption from Chapter 1, Title 53 of the 1976 Code. This benefit would be a result of an expanded tax base thereby reducing the burden placed on property owners through the property tax. Allowing the operation of establishments on Sunday in these areas would also reduce the property tax burden through additional accommodation tax revenue which allows these areas to provide necessary governmental service from these revenues.[167]

The provision defined the counties in which merchants and operators of sporting and entertainment events would not have to wait until 1:30 p.m. before opening on Sunday as being those that collected more than nine hundred thousand dollars per year from the accommodations tax. This is yet another example of the retreat of the Sunday laws in the face of an economic show of force, in this case the need to expand the tax base and avoid increased property taxes. Money changers can enter the temple of the Sabbath if they can keep those property taxes down. Another concession to the restaurant and tourism industry had been adopted a year earlier in 1984. Section 61-5-180 authorizes the holding of referenda "upon petition of at least ten per cent but not more than twenty-five hundred qualified electors of the county or municipality . . ." to determine whether or not the Alcoholic Beverage Commission may issue temporary alcoholic beverage sales licenses for periods not to exceed twenty-four hours.[168] Neither the basic law or the wording of the referendum question which is set forth in the law mentions the authorization of Sunday sales in particular, but upon a positive vote in the referendum, temporary permits could be issued on that day as well as any other day on which sales normally could not take place. A stiff fee of one hundred dollars for processing and fifty dollars for the permit itself are the price exacted for these temporary bacchanalian revels. Expensive though the permits may be, the provision shows how far the state has traveled from the early eighteenth-century laws discussed above which gave Anglican Church wardens the power to enter taverns on Sunday and roust out the idle tipplers in order that they might meet church attendance requirements.

The provisions in section 53-1-5 that protect an employee from dismissal or demotion, and a store operator from termination of his lease or franchise because he conscientiously objects to Sunday or Saturday work, pose a constitutional dilemma. The free exercise and establishment clauses of the United States Constitution are designed to work together to assure that the government remains neutral toward religion. However, the two clauses are not a matched pair that always move together. Sometimes they work at cross purposes. Provisions designed to protect an employee from adverse personnel action because of a conscientious objection to work on his Sabbath are designed to facilitate the free exercise of religion of those persons. However, a thin line separates a measure that properly protects free exercise from one which improperly favors certain religions with days of worship that are the Sabbath of the predominant elements of the population or of the most respected religious minorities. Even if such laws do not favor particular religions, they may improperly favor persons who choose their day off for religious reasons no matter what day they choose. As more and more states enact laws loosening restrictions on Sunday commercial activity, the dilemma grows more acute — how do we protect free exercise without endorsing religion in a way that violates the establishment clause. In *Estate of Thornton v. Caldor, Inc.*,[169] the Supreme Court of the United States was confronted with a Connecticut attempt to walk the tight wire between establishment and free exercise clause violations. Upon revision of its laws to permit more Sunday retailing, Connecticut passed a statute which provided that:

> No person who states that a particular day of the week is observed as his Sabbath may be required by his employer to work on such day. An employee's refusal to work on his Sabbath shall not constitute grounds for his dismissal.[170]

Thornton was a management-level employee in the respondent's store. Thornton refused to work on Sunday and rejected the respondent's offer to transfer him to an out-of-state store that did not open on Sunday or to another in-state store at a lower position not requiring Sunday work. Thornton resigned contending that he had in effect been discharged from his management level position. A state mediation board ordered the store to reinstate Thornton with back pay. The Connecticut Supreme Court found that the statute did not have a secular purpose and thus constituted a law respecting the establishment of religion. The United States Supreme Court agreed. The Court observed that in order to avoid violating the establishment clause, the law must ". . . have a secular purpose and not foster excessive entanglement of government with religion, [and] its primary effect must not advance or inhibit religion."[171] The Connecticut law had an improper primary effect of advancing religion. Although it was formally based on establishment clause reasoning, the opinion also had free exercise implications from the employer's perspective since the employees were given ". . . an absolute and unqualified right not to work on (whatever day they designated as) their Sabbath" and the employer was required to reorganize his personnel schedule to meet those demands, thus mandating that the employer indirectly join in the employee's Sabbath observation.[172]

The Connecticut law improperly advanced religion by requiring that Sabbath observance take precedence over all secular concerns in organizing the work schedule.[173] In addition, those preferring to take a day off for religious reasons are given a preference over those who want time off for non-religious reasons. Employees not seeking the day off for religious reasons must take up the slack left by the employee absent for religious reasons. The employers' legitimate commercial concerns were given no weight under the law which provided an absolute right to take the day of worship off no matter how short-handed it might leave the employers. The law was too rigid and unyielding. Reasonable attempts by the employer to accommodate the employee's religious needs, even if the employee's demands of a religious day off were not met one hundred percent, were given no weight.[174] This cuts too deeply into the retailer's property right to manage its business. Property clause rhetoric was not used but in essence that is what the court was saying.

Section 53-1-5 of the South Carolina Code carries even heavier constitutional freight. The South Carolina statute, like its Connecticut counterpart, appears to confer an absolute right to a day off to those who are conscientious believers in a religion that demands that the day be devoted to worship. Hence again, those seeking the day of rest for religious reasons are given an absolute preference over those who seek time away from work for secular reasons. Also, like the Connecticut statute, the

South Carolina law grants the preference despite the economic difficulties, schedule disruption, and loss of income it might cause to the employer. However, the South Carolina law compounds the difficulties. It specifies those who celebrate Sunday or Saturday as the day of worship as those who are entitled to conscientiously object to working on a particular day for religious reasons. This has a primary effect of advancing the predominant Judeo-Christian religions. As society grows more complex with the presence of emerging ethnic groups, the days held sacred by people grow more varied. Even those who choose Sunday and Saturday as the appropriate days of worship may occasionally choose other days to signify particular religious holidays or seasons. Society, and the number of religions found in it, have grown more varied since the *Braunfeld* case which seemed to tacitly accept the indirect preference given to the Sunday worshipper by choosing Sunday as the universal day of rest. As a policy matter, even if not strictly demanded by a constitutional imperative, greater freedom of choice among religious and secular days off should be given. However, the employer must not be made to sacrifice his business for another's religion. That trenches not only upon his property, but also his free exercise rights (assuming we are dealing with a natural person as an employer) by requiring that he make financial and business adjustments for another's religion. Perhaps the approach suggested by Justice O'Connor in her concurring opinion in *Thornton* merits consideration. She praised the approach of the federal Civil Rights Act of 1964 which forbids religious discrimination except where the religious orientation of the employee may be a genuine job qualification. However, it does not grant employees absolute rights to demand certain conditions based on religious preference. It merely requires ". . . employers to reasonably accommodate the religious practices of employees unless to do so would cause undue hardship to the employer's business."[175] The South Carolina law constitutes an admirable attempt to permit a broader range of activities on Sunday but to do so in a manner that does not unduly force people to abandon their religions to keep their jobs. However, perhaps some consideration should be given to adjustments in its provisions.

The Sunday laws confront states with a difficult balancing act: affording a uniform day of rest but doing so in a manner that does not create a legal preference for certain religions. An equally difficult balancing act must be performed when courts are asked to resolve internal church disputes. Court attempts to adjudicate such disputes without taking sides in controversies regarding church doctrine are discussed in the next chapter.

NOTES

1. The Sunday Observance Act 1677, 29 Car. 2c 7, 8 HALSBURY'S STATUTES OF ENGLAND 23 (3d ed. 1969). [hereinafter the Sunday Observance Act 1677].

2. The Sunday Observance Act 1677 at 23.

3. The Sunday Observance Act 1677 at 24.

4. The Sunday Observance Act 1677 at 24-25.

5. The Sunday Observance Act 1677 at 25.

6. The Sunday Observance Act 1677 at 25.

7. Act No. 28 of 1685, 2 S.C. STATUTES AT LARGE 13 (Cooper 1837).

8. Act No. 74 of 1691, 2 S.C. STATUTES AT LARGE 68 (Cooper 1837).

9. Act No. 74 of 1691, 2 S.C. STATUTES AT LARGE 68, 68-69 (Cooper 1837) [hereinafter cited as Act No. 74 of 1691].

10. Act No. 74 of 1691 at 69.

11. Act No. 74 of 1691 at 69.

CHAPTER FIVE—NOTES

12. Act No. 74 of 1691 at 69.

13. Act No. 74 of 1691 at 69.

14. Act No. 74 of 1691 at 69.

15. Act No. 74 of 1691 at 69.

16. Act No. 74 of 1691 at 69.

17. Act No. 74 of 1691 at 70.

18. Act No. 74 of 1691 at 70.

19. Act No. 74 of 1691 at 70.

20. Act No. 320 of 1712, 2 S.C. STATUTES AT LARGE 396, para. I (Cooper 1837) [hereinafter cited as Act. No. 320 of 1712].

21. Act No. 320 of 1712 at 396-97, para. II and III.

22. Act No. 320 of 1712 at 397, para. IV.

23. Act No. 320 of 1712 at 397, para. V.

24. S.C. CODE ANN. § 53-1-10 (Law. Co-op. 1976) (In the 1985 Supplement § 53-1-10 forbids professional athletic, musical, historical and similar events on Sunday unless local government permission is obtained).

25. Act No. 320 of 1712 at 397, para. VI and VII.

26. Act No. 320 of 1712 at 397, para. VIII.

27. Act No. 320 of 1712 at 398, para. IX.

28. Act No. 320 of 1712 at 398, para. XII.

29. C. WOODMASON, THE CAROLINA BACKCOUNTRY ON THE EVE OF THE REVOLUTION 47 (Hooker ed. 1953) [hereinafter cited as C. WOODMASON].

30. JOURNAL OF JOSIAH QUINCY, 49 MASS. HIST. SOC. PROCEEDINGS 424, 455 (1915-16).

31. C. WOODMASON at 96-97.

32. J. BRINSFIELD at 71.

33. G. ROGERS, CHARLESTON IN THE AGE OF THE PINCKNEYS 21-22 (1969).

34. *Ex Parte* Duke, 33 S.C.L. (2 Strob.) 530 (1833) (appendix to City of Council of Charleston v. Benjamin, 33 S.C.L. (2 Strob.) 508 (1846).

35. *See* Cantwell v. Connecticut, 310 U.S. 296, 60 S. Ct. 900, 84 L. Ed. 1213 (1940) and Everson v. Bd. of Educ., 330 U.S. 1, 67 S. Ct. 504, 91 L. Ed. 711 (1947) (held that the free exercise clause (*Cantwell*) and the establishment clause (*Everson*) were incorporated into the due process clause of the Fourteenth Amendment and applied to state and local governments).

36. *Ex Parte* Duke, 33 S.C.L. (2 Strob.) at 532.

37. Braunfeld v. Brown, 366 U.S. 599, 81 S. Ct. 1144, 6 L. Ed. 2d 563 (1961); State v. Solomon, 245 S.C. 550, 141 S.E.2d 818 (1965).

38. *Ex Parte* Duke, 33 S.C.L. (2 Strob.) at 532.

39. *Ex Parte* Duke, 33 S.C.L. (2 Strob.) at 532.

40. *Ex Parte* Duke, 33 S.C.L. (2 Strob.) at 533.

41. *Ex Parte* Duke, 33 S.C.L. (2 Strob.) at 534.

42. Act No. 320 of 1712, 2 S.C. STATUTES AT LARGE 396 (Cooper 1837).

43. 33 S.C.L. (2 Strob.) 508 (1846).

44. 33 S.C.L. (2 Strob.) at 512.

45. 33 S.C.L. (2 Strob.) at 512.

46. 33 S.C.L. (2 Strob.) at 513.

47. 33 S.C.L. (2 Strob.) at 514.

48. 33 S.C.L. (2 Strob.) at 515.

49. 33 S.C.L. (2 Strob.) at 515.

50. 33 S.C.L. (2 Strob.) at 511.

51. 33 S.C.L. (2 Strob.) at 518-21.

52. 33 S.C.L. (2 Strob.) at 519.

53. 33 S.C.L. (2 Strob.) at 521.

54. 33 S.C.L. (2 Strob.) at 522.

55. 33 S.C.L. (2 Strob.) at 522.

56. 33 S.C.L. (2 Strob.) at 522.

57. 33 S.C.L. (2 Strob.) at 522-23.

58. 33 S.C.L. (2 Strob.) at 523.

59. 33 S.C.L. (2 Strob.) at 524-25.

60. 33 S.C.L. (2 Strob.) at 529.

61. 33 S.C.L. (2 Strob.) at 529-30.

62. *Braunfeld,* 366 U.S. at 599.

63. *Benjamin,* 33 S.C.L. (2 Strob.) at 530.

64. M. BORDEN, JEWS, TURKS AND INFIDELS 114-15 (1984) [hereinafter cited as M. BORDEN].

65. M. BORDEN at 114.

66. M. BORDEN at 114 (emphasis in original).

67. M. BORDEN at 115.

68. M. BORDEN at 115 (emphasis in original).

69. M. BORDEN at 115.

70. M. BORDEN at 115.

71. M. BORDEN at 142 n.2.

72. M. BORDEN at 142 n.2. But note that in 1797 and 1805 the United States entered into two treaties with Tripoli, the first of which stated that "...the United States is not, in any sense, founded on the Christian religion." That language was omitted from the second treaty. *See* A. STOKES AND L. PFEFFER, CHURCH AND STATE IN THE UNITED STATES 89 (1964) [hereinafter cited as A. STOKES AND L. PFEFFER].

73. County of Allegheny v. ACLU, 492 U.S. 573, 109 S. Ct. 3086, 106 L. Ed. 2d 472 (1989).

74. County of Allegheny v. ACLU, 492 U.S. at 604 n. 53.

75. *See* C. BLESER, SECRET AND SACRED, THE DIARIES OF JAMES HENRY HAMMOND, A SOUTHERN SLAVEHOLDER (1988), *see especially* the diary entries for December 12, 1844 at pp. 137-38; February 8, 1845 at p. 142; *and see* pp. 125-26.

76. Both proclamation incidents are discussed in C. REZNIKOFF at 111-12.

77. A. STOKES and L. PFEFFER at 87-89.

78. A. STOKES and L. PFEFFER at 53, 60, 184.

79. State v. Hondros, 100 S.C. 242, 84 S.E. 781 (1914).

80. Cain v. Daly, 74 S.C. 480, 55 S.E. 110 (1906).

81. State v. James, 81 S.C. 197, 62 S.E. 214 (1908).

82. O'Hanlon v. Myers, 44 S.C.L. (10 Rich.) 128, 130 (1856).

83. Charleston Oil Co. v. Poulnot, 143 S.C. 283, 141 S.E. 454 (1928).

84. Palmetto Golf Club v. Robinson, 143 S.C. 347, 141 S.E. 610 (1927).

85. Xepapas v. Richardson, 149 S.C. 52, 146 S.E. 686 (1928).

86. Carolina Amusement Co. v. Martin, 236 S.C. 558, 115 S.E.2d 273 (1960).

87. *Martin*, 236 S.C. at 561, 115 S.E.2d at 274.

CHAPTER FIVE—NOTES

88. 2 S.C. STATUTES AT LARGE 707 (Cooper 1837); *and see generally*, D. MALONE, THE PUBLIC LIFE OF THOMAS COOPER (1961).

89. Hennington v. Georgia, 163 U.S. 299, 16 S. Ct. 1086 (1896).

90. Soon Hing v. Crowley, 113 U.S. 703, 5 S. Ct. 730, 28 L. Ed. 1145 (1885).

91. Zorach v. Clauson, 343 U.S. 306, 72 S. Ct. 679, 96 L. Ed. 954 (1952).

92. S.C. CONST. OF 1895, art. I, § 4 (1895).

93. Joseph Burstyn, Inc. v. Wilson, 343 U.S. 495, 72 S. Ct. 777, 96 L. Ed. 1098 (1952).

94. Carolina Amusement Co. v. Martin, 236 S.C. 558, 581, 115 S.E. 2d 273, 284 (1960), *appeal dismissed and cert. denied*, 367 U.S. 904, 81 S. Ct. 1914, 6 L. Ed. 2d 1248 (1961).

95. Braunfeld v. Brown, 366 U.S. 599, 81 S. Ct. 1144, 6 L. Ed. 2d 563 (1961).

96. 366 U.S. at 607.

97. 366 U.S. at 610-16.

98. Sherbert v. Verner, 374 U.S. 398, 83 S. Ct. 1790, 10 L. Ed. 2d 965 (1963).

99. McGowan v. Maryland, 366 U.S. 420, 81 S. Ct. 1101, 6 L. Ed. 2d 393 (1961).

100. 366 U.S. at 426.

101. 366 U.S. at 427.

102. 366 U.S. at 427-28.

103. 366 U.S. at 429.

104. 366 U.S. at 429.

105. 366 U.S. at 449.

106. 366 U.S. at 431.

107. 366 U.S. at 442.

108. 366 U.S. at 431.

109. 366 U.S. at 435, 448.

110. 366 U.S. at 452.

111. Two Guys from Harrison-Allentown, Inc. v. McGinley, 366 U.S. 582, 81 S. Ct. 1135, 6 L. Ed. 2d 551 (1961).

112. Gallagher v. Crown Kosher Super Market, 366 U.S. 617, 81 S. Ct. 1122, 6 L. Ed. 2d 536 (1961).

113. State v. Solomon, 245 S.C. 550, 141 S.E.2d 818 (1965), *appeal dismissed*, 382 U.S. 204, 86 S. Ct. 396, 15 L. Ed. 2d 270 (1965).

114. 245 S.C. at 561, 141 S.E.2d at 824.

115. 245 S.C. at 560-62, 141 S.E.2d at 824-25.

116. 245 S.C. at 566-67, 141 S.E.2d at 827; *but see* State v. James, 81 S.C. 197, 200, 62 S.E. 214, 215 (1908) (noting that the purpose of Sunday closing was to permit "contemplation of higher things.").

117. 245 S.C. at 567-68, 141 S.E.2d 827-28.

118. Lyng v. Northwest Indian Cemetary Protective Ass'n., 485 U.S. 439, 108 S. Ct. 1319, 99 L. Ed. 2d 534 (1988).

119. *See* The Sunday Observance Act of 1677, 29 Car. 2c 7, 8 HALSBURY'S STATUTES OF ENGLAND 23-26 (3d ed. 1969) (exempting works of "necessity and charity" from the prohibition of worldy labor on Sunday).

120. *Solomon*, 245 S.C. at 570-71, 141 S.E.2d at 829.

121. The Court cited numerous cases interpreting the meaning of "work of necessity." *See* Charleston Oil Co. v. Poulnot, 143 S.C. 283, 141 S.E. 454 (1928) (routine sale of oil on Sunday is not a necessity); State v. James, 81 S.C. 197, 62 S.E. 214 (1908) (sale of ice and fresh meat on Sunday is not a necessity in absence of an emergency). *See* Smith v. Western Union Tel. Co., 72 S.C. 116, 51 S.E. 537 (1905) (delivery of telegram informing recipient of sister's impending death is a work of necessity). *See also* Oliveros v. Henderson, 116 S.C. 77, 106 S.E. 855 (1921) (interpreting the meaning of another exempted activity, the work of charity of selling ice cream on Sunday and donating proceeds to Red Cross is not legally an act of "charity").

122. *Solomon*, 245 S.C. at 570, 141 S.E.2d at 829.

123. 245 S.C. at 571, 141 S.E.2d at 829.

124. 245 S.C. at 572, 141 S.E.2d at 830.

125. S.C. CODE ANN. § 64-2 (Michie Co. 1962 and Supp. 1975).

126. S.C. CODE ANN. § 53-1-50 (Law. Co-op. 1976 and Supp. 1984).

127. *Solomon*, 245 S.C. at 572-73, 141 S.E.2d at 830.

128. 245 S.C. at 573, 141 S.E.2d at 830.

129. 245 S.C. at 573-74, 141 S.E.2d at 830-31.

130. 245 S.C. at 574-75, 141 S.E.2d at 831.

131. S.C. CODE ANN. § 53-1-40 (Law. Co-op 1976).

132. *See* J. UNDERWOOD, THE CONSTITUTION OF SOUTH CAROLINA VOLUME I: THE RELATIONSHIP OF THE LEGISLATIVE, EXECUTIVE AND JUDICIAL BRANCHES 108 (1986).

133. Whitney Stores, Inc. v. Summerford, 280 F. Supp. 406 (D.S.C. 1968), *aff'd*, 393 U.S. 9, 89 S. Ct. 44, 21 L. Ed. 2d 9 (1968).

134. Solomon v. South Carolina, 245 S.C. 550, 141 S.E.2d 818 (1965), *appeal dismissed* 382 U.S. 204 (1965).

135. *Whitney Stores, Inc.*, 280 F. Supp. at 411.

136. 280 F. Supp. at 411.

137. Whitney Trading Corp. v. McNair, 255 S.C. 8, 176 S.E.2d 572 (1970).

138. State v. Johnson, 255 S.C. 14, 176 S.E.2d 575 (1970).

139. McLeod v. Whitney Stores, Inc., 250 S.C. 273, 157 S.E.2d 254 (1967).

140. *Johnson*, 255 S.C. at 17, 176 S.E.2d at 577.

141. State v. Smith, 271 S.C. 317, 247 S.E.2d 331 (1978).

142. *See* S.C. CODE ANN. § 53-1-50 (Law. Co-op. 1976).

143. *See also* Arnold v. City of Spartanburg, 201 S.C. 523, 23 S.E. 2d 735 (1943) (which rejected equal protection attacks on local government ban on Sunday sale of alcoholic beverages since the ban was uniformly applicable to all vendors of such products).

144. Mullis v. Celanese Corp. of Am., 234 S.C. 380, 108 S.E.2d 547 (1959).

145. *See* S.C. CODE ANN. § 64-6 (Michie 1962 and Supp. 1954).

146. *See also* S.C. CODE ANN. § 53-1-130 (Law. Co-op. 1976) (extending the exemption to plants requiring "...continuous and uninterrupted operation" whether they used chemical processes or other technology).

147. *See* 1966-67 Opinions of the Attorney General of South Carolina, pp. 166-69, Opinion No. 2337 November 10, 1967.

148. S.C. CODE ANN. § 53-1-10 (Law. Co-op. 1976).

149. Eason v. Witcofskey, 29 S.C. 239, 7 S.E. 291 (1888). In the 1793 case, Shaw v. M'Combs, 2 S.C.L. 93, 2 Bay 232, the court invalidated a verdict because the jury rendered it on Sunday.

150. Trakas v. Charleston & W. C. Ry. Co., 87 S.C. 206, 69 S.E. 209 (1910).

151. Rosamond v. Lucas-Kidd Motor Co., 182 S.C. 331, 189 S.E. 641 (1937).

152. Greenville Baseball, Inc. v. Bearden, 200 S.C. 363, 20 S.E. 2d 813 (1942).

153. 200 S.C. at 369, 20 S.E.2d at 816.

154. Bishop v. Hanna, 218 S.C. 474, 63 S.E.2d 308 (1951).

155. 218 S.C. at 479, 63 S.E.2d at 310.

156. 218 S.C. at 480, 63 S.E.2d at 310.

157. *See* S.C. CODE ANN. § 53-1-15 (Law. Co-op. 1976 and Supp. 1983).

158. *See* S.C. CODE ANN. § 53-1-10 (Law. Co-op. 1976 and Supp. 1980).

CHAPTER FIVE—NOTES

159. S.C. CODE ANN. § 53-1-10 (Law. Co-op. 1976 and Supp. 1980).

160. State v. Galloway, 240 S.C. 136, 124 S.E.2d 910 (1962).

161. The State, December 31, 1989, at 4G, col. 1.

162. The State, December 31, 1989, at 4G, col. 1.

163. S.C. CODE ANN. § 53-1-5 (Law. Co-op. 1976 and Supp. 1989).

164. S.C. CODE ANN. § 53-1-10 (Law. Co-op. 1976 and Supp. 1989).

165. S.C. CODE ANN. § 53-1-15 (Law. Co-op. 1976 and Supp. 1989) (But note this exemption traces its origins back to 1983 Act No. 28. Even though the 1985 revision was the centerpiece of the Sunday law revamping, other changes had preceded it).

166. S.C. CODE ANN. § 53-1-50 (Law. Co-op. 1976 and Supp. 1989).

167. S.C. CODE ANN. § 53-1-150 (Law. Co-op. 1976 and Supp. 1989).

168. S.C. CODE ANN. § 61-5-180 (Law. Co-op. 1976 and Supp. 1984).

169. Estate of Thornton v. Caldor, Inc., 472 U.S. 703, 105 S. Ct. 2914, 86 L. Ed. 2d 557 (1985).

170. CONN. GEN. STAT. ANN. § 53-303e(b) (West 1985).

171. *Estate of Thornton*, 472 U.S. at 708.

172. 472 U.S. at 710-11.

173. 472 U.S. at 709.

174. 472 U.S. at 709-10.

175. 472 U.S. at 712 (Connor, J., concurring); *see also* 42 U.S.C. § 2000e(j) (1989).

CHAPTER SIX

MAINTAINING STATE NEUTRALITY IN COURT: RESOLUTION OF INTERNAL CHURCH DISPUTES

Churches, like all other organizations, often have disputes among the members concerning the type of programs to which they should direct their attention, how they should spend their money and utilize their property. Because religion by its very nature is something that deeply engages the emotions, and because those who have sought spiritual truth sometimes believe that the answer that they have found should govern church temporal, as well as religious decisions, internal church disputes often have an unusually bitter quality. Sometimes such bitter disputes cannot be ended through the normal internal conflicts resolution procedures of the church. Court help must be sought. Courts often have a legitimate role to play in such controversies, especially those involving property, because of their impact on businessmen and others outside the church family. When property disputes are interwoven with controversies involving doctrinal matters such as the proper mode of worship, the answer to theological puzzles, or the selection of ministers, the court is confronted with a dilemma. When the court receives such a case, it enters a minefield. Can it resolve the controversy without taking sides in doctrinal disputes? Can it declare legal principles without also assuming the mantle of prophets revealing religious truth? Can it undertake traditional court fact-finding exercises such as determining the intent and reasonable expectation of the parties to a dispute without also conducting an inquisition into the genuineness of the faith of the parties and undertaking to declare who is and who is not a true believer? The South Carolina courts generally have done a good job rendering balanced, neutral judgments in internal church disputes without straying into religious preachments or basing their decisions on the doctrinal merits of one side's position rather than another. In rendering these decisions, the courts have emphasized neutral legal principles such as contract and property law, and the law governing corporate bodies. However, occasionally the courts could not resist injecting avuncular advice concerning what the proper Christian attitude would be in resolving a dispute.

One of the earliest full-dress opinions in which a court decided a squabble that had broken out within a church organization was *Harmon v. Dreher.*[1] This case involved a dispute between St. Peter's Church and the synod of which it was a member. The synod had originated as a coalition of a number of German Protestant churches, some Lutheran and some Presbyterian. It was organized in the late eighteenth century in the Lexington area between the Broad and Saluda Rivers. In the 1830's, a dispute broke out concerning a controversial minister, Reverend Dreher, who was charged by the synod with aligning himself with itinerate preachers who espoused unsound doctrine. Dreher was tried for heresy by the synod and expelled from its ranks. However, he continued to be minister of St. Peter's Church, a synod member. One faction of the church allied itself with the synod and contended that after his expulsion, Dreher could no longer be the church's minister, and that by continuing him as minister it had forfeited its membership in the synod and thus it could no longer exercise control over church property. This faction contended that control over the property must be exercised by the synod or church members allied with the synod in the disputes regarding Dreher. Dreher's right to continue preaching on the premises was questioned. After a period in which shared use of the church was attempted by the factions, the group supporting Dreher attempted to exclude the other contingent. The court concluded that St. Peter's had not resigned from the synod by continuing Dreher as minister since the congregation had never received proper notice of Dreher's expulsion from the synod. Church policy would continue to be set by majority vote of St. Peter's members rather than by the synod or a rump faction. The majority could employ whatever minister it desired.

In reaching these conclusions, the court announced several principles designed to maintain court neutrality in resolving disputes where church doctrine had played a role in dividing the contending parties. Among these were the following: (1) a civil court should not examine the correctness of the decision of a church body, such as the synod, in expelling a minister for heresy; (2) a civil court cannot tell a church whom to employ as a minister. In other words, separation of church and state demands that civil courts not exercise religious decision-making power. Instead, disputes should be resolved when possible by general principles of law, such as that which governs what is fair notice (in this case, notice of the results of the heresy trial) and the general principles that govern the construction of the traditions and agreements which define the relationship of a constituent organization to its parent body. The opinion was long and convoluted, taking many unnecessary side trips. However, the above principles can be gleaned from the case at least by implication. Even though the court used neutral principles in resolving the dispute, the trial judge, whose opinion was adopted by the appellate court, could not resist frequent asides concerning the conduct of some of the parties as being inappropriate for Christians.

Courts are frequently confronted with property disputes when a majority of a particular congregation has defected from national and regional governing authorities of the church but the minority of the local church remains loyal to the national and regional organizations. In such situations the court can examine tradition and documents to determine who has ultimate control under the form of governance chosen by the national organization, and it can examine documents and customs that might indicate acceptance by the local entity of the mode of governance employed by the national body. In making such decisions, the court can examine statements that give clues as to where the allegiance of particular factions lie as between the national and local church, but the courts cannot declare what is religious truth and they normally avoid delving into the sincerity of someone's professed beliefs else its proceedings will degenerate into a state-sponsored inquisition. In the 1846 case of *Wilson v. The Presbyterian Church of John's Island and Wadmalaw*,[2] the court was confronted with the question of who could control property of the local church, including a bequest for the support of a minister professing the Presbyterian faith at John's Island. A majority of the local congregation had broken with the national and regional organizations but a minority remained loyal. The court concluded that the minority could control the property. The court could not determine what was true Presbyterian doctrine and who sincerely believed those concepts. It could, however, determine the traditional balance of power among national, regional, and local entities and examine external clues, such as which group espoused loyalty to the national, and use that as a basis of determining who could properly supervise the property. This entire adjudication process is fraught with peril for the concept of separation of church and state. It only takes a slight misstep in the reasoning process to stray from examining external clues concerning a person's loyalty to an organization to an improper inquiry into the sincerity of one's beliefs and how close they are to traditional doctrine.

In 1846, the same year that the *Wilson* decision was rendered, the South Carolina court ruled in *State ex rel. Ottolengui v. Ancker*[3] that it was not proper for a civil court to resolve disputes within a religious congregation concerning the proper mode of worship or controversies concerning such basic questions of faith as the true meaning of the Messianic prophecy. However, a civil court can decide disputes concerning the allocation of power within the congregation when the ruling can be based on neutral principles of general law governing the construction of documents such as corporate charters and by-laws. Even these decisions should be rendered cautiously lest the court trample upon rights of free exercise of religion by decreeing that judicial orthodoxy, rather than the beliefs of the congregation, control decisions. Court decisions should focus more upon the process by which a religious body reaches a decision, such as whether the decision is in accord with its charter and bylaws, than upon whether the ultimate decision was the correct one. Questioning the theological correctness of the ultimate decision makes the court set aside the surer compass of the law for the quagmire of matters of faith in which it has no particular competence.

The *Ottolengui* case involved a fractious quarrel that shook the historic synagogue of Beth Elohim in Charleston. The narrow legal focus of the dispute concerned who was a proper member of the congregation entitled to influence matters of church governance. The broader theological dispute concerned whether or not it contradicted the Jewish traditions upon which the congregation had been founded to change the style of worship to include organ music. Additionally, the doctrinal dispute concerned whether or not the Rabbi should teach that the Messiah would take the form of an actual being who would come to earth or should the Messiah be considered an idealized, intangible concept rather than one that would achieve physical existence. The court eschewed the opportunity to resolve these broader theological questions and focused on the narrower legal dispute.

The case had been brought by a majority of the corporation, technically known in law as the relators, who pressed the case in the name of the state, presumably because the dispute involved construction of the synagogue's corporation charter granted by the legislature. The relators alleged that a strong minority faction had been participating improperly in church governance. They were not bona fide members of the congregation. Many of them had been members of the congregation, but had resigned. Other members of the dissident group had never properly become members of the organization. The relators claimed that meetings of the trustees and the general congregation that purported to readmit the minority who allegedly had resigned, and to admit the other dissidents as new members, had not been properly called since the President had refused to assent to the meetings. The dissidents argued that those who had been longtime members of the congregation had not really resigned but had temporarily left because of the disputes concerning the mode of worship and the doctrine of the Messiah. To fortify this last point, they offered evidence concerning the proper traditional style of worship and what they considered the true nature of the Messiah to be. The trial court refused to accept this theological evidence. The appellate court confirmed and refused to rule on matters of doctrine. It considered its proper role to be limited to construing standard legal documents such as statutes, corporate charters and bylaws. The question of what constituted theological truth lay beyond its grasp.

The court justified the narrow role it had permitted itself in such internal church disputes by stating that:

> There should be great caution observed, in relation to cases like the present. The court should only take cognizance of such matters as may fairly come

> within the scope of a judicial judgment. From his habits of thinking and education, a judicial magistrate is not very well qualified to give a definite and enforceable judgment on questions of Theological doctrine, depending on speculative faith, or ecclesiastical rites. It is to be regretted that they have of late become such frequent themes of forensic discussion.[4]

Later in the opinion, the court cited as an additional reason for caution, beyond its incompetence on theological matters, its fear of encroaching upon religious freedom. It stated that: "If the court can be called on to settle by its decisions such disputes, it would be bound to require parties to conform to its standard of faith -- a judicial standard for theological orthodoxy!"[5]

The court observed that it could resolve certain congregational disputes if internal procedures failed to settle them. Among these proper areas of court focus were:

(1) whether the organization had blatantly deviated from the purposes for which it was founded, as expressed in the corporate charter. As a hypothetical example of a blatant deviation from the legally authorized corporate purpose, the court gave the changing of a Jewish synagogue into a Turkish Mosque. Presumably, the deviation would have to be outrageous and obvious or else the court would become entangled in resolving fine points of doctrine.

(2) whether or not bona fide members had been deprived of their rights under the corporate charter and bylaws. Perhaps the type of deprivation to which the court was referring was having one's voting rights stripped away by parliamentary maneuver.

(3) whether one power center within the organization had usurped a role properly belonging to another under the corporate charter and bylaws.[6]

Even these matters, which theoretically could be resolved under standard rules for construing legal documents, could have theological implications that would place the court in the position of endorsing one religious doctrine over another. Thus, the court should cautiously examine each case to determine whether or not taking jurisdiction would suck it into a whirlpool of theological dispute.

The court concluded that it could resolve the Beth Elohim dispute by using general tools for construing documents without trespassing into the dispute over the proper mode of worship, and the doctrine of the

Messiah. Using the corporate charter, bylaws and general standards of corporate governance, it concluded that the dissidents who had earlier been members of the congregation, in fact had resigned and that the trustee and congregational meetings that purported to readmit them had not been properly convened since the President, a key figure under the bylaws, had not agreed to call the meetings.

It is notable that this case was decided in the same year as *Benjamin, supra,* the famous Sunday closing case,[7] and only two years after Governor James H. Hammond's 1844 Thanksgiving Day Proclamation which called upon all South Carolina citizens to give thanks to Christ. The Thanksgiving Day Proclamation provoked a strong protest from Charleston Jews as excluding them from an equal role in the political community. The *Benjamin* decision ruled that the Sunday closing laws did not trespass upon the religious freedom of Orthodox Jews whose religion demanded that they close on Saturday and who wanted to open on Sunday to make up for the economic loss. The court concluded that there was no violation of the freedom of religion provisions in Article VIII, section 1, of the 1790 Constitution[8] since the closing laws did not forbid Saturday worship but only prohibited Sunday opening. However, this fairly orthodox legal conclusion was accompanied by divisive rhetoric in which the court concluded that the religious freedom provisions of the constitution were founded on Christian doctrine and that they should be interpreted in ways that advanced that faith.

By contrast, the *Ottolengui* decision contained no divisive rhetoric declaring Christianity to be the basis of the constitution and the common law. The court displayed the greatest respect for the Jewish faith, and it took great care to make sure that its decision did not encroach upon the free exercise rights of the members of the congregation. The entire opinion was permeated by a philosophy that courts should remain neutral in matters of religious doctrine. Why the difference in the manner in which these nearly contemporaneous matters were handled? Perhaps the key is that the *Ottolengui* case involved a dispute that was largely internal to the synagogue. It posed no threat to the traditions of the predominant Christian population as might approval of Sunday opening.

In a 1903 case, *Morris Street Baptist Church v. Dart,*[9] the court was even more circumspect about second-guessing the internal resolution of church disputes. In *Harmon v. Dreher* and *State ex rel. Ottolengui v. Ancker,* the court had concluded that it was improper for courts to determine questions of spiritual doctrine and to delve into the sincerity of a person's faith, but it did address itself, to some extent, to whether or not church decisions had been reached by proper procedure under its traditions or bylaws but, absent a serious procedural misstep, the court was unwilling to question the wisdom of decisions ultimately reached by the church. In *Harmon* it addressed itself to the fairness of the synod's procedure by questioning whether that body had properly informed the St. Peter's congregation of Reverend Dreher's dismissal and concluded that proper notice had not been given. In *Ottolengui* the court addressed itself to the question of which officials had the authority to call meetings of the trustees and the congregation. To the extent possible, the court resolved these issues by looking at the congregation's bylaws rather than by imposing an external standard upon it. In the *Dart* case, the court was even more cautious. It noted that a civil court should avoid, if possible, even questioning the regularity of the congregation's procedure as well as avoiding second guessing the wisdom of the corporation's ultimate decision. The court should try to limit its intrusion into the church decision-making process to determining whether or not the decision was made by the proper authority under the church's usual procedure of governance. Even this limited role should be played only when the problem concerns matters normally considered by civil courts, such as a contract dispute. Despite this cautious approach, the court in *Dart* was drawn into forming some limited conclusions about the propriety of the church procedure.

The *Dart* case involved an action brought by the Morris Street Baptist Church to enjoin the defendant minister from occupying the pulpit from which the plaintiffs said he had been dismissed. The minister questioned the propriety of the dismissal and claimed that it had been revoked by a subsequent meeting. The court disavowed any authority to tell a church whom to hire and fire but did conclude that under Baptist tradition, the congregation was the proper decision-making authority and that the minister had been duly dismissed.

When an ecclesiastical body has adopted a different mode of decision-making than congregational control (for example, control by centralized legislative and judicial bodies) and the state court must decide matters of civil law that depend upon the decision of the proper church authorities, the court will not substitute what it believes would be a better form of governance for the church. It will merely ascertain whether the decision was rendered by the proper authority under the church's constitution. If the proper authority rendered the decision, the court will not question its wisdom so long as no fraud or arbitrariness is found. In the absence of such irregularities, the court will defer to the church decision-maker's conclusions with regard to matters of church law, tradition and precedent. This is not to say that civil courts will supinely become conduits for church decisions, but that when an ingredient of a civil dispute, such as a property or contract dispute, depends on the manner in which an ecclesiastical issue was resolved, the court will not dictate the outcome of the theological or church governance controversy because to do so would encroach on the free exercise rights of the church organization. An example of the application of this approach is found in *Turbeville v. Morris.*[10]

In the *Turbeville* case the court was confronted with a church property dispute growing out of the nationwide merger of various units of the Methodist church that had split prior to the Civil War. Unlike the church in the *Morris Street Baptist Church* case, the Methodists did not utilize a congregational form of government but instead employed a more centralized decision-making process involving an ascending hierarchy of conferences covering progressively larger geographical areas. The court did not impose a congregational form of rule on the Methodists but determined whether or not decisions had been made by the appropriate centralized body. When it found that the decision had been made by the proper body, the court asked whether or not the decision was tainted by fraud, collusion, or arbitrariness and when it answered in the negative, it deferred to the decision of the church tribunal on matters of ecclesiastical law, retaining for itself the right to rule on the civil law issues and the right to determine how the civil and ecclesiastical elements combine to reach the ultimate decision.

A faction of the Pine Grove Church in Turbeville in Clarendon County objected to the national merger. This faction composed a majority of the local congregation. The pastor appointed by the Bishop and annual state conference, according to the Methodist mode, sought to oust the majority faction from control of the church property. The court concluded that congregational majority rule did not prevail in the Methodist church but control was in the centralized authorities represented by the various levels of geographical conferences. Who those centralized authorities were depended on whether the merger had properly taken place under church law. The ultimate disposition of property also depended upon the answer to certain questions of civil trust law. The state law combined these civil and ecclesiastical elements, without dictating the church-law decisions, in the following manner:

(1) Under state trust law the property had been properly deeded to the Methodist church for the use and benefit of its ministry.

(2) Who now constituted the Methodist church? Had the merger been properly consummated? If so, the merged body, and not the local congregation, controlled the property. With regard to the propriety of the merger, the court deferred to the church general conference judicial council that had concluded that the merger had been properly completed. Thus, the Pine Grove property should be controlled by the faction loyal to the merged national body and not by the dissident local body.

The *Turbeville* court made several important statements with regard to how church property disputes could be resolved by civil courts without those courts violating the constitution by endorsing, and thus establishing, some religious doctrines in preference to others, and without the state courts imposing a mode of governance on a church and thus harming its free exercise rights. All of this must be accomplished without the civil court abdicating its role as decision-maker and becoming a mere pipeline through which decisions of church groups are channeled.

In making these statements, the *Turbeville* court relied heavily on the leading United States Supreme Court case of *Watson v. Jones.*[11] The *Watson* court stated:

> In this class of cases we think the rule of action which should govern the civil courts, founded in a broad and sound view of the relations of church and state under our system of laws, and supported by a preponderating weight of judicial authority is, that, whenever the questions of discipline, or of faith, or ecclesiastical rule, custom, or law have been decided by the highest of these church judicatories to which the matter has been carried, the legal tribunals must accept such decisions as final, and as binding on them, in their application to the case before them.
>
> . . . .

> All who unite themselves to such a body do so with an implied consent to this government, and are bound to submit to it. But it would be a vain consent and would lead to the total subversion of such religious bodies, if any one aggrieved by one of their decisions could appeal to the secular courts and have them reversed.[12]

The *Turbeville* court based its conclusion (that it should question the decision of church tribunals on matters of ecclesiastical law and issues concerning the allocation of power within the church only if the church decision-making process was blatantly flawed) on another United States Supreme Court case, *Gonzalez v. Roman Catholic Archbishop.*[13] In *Gonzalez* the Supreme Court noted:

> In the absence of fraud, collusion, or arbitrariness, the decisions of the proper church tribunals on matters purely ecclesiastical, although affecting civil rights, are accepted in litigation before the secular courts as conclusive, because the parties in interest made them so by contract or otherwise. Under like circumstances, effect is given in the courts to the determinations of the judicatory bodies established by clubs and civil associations.[14]

The South Carolina court in *Turbeville* firmly rooted its deference to church tribunals with regard to matters of church law, theology and organization power on the constitutional concept of the separation of church and state when it stated:

> These matters present questions of a purely ecclesiastical nature. They depend upon the constitution and discipline, the faith and doctrine of this great denomination. It may be that in countries which have a State religion such questions could be inquired into by the civil Courts, but with us freedom of religion and the separation of church and state are among our most highly cherished principles. The Courts of South Carolina will not go behind the decisions of ecclesiastical tribunals on questions of this nature, by making the slightest inquiry into their wisdom. We take such decisions as we find them, after making the preliminary inquiries stated above.[15]

Although it ruled for the merged church and its loyalists on the local church property dispute, the *Turbeville* court refused a request from the united body that the dissidents be enjoined from using the words "Methodist Episcopal South" in the title of their group.[16] The South

Carolina court reasoned that while the merged body still used the term "Methodist" in its name, that it had abandoned the use of "Methodist Episcopal," and no confusion among potential donors and would-be members would be produced by the dissidents assuming the use of "Methodist Episcopal." A contrary conclusion was later reached in *Purcell v. Summers,*[17] a federal court of appeals decision, in a suit brought by different plaintiffs, a group of Bishops of the merged church. In concluding that the plaintiffs were entitled to enjoin the defendants from using the name "Methodist Episcopal" the court of appeals stated:

> No question of religious liberty is involved. Men have the right to worship God according to the dictates of conscience; but they have no right in doing so to make use of a name which will enable them to appropriate the good will which has been built up by an organization with which they are no longer connected.[18]

In other words, free expression of religious beliefs does not entitle a group to take what might be called a religious trademark belonging to another body. One wonders how far you would carry this reasoning, however. Could any group, as a prior user, be entitled to exclusive use of words such as "God" or "Christ"? Perhaps matters could not be carried to such an extreme since it is only in combination with other words that such terms become unique and proprietorial if consistently used by a particular group.

In a 1956 case, *Bramlett v. Young,*[19] the South Carolina court again wrestled with the problem of what is the appropriate disposition of the property of a local church when a majority of its members seceded from the national and regional organizations with which it had voluntarily affiliated, but a minority continued to adhere to the parent organization. The court made it clear that membership in a group is not a prerequisite to free exercise of religion and that an ingredient of free exercise is the ability to withdraw from a group and worship alone or pursuant to another affiliation. However, when a local group has affiliated voluntarily with a larger organization and accepted the discipline of that parent group, including property control, secession by the local church could result in loss of control of the property by a dissident majority of the local church to a minority who retains allegiance to the national organization.

In *Bramlett* a majority of the members of the McCarter Presbyterian Church became disenchanted with the national organization when a merger was begun between the northern and southern branches of the church. In addition they became estranged from the regional governing organization, the Enoree Presbytery, because of a dispute over who could serve as a substitute minister of the church. As a consequence, the majority voted to secede from both the Enoree Presbytery and the Presbyterian Church in the United States. The dissident majority adopted the name McCarter Independent Presbyterian Church and purported to convey the church property to an organization, known as the Bible Mission, as trustees for the new independent church. The minority members who were loyal to the Presbytery and the national organization brought suit to reform the deed of trust so that the property would be used for the benefit of the loyal minority, the Presbytery, and the national organization. The plaintiffs also sought to enjoin the secessionists from interfering with their use of the property. The court ruled in favor of the plaintiffs. It noted that, although the religious freedom provisions of Article I, Section 4 (now 2), of the Constitution of 1895 did not require group affiliation before freedom of worship could be exercised, and the constitution recognized the right of individuals or factions to withdraw from a group and worship on their own, those who had affiliated with larger organizations and pledged property to their use could not unilaterally decide to withdraw the property.[20] Control was lodged with the national and the local members remaining loyal to it. Even though it is not proper for a court resolving a factional dispute to decide which contingent is doctrinally correct, and it should be reluctant to test the sincerity of one's professed faith, it can make objective determinations of who does and does not purport to be loyal to a national organization.

There is a vast difference between determining organizational loyalty according to objective standards, as was done in *Bramlett*, and determining the disposition of property according to which group most closely adheres to church doctrine. Under the principle of separation of church and state, no civil court has any business in deciding which group most truly follows a body of theological doctrine. Jury members who are not of a faith, or even those who are, but who act not in their capacity as members but as agents of the state, should not dictate what beliefs must be held in order to be entitled to hold property for the church. These principles were applied in an important United States Supreme Court case, *Presbyterian Church in the United States v. Mary Elizabeth Blue Hull Memorial Presbyterian Church.*[21] In that 1969 case, two Presbyterian churches in Savannah, Georgia, objected to the doctrinal direction being taken by the Presbyterian Church in the United States. Among other things, they contended that the national church had approved the ordination of women, opposed prayer in the public schools, espoused civil disobedience as a means of gaining civil rights and involved itself in many controversial social issues such as the debate over the propriety of the Vietnam War. The local churches argued that this deviated from church doctrine and practice observed at the time that they had affiliated with the national church. This deviation from traditional doctrine allegedly breached an implied trust under which the national church controlled property used by the local church. The national church took over the local church's property. Rather than pursuing avenues of appeal available within the national church, the local congregations brought suit against the parent body for trespass in state court. Under Georgia law, the jury was asked to determine ". . . whether the actions of the general church 'amount to a fundamental or substantial abandonment of the original tenets and doctrines of the [general church], so that the new tenets and doctrines are utterly variant from the purposes for which the [general church] was founded.'"[22] Under this instruction, the jury found for the local church and the judgment was affirmed by the state supreme court.[23] The United States Supreme Court concluded that it violated basic principles of the separation of church and state for a civil court to determine the degree to which a church adhered to or deviated from its original doctrine. In reviewing church decisions as an essential part of resolving civil law disputes, the civil courts should confine themselves to the most "marginal" role.[24] According to the standards announced in *Gonzalez v. Archbishop,* this usually should involve no more than insuring that the church decision had been reached without fraud, arbitrariness or collusion. The "departure-from-doctrine" approach used in Georgia not only ran the risk of creating an establishment of religion by endorsing one set of doctrines over another, it also intruded on free exercise of religion by:

(1) "inhibiting the free development of religious doctrine," and

(2) "implicating secular interests in matters of purely ecclesiastical concern,"[25] and

(3) abrogating to a civil court the authority to determine how important a doctrine is to a church.[26]

A year later in *Maryland and Virginia Eldership of the Churches of God v. Church of God at Sharpsburg, Inc.,*[27] the United States Supreme Court continued in the same vein when it approved a Maryland court's resolution of a church property dispute because the state court had not attempted to resolve matters of church doctrine but instead had relied on a neutral state statute regulating the disposition of church property, the wording of deeds, church corporate charters and the constitution of the general church.[28] In a cautionary concurring opinion, Justice Brennan for himself, Justice Douglas and Justice Marshall, noted with general approval, as one possible route for resolving such church property disputes, deference to the decisions of the appropriate church authorities. This was the approach of *Watson v. Jones.* However, this usually neutral approach can embroil the court in internal church affairs if there is controversy concerning who the appropriate church authorities are.[29] In resolving such controversies the court would in essence be deciding church doctrine. If this approach gained ascendancy, then the actions of the South Carolina court in ruling upon the relative power of the president and trustees of the Beth Elohim congregation in the 1846 *Ottolengui* case would be questionable. It would be virtually impossible in many of these cases to render any meaningful decisions in church property disputes without resolving disputes concerning who are the proper church decision-makers.[30]

When a church property dispute is merely one incident of a larger dispute that primarily focuses upon theology, church organization, or who is fit to be a minister or high official of a religious organization, civil courts should be especially loath to question the decision of recognized church authorities. When a church has a settled hierarchy of decision-makers and the ultimate authority has spoken, civil court interference runs a serious risk of violating free exercise principles. Such a cautionary note was struck by the United States Supreme Court in *Serbian Orthodox Diocese v. Milivojevich.*[31] In that case the bishop of the American-Canadian Diocese of the Serbian Eastern Orthodox church had been removed by the church's highest authorities in Yugoslavia, the Holy

Synod and the Holy Assembly, and his diocese divided into three new dioceses, of one of which he was named bishop. The deposed bishop brought suit in Illinois state courts to enjoin the general church from interfering with the assets that had been in his charge, and to have himself declared the true bishop. The Illinois high court asserted that under the *Gonzalez* case, it had a right to review the decision to remove the bishop to determine whether or not the church authorities had acted with fraud, arbitrariness or collusion. Applying these due process standards, the court concluded that the bishop's removal was invalid. It further concluded that the reorganization of the diocese into three new dioceses was beyond the power of the church authorities under the general church constitution. The United States Supreme Court held that the Illinois court had interjected itself into a dispute that was primarily ecclesiastical rather than a property dispute with some peripheral theological issues. The Court drained much of the vitality from the *Gonzalez* case statement that civil courts could engage in minimal review of the decisions of religious organizations if the review went no further than examining whether or not the decision had been rendered fraudulently, arbitrarily or with collusion. The Court observed that the *Gonzalez* statement was dictum, and since it had been unnecessary to the resolution of the case, it should not have been given expansive weight. In particular, the *Gonzalez* standard should not be applied when the focal point of the dispute is theology or ecclesiastical politics, and involves only a peripheral property dispute. In such a situation even a limited review of the church decision to determine whether the decision was arbitrary, fraudulent or collusive could seriously harm free exercise of religion by substituting judicial orthodoxy for church doctrine. The Court noted that "constitutional concepts of due process, involving secular notions of 'fundamental fairness' or impermissible objectives, are therefore hardly relevant . . ." to religious decisions based more on faith than the marshaling of trial-type evidence.[32] The Illinois court also overstepped its authority when it ruled that the Serbian Eastern Orthodox hierarchy had exceeded its authority in reorganizing the diocese into three parts. As Justice Brennan had noted in his concurring opinion in *Maryland and Virginia Eldership of the Churches of God*, civil court resolution of controversies concerning which church agency has the authority to make certain decisions can plunge the civil courts into a theological maelstrom that is beyond their competence. Such decisions should be rendered, if at all, only when essential to resolving a primarily secular dispute with only peripheral church political issues. By contrast the reorganizational issues in the *Serbian Eastern Orthodox* case lay at the heart of the dispute and involved matters at the very core of the church's identity.[33]

In the wake of the *Serbian Eastern Orthodox* case, the casual reader might easily assume that the policy that civil courts not substitute their judgment for those of religious organizations' officials with regard to theological and organizational matters, meant that when a church was organized in a hierarchial manner that the civil courts always had to defer to the judgment of the church's hierarchy. However, the separation of church and state does not require such automatic genuflection to the church hierarchy. What is required is a neutral approach in which the civil courts neither (1) endorse a particular set of beliefs by declaring that only its adherents are entitled to control policy and property of a religious organization, nor (2) attempt to settle church political and theological disputes by substituting its views on such ecclesiastical matters for those of the church. The first approach risks violating the establishment clause and the latter risks violating the free exercise clause by imposing judicial orthodoxy on the religion.

In the 1979 case of *Jones v. Wolf*,[34] the United States Supreme Court concluded that this neutral approach did not necessarily dictate automatic obeisance of civil courts to a church hierarchy even when the affairs of a particular church are normally conducted according to an ascending scale of superior authority. The real essence of the neutral principles approach is the determination of the intentions of the parties to the religious compact.[35] Did they intend for particular issues to be determined by hierarchial superiors or by a majority of a local congregation? Even within the context of a church generally organized along hierarchial lines, the parties to a religious compact may have desired a particular issue to be resolved by the majority of a local congregation. The Court even refused to reject out of hand a state rule that presumed majority rule as the normal means of decision-making within local congregations of religious organizations if the state provided that such a presumption could be rebutted by demonstrating that the true intent of the parties was that the hierarchy should control on that issue. In order to reduce the risk that civil courts would rewrite fundamental church documents in the guise of interpreting them, the Court applauded the approach adopted by the Georgia courts in the wake of the *Presbyterian Church* case. The approach emphasized resolving disputes on the basis of ". . . objective, well established concepts of trust and property law . . . ."[36] The United States Supreme Court gave the state courts considerable flexibility in developing their own versions of this approach. Among the sources that might be appropriate in applying such standards were deeds, neutral state statutes concerning the disposition of church property, corporate charters and church constitutions viewed according to the standard principles for construing legal documents.[37] Despite the use of such traditional neutral legal sources the courts run a great risk of trespassing on religious freedom of the parties to church compacts whenever they attempt to discover the true intent of the parties. The risk may be tolerable when the dispute is primarily an internal church dispute concerning the control of property as was the case confronting the South Carolina court in *Bramlett*. When the dispute is primarily theological with only incidental property law dimensions, as in the *Serbian Eastern Orthodox* case, the courts are well advised to abstain because their decisions will invariably lead to the state taking sides in a theological dispute.[38]

The riddle that has consistently confronted the courts in resolving property and other disputes internal to a religious organization is how can they exercise their legitimate roles as resolvers of legal disputes without being drawn into the role of religious oracle. Perhaps the better course would be for the civil courts to abstain from deciding such disputes unless (1) the dispute involves third parties, such as purchasers of real property who have not consented to a dispute resolution mechanism within the church, or (2) dispute resolution machinery within the church has failed and a violent confrontation is likely. This policy of abstention would force the churches to devise better means for resolving controversies within their own ranks.

NOTES

1. Harmon v. Dreher, 17 S.C. Eq. (Speers Eq.) 87 (1843).

2. Wilson v. Presbyterian Church of John's Island and Wadmalaw, 19 S.C. Eq. (2 Rich. Eq.) 192 (1846).

3. State *ex rel.* Ottolengui v. Ancker, 31 S.C.L. (2 Rich.) 245 (1846).

4. *Ottolengui,* 31 S.C.L. (2 Rich.) at 268.

5. *Ottolengui,* 31 S.C.L. (2 Rich.) at 274.

6. *Ottolengui,* 31 S.C.L. (2 Rich.) at 269.

7. City Council of Charleston v. Benjamin, 33 S.C.L. (2 Strob.) at 508 (1846). M. BORDEN, JEWS, TURKS AND INFIDELS 142 (1984).

8. Art. VIII, § 1, S.C. CONST. 1790.

9. 67 S.C. 338, 45 S.E.2d 753 (1903).

10. Turbeville v. Morris, 203 S.C. 287, 26 S.E.2d 821 (1943).

11. Watson v. Jones, 80 U.S. (13 Wall.) 679 (1871).

12. 80 U.S. (13 Wall.) at 727, 729.

13. Gonzalez v. Roman Catholic Archbishop of Manila, 280 U.S. 1, 50 S. Ct. 5, 74 L. Ed. 131 (1929).

14. 280 U.S. at 16-17.

15. *Turbeville,* 203 S.C. at 315, 26 S.E.2d at 832.

16. 203 S.C. at 317-18, 26 S.E.2d at 832-33.

17. Purcell v. Summers, 145 F.2d 979 (4th Cir. 1944).

18. 145 F.2d at 987.

19. Bramlett v. Young, 229 S.C. 519, 93 S.E.2d 873 (1956).

20. 229 S.C. at 538-47, 93 S.E.2d at 882-88. *See also* Dillard v. Jackson, 403 S.E.2d 136, 138 (1991) in which the Court of Appeals stated that:

> The South Carolina Supreme Court has held that when a church splits, the courts will not undertake to inquire into the ecclesiastical acts of the several parties, but will determine property rights in favor of the party or division maintaining the church organization as it previously existed....We accordingly hold that when the entire congregation withdraws from the hierarchial church, the title to the church property remains in the church and does not follow the congregation.

21. Presbyterian Church in U.S. v. Mary Elizabeth Blue Hull Memorial Presbyterian Church, 393 U.S. 440, 89 S. Ct. 601, 21 L. Ed. 2d 658 (1969).

22. 393 U.S. at 443-44.

23. Presbyterian Church in U.S. v. Eastern Heights Presbyterian Church, 224 Ga. 61, 159 S.E.2d 690 (1968), *rev'd.*, 393 U.S. 440, 89 S. Ct. 601, 21 L. Ed. 2d 658 (1969).

24. *Eastern Heights*, 393 U.S. at 447.

25. *Eastern Heights*, 393 U.S. at 449.

26. *Eastern Heights*, 393 U.S. at 450. On remand, the Georgia court replaced its deviation from doctrine approach with a technique emphasizing neutral principles of property law focusing on the examination of statutes, deeds, articles of incorporation and church documents. The state court found no implied trust in favor of the national organization or local members loyal to it and thus again ruled in favor of the local congregation majority. *See* 225 Ga. 259, 167 S.E.2d 658 (1969), *cert. denied*, 396 U.S. 1041, 90 S. Ct. 680, 24 L. Ed. 2d 685 (1970).

27. Maryland and Virginia Eldership of Churches of God v. Church of God at Sharpsburg, Inc., 396 U.S. 367, 90 S. Ct. 499, 24 L. Ed. 2d 582 (1970).

28. 396 U.S. 367.

29. 396 U.S. at 368-70.

30. For a discussion of the *Sharpsburg* case, *see* 1974 Opinions of the Attorney General of South Carolina, No. 3757, April 22, 1974 at 127.

31. Serbian Orthodox Diocese for United States of Am. and Can. v. Milivojevich, 426 U.S. 696, 96 S. Ct. 2372, 49 L. Ed. 2d 151 (1976).

32. 426 U.S. at 715.

33. *See also* Kedroff v. St. Nicholas Cathedral of Russian Orthodox Church, 344 U.S. 94, 73 S. Ct. 143, 97 L. Ed. 120 (1952) (the court ruled that state legislation which prescribed matters of ecclesiastical administration, shifted control from one faction to another and influenced the selection of the clergy, violated the First and Fourteenth Amendments).

34. Jones v. Wolf, 443 U.S. 595, 99 S. Ct. 3020, 61 L. Ed. 2d 775 (1979).

35. 443 U.S. at 603.

36. 443 U.S. at 603.

37. 443 U.S. at 600.

38. 443 U.S. at 610-21 (Powell J., dissenting) (scolding the court for departing from the principles of Watson v. Jones, by permitting the states to develop so-called "neutral" principles of property law that have the potential of overriding the wishes of the religious body concerning which agency within it can make basic decisions).

CHAPTER SEVEN

SOUTH CAROLINA CONSTITUTIONAL PROVISIONS CONTROLLING GOVERNMENT FINANCIAL AID TO RELIGIOUS INSTITUTIONS

The South Carolina Constitution of 1868 was a broad democratic document that contemplated the extensive use of public funds to make educational and health benefits widely available to the newly-freed slave and the rest of society. A keystone of this program was Article X which mandated a system of free public schools open to all youths of the state. Broad educational opportunities were essential to the success of the universal adult male suffrage provisions of Article VIII, section 2. The greater infusion of public funds into the educational system and the opening of that system to a diverse group of students would prompt maneuvering for control of those funds as well as attempts to control the curriculum. In order for a diverse student body to be able to learn in a harmonious environment, the government could not afford to let funds raised for education from all property taxpayers under Article X, section 5, be used to spread the ideological message of any particular religion. For the first time, a South Carolina constitution had a provision prohibiting government establishment of religion as well as a clause insuring free exercise of religion. Article I, section 10, stated that "[n]o form of religion shall be established by law; but it shall be the duty of the General Assembly to pass suitable laws to protect every religious denomination in the peaceable enjoyment of its own mode of worship." General neutrality of the state toward religion was inherent in this broad provision. However, the plan for opening the schools to a diverse student body and burdening all property taxpayers with the support of this system made more concrete guarantees of fiscal and ideological neutrality toward religion in the schools desirable. Accordingly, at the end of Article X, section 5, providing for support of the public schools by property and poll taxes, was inserted a provision which stated that:

> No religious sect or sects shall have exclusive right to, or control of, any part of the school funds of the State, nor shall sectarian principles be taught in the public schools.

This was a strong provision. However, it was still possible to interpret the language as permitting significant influence to be wielded by religious organizations over the disposition of public education funds if the sects did not exercise "exclusive" control over any portion of the school funds but only enjoyed a substantial voice in determining disposition of the funds. This loophole was plugged by a far more detailed provision adopted as Article XI, section 9, of the original Constitution of 1895. The provision stated that:

> The property or credit of the State of South Carolina, or of any County, city, town, township, school district, or other subdivision of the said State, or any public money, from whatever source derived, shall not, by gift, donation, loan, contract, appropriation, or otherwise, be used, directly or indirectly, in aid or maintenance of any college, school, hospital, orphan house, or other institution, society or organization, of whatever kind, which is wholly or in part under the direction or control of any church or of any religious or sectarian denomination, society or organization.[1]

Not only did this provision prevent government financial aid from going to recipients that were only controlled partially by a religious organization, it further restricted government aid to religious organizations by (1) prohibiting aid to religious institutions from flowing from local as well as state government, (2) prohibiting not only the appropriation of tax funds for religious use but also the grant of other forms of aid including gifts, donations, loans or contracts, (3) prohibiting aid not only to schools operated in whole or in part by religious organizations but also to other agencies of church "good works" such as hospitals and orphanages, (4) prohibiting not only *direct* but *indirect* aid from flowing to religious organizations. As we shall see later, this outlawing of indirect as well as direct aid to religious organizations eventually would raise questions concerning whether or not the state could grant scholarships to students attending colleges operated by religious denominations. Even though technically the recipients of the aid were private citizens, the students and their parents, an argument could be made that the schools benefitted indirectly because the scholarship program made it possible for more people to attend expensive private colleges than would otherwise be the case.

At first the 1895 provision attracted little attention from litigants. *Forrest v. City Council of Charleston*[2] involved saber-rattling by a doctor over a $5,000 Charleston appropriation to an orphan asylum which the doctor believed to be controlled by the Roman Catholic church, but the case ended inconclusively with the doctor withdrawing from the field after a few minor procedural skirmishes. The case was withdrawn before trial, and it was never established whether or not the orphanage was Catholic controlled, and the appellate decision reached no constitutional issues and considered only whether or not the petition to withdraw the case had been timely filed.

In 1949, *Parker v. Bates*[3] involved a challenge to the state's use of surplus funds for the aid of eleemosynary hospitals. Since the program was structured in such a manner that some of the funds might accrue to religiously sponsored organizations the plaintiff challenged it as violating Article XI, section 9. Even though the court concluded that since there was no showing that funds would actually go to religiously controlled hospitals, the case was not yet ripe for decision. However, the court went ahead and explored the contours of Article XI, section 9, anyway. The court observed that the prohibition against using public funds, credit or property for aiding schools, hospitals, and orphanages, controlled at least in part by religious organizations was to be strictly interpreted. The prohibition was not to be ignored just because public benefit would accrue from the grant. It did not matter that the hospital was nonprofit.

It did not matter that it was open to patients without regard to their religious affiliation. It did not matter that the hospital was not used to proselytize for the sponsoring organization's religion. The test was: did the funds directly or indirectly aid an organization, controlled in whole or in part by a religious body? The test did not depend upon whether the funds were put to a religious use or not.[4]

The court refused to be swayed by cases from other states having more flexible constitutional provisions. The court distinguished the South Carolina Constitution from Kentucky standards interpreted in *Kentucky Building Commission v. Effron*.[5] In that case, Kentucky had appropriated ten million dollars for non-profit hospitals that were not government owned. The appropriation was made so that the state could qualify for federal matching funds. The *Parker* case indicates that the South Carolina hospital grant program also grew out of desire to qualify for federal funds.[6] The Kentucky case was ripe for adjudication since there had already been an appropriation to a hospital that was sectarian but open to the general public. The Kentucky court held that the appropriation did not transgress the state constitution. Section 5 of the Kentucky Constitution stated that:

> No preference shall ever be given by law to any religious sect, society or denomination.[7]

This was a general provision against religious discrimination by state law and did not have specific reference to the appropriation of funds as did the South Carolina standard. There was no *per se* rule that religious control of the grant recipient was fatal. If the ultimate beneficiaries — the general public — received health services without religious discrimination then the programs passed constitutional muster. The Kentucky court was aided in its conclusion that the grant program created no religious preference by the fact that not only were these non-profit hospitals open to members of the general public without regard to religious affiliation, but that the hospitals were not used as the instrument of religious teaching or evangelizing. It was true that the members of the board of one grant recipient were drawn entirely from one denomination. However, these officials of the private institution served as mere pipelines through which the government funds flowed to the ultimate recipient —

the patient. These officials exacted no religious toll for the passage of the funds. The Kentucky court stated that:

> On the contrary, the governing boards of such hospitals are but the channels through which the funds flow. Courts will look at the use to which these funds are put rather than the conduits through which they run.[8]

By contrast, the South Carolina Constitution sought to strike a preemptive blow — to stop the funds before they began to flow through the religious conduit — without waiting to see whether or not the eventual impact of the funds created a religious preference.

The Kentucky approach was reminiscent of the late-nineteenth-century United States Supreme Court case *Bradfield v. Roberts.*[9] That case questioned the validity of using federal funds from the District of Columbia to establish a hospital for communicable diseases in the Washington area. Although the hospital was to be built by federal funds it was to be operated by a sisterhood of nursing nuns. The courts looked at the nature of the aid — funds for building a health services facility that would benefit the general public. Even though it was conceivable that the health services could be directed to religious ends, medical care was not an intrinsically religious function. It is not designed to advance the cause of the church or gather in new converts. The immediate recipients of the aid — the sisterhood of nuns — even though they were associated with the Catholic church, administered the healing arts in a secular, neutral manner and were not expected to use the hospital as a tool to seek converts. They were not a pervasively religious organization. It was possible to separate their secular health care from their religious adherence.

By South Carolina standards, this left too much to chance. Even the possibility of the diversion of public funds toward religious ends should be stopped. This is a complete about-face from the early eighteenth-century custom, discussed above, of channeling many social services, such as aid to the poor, not only through the church but through one particular denomination, the Church of England. Society was more diverse now, and the government representing it had to be more neutral or else fractious quarrels would be set off as the various denominations would vie for the biggest share of public funds. Article X of the Constitution of 1895 is a document that reeks of fiscal restraint. Especially abhorrent to Article X is the use of public funds by private entities whether they be railroads or hospitals.

In a sense Article XI, section 9, of the original 1895 Constitution, and its current counterpart Article XI, section 4, are an extension of the traditional South Carolina fiscal conservatism to the educational and social services area with specific emphasis upon prohibiting grants to religious organizations as those most likely to be operating in those fields. Let private organizations look to private sources.[10]

As the competition for private funds increased and expenses mounted, many private educational institutions were under enormous pressure to seek government assistance from state and federal agencies. Article XI, section 9, loomed as a gigantic boulder blocking the path toward government aid.

In 1969 the Committee to Make a Study of the Constitution of 1895, colloquially known as the West committee after its chairman Lieutenant Governor John West, considered proposals to loosen the restrictions found in Article XI, section 9, to permit tuition grants to students attending religiously sponsored colleges. Should the prohibition on the use of government funds in a manner that only *indirectly* aids a church-operated college, such as scholarships that make it more feasible for low- and middle-income students to attend such schools, be removed from the constitution? The benefits of preserving a variety of higher education providers in the form of private institutions, both secular and religious, as well as state-operated schools would be many. Debate on public issues is more incisive if not all participants in the debate draw their perspectives from the same fountainhead. However, government support of private, religiously-operated educational institutions, could lure such institutions away from the purity of their religious perspective and make them cater to the whims of government as a means of attracting more funds. Even indirect aid ran the risk of taking one person's tax money to support another's religion or creating the appearance that the state endorsed the ideological message of the religious institutions it aided. To be sure if the direct recipient of the aid were the student rather than the institution and if the student were pursuing a secular course of study, those dangers would be muted, but they would still be present.

The West committee was presented with testimony on both sides of the issue. The South Carolina Baptist Committee on Religious Liberty submitted a statement in opposition to tuition equalization programs that would involve grants to students attending private schools so that the financial burden on them would be comparable to what they would incur attending a state school. The Baptist committee argued that even if government tax-raised funds did not go directly to church-operated schools for use in religious instruction or proselytizing activities, it could free funds that the school would otherwise use for scholarships and permit them to be used to spread a religious message. This not only would violate constitutional principles on the separation of church and state, it would contravene historic Baptist doctrine. The statement noted that Article 8, section 2, of the South Carolina Baptist Convention Constitution[11] stated that "No funds, gifts, or allowances that infringe upon the historic principle of the Separation of Church and State shall be accepted by the Convention, the General Board, or any Institutions or agencies of the Convention."[12]

The Baptist statement was presented in opposition to a position paper submitted by the South Carolina Association of Independent Colleges in support of a tuition equalization plan. Dr. Paul Hardin, III, the President of Wofford College, and former Duke Law School professor, testified in favor of tuition equalization and constitutional changes that would remove any shadow of invalidity from such programs. President Hardin directed his remarks to the proposed revision in Article XI that was then before the committee. That proposal eventually became Article XI, section 4, which states that:

> No money shall be paid from public funds nor shall the credit of the State or any of its political subdivisions be used for the direct benefit of any religious or other private educational institution.

The provision removes the prohibition of aid that only *indirectly* benefits private educational institutions. The remaining prohibition of direct aid applies not only to grants going to church-operated private institutions but also to ". . . other private educational institution[s]." This removes the taint of singling out religious institutions for hostile treatment, which could be just as much of a deviation from the ideal of state neutrality toward religion as would be a provision singling out religious institutions for favorable treatment. Dr. Hardin applauded the removal of the rule against indirect aid to sectarian institutions, but he preferred to go farther and excise the prohibition of direct aid as well. He noted that Wofford had received direct aid from the federal government in the form of a grant to build a library. Wofford also received federal funds for scholarship assistance which the school was matching. Such direct aid would probably not be permitted even under the revised Article XI. He believed that such aid could be structured in such a way as to avoid "political interference" with the operation of the schools. In response to committee questioning about whether or not it was wise to make such a sweeping change as would remove the prohibition of direct as well as indirect aid, he offered a compromise that would permit aid that would go directly to the institution but which would outlaw aid that would pay for the teaching of religion at private sectarian colleges. However, he was unenthusiastic about this compromise position and preferred that there be no restraints on direct or indirect aid to sectarian institutions. Whether or not there was to be any aid to religious or other private institutions, and the form it would take, should be a matter left entirely to the discretion of the legislature.[13]

In recommending what eventually became Article XI, section 4, of the revised 1895 Constitution, the West committee took the more modest position of recommending the deletion of the ban on indirect aid but retained the prohibition on direct grants. In its final report the committee explained its cautious approach to amending Article XI in the following terms:

> . . . .
>
> The Committee fully recognized the tremendous number of South Carolinians being educated at private and religious schools in this State and that the educational costs to the State would sharply increase if these programs ceased. From the standpoint of the State and the independence of the private institutions, the Committee feels that public funds should not be granted outrightly to such institutions. Yet, the Committee sees that in the future there may be substantial reasons to aid the students in such institutions as well as in state colleges. Therefore, the Committee proposes a prohibition on direct grants only and the deletion of the word "indirectly" currently listed in Section 9 [of Article XI]. By removing the word "indirectly" the General

> Assembly could establish a program to aid students and perhaps contract with religious and private institutions for certain types of training and programs. The prohibition against using public money and credit for private hospitals, orphanages etc. presently listed in Section 9 is continued, but is included in . . . [the article on finance and taxation].[14]

As suggested by the committee, the prohibition against aid to private hospitals, orphanages, etc., was moved to the article on finance and taxation. After the 1977 revisions of Article X, section 11 contained the following language:

> The credit of neither the State nor of any of its political subdivisions shall be pledged or loaned for the benefit of any individual, company, association, corporation or any religious or other private education institution except as permitted by Section 3, Article XI of this Constitution.

The language does not explicitly mention orphanages or hospitals, whether supported by religious or other secular groups, as forbidden recipients of government loans or credits. However, such organizations are subsumed under the broader terms forbidding government fiscal assistance to all forms of private entities. This was the apparent intent of the West committee as seen from the interaction of its recommendation on the education article with its proposals for the tax and finance article.[15] The committee's recommendations became Article XI, section 4, of the Constitution in 1973.[16] The repetition in both the education and tax articles of the limitations on the use of government credit and funds for religious educational institutions, and the inclusion of limitations on government assistance to private *secular* educational institutions as well as other types of private secular organizations, reinforces the conclusion that the policy is as much an expression of the fiscal conservatism of the state as it is a reflection of separation of church and state doctrines. Promiscuous state fiscal aid to all forms of private endeavor, whether religious or not, was to be viewed with deep skepticism.

The West committee's conclusions that retention of the limitation on indirect aid to religiously sponsored schools would inhibit state and local government aid to students attending parochial schools as well as prohibit aid to the schools themselves, was borne out by an attorney general's opinion issued shortly after the West committee's final report, but before its recommendations had become a part of the constitution. The opinion also illustrated how the old Article XI, section 9, could be even more restrictive of government aid to religious schools than could the religious clauses of the federal First Amendment. In this 1970 opinion, the attorney general ruled that the prohibition on aid that indirectly benefitted religious institutions forbade the state or local governments from providing transportation to and from school for students attending Catholic parochial schools. The word "indirect" meant that such a program would not be saved by the fact that the immediate beneficiaries of the aid would be the students and their parents and that funds presumably would not go to the parochial school treasury.[17] This approach stands in stark contrast to the interpretation given to the establishment clause of the United States Constitution by the federal Supreme Court in the 1947 case *Everson v. Board of Education.*[18] In that case the Supreme Court upheld as not being violative of the establishment clause of the First Amendment, as applied to the states through the Fourteenth Amendment, a New Jersey program under which local governments would provide free transportation to school for students whether they attended public schools or private sectarian or secular schools. In some communities, this took the form of reimbursing parents for funds that they had expended in paying for their children's transportation to and from parochial schools. The program was challenged by a taxpayer as being a law creating an establishment of religion by appropriating public funds to aid religious education. The Court rejected this challenge noting that the program did not constitute endorsement or financial support of religious education since:

(a) The purpose of the program was to assure the health and safety of all students attending school, whether public, private secular, or private parochial schools. Thus the program was designed to achieve neutral health safety goals rather than the advancement of religion.

(b) Any impermissible effect of advancing religion was avoided because (1) the students and parents were the direct beneficiaries of the program since no state funds were transferred to school treasuries, and (2) the program helped the general student population and not just those attending parochial schools.

(c) In maintaining the neutral government stance toward religion that was required by the First Amendment, the state must not only avoid granting a preference to religion, it must also avoid punishing people for religious affiliations by denying them generally available benefits. Even though the court was reluctant to say that the states *had* to extend the benefit to parochial, as well as other students, the state could at least justify giving the benefit to them as an act of state neutrality rather than favoritism toward religion.

Under Article XI, section 9, of the South Carolina Constitution, as it existed prior to adoption of the amendment deleting the prohibition of indirect aid to religious schools, it is doubtful that the fact that the direct beneficiaries were the students and parents rather than the parochial school itself even could have been considered as part of the chain of reasoning if a program similar to that in *Everson* had been attacked under the South Carolina Constitution. The chances that the program would have been declared unconstitutional would have been greater than they would have been had such a program been considered solely under general establishment clause language, or language similar to Article XI, section 9, without the prohibition of indirect aid. However, if the program considered in the 1970 attorney general's opinion was structured in such a manner as to benefit only parochial school students, then it was likely that it would be invalid even if there were no prohibition of indirect aid since such a program would prefer some citizens over others based on their religious adherence.[19]

After the West committee recommended deletion of the prohibition against indirect aid to religious schools but before the amendments were adopted, the most persistent problem continued to be interpreting the scope of Article XI, section 9, with regard to tuition grant programs aiding students attending colleges operated by religious denominations. The state tried to walk a narrow path that would avoid constitutional transgression but that would permit it to aid private religious schools that took a great deal of the burden of providing higher education off the backs of state institutions. With surplus space, private institutions could assume still more of the burden. A good mix of state, secular-private, and religious-private schools educating future leaders adds to the quality of debate on public issues. As tuition increased it became harder for many students to attend private schools without financial assistance. Private schools had difficulty providing such assistance from their own resources and sought government help.[20]

One attempt by the state to provide tuition grant assistance to private schools, including those operated by religious bodies, came before the Supreme Court in *Hartness v. Patterson.*[21] The *Hartness* case involved a taxpayer's attempt to enjoin the state treasurer from implementing a program to provide tuition assistance to students attending private colleges, both secular and sectarian. However, the program did not permit aid to be given to students pursuing courses of theology or religious education. Sixteen of the twenty-one private schools whose students would be eligible for the assistance were under the "...direction or control..." of churches, thus making even indirect aid to them suspect under the language of Article XI, section 9. The tuition grant program was administered by a committee consisting of eight representatives of the participating colleges and two *ex officio* representatives of the General Assembly. The Court noted that it was at least possible that a majority of the committee could be representatives of private religious schools. The committee had extensive powers to make rules governing the award of tuition grants.

The state Supreme Court concluded that the program violated the strictures of Article XI, section 9. The court began its justification for striking down the program by noting that no matter how circuitous the path, the aid still benefits the school. The student receives the grant only after he has been accepted or is enrolled in a participating school. He or she has no status as a recipient except by virtue of affiliation with a qualified school. The student can not dispose of the funds as he likes but must use them to attend a participating school which he selects and which has accepted him. Even though the grant was to the student, the conditions and restrictions placed on the grant make it certain that a private school, most of which are religiously controlled, ultimately would receive the funds. The path was indirect but the destination was sure. The student benefitted from the education, but in an accounting sense he or she was a mere conduit through which funds flowed to the school.[22] In addition to providing a variety of educational opportunities to the young people of the state, the program had a purpose of boosting the financial health of private educational institutions, and that was the eventual impact of the program.

One of the basic philosophical themes underlying Article XI, section 9, was that it was improper for private entities, especially religious educational institutions with great influence over young minds, to exercise government power by controlling the disposition of public funds. This abhorrence of secular power being wielded by sectarian institutions is revealed by the language of Section 9 that labelled as improper recipients of public funds, loans, gifts or contracts, colleges, hospitals or orphanages ". . . wholly or in part under the *direction or control* of any church . . ." (emphasis added). It is contrary to our concept of separation of church and state for religious bodies to direct or control the civil government decision-making process whether it relates to the disposition of government funds or other crucial decisions.

A similar theme was struck with regard to another type of government decision by the United States Supreme Court in *Larkin v. Grendel's Den Inc.*[23] In that case, the Court struck down as violative of the establishment clause of the federal First Amendment a Massachusetts law that gave churches and schools, whether public or private, a veto power over liquor licenses being granted to restaurants or bars within 500 feet of the church or school. The Court pursued its traditional establishment clause analytical system by asking whether giving churches such power was designed to serve the purpose of advancing religion, or had the primary effect of advancing religion, or excessively entangled the church and state power structures. The Court concluded that even though the statute could have the legitimate secular purpose of preserving a zone of quiet and decorum around churches and schools, as institutions uniquely in need of such quiet, the state chose unnecessarily religious means of accomplishing that goal. The same goal could have been achieved without granting churches veto power over nearby liquor licenses by either a flat legislative decree that a liquor license could not be granted to establishments within 500 feet of schools or churches, or by holding hearings on the wisdom of granting such licenses and permitting the schools and churches as well as other interested parties an opportunity to present testimony. Neither alternative would cede secular power to religious entities. The church veto system could have had a primary effect of advancing religion as it would have permitted the churches to use the veto power as an inducement to get would-be licensees to join or make contributions, or otherwise support the church. Even though such crude use of the veto power might never have taken place, the mere existence of such power might entice people to pander to the church in ways that would be repugnant. Finally, the system entangled church and state power in ways that might make those possessing such concentrated powers insensitive to the needs of the general population. The church authorities were not elected officials. The wielding of secular power by church authorities might prove to be divisive in the political community. Even though the South Carolina court in *Hartness* was interpreting a different constitutional provision, as applied to a different government program, the same disdain for the exercise of secular power by religious officials would seem to underlie both decisions.

The lesson of the *Hartness* case was not lost on the legislature. In *Durham v. McLeod*[24] the state Supreme Court upheld a tuition loan guarantee program which corrected the flaws in the earlier system. Secular power was not wielded by church authorities since the grant program was administered by the state Budget and Control Board. Article XI, section 9, of the state constitution was not violated because (1) neither state funds nor credit were involved, and (2) the religious schools did not benefit even indirectly. State funds were not involved since the money for the tuition grants did not come from taxes or other normal state revenue sources but instead came from bonds issued by the state but payable not out of the state treasury but from loan repayments from the students. The bonds were so-called revenue bonds rather than general obligation bonds. Such bonds do not pledge to the purchaser the full faith credit and taxing power of the state as a source of repayment. Thus the bonds did not constitute a true debt of the state. Payment of interest and principal on the loans was to come from a particular revenue source: repayment of the loans by the students. Since state funds were no longer linked to education provided by religious institutions the danger of state endorsement of the contents of such education was reduced.

Under the new scheme it was difficult to consider religiously controlled schools to be even indirect beneficiaries of state fiscal aid. Not only were state funds not involved, the class of student beneficiaries had been broadened to include those with no links to religious schools. Under the program considered in *Hartness*, receipt of the tuition grant was conditioned upon acceptance of the students by a narrow range of private schools, most of which were religious. In the new program, the student first received the loan, then he could decide what school he wanted to attend whether it be a public college, private secular or religious school.

Religious schools, as well as other public and private schools, could compete for the patronage of the student loan recipient, but they did not have a lock on any part of the funds.[25] Since quite a few students receiving loans would elect to attend church-sponsored colleges, it could be argued that in a highly remote, speculative sense that the sectarian schools were beneficiaries. However, this system was a far cry from that in *Hartness* in which the restrictions and conditions placed on the grants assured the church schools that formed a majority of the participating colleges of receiving substantial state funds even though indirectly through the students as conduits.

In addition to the charges of Article XI violation, the South Carolina court in *Durham* considered allegations that the loan program violated the establishment clauses of the state and federal constitutions. The court stated that:

> We find no merit in this claim. The Act is scrupulously neutral between religion and irreligion and as between various religions. It simply aids and encourages South Carolina residents in the pursuit of higher education, and leaves all eligible institutions free to compete for their attendance and dollars, neither advantaged or disadvantaged by the operation of the Act. If, on the other hand, sectarian schools had been excluded from the category of eligible institutions, such schools would have been materially disadvantaged by the intervention of the State's loan program.[26]

This last sentence is especially notable since it is often forgotten that the concept of neutrality is a river that flows in both directions. The state must not discriminate in favor of religious adherents but it must not deprive them of generally available benefit programs, or the state would be guilty of hostility toward religion.[27] In determining that the loan program did not violate the state or federal establishment clauses, the South Carolina court adopted the analytical scheme used by the United States Supreme Court in *Lemon v. Kurtzman*,[28] a case which struck down Pennsylvania and Rhode Island programs which provided state supplements to the salaries of instructors of secular subjects in parochial schools. Under this system a government program violates the establishment clause if it either has a (1) *purpose* of advancing or inhibiting religion, or (2) a *primary effect* of advancing religion, or (3) results in excessive *entanglement* of government and church authorities by church officials wielding secular power, or vice versa, or the government conducting excessive surveillance of church administrative activities, or by creating a divisive atmosphere in which political contests are fought along religious lines. In the *Durham* case, the South Carolina court found that the tuition loan program violated none of the prongs of the purpose, effect, entanglement doctrine. Although the court did not provide a point-by-point discussion of each element of the *Lemon* test, perhaps the key to analyzing all three points was that the students were the primary beneficiaries of the program and that students attending public and secular-private schools were eligible as well as students attending private parochial schools.

A similar approach was taken in a later United States Supreme Court case, *Mueller v. Allen.*[29] In that case the Court approved a Minnesota program authorizing state taxpayers to deduct expenses that they had paid for providing tuition, textbooks, and transportation for their children to attend public, private secular, or private sectarian elementary and high schools. The program passed all three elements of the *Lemon* test. The purposes of the program were the secular goals of making education more accessible to all Minnesota young people and making it possible for private schools to continue to relieve public schools of some of the burden of providing education to large numbers of children. This secular purpose was evidenced by the breadth of the beneficiary class. This same fact, that the beneficiaries included public as well as private secular and sectarian school students, insured that the program did not have a primary effect of advancing religion. Any tendency the program had toward advancing religion was further diluted by the fact that the aid went to the parents claiming the tax funds and did not involve direct fund transfers to parochial schools. If the Minnesota program had been analyzed under a provision similar to old Article XI, section 9, of the South Carolina Constitution,[30] the indirectness of the aid may have been less likely to have saved the program, but it was a crucial factor under the more general establishment clause provisions.

The Minnesota program did not involve excessive entanglement between state and federal authorities. The nature of the tax-benefit program as one not requiring the direct transfer of government funds to religious schools was not such as to require the continuing surveillance of religious school records and classes to insure that government funds were not being used for religious purposes. Persistent government spying on religious school operations proved fatal to the program in *Lemon* and was carefully avoided in the Minnesota scheme. Some examination of private school textbooks was conducted by the state to insure that the textbooks were not used for religious instruction. However, when surveillance was this brief, it resembled the nonintensive sort that the court had found acceptable in a New York textbook loan program in *Board of Education v. Allen.*[31] It is notable that in both the *Allen* textbook loan program and the *Everson* school transportation program the class of beneficiaries had included all school children and not just those attending private schools. The pivotal nature of the range of beneficiaries was signaled in an earlier United States Supreme Court case, *Committee for Public Education v. Nyquist.*[32] In that case the Court struck down as violating the establishment clause a New York program that (1) granted government funds for the repair of nonpublic schools, (2) granted tuition reimbursement to low-income parents whose children attended nonpublic schools, and (3) gave tax deductions to higher-income parents whose children were enrolled in nonpublic schools. The Court considered all elements of the program to have a primary effect of advancing religion since the class of beneficiaries was limited to nonpublic schools (most of which were church-affiliated) and parents whose children attended such institutions. Because the beneficiary class was so narrowly defined, the fact that the tuition grants and tax deductions in *Nyquist* went to the parents rather than to the schools directly did not save the program. The South Carolina tuition grant program struck down in *Hartness* shared with the scheme invalidated in *Nyquist* a narrow — largely religious — class of beneficiaries. The Minnesota program upheld in *Mueller* and the South Carolina program upheld in *Durham* had broader classes of beneficiaries that included public school students. This reduced any appearance that the state was endorsing religion in violation of the establishment clause.

Tuition grants and loans were not the only means by which South Carolina sought to aid private colleges that carried much of the higher education load of the state but which lacked the fiscal resources of their state-run counterparts. One technique used by the state to aid such institutions was the issuance of revenue bonds to assist private colleges in erecting buildings and improving their physical plants. This program was the subject of a long series of state and federal Supreme Court decisions that ultimately resulted in the program passing constitutional muster. The state supreme court was first asked to rule on the validity of the program in what we shall call *Hunt v. McNair I* in 1970.[33] The statute under attack in a taxpayer's suit in *Hunt I* designated the state Budget and Control Board as the Educational Facilities Authority. In this role the Board was authorized to issue revenue bonds on behalf of higher education institutions, whether religiously affiliated or not, to assist them in the building or repairing of physical plant or the acquisition of equipment. Proceeds derived from sale of the bonds could be devoted to the refinancing of existing projects as well as the institution of new ventures. Since the bonds technically were issued by the state, even though the proceeds normally would be turned over to a private educational institution, the interest received by bond purchasers would be tax free, and thus the bonds could be sold at a lower interest rate than otherwise. The principal on the bonds, as well as the interest, was to be paid from funds generated by the projects rather than from tax-raised funds. The full faith, credit and taxing power of the state was not pledged for repayment. Thus the bonds were revenue bonds rather than general obligation bonds. As such, they did not constitute state debt. To protect the interest of the state and the bond holders, the project premises were conveyed by the school to the state and rented back to the school at a rate sufficient to meet payments due on the bonds. Upon repayment of all principal and interest obligations the premises were reconveyed to the school. If default occurred, the bond holders had a foreclosable interest against the project property and no claim against the full faith and credit of the state. Only the bondholders, not the state, possessed this foreclosure right. To further minimize the involvement of the state, the bondholders' interest was administered in trust by a private fiduciary. The state did have the ability to require an increase in the fee charged by the school for project use if the Board concluded that existing fees were insufficient to meet principal and interest obligations on the bonds. The bond proceeds could not be used to finance a worship or religious instruction facility. The state had a right of inspection to insure that these requirements were observed. Instruments reconveying the premises back to the school after it had discharged its obligations under the bonds had to contain a covenant prohibiting use of the facility for religious purposes. This covenant was enforceable not only against the school but also against a voluntary purchaser from the school but was not enforceable against a purchaser at an involuntary foreclosure sale.[34]

The revenue bond program was subjected to a variety of state and federal constitutional challenges, but for purposes of the present work we are concerned only with the attacks based on the religious clauses. These attacks focused upon revenue bonds issued to aid the Baptist College in Charleston to complete a dining hall, purchase trailers and other equipment that would be used in the educational program, and used to refinance ongoing projects. The plaintiff argued that this violated Article XI, section 9, of the state constitution by using state funds, credit, or property for the benefit of a school controlled in whole or in part by a religious denomination. The court admitted that the college was Baptist controlled since the state Baptist Convention elected the college's twenty-five trustees. Furthermore, sixty percent of the students were affiliated with the Baptist church. However, not only did the recipient of the funds have to be religiously controlled for there to be a violation of Article XI, but also state funds, credit, or property had to be involved. This requirement was not met, since:

(1) the funds were not raised by taxation but by the sale of revenue bonds. Thus public money was not involved. (2) The principal and interest on the bonds were payable out of revenues generated by the project and the full faith, credit and taxing power of the state were not pledged toward repayment. State credit was not involved. The court concluded that the same reasoning rebutted the attack on the program made on the basis of Article I, section 4 (now 2), of the state constitution which forbids enacting laws respecting an establishment of religion. Since no state funds or credit were conveyed to a religious institution, no law respecting an establishment of religion had been promulgated. This meant that the state had not committed the folly of taking one person's tax money and conveying it to another person's religion. Under one view of federal establishment clause analysis, a violation can be found not only by financial sponsorship of religion by a government, but also by government endorsement of the ideology of religion in general, or of any particular religion. Even though the South Carolina court did not emphasize the point, it would seem that the possibilities of such ideological endorsement were greatly reduced by the requirement that the funds not be used for facilities devoted to worship or religious instruction.

The South Carolina Supreme Court decision in *Hunt I* was appealed to the United State Supreme Court which remanded the case back to the state court[35] for reconsideration in light of the high court's opinions in *Lemon v. Kurtzman*[36] and *Tilton v. Richardson.*[37] As noted earlier, *Lemon* refined federal establishment clause analysis by focusing inquiry upon whether or not the government regulation displays either (1) a purpose of advancing or inhibiting religion, or (2) a primary effect of advancing or retarding religion, or (3) excessive entanglement between government and religious power structures. The *Tilton* opinion, issued on the same day as the *Lemon* decision, applied these concepts to a federal government program which aided private schools, including many with religious affiliations, in erecting buildings used for secular instruction.

In *Lemon* the Court considered a Pennsylvania plan by which the state reimbursed parochial schools for teachers' salaries, textbooks and instructional materials. Reimbursement was made directly to the schools but only for expenses incurred with respect to secular subjects. The Court also considered a Rhode Island plan by which the state paid salary supplements to parochial school teachers who taught secular courses. These payments were made directly to the teachers and were not channeled through the schools as in the Pennsylvania program. However, the Court considered both programs repugnant to the establishment clause. It was easy enough for the programs to surmount the first two prongs of the purpose, effect, entanglement test. The purpose was the secular one of raising the general level of education in the state by aiding parochial schools that shouldered a great part of the burden of educating the states' young people. Many of these schools were having a difficult time surviving and providing quality education during a time of rapidly escalating costs.

The states insured against their programs having a primary effect of advancing religion by providing funds only for teachers, materials and books used in secular subjects such as science, mathematics and foreign languages. The textbooks provided in Pennsylvania were the same or similar to those read in public schools, and had been inspected by state officials to make sure that they could not be used for religious instruction. However, the interaction of the primary effects prong of the test with the entanglement factor caught the states in a dilemma, a web of doctrine with no exit. The very steps they took to insure that the programs produced no primary effect of advancing religion plunged them into the bog of entanglement. In addition to textbook inspection which was no more intense than that approved in *Allen, supra,* the states had to inspect school instructional records and presumably even classes to insure that state funds were not being diverted to religious instruction. The *Lemon* Court was concerned with two forms of entanglement:

(1) administrative entanglement -- this could consist of surveillance by the state of religious school instructional programs to insure that state funds were not used for worship or instruction in religion. Such surveillance has a tendency to expand and become, or seem to be, omnipresent. The religious school loses its right of privacy. It thinks less of pursuing its own religious agenda and more of avoiding the wrath of its governmental patron. The instructional program may become more bland and less offensive. Such state-fostered alterations in the behavior of religious bodies have free exercise as well as establishment clause implications.

(2) political entanglement — this feature is significant when the government action under challenge is financial aid to a religious institution. Such aid programs, depending on the circumstances, can lead to divisive political fights along religious lines as sects lobby for a greater share of government largesse. Such entreaties can take the form of an argument that one group is more deserving than another because its theology represents the true path to salvation. As society grows more diverse, such grounds grow more fractious.

The *Lemon* Court identified several features of government aid programs that were especially sensitive indicators of excessive entanglement. Chief among these were (a) the nature of the recipient institution, and (b) the nature of the aid.

Was the recipient institution so pervasively religious that its secular functions could not be separated from its religious role? If so, even aid targeted for a secular function would be invariably diverted to serve religious goals. In determining whether or not a recipient institution was pervasively religious, the Court would consider such matters as the purpose for which the institution was founded, the nature of its staff, the age and impressionability of its client-class (students) and the degree to which its functions were superintended by higher religious authority. Under these standards, the parochial schools were so pervasively religious that an intense surveillance program was essential to assure that the aid was not used to religious effect. This surveillance program had to be so continuous and detailed that it violated establishment clause standards. The Court concluded that the parochial grammar and high schools in *Lemon* were pervasively religious by looking first at the purpose for which the schools were founded. The schools, largely Catholic, were created primarily to transmit the beliefs of that faith to young children. Even though a growing number of teachers were lay men and women, many instructors still were members of religious orders subject to strict discipline requiring them to bring religion to bear upon every aspect of their lives. The students were young and impressionable. They could have concluded that state aid amounted to state endorsement of religious doctrine. This combination of religious purpose, staff, and clientele (students) created an intensely devout atmosphere in which even the most secular event could be viewed in a religious light. Aid to such a school would be sure to have a significant effect of advancing religion unless impermissible, heavy-handed surveillance were conducted to avoid that result. In addition, political entanglement was likely as parochial schools of various denominations competed for larger and larger shares of the public fisc with equally hungry public schools. Tempers run hot when parents seek to provide their children with high quality education. They run hotter still when religious divisions enter the scene.

Not only did the nature of the recipient institutions increase the need for surveillance to avoid a primary effect of advancing religion, but so did the nature of the aid. A textbook loan program such as that approved in *Allen* involves a one-shot inspection of the books' contents. Aid to teachers is different. Since a teacher may at anytime divert his instruction in a religious direction, repeated inspections would be necessary. Religion should not be subjected to such a steady stare by the baleful eye of a government cyclops.

Even though the aid to public grammar and high schools was struck down in *Lemon* as involving excessive entanglement between church and state, a different form of federal aid (building construction) to a different level of institution (colleges) was approved in *Tilton* but with the Court insisting on additional controls to avoid a primary effect of advancing religion. The federal program in *Tilton* involved grants to higher education institutions, many of which were religiously affiliated, for the construction of facilities that would be used entirely for secular education. The buildings constructed under the grants challenged in *Tilton* included a library, language laboratory, a science building and an art, music and drama facility. The schools that received grants to build libraries placed no religious restrictions on the contents of the books housed in the facilities and the colleges constructing laboratory and classroom buildings did not use them for worship or religious instruction. Federal grant restrictions forbade use of the facilities for religious purposes for twenty years and inspections were made by government officials to insure that the requirements were met.

As in the *Lemon* case, the grant program soared easily over the hurdle requiring that there not be a purpose of advancing religion. The secular purpose underlying the program was to improve the security and welfare of the country by increasing the educational opportunities of the growing number of youths who were seeking a college education.

The program sailed smoothly over the usually jagged rocks of the entanglement doctrine but temporarily ran aground on the primary effects prong of the *Lemon* test. The nature of the recipient institutions and the nature of the aid were such that some surveillance was required to avoid a primary effect of advancing religion but it did not need to be as intense as that found excessive in *Lemon.* The problem was that the grant contracts placed no restrictions on the uses to which the buildings could be put after twenty years and surveillance would cease after that time. There was thus nothing to stop use of a facility paid for by federal funds for worship or religious instruction after expiration of the twenty-year period. Apparently the Court felt that the ban on religious use of government-financed facilities, and the inspection program should extend throughout the life of the building. It was ironic for the Court to be requiring a longer period of entanglement through government surveillance of government-financed church-college buildings on the same day it was complaining about excessive state surveillance of parochial grammar and high schools in *Lemon.* The only reconciliation of the-two cases is that even though the Court insisted upon lengthy (twenty-plus years) surveillance in *Tilton* to avoid religious use of the buildings, the nature of the recipient institutions and the character of the aid was such that there did not need to be as much intrusion on school privacy as in *Lemon.*

The recipient institutions in *Tilton* were church-affiliated colleges. Even though the founding denominations undoubtedly wanted to extend the influences of their beliefs through college instruction, they also had a strong desire to further education in secular subjects. The students were older and more skeptical. They were less likely to consider government aid to be endorsement of the beliefs of the churches sponsoring the college. The instructional staff members were less likely to be priests, nuns or ministers than would be the case in a parochial grammar or high school. The curriculum would be as much influenced by secular accrediting agencies as by the religious hierarchy. Thus the recipient schools were not so pervasively religious that it was impossible to separate the secular from the religious functions of the school. Aid designed for secular instruction would not be swept into a religious vortex.

The nature of the aid was also different from that in *Lemon* and was less susceptible to being diverted from its intended secular purpose toward religious ends. The buildings constructed under the federal program in *Tilton* would play roles predestined by their architecture, configuration and furnishings. A library, scientific laboratory, and a modern language center, expensively equipped for those purposes, could not be changed overnight into a chapel. Since any building has some flexibility permitting changes to other uses, some surveillance would be necessary throughout the life of the building to make sure that it was not altered for religious use. However, since buildings usually can not undergo the quick, chameleon-like changes that teachers receiving salary supplements in *Lemon* could achieve in altering the content of their classes, the surveillance need not be so frequent. The combination of aid recipients who were not pervasively religious and a form of aid that was more difficult to manipulate in a religious direction greatly reduced the level of surveillance needed to avoid having government funds diverted towards religious ends. The entanglement between church and state administrative structures was kept well within permissible limits.

Political entanglement was also less bothersome than in the *Lemon* case parochial school teachers' salary supplements. The building construction aid in *Tilton* came from the federal government. Federal election contests involve such a variety of foreign policy, national security and domestic issues that it is unlikely that rancorous denominational feuds over who is entitled to the largest share of construction funds will dominate the elections. The political impact of such grants is also reduced by the fact that many colleges draw their students from wider geographical areas than do grammar and high schools. Thus any dissatisfaction arising from inadequate grants or losing a grant to a school of another denomination, is likely to be dispersed over several political boundary lines and not dominate any election. The lessened threat of political as well as administrative entanglement meant that the college construction grant program in *Tilton* survived constitutional challenge except for the need to extend the prohibition against religious use throughout the life of the buildings.

In *Hunt II,* upon remand by the United States Supreme Court for reconsideration in light of *Lemon* and *Tilton,* the South Carolina high court reaffirmed its earlier view that the revenue bond program for constructing and repairing college buildings was valid.[38] Many of the features in the federal construction grant program in *Tilton* that made it constitutionally innocuous were also present in the South Carolina revenue bond scheme. In addition, other features of the South Carolina program further reduced the risks of constitutional violation under the entanglement doctrine. Before reaching the question of excessive entanglement, the court quickly disposed of the issues of whether or not the revenue bond act had an invalid purpose or primary effect of advancing religion. The answers echoed the court's opinion in *Hunt I.* The purposes were the valid secular goals of increasing the vigor of the state's economy and the health and welfare of its citizens by encouraging higher education in a variety of institutions. A primary effect of advancing religion was avoided by forbidding the use of college facilities financed by revenue bonds for worship or religious instruction and by giving state officials a right to inspect the premises to insure that they were not being diverted to religious use. The bulk of the discussion focused on whether or not the state Budget and Control Board, acting as the Educational Facilities Authority, had improperly entangled itself with church school operations not only by conducting surveillance to guard against religious use of the facilities, but also by the lease-back arrangement under which the school conveyed project premises to the state which leased the property back to the school until it regained full ownership upon satisfaction of all of its bond obligations, and by retention by the Authority of power to see that the fees set by the college for use of the facilities were sufficient to pay principal and interest on the revenue bonds. The institutions that received the aid in *Hunt*, though religiously affiliated in some cases, were no more pervasively religious than the colleges in *Tilton*.

Like the grants in *Tilton*, the nature of the aid in *Hunt* was the provision of construction funds for college buildings as well as money for repairs and equipment. Such aid does not require the constant monitoring to guard against use for religious purposes as was required for the parochial school-teacher salary supplements in *Lemon*. The South Carolina court, however, did not focus on these similarities of the state scheme to the plan approved in *Tilton* so much as it did other features of the revenue bond plan that greatly reduced state interference with private school decision-making.

The state's role was largely the passive one of conduit for the funds from the bond purchaser to the college. This state sponsorship enabled the bond interest to be tax free, thus making it feasible for the bonds to be sold at a lower interest rate. After issuing the bonds and taking title to the project premises as security for repayment, the Authority stepped out of the picture. A mortgage interest was transferred to a private bank as trustee for the bondholders. The bank would disperse the funds to the recipient institution and collect project revenues from the institution for repayment of principal and interest. At that point the transaction was largely one of a private bank trustee dealing with a private college on behalf of private bondholders. True the state retained certain fee-setting and inspection rights to insure adequate revenues for repayment and to guard against religious use of the premises, but given the fact that the institutions were not pervasively religious, intrusive surveillance was not likely. In addition, the pressure for officious meddling by the state in private school affairs was further reduced by the fact that no tax funds were involved, and the state's credit did not guarantee the bonds which were to be repaid only from funds generated by the project premises. Thus the state did not violate the establishment clause either by spending state funds to finance a religious project or by exercising state power over the decision-making process of religious institutions.[39]

The state court noted that the South Carolina program did not even have the minor blemish that required correction in the federal program in *Tilton*. The ban against religious use of buildings financed by the revenue bonds was not limited to twenty years but applied throughout the life of the building. Only a purchaser at an involuntary foreclosure sale could take free of the prohibition against religious use. The chances of this actually occurring were too remote for the act to have a primary effect of advancing religion.[40]

After the case had been thoroughly dissected by the state court under the *Lemon* and *Tilton* principles, it returned to the United States Supreme Court which affirmed the South Carolina court's decision in favor of the constitutionality of the revenue bond program.[41] Again, the program easily surmounted the requirement that the state action not have a purpose of advancing or inhibiting religion. The Supreme Court accepted the state court's conclusion that the act's purposes were the secular ones of improving the economy, general welfare and health of the state by improving educational opportunities through a system of strong private as well as public colleges. The court emphasized that all institutions of higher education in the state, not just those with a sectarian orientation, could take advantage of the revenue bond program.[42]

In concluding that the program did not have a primary effect of advancing religion, the Court observed that the establishment clause did not forbid every program ". . . which in some manner aids an institution with a religious affiliation. . . ."[43] A financial aid program violates the establishment clause only if it (a) goes to a distinctly religious function performed in a largely secular institution, or (b) is a contribution to a pervasively religious school in which religion so dominates every facet of the school's operation that it is impossible to isolate the aid and use it only for secular purposes. The Court noted that if a recipient is not pervasively religious and the aid is directed toward a secular part of its operations that the court would not find an establishment clause violation simply because the state contribution to the secular functions might free the recipient to devote more of its own funds to religious purposes.[44] The Supreme Court did not consider the Baptist College to be a pervasively religious institution. The South Carolina Baptist convention elected the college trustees and retained power to approve several key financial transactions. Sixty percent of the students were Baptist. However, this did not produce a cloistered island of the Baptist faith. The percentage of students who were Baptist was no greater than the proportion of Baptists in the general population of the area. No religious qualifications were exacted for admission as a student or employment as a faculty member. The educational program was predominantly secular.[45]

Since the institution was not pervasively religious, aid targeted toward secular functions of the school would not inevitably advance a sectarian program. The revenue bond proceeds accruing to the Baptist College would be used for such distinctly secular projects as completing a dining hall. The combination of an institution that was not pervasively religious and aid that was channeled toward the standard needs of an academic institution meant that the program did not produce a primary effect of advancing religion. The form of the aid itself helped reduce chances of there being a primary effect of advancing religion. The use of revenue bonds, payable out of funds produced by school use of the project property, rather than the appropriation of tax funds to religious institutions reduced the appearance of state endorsement of religion.[46] Like the South Carolina court, the United States Supreme Court was unimpressed with arguments that the program endorsed religion since the ban on religious use of premises financed by the revenue bonds did not apply to a purchaser at an involuntary foreclosure sale. The chances of this happening were too remote and speculative.[47]

The Supreme Court then plunged into the thicket of the entanglement doctrine. The Court's disposition of these issues reflected the approach it had taken in *Tilton, supra,* that church-sponsored colleges were generally less distinctly religious than their elementary and high school counterparts. Their curriculum more closely tracked that of colleges in general than a rigid religious regime. The faculty and students were less likely to be preoccupied with religion. Since the recipient was not pervasively religious, the level of surveillance necessary to insure that state aid would not be used for religious purposes would not be excessive. Most of the Court's entanglement doctrine analysis focused on two powers by which the state authority could influence school decision-making. These were: (1) the ability to intervene and adjust rates that the school charged for use of the project premises if the state concluded that the institution was not charging enough to meet its obligations to repay principal and interest on the revenue bonds, and (2) the ability to inspect the use of the premises to insure that the buildings were not being used for religious purposes. The Court concluded that these powers did not violate the establishment clause. Since the institution was not pervasively religious, the inspections did not have to be frequent. The fee-adjusting authority, if actively and frequently exercised, could cause serious establishment clause problems by involving the state deeply in the decision-making process of religious institutions. However, the state's power was largely latent. It was contingent power that could be exercised only if the institution failed to set fees adequate to repay the bonds. Such slumbering entanglement was virtually no entanglement. The program did not result in an impermissible intermixture of government and religious authority.[48]

Justice Brennan in a dissent joined by Justices Douglas and Marshall viewed the revenue bond program in a more sinister light.[49] The program did more than permit the state to cast an occasional benign, avuncular eye on the grant recipients' operations to insure that repayment of the bonds is not being jeopardized and that religious exercises are not being conducted in project buildings. It laid the groundwork for a virtual takeover of the fiscal affairs of a grant recipient by the state. To assume that these powers will always remain latent and never be abused is unjustified. The revenue bond scheme gave the government power to do more than adjust building fees and conduct inspections to prevent religious use of project-financed buildings. The state could determine the nature of the project and its location and, in adjusting fees charged for building use, the state could decisively influence such basic matters of school policy as the amount of tuition charged. Exercised in its fullest scope, the power to conduct surveillance to guard against religious instruction in project buildings could result in a school's ceding control over curriculum planning to the state.[50] Latent power, lying coiled and ready to strike when provoked, is bound to affect the behavior of the recipients in ways that intrude on the freedom of the schools to act in the manner they think best serves the interest of its founding church. In addition, one must never assume that potential power will never become actual power. Once exercised, the use of such power may become customary, even demanded.

The South Carolina revenue bond program certainly avoided many of the problems associated with government financial sponsorship of religious institutions. The fact that government tax funds were not involved and the full faith and credit of the state were not pledged for repayment of the principal and interest of the bonds meant that citizens would not be forced to contribute to religion through the state treasury. It meant that religions were less likely to become slothful and overly dependent on government funding. After all, the ultimate responsibility for repayment rested with the church-sponsored schools themselves. This lower risk of fiscal dependency of the church schools on the state reduced the likelihood that they would abandon their own religious goals to pander to the state.[51] However, real dangers remain. Even if latent state power is never used to force change in the behavior of church-related institutions, it still may subtly alter the policy of such institutions who do not want to offend those who guard the gateway to the ability to issue bonds with tax-free interest. In *Larkin v. Grendel's Den, Inc.*,[52] the Court was troubled by the grant of power to churches to veto the issuance of liquor licenses to bars or restaurants within 500 feet of church premises. If the wielding, or latent possession, of secular power by religious organizations is offensive, then the possession of power by the state to influence the policy of sectarian institutions could be equally troubling.

As troubling as these dimensions of the revenue bond program may be to the constitutional purist, they do not even remotely approach the historical high-water marks of established religion in South Carolina. It does not use tax funds to pay ministers, build churches, and support social welfare programs of a church that was endorsed by the state as was the Church of England prior to the replacement of the system in Article 38 of the Constitution of 1778 by a general establishment of the Protestant Christian religion. The 1778 establishment was more psychological than fiscal and broadly embraced all Protestant faiths meeting certain basic belief standards. However, Article 38 of the Constitution of 1778 did impose an ideological litmus test that had to be met by an organization in order to be recognized as an established church. The revenue bond program, enacted within the circumference of the federal and state constitutional provisions prohibiting government establishment of religion, did not demand fealty to any ideology. Nor did it involve state endorsement of the beliefs taught in the schools wishing to take advantage of the revenue bond program. The state was the fiscal sponsor of the institution, not its ideological patron. Any ideological endorsement would wither under the cold gimlet eye of the bond market. The program is part of a wider scheme to raise the quality of education whether it be public, private, secular or sectarian. Indeed, like its first cousin, the industrial revenue bond, it seeks the economic betterment of the state rather than advancement of an ideological agenda. Still, the potential for intrusion of state power into the decision-making process of religious institutions was there. Such programs should be approached warily with the understanding that human nature and good intentions are no guarantee that latent power will never be exercised.

Government tax relief for religious organizations sometimes takes a less acceptable form than the revenue bond approach. In *Thayer v. C&R Marketing* (Slip Op. No. 23553, Jan. 13, 1992), the state Supreme Court struck down a use tax exemption that helped only religious publications. This exemption violated the establishment clause because it betrayed a purpose of favoring religious publications over most others, and it had a primary effect of advancing religious proselytization by not only granting a financial benefit but also by bestowing the state's imprimatur on sectarian literature. To be valid, exemptions should benefit a broad class of nonsectarian as well as religious organizations. *Jimmy Swaggart Ministries v. Bd. of Equalization* (493 U.S. 378 (1990)) said that the free exercise and establishment clauses do not require that religious organizations be granted exemption from general sales or use taxes if the assessments: (1) do not single them out for unfavorable treatment, (2) payment is not a precondition to religious activity, (3) the tax is not an unduly burdensome flat fee, and (4) administration of the tax does not require excessive government entanglement with religious affairs such as continuous inspections that involve inquiry into the religious content of a message.

NOTES

1. In adopting this provision the 1895 convention may have been influenced by the lobbying efforts of The National League for the Protection of American Institutions which contacted state conventions and legislatures throughout the country in an effort to enlist support for insertion in the federal and state constitutions of an amendment forbidding the use of federal or state funds to support organizations, especially schools, controlled wholly or in part by religious denominations. Apparently one purpose of this lobbying effort was to protect appropriations for public schools from being undermined by diversion of government funds to sectarian schools. *See* The State, September 22, 1895 p. 1, col. 1 and p. 2, col. 1.

State constitutions can make a difference. *See* Witters v. Washington Dept. of Services for the Blind, 474 U.S. 481 (1986) (neutral tuition aid program for visually impaired valid under U.S. Constitution even if used by ministerial student but invalid under state constitution prohibiting state grants for religious instruction. 771 P.2d 1119 (Wash. 1989).

2. Forrest v. City Council of Charleston, 65 S.C. 500, 43 S.E. 952 (1903).

3. Parker v. Bates, 216 S.C. 52, 56 S.E.2d 723 (1949).

4. 216 S.C. at 62-63, 56 S.E.2d at 727.

5. Kentucky Bldg. Comm'n v. Effron, 310 Ky. 355, 220 S.W.2d 836 (1949).

6. *Parker*, 216 S.C. at 63, 56 S.E.2d at 727-28.

7. KY. CONST. § 5.

8. *Effron*, 310 Ky. at 359, 220 S.W.2d at 838.

9. Bradfield v. Roberts, 175 U.S. 291, 20 S. Ct. 121, 44 L. Ed. 168 (1899).

10. For a discussion of the constitutional restraints upon using public funds to aid private organizations, *see* J. UNDERWOOD, THE CONSTITUTION OF SOUTH CAROLINA, VOLUME II: THE JOURNEY TOWARD LOCAL SELF-GOVERNMENT 55-61, 75-83, 139-51, 215-38 (1989).

11. S.C. Baptist Convention Const. Art. 8, § 2.

12. *See* Statement of the South Carolina Baptist Convention on Religious Liberty, Minutes of the Committee to Make a Study of the South Carolina Constitution of 1895 13-14 (Mar. 4, 1969) (statement of Mr. G.E. Hinson) [hereinafter cited as WEST COMMITTEE MINUTES].

13. *See* Statement of the South Carolina Association of Independent Colleges, WEST COMMITTEE MINUTES, 14-17 (Mar. 4, 1969) (statement of Dr. Paul Hardin, III).

14. Final Report of the Committee To Make A Study of the South Carolina Constitution of 1895 99-101 (1969) [hereinafter cited as WEST COMMITTEE FINAL REPORT].

15. WEST COMMITTEE FINAL REPORT 78-79, 98-101.

16. *See* 1973 S.C. ACTS AND JOINT RESOLUTIONS 44-45.

17. *See* 1970 Opinions of the Attorney General of South Carolina, No. 2906, May 26, 1970 at 152-53.

18. Everson v. Bd. of Educ. of Township of Ewing, 330 U.S. 1, 67 S. Ct. 504, 91 L. Ed. 711 (1947).

CHAPTER SEVEN—NOTES

19. Committee for Pub. Educ. & Religious Liberty v. Nyquist, 413 U.S. 756, 93 S. Ct. 2955, 37 L. Ed. 2d 948 (1973).

20. *See* WEST COMMITTEE MINUTES, 15-17 (statement of Dr. Paul Hardin, III).

21. Hartness v. Patterson, 255 S.C. 503, 179 S.E.2d 907 (1971).

22. 255 S.C. at 506-08, 179 S.E.2d at 908-09.

23. Larkin v. Grendel's Den, Inc., 459 U.S. 116, 103 S. Ct. 505, 74 L. Ed. 2d 297 (1982).

24. Durham v. McLeod, 259 S.C. 409, 192 S.E.2d 202 (1972) *appeal dismissed,* 413 U.S. 902, 93 S. Ct. 3060, 37 L. Ed. 2d 1020 (1973).

25. 259 S.C. at 413, 192 S.E.2d at 203-204.

26. 259 S.C. at 413, 192 S.E.2d at 204.

27. Sherbert v. Verner, 374 U.S. 398, 83 S. Ct. 1790, 10 L. Ed. 2d 965 (1963).

28. Lemon v. Kurtzman, 403 U.S. 602, 91 S. Ct. 2105, 29 L. Ed. 2d 745 (1971).

29. Mueller v. Allen, 463 U.S. 388, 103 S. Ct. 3062, 77 L. Ed. 2d 721 (1983).

30. S.C. CONST. Art XI, § 9 (Original Const. of 1895).

31. Board of Educ. of Cent. School Dist. No. 1 v. Allen, 392 U.S. 236, 88 S. Ct. 1923, 20 L. Ed. 2d 1060 (1968).

32. *Nyquist,* 413 U.S. 756, 93 S. Ct. 2955, 37 L. Ed. 2d 948 (1973).

33. Hunt v. McNair, 255 S.C. 71, 177 S.E.2d 362 (1970). The following description of the state's program for issuing revenue bonds to assist institutions of higher education to build, repair, or refinance work on educational institutions is based in part on later installments of the *Hunt* case found in 258 S.C. 97, 187 S.E.2d 645 (1972), *aff'd,* 413 U.S. 734, 93 S. Ct. 2868, 37 L. Ed. 2d 923 (1973).

34. This description of the program is based in part on information assembled by the author for an earlier work. *See* J. Underwood, *Permissible Entanglement Under the Establishment Clause,* 25 EMORY L.J. 17 (1976).

35. Hunt v. McNair, 403 U.S. 945, 91 S. Ct. 2276, 29 L. Ed. 2d 854 (1971).

36. Lemon v. Kurtzman, 403 U.S. 602 (1971).

37. Tilton v. Richardson, 403 U.S. 672, 91 S. Ct. 2091, 29 L. Ed. 2d 790 (1971).

38. Hunt v. McNair, 258 S.C. 97, 187 S.E.2d 645 (1972).

39. It is notable that the South Carolina court considered the state constitution's establishment clause, Art. 1, § 4 (now § 2) and the counterpart clause in the First Amendment of the U.S. Constitution to have the same meaning and be subject to the same analytical process. 258 S.C. at 103, 187 S.E.2d at 648.

40. 258 S.C. at 109-110, 187 S.E.2d at 652.

41. Hunt v. McNair, 413 U.S. 734, 93 S. Ct. 2868, 37 L. Ed. 2d 923 (1973).

42. 413 U.S. at 741.

43. 413 U.S. at 742-43, citing Bradfield v. Roberts, 175 U.S. 291, 20 S. Ct. 121, 44 L. Ed. 168 (1899).

44. 413 U.S. at 743.

45. 413 U.S. at 743-44. *But see* Comment, *Beyond the Establishment Clause: Enforcing Separation of Church and State Through State Constitutional Provisions*, 71 VA. L. REV. 625, 632-33 (1985) (which asserts that Art. XI, § 4 of the South Carolina constitution forbids any financial aid to religious schools, not just aid to religious functions).

46. 413 U.S. at 745 n. 7.

47. 413 U.S. at 743-44.

48. 413 U.S. at 745-49.

49. 413 U.S. at 749-55 (Brennan, J., dissenting).

50. 413 U.S. at 752-53 (Brennan, J., dissenting).

51. *See* J. Underwood, *Permissible Entanglement Under the Establishment Clause*, 25 EMORY L.J. 17, 59-60 (1976).

52. Larkin v. Grendel's Den, Inc., 459 U.S. 116, 103 S. Ct. 505, 74 L. Ed. 2d 297 (1982).

CHAPTER EIGHT

FREEDOM OF THE UNORTHODOX WORSHIPPER

The centuries-old struggle over the validity and meaning of the Sunday closing laws, first justified as essential to encourage religion, then as a means to preserve health by a universal day of rest, was in part a struggle between the mainstream religions that used Sunday as their primary day of worship and less orthodox groups that preferred a different time and mode of worship. Disputes over government financial support of religion often pitted safely entrenched orthodox religions, which received support because of their respectability, against "upstart" groups with rites and practices that struck traditionalists as strange. Tensions between dominant religions and their more "off-beat" rivals took many other forms and gave rise to a number of legal issues. These include: (1) to what extent does the state properly recognize an affirmative duty to protect the less orthodox worshippers against those who find their religion offensive and would disrupt it; and (2) when can worship or evangelizing activities be curbed as disturbing the public peace, invading the rights of others, or creating a physical danger for the worshipper, his family or the casual onlooker.

A. GUARANTEEING THE RIGHT TO HOLD UNPOPULAR BELIEFS

An 1818 case, *Bell v. Graham*,[1] explored the degree to which the state was obligated to affirmatively protect worship services of an unorthodox group from those who disagreed with its form of devotion or the composition of its membership. The *Bell* case involved a Methodist congregation of blacks and whites, slaves and freemen. Even though such a mixed congregation was not necessarily provocative in and of itself, it became controversial when the assembly was suspected of harboring slaves who were present without proper passes or when the assembly was suspected of harboring abolitionist tendencies. This created a situation that was fertile ground for officials, or those who thrust themselves forward in a quasi-official status, to break up church services, containing black and white members, under the guise of protecting the slave system.

In the *Bell* case a group of men purporting to be the slave patrol broke up a Methodist meeting at Shady Grove near Fairfield. It was never clear whether the group was indeed the official slave patrol or only a group of bullyboys, a gang out for a strange form of sport, or a citizens' vigilante group. After the "patrol" dispersed the meeting, the head of the congregation went before a magistrate and applied for a warrant against members of the patrol for illegally disturbing a worship service. The magistrate found probable cause that a violation had occurred and issued the warrant. The chief agent of the "patrol" was arrested but refused to post bail. Prosecutors requested an indictment from the grand jury. The grand jury refused to issue the indictment and the "patrol" agent sued the head of the congregation for malicious prosecution. Despite the trial judge's direction of a verdict in behalf of the defendant, the jury found against the head of the congregation and directed him to pay damages to the "patrol" agent. The defendant's motion for a new trial was granted by Judge Johnson, whose opinion accompanying his order provides us with our sole source of reliable information about the case. He began by noting that freedom of worship was a right enjoyed by all men regardless of their status in society. He traced the right to conduct peaceful worship services free from those who would disrupt it back to English common law. He stated:

> To worship *God,* after the dictates of our consciences, is a privilege that all men claim as a birth right from heaven. Millions have shed their blood in defence of it; and a conviction of its justness has sustained the martyr at the stake. But feeble indeed, would be the protection of our inestimable constitution, which professes to secure to us this privilege, if a petty patrol officer was permitted to mar and disturb our devotions at his pleasure, and with impunity. The English Common Law held this privilege so sacred, that it would not justify one in striking, even in his own defence, during worship; and it is a principle so clear that those who unlawfully disturb the devotion of a religious assembly, by any indecency or violence, may be punished by indictment, that authorities are unnecessary to support it.[2]

The judge was no maverick dissenting from the firmly entrenched system of slavery and the prevailing view that a patrol system was necessary to guard against incipient revolt and to capture escapees. In his view, however, the need for a patrol did not justify disturbing a peaceful worship service displaying no characteristics of rebellion or disorder, just because the congregation was a mixed black and white, slave and free group. The judge appeared to believe that the patrol agent was so intoxicated by his real or supposed power that he was infringing the right of worship on a personal whim. In his view there was a sufficient basis for the head of the congregation to apply for, and the magistrate to issue, a warrant. The element of malice necessary for a successful suit against the head of the congregation for seeking the warrant was absent.

It would be nice to believe that the *Bell* case constituted a ringing affirmation of the slaves' right to worship, even in a mixed black-white congregational setting. At best the case represents a standoff. The failure of the grand jury to indict, even though the judge thought such an indictment was clearly justified, may indicate more community adherence to the slave system than to the principle of freedom of worship when practiced in a setting suspected of posing a threat to that system. The principle against disturbing a peaceful worship service was enshrined early in South Carolina constitutional law as was the right of slaves to worship as long as their worship did not weaken the control of their masters over them. These principles are found in the July 21, 1669 version of the Fundamental Constitutions.[3] No liberty can exist in isolated splendor. Freedom of worship cannot come to full flower in a garden of sandy soil devoid of the freedoms of movement, speech, and the rights to vote and receive an education. Without such freedoms undergirding the freedom of religion, the worshipper can fall prey to just the sort of bullyboy tactics displayed by the "patrol" agent in *Bell v. Graham.*[4]

The most notorious exponent of unorthodox religious views in early nineteenth-century South Carolina was Dr. Thomas Cooper, medical doctor, lawyer, compiler of South Carolina laws and President of South Carolina College. In his book *The Public Life of Thomas Cooper*, Dumas Malone describes Cooper as a broad-ranging intellect whose life was a nearly never-ending tissue of controversy with those espousing traditional religious views.[5] For our purposes we are concerned with the charges brought against him in 1830 during his tenure as president of the college, his subsequent trial and acquittal by the trustees, his constitutional defense against the charges and his eventual resignation and loss of influence after the acquittal.[6] Cooper provoked powerful religious figures in several ways. In 1829 he railed against proposed federal legislation that would stop Sunday mail service. He described the Sabbath as the contrivance of ministers who wished to prevent anyone else from making a profit on that day.[7] He accused the professional clergy, particularly the Presbyterians, of trying to gain political power.[8] He attacked the employment of chaplains at public expense to offer prayers in Congress.[9] Popular opinion in South Carolina was that he did not believe in the immortality of the soul and trusted only in concepts capable of physical or economic proof.[10] He was controversial politically as well as religiously. He was outspoken in behalf of the nullification party that believed that a state could interpose itself between an invalid federal law and the state's citizens, thus nullifying the law's effectiveness within its borders. The laws the nullifiers wished to render ineffective were tariff rules injurious to the state's economy. Thus, he earned the ire not only of those with more orthodox religious views but also of the unionists' party which believed in greater ascendency of federal power.[11] Pursuant to a request from the legislature, the college trustees conducted a hearing of charges against Cooper. Among the charges against him were accusations that he had attacked the Mosaic version of creation in classes and in addresses to the college community, and that he had maligned the Presbyterian clergy for accepting pay for their work. He was accused of using his position to impose his views on the students in contravention to the wishes of their parents.[12] Many of these charges were disputed factually at the hearings. For our purposes, Cooper's defense based on the constitutional principles of freedom of religion and speech and press are more important. The heart of his constitutional defense is found in a pamphlet he circulated in December of 1831 before the hearings which occurred in December 1832.[13] The pamphlet is entitled *The Case of Thomas Cooper MD, President of South Carolina College Submitted to the Legislature and the People of South Carolina December 1831.*[14] His defense was based on both the federal Constitution and the South Carolina Constitution of 1790. On the flyleaf of the pamphlet he quotes Article VI, section 3, of the United States Constitution which states in part that ". . . no religious test shall ever be required as a qualification to any office or public trust under the United States." Despite the phrase ". . . under the United States," apparently he considered the provision applicable to state offices as well as federal. He charged that not only were members of the clergy who were covetous of political power trying to impose a religious test for the presidency of the college but also that they were seeking to force members of the legislature to run for election on the basis of their religious beliefs.[15]

Cooper argued that neither the legislature nor the trustees of the college had a right to even inquire as to what the beliefs of the president of the college were, much less to censure him for expressing certain views or to require him to express others.[16] Article VIII, section 1, of the South Carolina Constitution of 1790[17] guaranteed "to all mankind" free exercise of religions ". . . without discrimination or preference . . ." so long as religious acts are not licentious or ". . . inconsistent with the peace or safety of this State." Article IX, section 6, stated that ". . . the liberty of the press shall be forever inviolably preserved." Dr. Cooper noted that his clerical enemies, while admitting that the general run of citizen possessed these rights, argued that when he assumed the college presidency he forfeited his rights to speak freely on matters of religion and politics.[18] He charged that such a view, narrowing the scope of freedom of religion and the press, amounted to an amendment of the constitution and that such a change could not be accomplished except by the procedure specified in Article XI which required approval by two-thirds of both branches of the legislature, publication three months prior to the next election, and approval again by two-thirds of the members of both branches of the new legislature.

Cooper viewed freedom of religion as being so broad that the legislature could not pass any law that even touched upon the subject because such a statute invariably would discriminate or express a preference for certain views in violation of Article VIII, section 1.[19] Presumably he would extend this prohibition of any legislative action touching upon the subject of religion to any religiously motivated action by the legislature's agents (the trustees) including dismissal of the president for his religious or political views.

On December 18, 1832, the trustees adopted a resolution saying that the charges against Dr. Cooper had not been substantiated and his removal from the presidency was not justified.[20] It would be nice to attribute Dr. Cooper's vindication to a strong commitment by the state to the principles of freedom of religion and the press. Cooper's effective marshaling of constitutional arguments in his defense and the broad scope of the language protecting freedom of religion and the press in Articles VIII and IX of the South Carolina Constitution of 1790 probably contributed to the trustees' refusal to dismiss him from the college presidency. However, Malone attributes the favorable outcome to the political influence of Cooper's allies in the nullification party.[21] After all, some of the animus against him grew out of his views on political economy, and those who shared his views could not afford to see him sacrificed on a unionist altar. In addition, the trustees' vote cannot be viewed as a complete victory for Cooper and freedom of religion and speech. As a result of the controversy, college enrollment dropped, and in November 1833 Cooper resigned the presidency.[22] The old curmudgeon had shouted into the whirlwind once too often.

The 1790 Constitution greatly expanded the scope of religious liberty and abolished establishment of Protestant-Christianity, but it was a post-Civil War constitution that sought to give government an aggressive role in insuring freedom.

The Constitution of 1868, passed during the Radical Reconstruction era, had woven throughout it a theme that participation in government and the guarantees of liberty should be widely available to all segments of society. In addition, that constitution viewed it as the obligation of government to not only refrain from harming the citizens but to pursue a positive course of improving the lot of the people, including the manner in which they were treated by other individuals as well as the government. Thus, the language guaranteeing freedom of religion and prohibiting the establishment of religion seemed to invite government intervention to insure that one individual did not trample on the religious freedom of another. It also could be interpreted as barring the government from aiding and abetting one individual in injuring the freedom of another. In civil rights as well as in economics, and education and social services, the 1868 Constitution called for a positive, active state government. Thus Article I, section 9, stated that:

> No person shall be deprived of the right to worship God according to the dictates of his own conscience: *Provided*, That the liberty of conscience hereby declared shall not justify practices inconsistent with the peace and moral safety of society.

This free exercise of religion provision was augmented by an explicit provision prohibiting the establishment of religion. The 1790 Constitution had omitted the establishment of the Protestant Christian religion that was contained in Article 38 of the Constitution of 1778, but it did not contain a concrete, general prohibition of laws respecting an establishment of religion. The first post-Civil War constitution, that of 1865, also failed to contain an explicit antiestablishment provision. The 1868 Constitution did contain such a provision but coupled it with a requirement that government be active in insuring free worship for all religions. Article I, section 10 stated that:

> No form of religion shall be established by law; but it shall be the duty of the General Assembly to pass suitable laws to protect every religious denomination in the peaceable enjoyment of its own mode of worship.

The last clause seemed to direct the government to not only avoid oppressing minority religions itself, but also to buttress such religions, and all others, against interference with their worship by private individuals. These remarkable provisions received interpretation in *Magee v. O'Neill.*[23] That case showed the court demonstrating considerable solicitude for the Catholic religion. In the late twentieth century, the Catholic religion would be regarded as a large, respected, mainstream denomination. However, the reader will recall from the earlier discussion in this volume that until the enactment of the broad religious freedom provisions in

Article VIII of the Constitution of 1790, Catholic churches could not incorporate, and they were by definition precluded from the Protestant establishment prevalent under Article 38 of the Constitution of 1778. By contrast, the court in *Magee* took seriously its responsibility under Article I, section 10, to protect ". . . every religious denomination. . . ." Oddly enough, however, the case also revealed that under some circumstances, the government's obligation under section 9 to insure that no one was ". . . deprived of the right to worship God according to the dictates of his own conscience . . ." could conflict with its duty to insure that every denomination shall be able to enjoy its own mode of worship so long as it is peaceful. Surprisingly, these dilemmas in *Magee* arose not out of an overt interference with a worship service but from a contest over conditions placed on a devise contained in a will. The testator had left a sum of money in trust for the education and maintenance of his granddaughter on condition that she be reared in the Catholic faith and educated in a school operated by that religion. When she reached adulthood, the granddaughter brought suit to have the condition declared invalid and the trust funds paid over to her. The trial court ruled that the condition was invalid and the granddaughter, Elizabeth Magee, could receive the devise even if she had not been reared in the Catholic faith. The judge concluded that the Catholic upbringing requirement in the will violated the freedom of conscience of both the granddaughter and her mother. Part of the free exercise of religion guaranteed by Article 1, section 9, was the right of parents to determine the religious education, if any, which their child would be given. Upon reaching an appropriate age, the child's own freedom of conscience became effective and she could choose her own mode of worship. If a civil court enforced such a condition in a will, then the state would become an instrument of religious oppression. If the government could no longer interfere with religious freedom then neither could an individual, especially one who sought the aid of the state laws in effectuating the coercion.[24]

The state supreme court reversed, holding the Catholic upbringing requirement to be an enforceable condition of the devise. It gave little weight to the contentions that court recognition of the validity of the provision mandating a Catholic upbringing would invade the freedom of conscience of the granddaughter and her mother. Instead, the court gave ascendency to the Article I, section 10, obligation of the state ". . . to protect every religious denomination in the peaceable enjoyment of its own mode of worship." The court noted that every testator had a right to choose how he would dispose of his property by will. It noted that "[t]his right is secured alike to every citizen, whatever is his religious faith, be he Jew or Gentile, Protestant or Catholic."[25] The court had no difficulty in reconciling the government's obligation to make no law establishing a religion and its duty to insure freedom of worship to every denomination. To insure freedom to all denominations did not require the establishment of any of them. The establishment clause did not require indifference to religion. The state could take cognizance of religious beliefs to the extent necessary to discharge its obligation to insure the freedom of worship of each denomination.[26] The court summed up this philosophy in the following terms:

> We assume that the separation of church and State was made because it was conceived that matters of faith are too elevated and spiritual for human control, and possibly for the additional reason that the diversity of creeds rendered hopeless the task of giving authoritative sanction to one without unjustly depressing others; all being equally sound and essential in the views of those entertaining them respectively. Instead of saying that the government has renounced all, it is more correct to say that the government recognizes all religious denominations.[27]

Since the government had not renounced all religions but had embraced them all and assumed the obligation to insure the freedom of worship of all denominations, the courts could enforce conditions placed upon devises such as that requiring a Catholic upbringing for the devisee. Indeed, a failure to enforce such conditions would itself be an encroachment upon religious freedom. The court asked:

> Can it be properly said to be against the spirit of the constitution, for a member of one of these religious denominations, so protected, to endeavor by peaceable and legal means to extend his faith and to influence his children and grandchildren to adhere to the church of their fathers — for one belonging to the Presbyterian or Methodist, or any other denomination, to use such influences as argument, association, schools, colleges, donations, etc., to impress the minds of others, and particularly the youth of the country? Because such things may have some effect in determining religious opinions,

can it be truly said that, therefore, they violate liberty of conscience, and are productive of evil consequences to the public against public policy?[28]

At first glance, the *Magee* case seemed to involve a face-off between two aspects of the freedom of religion. The freedom of the granddaughter and her mother to determine their preferred mode of worship and the manner of the child's education seemed to be juxtaposed against two rights of the testator, the right to decide the disposition of his own property and the right to express his religious preference by the conditions placed on the devise to his granddaughter. However, the granddaughter was not deprived because of her religious convictions of any property in which she had a vested interest; nor was she denied a generally available government benefit because of her religious preference. She had a right to believe and practice whatever peaceful faith she chose but this did not include a right to force another to disgorge his property in her behalf. As the court viewed it, the case did not involve a clash between two equally revered dimensions of the right of freedom of conscience, but it instead called for the vindication of the testator's combined property and freedom of religion rights against one who asserted no cognizable right. To have ruled in favor of the granddaughter would have meant invading the grandfather's right to express his religious preference through one of the most potent means available, the disposal of his property. Under Article I, section 10, the government not only had an obligation to avoid intruding on the religious freedom of individuals and groups but also to protect the freedom of each denomination from invasion by private parties. This is an interesting approach that is not continued in currently applicable constitutional provisions. Both the First Amendment to the United States Constitution and Article I, section 4 (now 2), of the 1895 Constitution provide direct protection only against government intrusion. This, of course, does not preclude the enactment of statutory provisions protecting against religious discrimination in matters such as employment, assuming the law does not favor the protected religion.[29]

B. RELIGIOUS PRACTICES POSING PHYSICAL DANGER

The broad grant of religious freedom contained in the Constitution of 1790 was not absolute. Article VIII, section 1, contained a proviso stipulating ". . . that the liberty of conscience hereby declared shall not be so construed as to excuse acts of licentiousness, or justify practices inconsistent with the peace or safety of this State." The 1895 Constitution contains a free exercise clause virtually identical to that in the First Amendment of the United States Constitution.[30] Neither the federal nor state free exercise clauses now has such explicit language as did the Constitution of 1790 permitting the state to curb acts that are "licentious" or harm the "peace or safety" of the state. However, court interpretations and other authoritative analyses, such as attorney general's opinions, have read into the free exercise clauses limitations similar to those found in the 1790 fundamental law.

In the late nineteenth century in *Reynolds v. United States*[31] and *Davis v. Beason*,[32] the United States Supreme Court explored the limits of freedom of religion. In *Reynolds* it ruled valid federal criminal statutes outlawing the practice of polygamy in the Utah Territory even though certain Mormon groups then believed that their religion demanded that they engage in this practice. In *Davis v. Beason*, the Court held that an Idaho statute denying polygamists the right to vote or hold office did not violate the free exercise clause. In both cases the Court made a distinction between freedom of belief and freedom of action. The freedom of belief was absolute. No policeman knew what was in a person's mind. Unexpressed thoughts posed no danger to others. Even expressed thoughts should not be curbed unless they posed clear, palpable dangers. Unlike the freedom of belief, the right to exercise or act upon one's beliefs was not absolute. However, the First Amendment and comparable provisions of the state Constitution of 1895 (Article I, section 4, now 2) do expressly protect free *exercise* which connotes a right not merely to hold beliefs but to carry them out through a form of worship or other actions demanded by one's faith. This freedom of religious action is entitled to considerable protection even though it is not absolute.

Free exercise should be invaded only when it poses clear and serious dangers. *Reynolds* and *Davis* assumed that such dangers could be posed not only by acts creating physical dangers but also by acts that subvert morality and social order. To the *Reynolds* court, polygamy threatened to unravel the fabric of the family structure upon which civilization built not only a stable personal life but a stable government. Patriarchal dictatorship would replace democracy.[33] Carried to the extreme, however, the *Reynolds* reasoning can jeopardize religions that are shocking, unpalatable and unpopular but pose little danger to personal safety, social order or the survival of the government. However, *Reynolds* and *Davis* are the fountainhead cases demonstrating that free exercise of religion is not absolute and can be curbed if it poses significant dangers. It is easiest to justify such curbs if the danger posed threatens physical safety or health of either the practitioner, the on-looker or society in general. The government's interest becomes most compelling in the face of such clear physical dangers. The *Reynolds* opinion expressed the distinction between the absolute freedom of belief and the strong but more limited freedom of action. The Court described the special dangers presented by religious practices creating physical dangers in the following terms:

> Laws are made for the government of actions, and while they cannot interfere with mere religious belief and opinions, they may with practices. Suppose one believed that human sacrifices were a necessary part of religious worship, would it be seriously contended that the civil government under which he lived could not interfere to prevent a sacrifice? Or if a wife religiously believed it was her duty to burn herself upon the funeral pile of her dead husband, would it be beyond the power of the civil government to prevent her carrying her belief into practice?[34]

Physical dangers are not always accompanied by such dramatic circumstances as the *Reynolds* examples of human sacrifice and flaming funeral piles. Governments may exercise their police powers by taking prophylactic measures against the unseen but nonetheless real threat of disease.[35] One such health measure that has clashed frequently with freedom of religion is the requirement that people, especially school children, be vaccinated or otherwise immunized against such diseases as smallpox and polio. In 1919 the South Carolina Attorney General was presented with a query from a magistrate concerning the validity of compulsory vaccination laws. On behalf of the Attorney General, his assistant Morris Lumpkin replied that:

> It is true that the Constitution of the United States, Article 1 of amendments of the same, forbid the making of any law prohibiting the free exercise of religion, which is repêated in our State Constitution of 1895 in Article 1, Section 4, but such articles do not guarantee the practice of a religion which conflicts with the laws of the State of South Carolina in the exercise of its police power for the protection of its citizens and their health. Article VIII, Section 10 of the State Constitution of 1895, is as follows:
>
>> "It shall be the duty of the General Assembly to create Boards of Health wherever they may be necessary giving them power and authority to make such regulations as shall protect the health of the community and abate nuisances."[36]

Most courts confronted with a similar clash between religious beliefs that hold vaccinations repugnant and state or local health laws requiring such preventive measures have come to the same conclusion as the South Carolina Attorney General. In the 1905 case of *Jacobson v. Massachusetts*[37] the United States Supreme Court sustained a Cambridge, Massachusetts ordinance requiring compulsory vaccination. Jacobson attacked the ordinance as invading his right to control his own body, rather than as an intrusion on his freedom of religion, but the decision has been a frequently cited precedent in freedom of religion cases. Jacobson had refused to be vaccinated and had been assessed a five dollar fine. He alleged that the law, by requiring a government intrusion into his bodily integrity, violated the broad standards of liberty set forth in the preamble to the United States Constitution as well as his privileges and immunities as a citizen which were guaranteed by the Fourthteenth Amendment. He further asserted that a proviso to the ordinance which permitted children to be exempt if they obtained a physician's certificate that their health would be jeopardized by a vaccination violated his equal protection rights as an adult. The Court ruled that the preamble was not an independent source of federal power to control the exercise of state police powers to preserve health.[38] It also concluded that the ordinance made a legitimate distinction between adults and children because of the greater risks vaccination might pose to children.[39] The general analytical approach of the Court was that state and local public health regulations should be struck down only if they did not bear a real or substantial relationship to achieving legitimate health safety goals, or if they clearly invaded fundamental rights. The Cambridge vaccination law was closely related to the pursuit of the valid health goal of preventing the spread of disease, and it invaded no fundamental right.[40] However, the Court expressed the caveat that there could be individual instances in which the law did not prevent a real danger and was thus arbitrary and capricious, and there could be situations in which an otherwise legitimate law was applied in an oppressive manner.[41]

In *Zucht v. King*[42] the United States Supreme Court held that an attack on a San Antonio, Texas ordinance requiring that all children be vaccinated before attending a public or private school did not present a substantial federal question justifying review by the high court. The attack on the ordinance was largely based on the equal protection clause and alleged that the statute was defective in that the vaccination requirement did not apply to the entire population and was applied in such a selective fashion as to be arbitrary. The Court summarily rejected both contentions. It should be noted that both *Zucht v. King* and *Jacobson v. Massachusetts* dealt with challenges to compulsory vaccination laws that were not based primarily on religious freedom grounds, and both were decided before *Cantwell v. Connecticut* concluded in 1940 that the Fourteenth Amendment due process clause incorporated the free exercise clause of the First Amendment and applied it to the states.[43] However, they set in motion the habitual affirmation of such laws even when confronted with state or federal religious clause challenges. In a case decided after the application of the First Amendment religious clauses of the federal Constitution to the states, the Court directly addressed the question of whether or not compulsory vaccination requirements could be imposed upon those who have religious objections to such preventive measures. The comments made in *Prince v. Massachusetts*[44] were dicta in a case primarily concerned with upholding state child labor regulations against allegations that the laws prevented a child and her guardian from distributing religious literature in the streets in accordance with their religious convictions. By way of illustrating that freedom of religion is not absolute, even when fortified by the freedom of a parent or guardian to raise a child in the moral tradition the parent chooses, the Court made the following observations:

> But the family itself is not beyond regulation in the public interest, as against a claim of religious liberty. . . . neither rights of religion nor rights of parenthood are beyond limitation. Acting to guard the general interest in youth's well being, the state as *parens patriae* may restrict the parent's control by requiring school attendance, regulating or prohibiting the child's labor and in many other ways. Its authority is not nullified merely because the parent grounds his claim to control the child's course of conduct on religion or conscience. Thus, he cannot claim freedom from compulsory vaccination for the child more than for himself on religious grounds. The right to practice religion freely does not include liberty to expose the community or the child to communicable disease or the latter to ill health or death.[45]

The Court further noted that the state's powers to limit religious freedom to protect health of individuals and the community were even more extensive when the well-being of children were at stake.[46] Normally fundamental freedoms, such as free exercise of religion, should be curbed, if at all, only in the face of the clearest, most imminent threat.[47] However, when the nature of the threat not only involves serious physical danger but also is of such an insidious nature that, by the time proof of an imminent danger exists, preventive measures are too late, a court may be willing to approve needed prophylactic measures as a routine health policy even in the absence of proof of a current outbreak in the disease. Thus in *Wright v. DeWitt County School Dist. No. 1 of Arkansas County*[48] the Arkansas Supreme Court approved a law requiring the vaccination of children before they were permitted to attend school even though the plaintiffs claimed that the regulation violated their freedom of religion and did so without a showing of an imminent threat of an epidemic. The court noted that even if the plaintiffs' allegations that there had been no smallpox in the county for fifty years were accepted, communicable diseases posed such unique threats that preventive measures were justified, especially where children were concerned, despite the claimed intrusion on religious freedom and the absence of proof that an outbreak of the disease was eminent.[49]

In *McCartney v. Austin*[50] the court approved a requirement that all children be immunized against poliomyelitis, smallpox and measles unless the child's parents or guardian are genuine members of a recognized religion whose teachings reject immunization. The challenge was based on both the federal First Amendment and Article I, section 3, of the New York Constitution which, in language reminiscent of the 1790 South Carolina Constitution, guaranteed freedom of conscience but not if religious conduct became licentious or threatened the peace or safety. After summarily rejecting claims that the immunization regulation was so vague and discriminatory as to violate due process and equal protection rights, the appellate court confirmed the trial court's decision that the plaintiffs lacked standing to challenge the health measure as intruding on their religious freedom.

The court noted that the plaintiffs were Catholics and the Catholic Church did not teach opposition to immunization programs.[51] Thus the New York courts placed themselves in the bizarre position of not only presuming to declare what was orthodox within the Roman Catholic Church but also assuming that once someone had affiliated with a church, he could not entertain conscientious, religious-based scruples, except those condoned by that church. Any other scruples were likely to be based on general moral philosophy rather than religion. Even though the conscientious objector provisions in the law seemed to require that the objections be based on the teachings of a recognized religion of which the objector was a bona fide member, that should not limit the right to make constitutionally based objections or permit a civil court to assume the function of an ecclesiastical tribunal in declaring what is orthodox in a particular religion.[52] Permitting only members of recognized religions to make conscientious objections and allowing them to do so only according to church doctrine smacks of establishment of religion. In *Sherr v. Northport-East Northport Union Free School Dist.*[53] the federal district court held that the requirement that in order to be entitled to the exemption the child's parents must belong to a recognized religion which opposes immunization, violated both the free exercise and establishment clauses of the First Amendment. The court concluded that parents who were not members of recognized religious groups but whose objections to immunization were religiously based were entitled to conscientiously object.[54] Apart from such invalidly biased exemptions, the immunization laws have been upheld even against those who conscientiously object on religious grounds.

The remote mountains and passes of southern Appalachia have spawned many odd rites designed to test and demonstrate one's faith. One such practice, snake handling, has posed problems to law enforcement officers who seek to maintain public safety, but who try to do so in a manner that avoids unnecessary intrusions on free exercise of religion. In a 1948 opinion, South Carolina Attorney General John M. Daniel responded to a request from a sheriff seeking to learn the extent of his authority to prevent participation in snake-handling rites. The Attorney General stated that:

> Unless there is a threatened breach of the peace or disorderly conduct, the Courts have held that people have the right to practice their religion and no interference is proper just because we do not agree with them. No duty would rest upon a sheriff to stop religious sects from handling snakes *per se*. But if the snake were allowed to become a threat to those attending these meetings and the commission of a crime such as disorderly conduct, breach of the peace, etc. — *then* the sheriff should interfere, to prevent those things from happening — just as he would were no professed religious exercises in progress. If a snake should be allowed to bite a person and the person should die, then the handler of the snake might be subject to prosecution for murder.[55]

This opinion recognizes a generous ambit of free exercise of religion in that it cautions the sheriff not to intervene merely because he disagrees with the ritual. Furthermore, even though the opinion recognizes the authority of law enforcement officers to stop religious practices that clearly threaten public safety, it seems to adopt as its major premise a principle that the officer should act only when the danger becomes imminent. This is seen in the italics emphasizing the word "then" in the passage quoted above. Although it is less obvious from the language of the opinion, it also implies that the officer should act only when the threat extends to ". . . those attending these meetings . . ." and not just to the participants. The opinion admonishes the sheriff not to assume that snake handling is "*per se*" bad but to wait until a clear threat materializes in a concrete situation.

Some courts applying explicit state statutes forbidding snake handling have upheld, against federal and state constitutional challenges, the right of the state to prohibit the ritual as one that is inherently dangerous without requiring proof that it is dangerous in a particular situation. The court defers to a reasonable legislative judgment that the practice is one that is consistently fraught with danger. Such states assert the right of the police to protect the practitioner against the dangers of his own religion as well as the right to protect the on-looker and general public. The basis on which the state asserts this right to protect the practitioner against the excesses of his own religion is not developed by the courts, but it may be that one who appears to be a voluntary participant may actually be swept into the ritual by crowd pressure. The practice could create social costs in which the state has a strong interest even when participation is truly voluntary. The state may incur costs in investigating deaths, providing medical care, and providing support for survivors.

Lawson v. Commonwealth[56] is illustrative of the usual approach of the courts in upholding anti-snakehandling measures as legitimate uses of state police power. In that case the Kentucky court concluded that it was unnecessary to demonstrate a safety-threatening breach of the peace in the context of a particular snakehandling exercise. The legislature had made a rational judgment that such exercises were intrinsically threatening. The court considered challenges to the statute under the religious clauses of the federal First Amendment as well as the Kentucky Constitution which then stated that "[n]o human authority shall, in any case whatever, control or interfere with the rights of conscience."[57] The court observed that the religious freedom provisions of the state and federal constitutions were designed to guard against state-induced pressures toward religious conformity and not to shackle the state's power to guard the health and safety of its citizens. The court reiterated the distinction made in the *Davis* and *Reynolds* cases, between the absolute freedom to believe and the freedom to carry out religious acts, which, although a strongly entrenched right, could be limited to avoid a clear threat to public safety. The court observed that the state's regulatory power could be used to prohibit rites that threaten the health and safety of participants as well as other persons.[58] In *Harden v. State*[59] the Tennessee court concluded that anti-snake-handling provisions were valid even as applied to religions that believed that the ritual was a demonstration of their faith and was essential to their religion and that it was a core ingredient of their method of evangelism, a form of expression that was designed to gain converts by showing the depth of their conviction.[60]

The distinction between the state's ability to regulate religiously motivated actions that threatened health and safety and its inability to regulate beliefs formed the basis of the decision of the state court of appeals in *South Carolina Department of Social Services v. Father and Mother*.[61] In that case, the parents of a thirteen-year-old girl were charged with child abuse in the form of excessively severe corporal punishment which they claimed to be dictated by the Bible. The child had lied to her parents by claiming to be elsewhere when she was actually attending a party. As punishment, the father, with the mother's approval, beat the girl black and blue with his belt. As a result, extensive purple bruises covered the child's back and left thigh, and she complained of a ringing in her ears, apparently resulting from a blow to the face. Both parents were well-educated, the father being an engineer and the mother a school teacher. However, they took literally the injunction of Proverbs that the parents should "[w]ithhold not correction from the child: for *if* thou beatest him with the rod, he shall not die."[62] Thus, the parents believed that they not only were permitted to administer such severe corporal punishment, but that the Bible so required. Despite these beliefs, a child abuse proceeding was instituted in Family Court at the request of the State Department of Social Services. Even though the parents' beliefs presumably were sincere, and their interpretation of the Biblical directive was fortified by the testimony of a clergyman at the trial, the court found that the punishment was deliberate and excessive and thus constituted child abuse rather than permissible parental correction of an errant child. The trial court left the child in the custody of the parents but ordered them to undergo counseling monitored by the child's guardian ad litem. The court of appeals concluded that the child abuse finding and punishment were justified despite the parents' contentions that they had a right to correct their child in such a severe fashion because such action was part of their free exercise of religion and within the authority of parents to control the upbringing of their own child.

The court of appeals in an opinion by Chief Judge Sanders upheld the trial court's action. He noted that the First Amendment to the United States Constitution and Article I, section 2, of the South Carolina Constitution contained identical guarantees of the free exercise of religion. He reiterated the familiar distinction between the unfettered right to believe what you wish and the right to act on those beliefs that was subject to government regulation to maintain health and safety and good order. He demonstrated the absurdity of holding that the government had no authority to regulate religiously motivated actions by noting that:

If the law were otherwise, a Fundamental Mormon could have multiple wives, a Jehovah's Witness could withhold medical care from his child and a modern-day adherent to an early eastern religion could drown a virgin bride to appease a river god.[63]

For the paranoid, the case may raise the specter of state-reared children, children appealing their every punishment to the courts, and courts deciding which Biblical injunctions are to be taken literally and which are not, but the approach of the court was such that it clearly limited state intervention in the parent-child relationship and interference with religiously-based child rearing to situations in which the health, safety or moral welfare of the child were placed in serious jeopardy.

The use of drugs in religious ceremonies has not become a focal point of South Carolina jurisprudence, but should be mentioned briefly because of its similarity to the snake handler and vaccination cases in demonstrating the strength of state police power when religious practices pose physical dangers to health and safety. Courts have generally upheld criminal sanctions against the use in religious ceremonies of drugs that pose serious physical or psychological dangers. Under traditional analysis, religious exercise should not be curbed unless a state has a compelling interest in doing so. The avoidance of serious danger to the health of the user normally has been considered to meet this tough compelling interest standard. For example, in *United States v. Middleton,*[64] a defendant was convicted in federal court of importing and possessing marijuana. The defendant claimed that he was a devoted member of the Ethiopian Coptic Church and that marijuana use was a crucial part of the worship services of his church, especially in prayer ceremonies. Thus, his conviction for importation and possession of marijuana, incidental to such religious use, would violate his free exercise rights under the First Amendment of the federal Constitution. The court of appeals concluded that in order to succeed in such a constitutional defense the proponent must demonstrate that his practices were indeed religious in nature and that marijuana use formed a significant part of such rites. However, the court noted that even if the defendant succeeded in proving these elements his constitutional attack would fail because of the compelling interest the federal government had in preventing the clear and significant harms associated with marijuana traffic and use.

In *Lewellyn v. State of Oklahoma*,[65] the state court of criminal appeals was confronted by a defendant convicted of possession and use of marijuana who claimed that the religious use of the drug was essential to his personal religious faith because ". . . it brings a person closer to God, makes him less violent, more peaceful, and more loving toward his brother man."[66] The court was unimpressed with these contentions. It refused to inquire into the "truth or veracity of defendant's religious beliefs. . . ."[67] In fact, it did not even raise the balancing process components that were, at least, mentioned by the *Middleton* court. Thus it did not ask whether the defendant's actions were genuinely a significant part of a religious practice. It flatly declared that the dangers inherent in marijuana use were so substantial that no attempt at religious justification of the practice should carry any weight.[68] Even though the analytical routes chosen by the courts may vary from at least demonstrating a facade of a balancing process in which the government's compelling interest outweighs free exercise contentions to a simple flat statement, without balancing, that use of certain drugs is too dangerous to permit, the usual result is sustaining the government's regulation.[69]

An interesting exception to this approach is *People v. Woody*,[70] a decision rendered by the Supreme Court of California. The court reversed the conviction of members of the Native American Church for use of the hallucinogenic drug peyote in religious ceremonies. In reaching this result the court pursued the following analytical process:

(1) Was the religious use of peyote a key element of the religion? Yes. The inclusion of peyote use in religious ceremonies was not a modern day contrivance to justify drug use but was a tradition of the church traceable back to 1560. The drug use is supposed to enhance the participating member's ability to communicate with the Holy Spirit.

(2) Would government prohibition of the practice significantly injure an essential feature of the religion? Yes. The evidence was that the essential character of the religion could not exist without it.

(3) Does the government have a compelling interest which outweighs this injury to free exercise of religion? No. The state offered several justifications for the prohibition. It argued that since entire families participated in the worship, that children would be endangered. The court rejected this justification, noting that children were not allowed to participate in the drug use and that they were safeguarded during the

ceremony. The state argued that the prohibition was necessary to prevent the Indians from using peyote to alleviate pain rather than seeking medical treatment. The court concluded that no evidence supported this argument. The state argued that a judicially-granted exception to the anti-drug use laws that permitted use by such religious bodies would seriously undermine the state's effort to fight drug use since it would be confronted in every case by claims for religious exemptions. The court concluded that the general anti-drug use laws would not be undermined since juries could distinguish between genuine and fraudulent claims for religious exemption. What had been the clenching argument in most cases carried little weight with the *Woody* court. The state argued that peyote use caused serious physical and psychological harm including a reaction similar to schizophrenia. The court admitted that there were occasional adverse reactions but that they were rare in the careful, controlled environment of the religious ceremony. Of course, the court's conclusions were reached in 1964 when knowledge of the adverse effects of drugs was not so great as it is today. Finally, the court rejected the state's attempt to justify the prohibition as a measure essential to save the Indians from maintaining a primitive culture. The court dismissed this as a patronizing, elitist argument that assumed that everyone should pursue an orthodox lifestyle.

A strikingly different analytical approach was taken by the United States Supreme Court in the 1990 case *Employment Division, Department of Human Resources of Oregon v. Smith*.[71] In that case the Court held that Oregon was justified in denying unemployment benefits to members of the Native American Church who had been dismissed from their jobs as drug counselors at a private agency because they had used peyote as part of a religious ceremony. The state denied the benefits because the Indians had been dismissed from their jobs because of employment-related misconduct, drug use that was a criminal offense. The Court determined that it was unnecessary for the state to demonstrate that its benefits denial was justified by a compelling rather than a merely legitimate state interest. Such strict scrutiny analysis was not necessary where the religious practice was not the direct target of the government regulations but religion was harmed only incidentally to the application of a general measure designed to preserve public safety. If a religious practice was not the direct target of the regulation, strict scrutiny would be employed only if injury to religious liberty was combined with injury to other rights, such as the free speech rights or the right of parents to control the upbringing of their children. The anti-drug use laws in Oregon were not specifically aimed at prohibiting the religious use of harmful drugs but forbade the use of such drugs in virtually all contexts. Since religious use was not discriminated against by the anti-drug laws, there was no need for the strict scrutiny (compelling state interest) analysis.

An element of the *Woody* approach also involved assessing the degree of injury to the religion that was imposed by the regulation. A feature of this analysis was determining whether or not there was significant injury to a central, or essential, element of the religion. If such a severe injury were present, it could be justified only by the state's demonstrating that the regulation was essential to accomplishing a compelling interest. In the *Smith* case the Court refused to inquire into whether or not the harmed practice was central to a particular religion because to do so would make the court the ultimate authority on what was and was not a key element of virtually every faith. This would transform the Court into an ecclesiastical tribunal. Such a role, in which the Court sanctions certain practices as essential to a religion and others as not, smacks of Court endorsement of some religious beliefs in a manner that at least approaches being an establishment clause violation. It will be recalled that cases such as *Middleton* used compelling interest analysis in approving criminal sanctions against drug use, despite free exercise clause objections, but that the balancing process was rather perfunctory and clearly skewed toward the government position.[72]

As Justice O'Connor observed in her concurrence in *Smith*, Oregon's denial of unemployment benefits to sacramental drug users could be upheld under the traditional compelling interest test.[73] Even when prohibiting ritualistic drug use severely harms the religion, such laws may serve a compelling state interest in avoiding serious physical and psychological harm. Subjecting government intrusions on free exercise of religion to strict scrutiny only when the religious practice is the deliberate target of the regulation, or when other rights are injured in combination with religious freedom, would permit severe injury to freedom of religion (even when the religion is merely unpopular and not physically dangerous) just by labelling the harm to religion as only incidental to the regulation. Furthermore, it downgrades religious freedom to the position of a right less lofty than freedom of speech and racial equal protection. Under this approach, free exercise of religion becomes a right that often does not receive the protection of strict scrutiny unless injured in combination with other rights. This approach ignores the Constitution itself to accommodate a judicial philosophy hostile to strict scrutiny analysis. Religious freedom is singled out for protection in the First Amendment itself. It is not a court-created or merely implied right. It should not be forced to ride into the domain of strict scrutiny protection piggy-backed upon other rights.[74]

C. REGULATING RELIGIOUS EXPRESSION THAT DISTURBS THE PUBLIC PEACE OR INVADES THE RIGHTS OF OTHERS

Even when the religious expression does not involve an act which is inherently dangerous, such as snakehandling or sacramental drug use, a state may regulate the practice under its police powers to avoid the interference with the rights of others such as would result from excessive noise, blocking public or private passways, or trespass. In addition, religious acts which are not intrinsically dangerous but show a clear likelihood of inciting or provoking violence may be regulated. These points can be illustrated by several South Carolina decisions occurring in the late 1930's and early 1940's, just before and just after the United States Supreme Court applied First Amendment free exercise clause standards to the states in the 1940 case of *Cantwell v. Connecticut.*[75] All of these cases involved minority religions that used modes of worship or evangelizing that offended the general population. Considered in combination, these cases indicate that state regulatory power is at its height when the religious expression invades the rights of others or poses a serious risk of immediate violence but is at its nadir when it merely offends the delicate sensibilities of the general population. We will first consider decisions rendered a few months before *Cantwell*, then we will examine *Cantwell* itself, not only because of its usefulness in delineating the kinds of speech that may be regulated but also because of its clarification of the Court's preference for so-called time, place and manner regulations over placing prior restraints on expression.

In *State v. Langston*,[76] the state supreme court reviewed the case of several Jehovah's Witnesses who had been convicted of breach of peace. These Witnesses had adopted a form of evangelism that consisted of going upon the piazzas (porches or verandas) of private homes and playing victrola records containing a religious message. Although accounts of the case are not clear on this point, the implication is that in at least some instances permission was not received from the owners of the premises. In addition, the Witnesses patrolled the town on Sunday mornings in cars with loud speakers proclaiming religious messages to the general public. The court did not describe the specific form of the practice. The degree to which the practice intruded on the rights of others would depend to a considerable extent on the sound volume of the message and whether the cars were constantly in motion or stationary for a long period at a location at which they might directly intrude on the rights of others. The fleeting presence of a speaker tuned to a moderate volume would not significantly intrude on the rights of others, whereas a loud message that drowns out the worship of others would be highly intrusive. There is no indication from the facts that the Witnesses used their message to inundate the views of others. At any rate, the court considered the case a simple breach of peace case.

Arguments were made on behalf of the defendants that the breach of peace convictions curbed their right to practice their religion by using effective means to evangelize. The court essentially concluded that freedom of religion arguments had no proper place in breach of peace cases. There were so many different religions with so many modes of spreading their messages that it would only confuse the analysis by placing too much emphasis on religious freedom. The court stated that:

> In this State there are so many religious beliefs, so varied in what they teach and with such great difference, that one of the most fruitful, and yet fruitless, sources of argument is some theological question. It certainly cannot be said that there is not in this State an absolute freedom of religion. A man may believe what kind of religion he pleases or no religion, and as long as he practices his belief without a breach of peace, he will not be disturbed.[77]

The supreme court accepted the circuit court's description of the means by which a breach of peace could be committed. Such a violation could occur by (1) a violation of public order, (2) a disturbance of public tranquility, (3) inciting to violence.[78] Many years later, item 2 of this list of breaches of the peace earned the ire of the United States Supreme Court in *Edwards v. South Carolina*, a case overturning the conviction of civil rights protesters who conducted a peaceful demonstration on State House grounds against segregation.[79] Permitting arrests for speech that merely disturbed the tranquility of the community could sweep so broadly as to allow charges against those who merely uttered non-inciting political messages with which the audience or the arresting officer disagreed. Merely making people uncomfortable by an unpopular message is not a constitutionally punishable breach of peace.[80]

However, a very noisy religious message played over a loud speaker at a time when it could disrupt the activities of others could constitute a constitutionally regulatable breach of the peace, as would a message broadcast without permission on the veranda of a private residence.

In addition to curbing intrusion on private property, the government can impose reasonable time, place, and manner regulations on religious as well as other forms of speech, even in a public forum, such as a street or park, so long as the regulation is not imposed because of the message contained in the speech, reasonable access to the audience is not blocked, and the regulations are narrowly drawn to accomplish a significant government interest such as permitting others to exercise their rights. Thus in the 1989 case of *Ward v. Rock Against Racism*[81] the United States Supreme Court sustained a New York City regulation of the volume and mix of sound at rock concerts and other performances at the bandshell in Sheep Meadow in Central Park. Residents in neighborhoods surrounding the park, as well as those using other portions of the park, had complained about the noise emanating from the bandshell. To alleviate the loudness problem and improve the sound quality for those attending the concerts, the city required all performers appearing in the bandshell to use a sound system operated by the city. Even though the park was a traditional public forum, dedicated to speech, the city's regulation was permissible as it pursued a significant noise abatement goal, was not prompted by disagreement with the content of the message, did not block access to the audience and was a narrowly drawn procedure well designed to achieve the city's goal. Although such regulations of the manner of speech had to be narrowly drawn to achieve an important government goal the city was not required to use the procedure that was least intrusive on free speech, so long as it did not broadly damage free speech. Even though it was decided long before all of these refinements were developed, the *Langston* case appears to fit well within this framework.

Another early 1940 case decided by the South Carolina Supreme Court shortly before the federal Supreme Court's *Cantwell* decision was *Morison v. Rawlinson.*[82] In *Morison* the South Carolina court rejected the application of the deacons of a church for an injunction against attempts by the Columbia Police Department to close the church as a public nuisance. The court described the church service as involving dancing, members who entered "hypnotic trances" as other worshippers gave "forth weird and unearthly outcries" often accompanied by "shouting, clapping of hands in unison, and stamping of feet."[83] The church music involved "drums, timbrels, trombones, horns, scrubbing boards and wash tubs."[84] Testimony indicated that the noise could be heard many blocks away, including adjoining residential sections. The meetings took place every day from early evening to early morning. Large, disorderly crowds of would-be worshippers who were unable to get in congregated outside the church with apparently some blockage of public passageways occurring. Allegations were made that the church sold beer, soft drinks and food in an adjoining building. The church denied these contentions. The church was located in a densely populated residential neighborhood. The residents complained that the noise continued into the early morning. The church denied that it contributed to the noise outside its doors, contending that these disturbances were created by idle on-lookers. Tension was added to the situation by the fact that church members were black and the complaining residents were white and had opposed the opening of the church.

The court found several due process violations in the manner in which the city council had adopted the resolution to close the church as a public nuisance. The resolution should have been preceded by passage of a general ordinance defining what constituted a public nuisance. This would have given potential offenders greater notice of what they could and could not do. The church had not been given an opportunity to appear before the council to contest the closing. However, the court concluded that these were technical defects that had been cured by a long common law tradition defining a public nuisance and by later opportunities in court for the church to present its case.[85]

On the merits of the public nuisance charge, the court observed that religious expression should not be abated as a nuisance unless the case that it was, in fact, a nuisance was ". . . clearly and conclusively made out."[86] A mere threat of a nuisance should be enjoined ". . . only where the Court is satisfied that the threat will become a certainty. . . ." The court concluded, however, that an adequate case had been made that the services and the accompanying disorder outside the church constituted a nuisance.[87] The pastor of the church testified that much of the noise was an integral part of worship. These contentions were fortified by Biblical references to ". . . clapping of hands, shouting, the making of a joyful noise, and the worship of the Lord both morning and evening."[88] Despite these free exercise of religion arguments, the court concluded that the nuisance could be abated. Freedom of belief was absolute but religiously-inspired action could be abated when it interfered with the rights of others.[89] Here the boisterous services interfered with the rights of residents to have enough peace and quiet to get a decent night's sleep and enjoy their homes. It will be recalled that there also was some blockage of the streets by the outside crowd. Although the court did not emphasize this point, it may have been concerned about the crowd's impeding the freedom of movement of others who wished to use the streets. A convincing case was made for government regulatory action. However, one wonders whether or not a less intrusive measure such as providing reasonable limits on how late at night the church could meet would not have been preferable since the shouting and clapping were integral parts of the worship. An attempt also could have been made to limit the decibel level of the instruments. Even this would be treading on dangerous ground as it could lead to police officials attempting to dictate the mode of worship.[90]

The *Langston* and *Morison* cases were decided in March 1940. In May of the same year, the United States Supreme Court decided *Cantwell v. Connecticut*[91] which concluded that the Fourteenth Amendment's admonition that states not deprive persons of life, liberty or property without due process of law incorporated the First Amendment free exercise of religion standards and applied them to the states.[92] Even though it is unlikely that the outcome of the *Langston* and *Morison* decisions would have been different after the *Cantwell* opinion, the analytical standards announced in *Cantwell* placed greater emphasis upon the need for identifying a palpable danger, not just offensive remarks, before religious expression was curbed, and also created stricter standards that must be met by states in fashioning the procedures by which they protect public health, safety and morals. We shall see the *Cantwell* approach exercising a strong influence on the South Carolina Supreme Court's reasoning in the 1941 case of *City of Gaffney v. Putnum.*[93] Before considering this case, more detailed consideration must be given to the *Cantwell* decision itself.

The *Cantwell* case, like the *City of Gaffney* case, the *Langston* case, and many others of that time, involved the intrepid Jehovah's Witnesses evangelists. A Connecticut law required that anyone soliciting anything of value for a religious, charitable or philanthropic cause from persons other than its own members must obtain permission form the local public welfare council. The secretary of the council had the authority to determine whether or not a particular solicitation was for a genuine religious, charitable or philanthropic cause. Cantwell was convicted of not complying with this ordinance and of committing a breach of the peace.

Cantwell and his sons went to a heavily populated, predominantly Roman Catholic neighborhood in New Haven equipped with books, phonograph records, and a portable record player, all of which explained doctrines of the church. The phonograph record contained a description of a book entitled *Enemies.* The Witnesses would ask passers-by on the public streets for permission to play the record which they would do if the passers-by agreed. The record contained a strong attack on all organized religion as the tool of Satan but made particularly vitriolic remarks concerning the Roman Catholic church. The Court described the record as containing a message that would not only offend Catholics but also would earn the ire of dedicated members of other organized religions.[94] Several members of the audience that heard the record said that they were "highly offended."[95] One testified that he felt like hitting Cantwell but that the trouble dissipated when Cantwell agreed to leave. Cantwell and his sons were convicted of failing to obtain the proper permission prior to soliciting contributions and were also convicted of breach of peace arising from the street confrontation. On appeal, the

United States Supreme Court found the convictions on both charges to be defective.

With regard to the conviction for failing to obtain permission to solicit, the Court observed that a state or local government had the power to adopt general non-discriminatory rules that regulated the time, place and manner of solicitation on its streets as a means of protecting the peace, good order, and comfort of the community.[96] However, the Connecticut solicitation statute went far beyond permissible regulatory bounds. It did not merely regulate the time, place, or manner of peaceful and honest, though offensive, solicitation. It prohibited such solicitation entirely unless a certificate were obtained from the council. The secretary of the council was given sweeping powers to determine whether or not the particular cause for which the solicitation was to be made was a religious one.

Such power amounted to the ability to impose a prior restraint on religious speech at the whim of the administrator. Prior restraints, because they (a) stop the speech in advance, (b) give the public no benefit of its contents, (c) give the authorities no chance to evaluate its danger before a real audience, (d) are often imposed by judicial or administrative fiat without a bilateral hearing, and (e) even if later dissolved, have lost forever the opportunity to speak at a particular time that may be crucial to the effectiveness of the speaker's message, are a law enforcement procedure that seriously injures freedom of expression.[97] Such prior restraint should be imposed only to avoid the gravest, most imminent harms that could not otherwise be averted.[98] The Court in *Cantwell* observed that a state could safeguard its citizens from fraud by requiring a newcomer in the area to identify himself and furnish evidence of his authority to solicit for the organization he purports to represent before allowing solicitation. The government can also impose reasonable time, place and manner regulations on the solicitation to avoid interference with the rights of others and to maintain peace and good order. Allowing an official to stop solicitation for a religious organization based on his unguided, subjective judgment of whether the cause is a proper religious one or not grants sweeping censorship powers not permissible in this country. Merely permitting the administrative decision to be reviewed by the Court does not save the law because a prior restraint imposed by a court is just as constitutionally infirm as one imposed by administrative fiat.[99]

The conviction for breach of the peace was also constitutionally infirm. The Court recognized the legitimate interest of the state in preserving good order within its borders.[100] However, the state's authority to regulate includes not only violent acts but ". . . words likely to produce violence in others."[101] The possibility of violence flowing from the words should not be remote and speculative but should present a ". . . clear and present danger of riot, disorder, interference with traffic upon the public streets, or other immediate threat to public safety, peace, or order. . . ."[102] This likelihood of violence can be created by a speaker who intends to incite the listener to immediate violent action and does so under circumstances in which it is probable that he will succeed. In addition, the likelihood of violence that can justify significant state penalties can occur even when the speaker does not intend to incite a violent action, but his statements occur under circumstances in which he reasonably can assume that violence is a likely result.[103]

A speaker who does not intend to incite violence may be subject to prosecution anyway if the nature of the words, together with the time, place and audience, create a likelihood that the listener will react violently. This probability of violence is not created by speech that is merely broadly insulting to a large group of which the listener is a member, or speech which merely offends the listener's political opinions. In order to trigger regulatory power the words must be highly insulting in a very personal manner. The Court in *Cantwell* emphasized that the defendant's verbal assaults on organized religion and the Catholic church were ". . . a general attack."[104] It noted that the remarks were not ". . . directed to the person of the hearer,"[105] and that they did not constitute ". . . personal abuse."[106] Even though the Court did not use the term in *Cantwell,* this concept is often called the "fighting words doctrine." *Chaplinsky v. New Hampshire,* decided two years after *Cantwell,* described fighting words as those that are "likely to provoke the average person to retaliation, and thereby cause a breach of the peace."[107] In the 1989 case of *Texas v. Johnson,*[108] the United States Supreme Court struck down the Texas statute which outlawed flag desecration. The Court observed that a state was not justified in punishing speech as "fighting words" unless a ". . . reasonable onlooker would have regarded [the expression] as a direct personal insult or an invitation to exchange fisticuffs."[109] If violence is likely or occurs because of the hot-headed nature of the audience rather than the incendiary quality of the speaker's words, it is the violent audience that should be the object of the regulatory effort and not the speaker.[110]

City of Gaffney v. Putnam[111] was decided a year after *Cantwell* and adopted its analytical framework and applied it to a factual setting reminiscent of *Cantwell*. Putnam, a Jehovah's Witnesses member, was convicted of violating a city ordinance that punished varied disorders including "disturbing noises" and "obscene, abusive and vulgar language" as well as violent acts.[112] One Sunday afternoon, Putnam was distributing a Jehovah's Witnesses' publication, *The Watchtower*, on a street corner in the Gaffney business district. Occasionally, in an effort to attract attention to the magazine, he would call out cryptically, "Religion is ruining the nations; Christianity will save the people." During the course of these declamations the police chief strolled by. Even though the chief did not believe that Putnam was violating the ordinance, he advised the speaker "to move on."[113] The chief later testified that he was afraid that some passerby might be offended enough by Putnam's remarks to react violently. However, other than advising Putnam to "move on," the chief did not communicate his fears of violence to Putnam. Despite the chief's admonition, Putnam continued his remarks. The chief proved to be prophetic. One Fowler blustered by, was offended by Putnam's "Religion is ruining the nations, Christianity will save the people" remarks, and told Putnam not to repeat them. Putnam refused to bow to Fowler's street corner censorship and repeated the statement. This provoked Fowler to beat Putnam repeatedly. Even though Fowler was much larger than Putnam, the latter kept getting back up. This only served to further inflame Fowler who, perhaps, was inspired by the crowd that had gathered. Oddly enough, it was Putnam that the police chose to arrest. The prosecution's case was not helped by Fowler's admission that he was the aggressor, although he also claimed that Putnam had flourished his fists in front of him. The South Carolina Supreme Court reversed Putnam's conviction as violating his rights under the First Amendment of the federal Constitution as well as Article I, section 4 (now 2), of the State Constitution of 1895. The court noted that these provisions permitted vigorous, even offensive, religious speech. Such speech should not be curbed unless it creates a significant danger such as the risk of an immediate violent reaction. Putnam's remarks did not deliberately incite listeners to violence; nor did they occur under circumstances in which he reasonably could have foreseen that an onlooker would have been so personally insulted that he would have reacted violently. Putnam's statements were not targeted at Fowler personally and thus did not constitute fighting words. The court stated that:

> It does not appear that he had ever seen Fowler before, or that he had any reason to believe that his words would be personally offensive to him by reason of the latter's religious views or convictions. There is no showing that the defendant's deportment was noisy, truculent, overbearing, or offensive. He indulged in no opprobrium or abuse of the public, or of Fowler. So far as the evidence shows, he wished only to interest those who passed by in his propaganda.[114]

Indeed, the defendant's remarks were even more general and less personal than those in *Cantwell* where the recording insulted the Roman Catholic Church, members of which were in the audience. It is true that, unlike *Cantwell* in which the speaker had moved rather than risk a violent confrontation, violence had in fact broken out. However, that seemed to be more the result of the listener's personal predilections than the nature of the speaker's words. The court noted that ". . . mere words, no matter how abusive, insulting, vexatious or threatening they may be, will not justify an assault or battery, unless accompanied by an actual offer of physical violence. . . ."[115]

The South Carolina Supreme Court was presented with another Jehovah's Witnesses case in the summer of 1941. *State v. Meredith*[116] was decided a few weeks after *City of Gaffney v. Putnam,* but this time the court finessed a possible religious freedom controversy by strictly interpreting a state regulatory measure in such a way as to avoid placing any roadblocks in the way of religious expression. Mr. Meredith was a Jehovah's Witnesses missionary in the rural area of Beaufort County. He would visit farmhouses and ask for permission to play his records. He would attempt to sell Jehovah's Witnesses literature such as *The Watchtower* magazine and booklets entitled "Refugees" and "Salvation." If the persons he was proselytizing had no money, he would give the literature to them if they indicated that they would read it. Any money received from the sale of literature was used to pay for the publication of additional literature. Mr. Meredith received no compensation for his services. He was arrested for failure to comply with state requirements that anyone who engaged in hawking and peddling must first obtain a license from the clerk of court. On the occasion of his arrest as he was evangelizing on a farmhouse porch with the occupant; he did not make a sale, but there was evidence that he had made a sale several weeks earlier. He was convicted in magistrate's court of violating the hawkers' and peddlers' licensing requirement. The conviction was affirmed by the circuit court, but the supreme court reversed. Defense counsel had argued that the licensing requirement, if applied to activities such as those of the defendant, would violate the free exercise of religion provisions of the state and federal constitutions. The court found it unnecessary to confront these issues since it concluded that such nonprofit, religious-oriented speech was not covered by a statute directed at commercial hawking and peddling. The court did not discuss establishment clause issues that might arise if a special exemption were carved out only for religious publications, but it noted that a variety of other publications also were exempt from the licensing requirement.[117] Meredith was charged only with violation of the licensing requirement, and no effort was made to convict him of uttering dangerous speech creating a breach of peace. However, the court noted in passing that there was nothing offensive, immoral or harmful to the general welfare about the publications.

At the close of its *Meredith* opinion the South Carolina court noted that a differently worded statute, with a scope that covered activities such as that of Meredith, would have presented additional questions for resolution. It cited the United States Supreme Court decision in *Lovell v. Griffin*[118] as an example of a case dealing with a broader statute that posed additional problems. Although the South Carolina court did not further explore the *Lovell* holding, it is worth noting that in it the federal Supreme Court struck down a Griffin, Georgia ordinance that required a license to be obtained from the city manager before any form of literature could be distributed in the municipality. The ordinance made no attempt to limit its broad sweep to literature that was likely to produce violence, damage morality or which was to be distributed in a manner that infringed on the rights of others. The city manager was set up as the czar of local literature with authority to ban any form of publication no matter how innocuous.

The South Carolina statute had no such broad sweep, and by interpreting it as not applying to activities such as Meredith's the court avoided much constitutional grief. The constitutional landscape of the early, and mid-1940's was littered with the corpses of state and local laws that attempted to limit the evangelizing activities of Jehovah's Witnesses and other groups. Licensing statutes, when applied to such activities, often fared no better than overly broad breach of peace statutes. In *Murdock v. Pennsylvania*[119] the United States Supreme Court cited with favor the South Carolina decision in *Meredith* but struck down an ordinance of Jeannette, Pennsylvania as applied to Jehovah's Witnesses' door-to-door evangelizing. The ordinance in the *Murdock* case required that a license be obtained by anyone prior to solicitation for goods and wares, including literature, within the town. A condition of obtaining a license was payment of a fee. This was no mere nominal fee to defray administrative costs but was a substantial charge. It was a flat tax, the same amount was exacted from everyone who solicited for a given length of time, no matter what the amount of profit they would make or the scope of their operation.[120] Such a fiscal roadblock could stop solicitation or evangelizing for a minority religion at its inception. In effect, such a tax amounted to a prior restraint on speech that presented no danger of violence or interference with the rights of others. The Court made several fundamental points concerning the scope of protection afforded free exercise of religion. Hand distribution of religious tracts is just as highly protected a form of religious expression as a worship service or a revival meeting.[121] Such expression does not lose its protected nature just because the pamphlets are sometimes sold. Religious organizations have financial needs just as do other going concerns.[122]

The ordinance was not saved by the fact that it did not single out religious literature solicitations, or even literature in general, for the license tax charge. The charge was exacted from those who solicited for all types of goods and wares. Despite this nondiscriminatory quality, the application of the ordinance in such a manner as to erect significant fiscal barriers to expression protected by the First Amendment religious clauses was a constitutional violation.[123]

Even though the United States Supreme Court commended the South Carolina court for its opinion in *Meredith*, the high court dealt harshly with a South Carolina decision in *Follett v. Town of McCormick*.[124] The *Follett* case dealt with a McCormick ordinance that exacted a license tax from a variety of occupations including that of book salesman. The defendant, another Jehovah's Witnesses evangelist, was convicted of violating the ordinance and fined fifty dollars.

The South Carolina Supreme Court upheld the conviction in *Town of McCormick v. Follett*.[125] The South Carolina court attempted to distinguish this case from its decision in *Meredith* and the federal Supreme Court's recent opinion in *Meredith*. The state court concluded that even though Mr. Follett was a Jehovah's Witnesses evangelist as was Meredith, and presumably was distributing different but similar literature to that disseminated by Meredith, and even though the material was unquestionably religious, Mr. Follett's status was significantly different from that of Meredith. He made his living by selling the books, whereas Meredith apparently reaped no material gain for himself. This placed Follett squarely within the bounds of the occupational license tax whereas Meredith, by contrast, was clearly not a commercial hawker or peddler. In addition, even though the McCormick ordinance appeared to exact the kind of flat license tax struck down in *Murdock*, it did not pose the same kind of roadblock to Follett's evangelizing as it did to the Jehovah's Witnesses preachers in *Murdock*. The *Murdock* Court had been concerned about the cumulative weight of such flat license taxes of itinerate ministers who went from town to town.[126] The South Carolina court concluded that since Follett was a local resident, not an itinerant, and would have to pay only the local tax, the fee would not pose the fiscal roadblock to his work that the aggregation of such taxes might pose to the itinerant.[127] It is interesting to note that the South Carolina court reviewed the literature and concluded that "[t]ested by the tenents [sic] of other forms of the Christian religion with which we are familiar, it is full of heresies."[128] It is impossible to tell to what degree, if any, these views influenced the Court's decision to uphold the conviction. However, they did not appear to be an integral part of the Court's rationale.

The United States Supreme Court was unimpressed with the South Carolina court's attempt to distinguish Follett's case from the *Murdock* and *Meredith* decisions. The Court observed that First Amendment free exercise protections applied to those who earned their living as evangelists as well as to those who could afford to donate their time. The Court pointedly noted that "[f]reedom of religion is not merely reserved for those with a long purse." [129] This does not mean that ministers or religious organizations can escape their fair share of the expense incurred by the operation of the government, but as the Court observed in *Murdock*, this did mean that the religious act itself could not be taxed. The *Murdock* Court stated:

> It is one thing to impose a tax on the income or property of a preacher. It is quite another thing to exact a tax from him for the privilege of delivering a sermon.[130]

The Supreme Court in *Follett* also was not persuaded by the South Carolina court's distinction between imposing a license tax on resident ministers rather than itinerant evangelists. It stated that "[a] preacher has no less a claim to that privilege when he is not an itinerant."[131] The philosophy of the United States Supreme Court in the *Follett* case was summed up in the following paragraph:

> But if this license tax would be invalid as applied to one who preaches the Gospel from the pulpit, the judgment below must be reversed. For we fail to see how such a tax loses its constitutional infirmity when exacted from those who confine themselves to their own village or town and spread their religious beliefs from door to door or on the street. The protection of First Amendment is not restricted to orthodox religious practices any more than it is to the expression of orthodox economic views. He who makes a profession of evangelism is not in a less preferred position than the casual worker.[132]

The United State Supreme Court's *Follett* opinion concluded with the observation that its decision should not be construed to mean that ". . . a preacher who preaches or a parishioner who listens . . . is free from all financial burdens of government, including taxes on income and property."[133] They, as well as other citizens, could be subjected to a generally applicable tax that did not have the impact that a flat license tax would of blocking religious expression at its inception.[134] In the 1990 case of *Jimmy Swaggart Ministries v. Board of Equalization*, the Court had an opportunity to describe the kinds of taxes to which religious organizations could be subjected without trampling upon their free exercise rights.[135] The court concluded that if the tax was a broadly applicable one that did not single out religion for special fiscal burdens, was not a flat tax that was a pre-condition upon disseminating a religious message but applied only after the completion of a sale, amounted to only a small percentage of the sales price, and did not entangle government officials with religious affairs, it might pass muster as an assessment that did not encroach upon freedom of religion. Entanglement that might invalidate a tax could consist of investigations by government agents into the religious contents of the articles sold or the continuous presence upon, or frequent inspections of, the premises of a religious organization by the tax authorities.

In addition to protecting their citizens against violence, injury to their health, disorder, interference with their freedom of movement, and fraudulent solicitations, state and local governments seek to guard the administrative efficiency and fairness of their operations against religiously inspired acts that may disrupt government operations. One area in which this government interest in the efficiency and fairness of its operations may clash with the practices of minority religions is in court administration. An especially vital interest of the judicial system is in getting the testimony of every person with information relevant to the case. The due process interest of the parties in receiving a fair trial demands as complete an airing of the facts as possible. In *State v. Bing*[136] the state court was confronted with a prison inmate who refused to testify in the trial of another prisoner who was accused of stabbing him. The witness waived his federal Fifth Amendment privilege against self-incrimination and attempted to justify his refusal to answer on free exercise of religion grounds. He argued that Islamic doctrines did not permit him to testify against another Moslem. The trial court rejected these contentions, held the witness in contempt for refusal to testify, and sentenced him to six months. The state supreme court affirmed the adjudication of contempt and the sanctions. The court observed that even if a witness holds religious beliefs which forbid him from testifying against a fellow member of his sect, this does not excuse him from his political duties as a citizen to cooperate in achieving the fair administration of justice.[137] To fortify its decision, the court cited several instances in which the judicial system's interest in conducting fair and accurate trials was sufficiently compelling to outweigh an individual's religious objections to giving evidence.

The South Carolina court noted that in the case of *In re Williams,*[138] the North Carolina Supreme Court upheld the conviction of a clergyman who refused to testify in a rape case in which members of his church were the defendant and the complainant. After the prosecutor argued that he was not asking the minister for confidential communications but only was trying to learn whether or not the pastor had gone to the defendant's house on a certain day, the defendant and other interested parties withdrew objections to the minister's testimony. However, the minister persisted in his refusal to answer, arguing that if he testified others would be discouraged from confiding in him. This would impede his ability to exercise his religious rights as a minister and would be contrary to his standards of ethics. The state supreme court sustained the trial judge's order holding the minister in contempt and committing him to jail for ten days. The court noted that the state should intrude on the free exercise of religion only to serve the most compelling interest. The fair and accurate adjudication of a criminal case in which the defendant could be sentenced to death was an interest of sufficient weight to overbalance the minister's freedom of religion objections. The court distinguished the case of a witness who was contumacious on religious grounds from *In re Jenison Contempt Proceedings*[139] in which the Minnesota Supreme Court upheld the right of a potential juror to refuse service on religious grounds. The state's interest was less compelling with regard to the juror since there were many other jurors available, whereas a witness may have information that is unique to him.

The South Carolina court in upholding the contempt citation in the *Bing* case also relied upon *Smilow v. United States*[140] in which the United States Court of Appeals rejected an attempt by a grand jury witness to overturn a contempt citation on the grounds that testimony by him would violate his religious obligations as a Jew not to be an informer. The court concluded that the grand jury had a vital interest in obtaining the testimony as part of its investigation into a firebombing that resulted in a fatality. The contempt sanction was narrowly drawn. The order did not harass or single out the witness because of his religious convictions and was no harsher than necessary to obtain the testimony.[141]

D. DENYING GOVERNMENT BENEFITS TO THE UNORTHODOX WORSHIPPER

In *Bing* and similar cases dealing with the clash between the needs of the judicial system for fair and accurate adjudication and a person's religious beliefs which dictate that he not cooperate with the system by giving testimony, the courts were dealing with one of the most compelling state interests, the integrity of the judicial process. This was not merely an internal administrative interest of the government but one upon which the due process rights of the parties depended and upon which depended the peaceful resolution of disputes by courts rather than by violence or other extra-legal means. This interest was powerful enough to outweigh incidental harm to a religious practice that was not the target of restrictive legislation but which suffered peripheral harm from a law of general applicability. When, by contrast, the state's interest focuses more on administrative convenience or fiscal integrity of the state treasury, and the harm to religion, although incidental to a generally applicable statute, is severe, and that statute is applied in a matter with a unique impact on certain religions, the courts may be more inclined to strike the balance in favor of religious freedom. This is seen in the unemployment compensation cases in which a person is denied benefits which are generally available to out of work people, and the reason for the denial is that he is unavailable for employment on a day set aside for worship by his religion. Such policies have had a uniquely harsh impact on minority religions that choose a day of worship other than Sunday, the preference of mainstream Christianity.

The seminal case in this line arose from South Carolina and resulted in the United States Supreme Court's reversal of the South Carolina court's approval of the denial of unemployment benefits to a Saturday worshipper. In the 1963 case of *Sherbert v. Verner*,[142] the South Carolina Supreme Court was confronted with the case of a Seventh Day Adventist who was fired from the textile job that she had held for thirty-five years because she was unwilling to accept a new schedule which required her to work on Saturday. Her religion dictated that she not work from sundown Friday until sundown Saturday. After her dismissal she was turned down for unemployment benefits by the state commission because her unemployment was not the result of general economic conditions or the inability of individual employers to furnish work but because she had for personal reasons made herself unavailable for employment. Thus, under the state statute, she was not entitled to benefits because she was responsible for her own unemployment. She claimed that the denial of benefits violated her rights to free exercise of religion as protected by the First and Fourteenth Amendments of the federal Constitution and Article I, section 4 (now 2), of the South Carolina Constitution of 1895. The state supreme court rejected these arguments, holding that the denial of benefits did not encroach upon her free exercise of religion since it did not forbid Saturday worship. The court stated that:

> . . . our Unemployment Compensation Act, as is hereinbefore construed, places no restriction upon the appellant's freedom of religion nor does it in any way prevent her in the exercise of her right and freedom to observe her religious beliefs in accordance with the dictates of her conscience.[143]

The court did not directly consider the fact that although Saturday worship was not forbidden by the statute, the state policy certainly made pursuing such a minority religion, choosing a day of worship other than Sunday, more expensive to pursue when generally available benefits were denied its practitioners.

The South Carolina court in *Sherbert v. Verner* also expressed concern that if it carved out an exception from the general statutory requirement that unemployment compensation beneficiaries be available for work during the hours considered acceptable by most of society, it would be creating a preference for such a religion that might constitute an establishment clause violation.[144]

Justice Bussey's dissent largely took issue with the court's conclusion that she had made herself unavailable for employment, thus rendering herself ineligible for benefits under the statute. With regard to the constitutional issues, he merely contended that the majority opinion had failed to meet them squarely.[145] The United States Supreme Court reversed, concluding that the state's unemployment compensation policy as applied to the Seventh Day Adventist constituted a significant intrusion on the right of free exercise of religion.[146]

In erecting an analytical framework upon which it could analyze the legitimacy of intrusions on the right to free exercise of religion, the Court stated that its inquiry should involve the following elements: (1) does the state action significantly burden free exercise of religion and, if so, (2) can the harm be justified by a compelling (not just a legitimate) state interest.[147] The Court expressly applied this strict scrutiny system, requiring a compelling state interest to justify even an ". . . incidental burden on the free exercise . . ." of religion as well as injuries deliberately inflicted on religious freedom.[148]

In applying the first element of this test, the Court found that there was a significant burden placed on religious freedom by the state's policy as applied to the Seventh Day Adventist. Even though the state policy did not expressly forbid Saturday worship, it placed the Seventh Day Adventist in the position of having to make a cruel choice between continuing to pursue the demands of her religion, which required Saturday as a day of rest and worship, and benefits which granted funds necessary for basic living expenses. No one should be put to such a stark choice between faith and livelihood except for the most compelling reasons.[149]

The Court noted that the state itself had recognized the unfairness of making people choose between religion and work. State law created exemptions from general employment laws to avoid such a cruel choice, but it did so only for practitioners of mainstream religions, those that chose Sunday as their day of rest and worship. The Court noted that South Carolina Code section 64-4 created an exception to the usual rule that Sunday would be observed as a day of rest that would permit textile plants, so authorized by the Commissioner of Labor, to operate on Sundays during times of national emergency. However, a provision was inserted to safeguard the rights of those conscientiously against working on Sunday. Their refusal to work on Sunday could not result in loss of seniority or any other sanction. This exemption from a general rule permitting Sunday work during national emergencies did not provide relief for those conscientiously opposed to working any other day. This seemed to undermine the force of the state supreme court's arguments that exemptions might result in the violation of the establishment clause by favoring certain religions.

Thus, not only did the South Carolina unemployment compensation policy intrude on the Seventh Day Adventist's free exercise of religion by forcing her to make the "no-win" choice between religion and benefits that provided necessary living expenses, it did so in a fashion which, when considered with other state employment laws, discriminated in favor of mainstream religions. To pass constitutional scrutiny, such a burden on free exercise must be justified by a compelling state interest. The state argued that if, indeed, the policy did intrude on free exercise of religion, it was justified by the compelling need to protect the state treasury from fraudulent unemployment compensation claims filed by people who pretended that they could not get work because available jobs conflicted with their religious day of rest. The Supreme Court noted that this argument had not been raised in the state courts and could not affect its decision. Even if the point had been properly raised, there did not appear to be any evidence to support the contention that granting unemployment benefits to Seventh Day Adventists who refused to work on Sunday would lead to a flood of fraudulent claims. If the argument had been properly raised and if it were supported by evidence, the Court concluded that the interest was still not sufficiently paramount to justify such a crippling invasion of the Seventh Day Adventist's free exercise rights. Even if the interest were considered to be a compelling one, the state should seek less harmful means of avoiding fraudulent claims than placing minority religions in the unfortunate position in which they found themselves.[150]

The United States Supreme Court made a less than convincing attempt to distinguish its decision in *Sherbert* from its holding in *Braunfeld v. Brown*[151] decided only two years earlier. Both cases involved attempts by minority religions, Orthodox Jews in *Braunfeld* and Seventh Day Adventists in *Sherbert*, both of which observed Saturday rather than Sunday as their primary day of rest and worship, to obtain exemptions from employment laws that did not forbid but made more expensive the observance of their day of rest. In *Braunfeld*, the Orthodox Jews sought an exemption from the general Sunday closing rules for stores so that they could make up for the economic loss incurred by closing on Saturday. In *Sherbert* the exemption sought by the Seventh Day Adventist was from the general rule that in order to be eligible for unemployment benefits, a person must be available for work on normal business days, including Saturday. The *Sherbert* case ruled that failure to grant the exemption violated the Seventh Day Adventist's free exercise rights, but in *Braunfeld* the Court ruled that the Sunday closing rules did not invade the Orthodox Jews' free exercise rights because they did not directly forbid Saturday worship but only prohibited Sunday store opening.

The cases would seem to involve similar economic pressures placed upon non-mainstream religions using the same day of worship. Why were the results different? In justifying the different results the Court first noted that the burdens placed on the Orthodox Jews by the Sunday closing laws were "less direct" than those placed on the Seventh Day Adventists by the unemployment compensation system in *Sherbert.*[152] However, both cases would seem to involve the same broad type of burden: forcing one to choose between his religion and his livelihood. In both instances, the religious practitioners were forced into a harsh choice. The Court then observed that the state's interest in *Sherbert* was less compelling than the government goals in *Braunfeld.*[153] One could just as easily argue the opposite: the government's interest in avoiding fraudulent unemployment compensation claims and protecting the public fisc is more important than insuring not only that everyone has a day of rest but that everyone rest on the same day. Why is avoiding a major crime such as fraud not compelling? The Court then argued that a further distinction in the two cases was that no feasible alternative to using Sunday as a uniform day of rest was available to accomplish the state's health safety goals, whereas less harmful alternatives were available in *Sherbert.*[154] The *Braunfeld* Court noted that allowing those who worshipped on Saturday the ability to choose their own day of rest would make the day of rest requirement more difficult to administer, force the state to conduct an inquisition into the sincerity of the beliefs of one who chose a day other than Sunday, and give economic advantage to those who were permitted to open on Sunday because they chose another day of rest.[155] By contrast, the Court in *Sherbert* concluded that less harmful alternatives than denial of benefits were available to accomplish the state's purpose of avoiding fraudulent, religious-based claims.[156] However, the Court gave few clues concerning what these less intrusive alternatives were. Perhaps the *Sherbert* Court should have given more consideration to overruling *Braunfeld.* However, as a practical matter overruling *Braunfeld* was unlikely because doing so would have involved the Court's disturbing the centuries-old custom of Sunday closing, a tradition so deeply entrenched that change might be more feasible by legislation. Striking down the unemployment compensation policy in *Sherbert* would not involve such a massive reworking of social mores.

The *Sherbert* Court had one more major issue to confront: does creating an exemption for Seventh Day Adventists from the requirement that those who seek unemployment benefits must be available for work on Saturday so favor that religion as to amount to a violation of the establishment clause? The Court concluded that no favoritism would result. Instead, unemployment benefits to Seventh Day Adventists who were available for employment, except for their Saturday rest and worship, would have a neutral impact since it merely would put them on a par with religions observing Sunday as their day of rest and worship, since the latter normally were not required to be available for Sunday work in order to be eligible for unemployment benefits.[157]

The *Sherbert* case set in motion a significant line of cases involving a clash between a state's interest in protecting the fiscal integrity and efficiency of its unemployment system and the rights of practitioners of minority religions who quit or were fired from jobs because their religion demanded that they refuse to work on certain days or refuse to take certain types of jobs. Until recently, the courts have required that a state which denies benefits to a person who loses his job for religious reasons prove that the denial of unemployment compensation was designed to serve a compelling state interest and was accomplished by the method that was least likely to result in significant harm to free exercise of religion. Thus, in *Thomas v. Review Board of the Indiana Employment Security Division,*[158] the Court held that the state's denial of unemployment compensation to a Jehovah's Witness who quit his position after being transferred to a job that required him to work on the production of weapons, a task that was contrary to his religious principles, violated the employee's freedom of religion. The Court held that even though the benefit denial did not directly command the employee to alter his religious practices, it created such intense economic pressure on him to change his religion that the state was required to furnish a compelling reason for injuring the employee's right to free exercise of religion. The Court stated that:

> Where the state conditions receipt of an important benefit upon conduct proscribed by a religious faith, or where it denies such a benefit because of conduct mandated by religious belief, thereby putting substantial pressure on an adherent to modify his behavior and to violate his beliefs, a burden upon religion exists. While the compulsion may be indirect,the infringement upon free exercise is nonetheless substantial.[159]

The employee's free exercise rights were not diluted by the fact that other Jehovah's Witnesses had a different view of their religion than he did and would not object to working on the production of weapons. The Court stated that ". . . the guarantee of free exercise is not limited to beliefs which are shared by all of the members of a religious sect."[160] Religious freedom is an individual as well as a group right. Any attempt by a civil court to sustain one scriptural interpretation over another in an intradenominational dispute, and label one as worthy of free exercise clause protection and the other as unworthy, would itself breach the wall of separation of church and state.

Indiana argued that the denial of benefits to one who quit his job because of conscientious objections was necessary to accomplish two compelling goals: (1) to avoid the extensive unemployment that would occur if people who resigned their jobs for personal reasons were given benefits, and (2) to avoid the necessity of an intensive inquiry into the sincerity of the employee's conscientious objections in order to detect fraudulent claims. The Court concluded that neither goal had sufficient factual support to be compelling. No evidence was presented that the grant of benefits to those with conscientious objections to certain kinds of work would result in widespread unemployment. Nor was there evidence that a detailed inquisition into the sincerity of the employee's conscientious objections would be necessary in order to distinguish genuine from spurious claims.[161] As in the *Sherbert* case, the Court in *Thomas* concluded that granting benefits to those who quit or were fired from their jobs because of religious objections to the time or nature of the work would not result in violating the establishment clause by favoring the employee's religion. Instead, the result would be a more even-handed distribution of benefits that would include practitioners of minority as well as mainstream religions.

In *Hobbie v. Unemployment Appeals Commission of Florida*[162] the Court was asked to abandon the strict scrutiny system it had adopted in *Sherbert* in favor of one that would make it easier for states to justify benefit denials. In the *Hobbie* case, the employee had been working for a jeweler for some time when she was converted to the Seventh Day Adventist religion which demanded that she cease the Saturday work which she previously had found unobjectionable. At first her immediate supervisor agreed to take her place on Saturday in exchange for the employee's agreeing to work on Sundays and evenings. When the general manager found out about the arrangement, he vetoed it and offered the employee the stark choice of either working a regular schedule, including Saturdays, or resigning. She refused to make the choice and was fired. When she applied to the state for unemployment compensation, the company intrepidly opposed her application on the grounds that she had been dismissed for misconduct on the job and thus was not qualified for benefits under state policy. The state denied the benefits and this decision was upheld by the state courts.

Florida urged the Court to abandon its strict scrutiny system under which a state was required to demonstrate that encroachments on free exercise of religion were justified by a compelling state interest and the least injurious means of accomplishing those goals were utilized by the state. Instead the state suggested that the Court adopt an analytical system that would make it easier for the state to justify its intrusion on free exercise rights. Florida argued that the Court should employ the system it had used in the 1986 case of *Bowen v. Roy*,[163] another case involving a clash between a government benefits system and an unorthodox religion, the practice of which collided with government administrative requirements. In that case an Indian family, members of the Native American Church, had refused to comply with the federal government requirement that a social security number be furnished before an applicant would be eligible for welfare benefits. The family objected to this requirement because of a belief that identifying their daughter by a number would rob her of her soul. Several members of the Supreme Court subjected the social security number requirement to the more easily met rational scrutiny system which demanded only that the government demonstrate that the policy is reasonably related (not absolutely necessary) to obtaining a legitimate (not a compelling) government goal.[164] The justices concluded that treating the governmental policy in such an indulgent, deferential manner was justified since the case dealt largely with the way in which the government ordered its own internal administrative affairs. The rule was a general, neutral requirement that was not aimed at religious practices, and it was only by an odd coincidence that the rule conflicted with anyone's religious beliefs.

Almost any government rule has the remote potential of conflicting with someone's religion, given the variety of views extant in America today. If all government programs were strictly scrutinized because of such an unintended, even unforeseeable impact on particular practitioners of unusual beliefs, the government would not be able to operate. In a sense, the social security number requirement subjected the Roys to the same harsh choice between their religious beliefs, and eligibility for benefits that might be desperately needed, that the Court had strictly scrutinized and struck down as unconstitutional in *Sherbert* and *Thomas*. However, in this case there were differences which the justices did not emphasize but may have had in mind. In the *Sherbert* and *Thomas* cases, even though the unemployment compensation requirements had not been fashioned in such a way as to intentionally harm the Seventh Day Adventists and Jehovah's Witnesses pacifists, it was reasonably foreseeable that the policies would have such an impact. In *Sherbert* in particular, it was foreseeable that Seventh Day Adventists and other Saturday worshippers would receive consistently less favorable treatment than those who believed in Sunday as a day of rest. In *Bowen v. Roy*, it was only by an odd, unforeseeable, and perhaps unique fluke that there was a clash between religion and the government's administrative requirements.

The Court in the *Hobbie* case refused to apply the deferential rational scrutiny system utilized in *Bowen v. Roy*. Only Chief Justice Burger and two other justices expressly utilized the rational scrutiny system in *Bowen v. Roy*. The Court noted that Florida put the Seventh Day Adventist to virtually the same kind of unsavory choice (between her religion and eligibility for benefits that might be essential for living expenses) as that with which South Carolina presented the unemployed Seventh Day Adventist in *Sherbert*. Such a choice, though not a direct prohibition of Saturday worship, created enough economic pressure to intrude on the employee's right to free exercise of religion. Florida tried to distinguish *Hobbie* from *Sherbert* by noting that in *Hobbie* the employee had adopted the Seventh Day Adventist religion *after* she had worked for the jeweler for some time. By converting to a religion with a day of rest and worship that she knew would clash with her employment schedule, the employee had, in a sense, deliberately provoked the clash. However, the Court rejected this argument, concluding that the free exercise clause protected the new convert from being required to choose between her religion and her livelihood just as fully as it protected long-time adherents to a faith.[165] After deciding that the Florida benefits policy significantly burdened free exercise, it concluded that the state had been no more successful in proving that the policy was essential to accomplishing a compelling interest than South Carolina had been in *Sherbert*. Also, as in *Sherbert*, it concluded that making the benefits available to Seventh Day Adventists as well as the unemployed in general would not result in the establishment of that religion by favored treatment but instead would have the neutral result of treating all alike.[166]

In the 1990 case of *Employment Division, Department of Human Resources of Oregon v. Smith*[167] the Court turned toward a strikingly different analytical approach. This case was discussed earlier in connection with state power to curb religious practices posing physical dangers. However, since *Smith* is a part of the *Sherbert* line of cases several points deserve reiteration here. In the *Smith* case the Court sustained Oregon's denial of unemployment benefits to members of the Native American Church, who were dismissed from their jobs as drug abuse counselors for a private agency because they had engaged in the sacramental use of the hallucinogenic drug peyote. In sustaining the state's benefits denial, the Court refused to employ the strict scrutiny test which required the government to demonstrate that any significant burden on free exercise was necessary to achieve a compelling state interest. This was the test employed in *Sherbert, Thomas* and *Hobbie,* all of which also involved the denial of employment benefits to members of unorthodox religions.

The Court in *Smith* reasoned that the compelling interest test was justified only when the religious practice was the direct target of the government regulation. When a religious practice was not directly prohibited or altered by a government regulation but only received incidental injury as the result of a generally applicable, neutral government rule, strict scrutiny was necessary only when other rights such as freedom of speech or the right of parents to control the upbringing of their children, were injured as well. This distinction between direct harms to religion, in which the religious practice is the target of the regulation, and incidental harms to free exercise flowing from generally applicable regulations is not borne out by the earlier cases such as *Sherbert* in which incidental burdens, if significant enough, could trigger strict scrutiny.[168] The *Smith* analysis also seems to denigrate free exercise of religion rights by deeming them important enough to be protected by strict scrutiny only when they are injured in the company of other rights, or subjected to frontal assault by the government. As noted earlier in this work, it was probably unnecessary to shift analytical systems to justify denying benefits to the peyote users in *Smith*. A strong argument could be made that the state government has a compelling interest in denying benefits to those who were dismissed for acts that were not only criminal but posed serious physical dangers to the user. On this basis the *Smith* case was factually distinguishable from the *Sherbert* and *Hobbie* cases which involved people who had done nothing more reprehensible than seeking to worship and rest on Saturday.

Perhaps *Smith* can be best understood alongside *Lyng v. Northwest Indian Cemetery Protective Association*,[169] which failed to find free exercise clause analysis triggered at all by a federal government decision to permit construction of a logging road through a forest preserve that had been used by Indians for centuries as a site at which they sought spiritual understanding. Since the Indians were not barred from the land and the area was only rendered slightly less tranquil, their religious practice was not directly prohibited. Perhaps the most telling point was the fact that the government owned the land. It could use its land as it saw fit. Free exercise of religion means that the government should not coerce or forbid a religious practice. It does not mean that the government has to provide the wherewithal for the practice of the religion. Similarly, a benefits program is, in a way, government property that can be doled out on whatever conditions the government likes. If members of a religion are denied benefits not because their religion is the target of the regulation, but because of an incidental clash with government policy, it may be argued that the result is well within the government's discretion to decide what to do with its property (benefits program). It is not yet clear whether or not that reasoning is an unarticulated major premise of *Smith*. If it is, it fails to recognize that although a government may be under no obligation to initiate a benefits program, once it does so it should administer the program even-handedly or it will be viewed as favoring some religions over others, thus risking an establishment clause violation.

The *Smith* Court did not require Oregon to grant an exemption from its drug regulations for the sacramental use of peyote. However, it did hint that it might be permissible for legislatures to grant such exemptions. This was a matter for the political process rather than constitutional adjudication. However, the crucial question is--should free exercise of religion rights be made to depend on the fickle whim of the political process?

Does this mean that the South Carolina General Assembly now could reimpose the requirement that unemployment compensation beneficiaries be available for work on Saturday, the rule that was struck down in *Sherbert* as applied to Seventh Day Adventists? Considered in its broadest sweep, the *Smith* Court's reasoning might suggest that. However, for now the *Sherbert* line of cases seems to be a relatively secure enclave when the reason for the state's denial of benefits was relatively innocuous religious conduct, rather than that having the criminal overtones of the drug use in *Smith.*

SUMMARY

At the close of this examination of South Carolina treatment of unorthodox or minority religions let us in review ask what types of religious conduct do we find most likely to be subject to constitutionally valid regulation and what responsibility have the courts assumed to protect the practice of unorthodox religions? In *Bell v. Graham* and *Magee v. O'Neil* courts displayed some degree of protective instinct toward minority religions when the practice did not pose an immediate physical danger. In *Bell* the court interpreted the law against disturbing religious worship services to afford protection to the head of a racially mixed, slave-freeman congregation, when he was sued for malicious prosecution by an "agent" of the slave patrol against whom he had brought charges of disrupting a service. In *Magee* the court sustained the right of a Catholic testator to propagate his religion by imposing a Catholic education condition on the receipt of a devise by his granddaughter.

The courts are most likely to approve state regulation of a religious practice when it poses a physical danger. An example of this is seen in the *Department of Social Services v. Father and Mother,* in which the court sustained sanctions against parents whose literal interpretations of certain scriptural passages led them to punish a daughter so severely that it became child abuse. Noisy, disruptive worship that interferes significantly with the rights of others may also be subject to regulation. In *Morison v. Rawlinson,* the court refused to enjoin city authorities from enforcing public nuisance laws against a church with such long and boisterous worship that it disturbed the sleep of surrounding residents and attracted a crowd that overflowed into the streets, making use of the streets by others difficult.

Religious beliefs may not form the basis of refusal to perform vital civil duties when the need for those services outweighs the harm to religion. Thus, in the *Bing* case the court insisted on a person's testimony in a criminal case, despite his religious objections to giving such testimony, when failure to receive the testimony could affect the fairness and accuracy of the adjudicative process and harm the rights of others.

When speech is merely offensive it is not subject to regulation. In *City of Gaffney v. Putnam,* the court refused to sustain punishment of offensive speech that did not create a clear and present danger of violence and did not interfere significantly with the rights of others, such as the ability to use the streets freely. When a religious practice does not cause physical harm or involve conduct that legitimately has been made criminal, it should not form the basis of the denial of benefits available to the general population. This is demonstrated by the United States Supreme Court's reversal of the state court decision in *Sherbert v. Verner* in which the state court had approved denial of unemployment benefits to a Seventh Day Adventist who refused to work on Saturday. Forcing a person to choose between her religion and eligibility for benefits that may be essential for her livelihood significantly burdens religious freedom and can be justified only if the state shows that the benefits denial was essential to accomplishing a significant state purpose. The United States Supreme Court decision in *Smith* has created an atmosphere of watchful waiting to see whether or not the strict protection of religious freedom is being abandoned or narrowed in its application.

CHAPTER EIGHT—NOTES

The tell-tale stain of government coercion, or the denial to practitioners of some religions of benefits available to the general population, has marked government action struck down as violative of the free exercise clause. However, more subtle government offenses do not escape the net of constitutional censure. The establishment clause has been applied to invalidate some government actions that endorse particular religions or religions in general. The most controversial applications of this approach have concerned religion in the public schools. These issues are discussed in the next chapter.

NOTES

1. Bell v. Graham, 10 S.C.L. (1 Nott. & McC.) 278 (1818).

2. *Bell*, 10 S.C.L. (1 Nott. & McC.) at 281.

3. *See* FUNDAMENTAL CONST. OF CAROLINA OF 1669, arts. 93 and 98 in M. PARKER, NORTH CAROLINA CHARTERS AND CONSTITUTIONS 150 (1963).

4. For other cases interpreting the laws prohibiting the disturbance of worship, *see* State v. Jones, 77 S.C. 385, 58 S.E. 8 (1907) (applying the law against such disturbances to a riot occurring not at the immediate site of the service but within forty feet of it); *and see* State v. Matheny, 122 S.C. 459, 101 S.E. 661 (1919) (court interpreted the laws against disturbing religious worship as protecting a congregation in at least three phases of its activities: (1) gathering for the service, (2) the service itself, and (3) when the congregation was dispersing after the service. Thus the congregation in the *Matheny* case was protected during a period of time when it had concluded its regular service, had left the sanctuary but was still on church property and proceeding to a nearby creek for baptismal service).

5. D. MALONE, THE PUBLIC LIFE OF THOMAS COOPER (1961).

6. D. MALONE, THE PUBLIC LIFE OF THOMAS COOPER 337-67 (1961).

7. D. MALONE, THE PUBLIC LIFE OF THOMAS COOPER 340-42 (1961).

8. D. MALONE, THE PUBLIC LIFE OF THOMAS COOPER 342 (1961).

9. *Id.*

10. D. MALONE, THE PUBLIC LIFE OF THOMAS COOPER 348 (1961).

11. D. MALONE, THE PUBLIC LIFE OF THOMAS COOPER 348-51 (1961).

12. D. MALONE, THE PUBLIC LIFE OF THOMAS COOPER 356 (1961) (summarizing the charges against Cooper).

13. D. MALONE, THE PUBLIC LIFE OF THOMAS COOPER 352-55 (1961).

14. The Case of Thomas Cooper, MD, President of South Carolina College, submitted to the Legislature and the People of South Carolina December 1831 (available in the South Caroliniana Library, University of South Carolina, in 1839 printed version) [hereinafter cited as *The Case of Thomas Cooper*].

15. *The Case of Thomas Cooper* at 2-3.

16. *The Case of Thomas Cooper* at 11-13.

17. S.C. CONST. OF 1790, art. VIII, § 1.

18. *The Case of Thomas Cooper* at 4-5.

19. *The Case of Thomas Cooper* at 5.

20. D. MALONE, THE PUBLIC LIFE OF THOMAS COOPER 359-60 (1961).

21. D. MALONE, THE PUBLIC LIFE OF THOMAS COOPER 360 (1961).

22. D. MALONE, THE PUBLIC LIFE OF THOMAS COOPER 361-62 (1961). For a useful account of the Cooper controversy in the legislature and in the trustee's hearing *see* D. HOLLIS, UNIVERSITY OF SOUTH CAROLINA, VOLUME I, SOUTH CAROLINA COLLEGE pp. 106-118 (1951).

CHAPTER EIGHT—NOTES

23. Magee v. O'Neill, 19 S.C. (Shand) 170 (1883).

24. *Magee*, 19 S.C. (Shand) at 175-77.

25. 19 S.C. (Shand) at 186.

26. 19 S.C. (Shand) at 186-87.

27. 19 S.C. (Shand) at 187.

28. 19 S.C. (Shand) at 187-88.

29. *See* Estate of Thornton v. Caldor, Inc., 472 U.S. 703, 711-12, 105 S. Ct. 2914, 2918-19, 86 L. Ed. 2d 557, 564 (1985) (O'Connor, J., concurring).

30. *See* S.C. CONST. OF 1895, art. 1, § 4 (now § 2).

31. Reynolds v. United States, 98 U.S. 145, 25 L. Ed. 244 (1878).

32. Davis v. Beason, 133 U.S. 333, 10 S. Ct. 299, 33 L. Ed. 637 (1890).

33. *Reynolds*, 98 U.S. at 165-66.

34. *Reynolds*, 98 U.S. at 166.

35. *See* J. NOWAK, R. ROTUNDA, and J. YOUNG, CONSTITUTIONAL LAW 1083-85 (3rd ed. 1986).

36. Opinion of the Attorney General of South Carolina October 7, 1919 pp. 76-77.

37. Jacobson v. Massachusetts, 197 U.S. 11, 25 S. Ct. 358, 49 L. Ed. 643 (1905).

38. 197 U.S. at 22.

39. 197 U.S. at 30.

40. 197 U.S. at 31.

41. *Jacobson*, 197 U.S. 38.

42. Zucht v. King, 260 U.S. 174, 43 S. Ct. 24, 67 L. Ed. 194 (1922).

43. Cantwell v. Connecticut, 310 U.S. 296, 303, 60 S. Ct. 900, 903, 84 L. Ed. 1213, 1217-18 (1940).

44. Prince v. Massachusetts, 321 U.S. 158, 64 S. Ct. 438, 88 L. Ed. 645 (1944).

45. 321 U.S. at 166-67.

46. 321 U.S. at 170.

47. West Virginia Bd. of Educ. v. Barnette, 319 U.S. 624, 639, 63 S. Ct. 1178, 1186, 87 L. Ed. 1628, 1638 (1943).

48. Wright v. DeWitt School Dist. No. 1 of Arkansas County, 238 Ark. 906, 385 S.W.2d 644 (1965).

49. 238 Ark. at 908-09, 385 S.W.2d at 646; *see also* Bd. of Educ. of Mountain Lakes v. Massachusetts, 56 N.J. Super. 245, 152 A.2d 394 (Super. Ct. App. Div. 1959), *aff'd*, 31 N.J. 537, 158 A.2d 330 (1960); *but see* Vonegut v. Baun, 206 Ind. 172, 188 N.E. 677 (1934) (partly predicated approval of a compulsory vaccination program on the decision of the city board of health that an epidemic was in progress).

50. McCartney v. Austin, 293 N.Y.S.2d 188 (Sup. Ct. 1968), *aff'd*, 298 N.Y.S.2d 26 (App. Div. 1969).

51. 293 N.Y.S.2d at 200.

52. Presbyterian Church v. Mary Elizabeth Blue Hull Memorial Presbyterian Church, 393 U.S. 440, 89 S. Ct. 601, 21 L. Ed. 2d 658 (1969).

53. Sherr v. Northport-East Northport Union Free School Dist., 672 F. Supp. 81 (E.D.N.Y. 1987).

54. *See also* Dalli v. Bd. of Educ., 358 Mass. 753, 267 N.E.2d 219 (1971).

55. 1948 Opinion of the Attorney General of South Carolina, July 21, 1948 at 204 (emphasis in original).

56. Lawson v. Commonwealth of Kentucky, 291 Ky. 437, 164 S.W.2d 972 (1942).

57. KY. CONST. § 5.

58. *Lawson*, 291 Ky. at 439, 164 S.W.2d at 974.

59. Harden v. State, 188 Tenn. 17, 216 S.W.2d 708 (1948).

60. *See also* State v. Massey, 229 N.C. 734, 51 S.E.2d 179 (1949) *appeal dismissed sub nom.* Bunn v. North Carolina, 336 U.S. 942, 69 S. Ct. 813, 93 L. Ed. 1099 (1949).

61. South Carolina Dept. of Social Serv. v. Father and Mother, 294 S.C. 518, 366 S.E.2d 40 (1988).

62. Proverbs 23:13 (emphasis in case).

63. South Carolina Dept. of Social Serv. v. Father and Mother, 294 S.C. at 523, 366 S.E.2d at 43.

64. United States v. Middleton, 690 F.2d 820 (11th Cir. 1982), *cert. denied,* 460 U.S. 1051, 103 S. Ct. 1497, 75 L. Ed. 2d 929 (1983).

65. Lewellyn v. Oklahoma, 489 P.2d 511 (1971).

66. 489 P.2d at 515.

67. 489 P.2d at 516.

68. 489 P.2d at 516.

69. *See* State v. Bullard, 267 N.C. 599, 148 S.E.2d 565 (1966), *cert. denied,* 386 U.S. 917, 87 S. Ct. 876, 17 L. Ed. 2d 789 (1967); State v. Big Sheep, 75 Mont. 219, 239-40, 243 P. 1067, 1073 (1926); *and see* Leary v. United States, 383 F.2d 851 (5th Cir. 1967), *rev'd on other grounds,* 395 U.S. 6, 89 S. Ct. 1532, 23 L. Ed. 2d 57 (1969), *appeal after remand,* 431 F.2d 85 (5th Cir. 1970), *appeal after remand,* 544 F.2d 1266 (5th Cir. 1977), *reh'g denied,* 548 F.2d 355 (5th Cir. 1977).

70. People v. Woody, 61 Cal. 2d 716, 394 P.2d 813, 40 Cal. Rptr. 69 (1964).

71. Employment Div., Dep't of Human Resources of Oregon v. Smith, 494 U.S. 872, 110 S. Ct. 1595, 108 L. Ed. 2d 876 (1990).

72. *See* J. NOWAK, R. ROTUNDA & J. YOUNG, CONSTITUTIONAL LAW 1084-85 (3rd ed. 1986).

73. *Smith,* 494 U.S. at _____, 110 S. Ct. at 1606-15 (O'Connor, J., concurring).

74. *See also Smith,* 494 U.S. at _____, 110 S. Ct. at 1615-23 (Blackmun, J., dissenting).

75. Cantwell v. Connecticut, 310 U.S. 296, 60 S. Ct. 900, 84 L. Ed. 1213 (1940).

76. State v. Langston, 195 S.C. 190, 11 S.E.2d 1 (1940), *cert. denied*, 311 U.S. 685, 61 S. Ct. 59, 85 L. Ed. 442 (1940).

77. 195 S.C. at 192-93, 11 S.E.2d at 2.

78. 195 S.C. at 193, 11 S.E.2d at 2.

79. Edwards v. South Carolina, 372 U.S. 229, 83 S. Ct. 680, 9 L. Ed. 2d 697 (1963).

80. 372 U.S. at 237.

81. Ward v. Rock Against Racism, 491 U.S. 781, 109 S. Ct. 2746, 105 L. Ed. 2d 661 (1989).

82. Morison v. Rawlinson, 193 S.C. 25, 7 S.E.2d 635 (1940).

83. *Morison*, 193 S.C. at 31, 7 S.E.2d at 638.

84. 193 S.C. at 31, 7 S.E.2d at 638.

85. 193 S.C. at 33-35, 7 S.E.2d at 639.

86. 193 S.C. at 36, 7 S.E.2d at 640.

87. 193 S.C. at 36, 7 S.E.2d at 640.

88. 193 S.C. at 36, 7 S.E.2d at 640.

89. 193 S.C. at 37, 7 S.E.2d at 640.

90. For a discussion of the *Langston* and *Morison* cases, *see* Herbert, *Freedom of Religion and Breach of the Peace*, IV SELDEN SOC'Y YEARBOOK PART II 60 (1940).

91. *Cantwell*, 310 U.S. 296, 60 S. Ct. 900, 84 L. Ed. 1213 (1940).

92. 310 U.S. at 303.

93. City of Gaffney v. Putnam, 197 S.C. 237, 15 S.E.2d 130 (1941).

94. *Cantwell*, 310 U.S. at 309.

95. *Cantwell*, 310 U.S. at 309.

96. *Cantwell,* 310 U.S. at 307-07.

97. *See* Near v. Minnesota *ex rel.* Olson, 283 U.S. 697, 51 S. Ct. 625, 75 L. Ed. 1357 (1931). For post *Cantwell* prior restraint cases *see* New York Times Co. v. United States, 403 U.S. 713, 91 S. Ct. 2140, 29 L. Ed. 2d 822 (1971); Organization for a Better Austin v. Keefe, 402 U.S. 415, 91 S. Ct. 1575, 29 L. Ed. 2d 1 (1971); and Nebraska Press Ass'n v. Stuart, 427 U.S. 539, 96 S. Ct. 2791, 49 L. Ed. 2d 683 (1976).

98. *Cantwell,* 310 U.S. at 308.

99. 310 U.S. at 305-07.

100. 310 U.S. at 307.

101. 310 U.S. at 308.

102. 310 U.S. at 308.

103. 310 U.S. at 309. *See also* Brandenburg v. Ohio, 395 U.S. 444, 89 S. Ct. 1827, 23 L. Ed. 2d 430 (1969) for a discussion of the incitement to violence doctrine which emphasizes that mere intellectual advocacy of violence is not enough to trigger state regulatory authority. The speaker must urge immediate violent action before an audience likely to act upon his words.

104. 310 U.S. at 309.

105. 310 U.S. at 309.

106. 310 U.S. at 310.

107. Chaplinsky v. New Hampshire, 315 U.S. 568, 574, 62 S. Ct. 766, 770, 86 L. Ed. 1031, 1036 (1942).

108. Texas v. Johnson, 491 U.S. 397, 109 S. Ct. 2533, 105 L. Ed. 2d 342 (1989).

109. 491 U.S. at 409, 109 S. Ct. at 2542.

110. For a United States Supreme Court discussion of these concepts in a South Carolina setting, *see generally* Edwards v. South Carolina, 372 U.S. 229, 83 S. Ct. 680, 9 L. Ed. 2d 697 (1963).

111. City of Gaffney v. Putnam, 197 S.C. 237, 15 S.E.2d 130 (1941).

112. 197 S.C. 237, 15 S.E.2d 130.

113. 197 S.C. at 240-41, 15 S.E.2d at 130-31.

114. 197 S.C. at 242, 15 S.E.2d at 131.

115. 197 S.C. at 242, 15 S.E.2d at 131.

116. State v. Meredith, 197 S.C. 351, 15 S.E.2d 678 (1941).

117. *Meredith,* 197 S.C. at 355, 15 S.E.2d at 679. For a discussion of establishment clause problems that can arise if religious publications are favored by an exemption from state tax or regulatory measures with which other publications must comply, *see* Texas Monthly Inc. v. Bullock, 489 U.S. 1, 109 S. Ct. 890, 103 L. Ed. 2d 1 (1989).

118. Lovell v. City of Griffin, 303 U.S. 444, 58 S. Ct. 666, 82 L. Ed. 949 (1938).

119. Murdock v. Pennsylvania, 319 U.S. 105, 112, 63 S. Ct. 870, 874, 87 L. Ed. 1292, 1298 (1943).

120. *Murdock,* 319 U.S. at 112.

121. 319 U.S. at 112-17.

122. 319 U.S. at 111.

123. 319 U.S. at 115.

124. Follett v. Town of McCormick, 321 U.S. 573, 64 S. Ct. 717, 88 L. Ed. 938 (1944).

125. Town of McCormick v. Follett, 204 S.C. 337, 29 S.E.2d 539 (1943), *rev'd,* 321 U.S. 573, 64 S. Ct. 717, 88 L. Ed. 938 (1944).

126. *Murdock,* 319 U.S. at 115.

127. *Follett,* 204 S.C. at 345.

128. 204 S.C. at 342, 29 S.E.2d at 540.

129. *Follett,* 321 U.S. at 576.

130. *Murdock,* 319 U.S. at 112.

131. *Follett,* 321 U.S. at 577.

132. 321 U.S. at 577.

133. 321 U.S. 577-78.

134. 321 U.S. at 578.

135. Jimmy Swaggart Ministries v. Bd. of Equalization, 493 U.S. 378, 110 S. Ct. 688, 107 L. Ed. 2d 796 (1990).

136. State v. Bing, 272 S.C. 544, 253 S.E.2d 101 (1979)..

137. 272 S.C. at 546, 253 S.E.2d at 102.

138. *In re* Williams, 269 N.C. 68, 152 S.E.2d 317 (1967).

139. *In re* Jenison, 265 Minn. 96, 120 N.W.2d 515 (1963), *vacated* 375 U.S. 14, 84 S. Ct. 63, 11 L. Ed. 2d 39 (1963), *remanded to* 267 Minn. 136, 125 N.W.2d 588 (1963).

140. Smilow v. United States, 465 F.2d 802 (2nd Cir. 1972), *vacated on other grounds,* 409 U.S. 944, 93 S. Ct. 268, 34 L. Ed. 2d 215 (1972), *remanded and decided on other grounds,* 472 F.2d 1193 (2nd Cir. 1973).

141. *See also* United States v. Fisher, 571 F. Supp. 1236 (S.D.N.Y. 1983), *cert. denied,* 474 U.S. 819, 106 S. Ct. 66, 88 L. Ed. 2d 54 (1985) which refused the request of a criminal case defendant of the Moslem faith who argued that the trial not be conducted on Fridays, a day on which he made religious devotions. The court concluded that the judicial system had a compelling interest in having that complex, lengthy, multi-defendant trial meet five days a week to avoid delaying justice for everyone. These judicial-efficiency-speedy-justice interests outweighed the defendant's somewhat belatedly raised religious objections to Friday sessions.

142. Sherbert v. Verner, 240 S.C. 286, 125 S.E.2d 737 (1962), *rev'd,* 374 U.S. 398, 83 S. Ct. 1790, 10 L. Ed. 2d 965 (1963).

143. 240 S.C. at 303-04, 125 S.E.2d at 746.

144. 240 S.C. at 304, 125 S.E.2d at 746.

145. 240 S.C. at 304-17, 125 S.E.2d at 746-53 (Bussey, J., dissenting).

146. Sherbert v. Verner, 374 U.S. 398, 83 S. Ct. 1790, 10 L. Ed. 2d 965 (1963).

147. 374 U.S. at 402-03.

148. 374 U.S. at 403.

149. 374 U.S. at 406-07.

150. 374 U.S. at 407.

151. Braunfeld v. Brown, 366 U.S. 599, 81 S. Ct. 1144, 6 L. Ed. 2d 563 (1961).

152. *Sherbert*, 374 U.S. at 408.

153. 374 U.S. at 408.

154. 374 U.S. at 408-09.

155. *Braunfeld*, 366 U.S. at 608-09.

156. *Sherbert*, 374 U.S. at 407.

157. 374 U.S. at 409-10.

158. Thomas v. Review Bd. Indiana Employment Sec. Div., 450 U.S. 707, 101 S. Ct. 1425, 67 L. Ed. 2d 624 (1981).

159. 450 U.S. at 717-18.

160. 450 U.S. at 715-16.

161. 450 U.S. at 718-19.

162. Hobbie v. Unemployment Appeals Comm'n of Florida, 480 U.S. 136, 107 S. Ct. 1046, 94 L. Ed. 2d 190 (1987).

163. Bowen v. Roy, 476 U.S. 693, 106 S. Ct. 2147, 90 L. Ed. 2d 735 (1986).

164. 476 U.S. at 708-09. This portion of Chief Justice Burger's opinion was joined by Justices Powell and Rehnquist.

165. *Hobbie,* 480 U.S. at 144.

166. *Hobbie,* 480 U.S. at 144-145.

167. Employment Div., Dept. of Human Resources of Oregon v. Smith, 494 U.S. 872, 110 S. Ct. 1595, 108 L. Ed. 2d 876 (1990).

168. *Sherbert,* 374 U.S. at 403. *See also Thomas,* 450 U.S. at 717-18, and *Hobbie,* 480 U.S. at 140-42.

169. Lyng v. Northwest Cemetery Protective Ass'n, 485 U.S. 439, 108 S. Ct. 1319, 99 L. Ed. 2d 534 (1988).

CHAPTER NINE

NON-COERCIVE VIOLATIONS OF THE RELIGIOUS CLAUSES AND THE DEBATE OVER RELIGION IN THE PUBLIC SCHOOLS

The popular conception is that only coercion by which the government forces one to engage in a practice obnoxious to his religion, or by which it forces him to cease a practice that is a part of his religion, are violative of First Amendment guarantees or comparable state constitutional standards. This view fails to recognize that there are two religious clauses in the First Amendment: the establishment clause which prohibits government action respecting the establishment of religion and the free exercise clause which forbids government interference with freedom of religious beliefs and actions inspired by such beliefs. Article I, section 2, of the South Carolina Constitution also has both a free exercise and an establishment clause. The essence of the free exercise clause protection is the guarantee it provides against a government's interference with religious practices either by physical force or intense economic or physical pressure. By contrast, the establishment clause can be violated by non-coercive government action that deviates from government neutrality toward religion either by (1) state ideological endorsement of a particular religion, or of religion in general or of attitudes hostile to religion; (2)

government fiscal support of religious activities; or (3) the intermixture of secular and ecclesiastical power.[1] No line of cases more clearly demonstrates the principle that government action devoid of overt coercion, but which creates social pressure encouraging religious conformity, can violate constitutional standards than that involving religious recitations in public schools.

Since most of the population considers the public school system to be an instrument for transmitting traditional values, there has been considerable pressure to instill moral values not merely by secular instruction in ethics but also by religious observances including school prayer. Since this is a nation composed of people with a large variety of religious traditions, religion in the schools poses complex problems. Would religious observances in tax-supported schools amount to taking one person's money to support instruction in another's religion? Does it give secular authorities impermissible power over religious training, or does it give religious authorities dominating influence in secular instruction? In a state utilizing compulsory school attendance laws, do religious observances in the public schools, even when a pupil may choose not to participate, create too much pressure toward religious conformity, even if it does not become intense enough to violate the free exercise clause? Does it create a divisive, religiously partisan element that harms the learning atmosphere for a student body that grows increasingly varied in background and tradition? By contrast, others may ask — is there any sound way to transmit moral values without religious instruction or observance? Does ethical instruction lose its moral imperative if it is devoid of religious foundation? This query in turn provokes the further question that if public schools do provide religious instruction or observances, will they have to be so watered down and all-embracing to avoid offending some segments of the student body that the result will be a tasteless moral pablum?

The United States Supreme Court began to confront these questions in *Illinois ex rel. McCollum v. Board of Education.*[2] In that case, the Court struck down a program in which public school classrooms were turned over to private religious instructors during the school day so that they could teach religion to students who chose to attend their classes. Students who did not participate in the religious instruction stayed in the school building as directed by the compulsory school attendance laws and did other work. Providing public school classroom space for religious instruction amounted to a form of government financial support of religious instruction since the schools were built with tax-raised funds. Even though an effort was made to provide a variety of instructors, and not to endorse a particular denomination, the program still encouraged a form of religious orthodoxy even though it was a multi-hued orthodoxy. Even though the students were not forced to participate, they were at least brought to the brink of participation by being required to remain in the building under the compulsory school attendance laws. This was high pressured, intense endorsement by the government of participation in religious training. The school board sought to justify the religious instruction program by arguing that the establishment clause was directed only at government actions that preferred a particular sect. Since its religious instruction system included Protestant, Catholic and Jewish teachers, it should escape establishment clause censure. The Court rejected this argument, concluding that the First Amendment forbade government endorsement and fiscal sponsorship of general ecumenical religious instruction as surely as it did proselytizing for a particular faith.[3] The Court reaffirmed its belief that the Fourteenth Amendment applied the First Amendment religious clauses to the state and local governments as well as the federal government.[4]

In *Zorach v. Clauson*[5] the Supreme Court upheld a New York religious instruction program that had been structured in such a manner as to avoid government financial support or ideological endorsement of religion as well as to remove the danger of a free exercise clause violation that would arise from coercing student participation. Under this program students whose parents so desired were released for a short period during the school day to attend religious instruction at privately operated, off-campus centers. Since neither government funds nor buildings constructed with tax-raised funds were used, the evil of government fiscal support of religion was absent. Since the program created a form of free market choice under which the students and their parents could choose that they remain in school or receive religious instruction, and if they opted for religious instruction, they could choose what form that would take, the government was not endorsing religion. It was merely accommodating religion by altering its schedule in such a manner as to facilitate free exercise of individual beliefs.[6] Separation of church and state does not require the government to be hostile to religion. However, the *Zorach* case raised troubling questions. Was there not at least some degree of endorsement and financial support present in the use of the school system's administrative machinery to insure that those students who were released to attend religious instruction did in fact do so? Had the schools thereby become truant officers for the religious instructors? Was there endorsement of religion present since the students were not given released time for constructive secular programs and thus they had to choose between staying in school or attending religious instruction? The Court concluded that the program was one that merely expanded personal choice rather than one that nudged the students in the direction of religious study.

After *Zorach* came *Engel v. Vitale*,[7] the famous school prayer case that most clearly illustrates the principle that establishment clause violations, unlike free exercise clause transgressions, do not require government coercion. In the *Engel* case, a local school board in New York, on recommendation of the State Board of Regents, adopted a directive that each school principal should cause a prayer, composed by the Regents, to be recited daily in each classroom. The prayer stated:

> Almighty God, we acknowledge our dependence upon Thee, and we beg Thy blessings upon us, our parents, our teachers and our Country.[8]

State authorities provided that students whose parents objected to their participation in the recitation could opt out of the exercise.[9] The wording of the prayer is obviously designed to offend as few people as possible and to not endorse a particular sect but to represent a consensus view of the Judeo-Christian mainstream ethic. Neither its non-coercive nature nor its ecumenical quality saved the rite in the Court's view. The Court stated that:

> Neither the fact that the prayer may be denominationally neutral nor the fact that its observance on the part of the students is voluntary can serve to free it from the limitations of the Establishment Clause, as it might from the Free Exercise Clause, of the First Amendment, both of which are operative against the States by virtue of the Fourteenth Amendment.
>
> . . . .

> The Establishment Clause, unlike the Free Exercise Clause, does not depend upon any showing of direct governmental compulsion and is violated by the enactment of laws which establish an official religion whether those laws operate directly to coerce nonobserving individuals or not.[10]

Why was government ideological endorsement of a prayer, even one as generalized as that composed by the Regents, violative of the establishment clause, when the recitation was not coerced? The Court concluded that one of the evils at which the establishment clause was directed was the attitude of ". . . hatred, disrespect and even contempt . . ." that would be directed at those with nonconforming beliefs when the government placed its imprimatur of support behind certain religious beliefs.[11] Acceptance of the government-approved religious beliefs would be considered a necessary attribute of patriotism. Those who disagree would not be merely religious dissenters but traitors as well.

Justice Douglas in his concurring opinion found that the Regent's prayer program violated the establishment clause for another reason in addition to its endorsement of certain religious views. It provided government financial support for religion. This may seem to be an odd conclusion since no large appropriation was provided specifically for the composition and recitation of the prayer. However, the recitation was led by state paid teachers in school rooms constructed with government funds. Douglas admitted that the recitation of the short prayer would utilize only a minuscule part of the teachers' salaries and the funds allocated to erect the school building. However, the principle that the establishment clause forbade government financial support of religion was the same whether the amount of money involved was great or small.[12] In addition, he saw at least the ghost of a free exercise clause violation. The voluntary nature of the prayer was somewhat illusory. Even though it was technically possible for a student to be excused from the observance, few would risk the social ostracism that might result from leaving the room during recitation of the prayer.[13]

Quickly following upon the heels of the *Engel* case was *Abington School District v. Schempp*,[14] colloquially known as the *Bible Reading Cases*. These cases dealt with public school religious observance programs adopted by Pennsylvania and Maryland that involved beginning the school day by the reading of Bible verses followed by the recitation of the Lord's Prayer. Students whose parents objected to their participation in the exercise were excused. These programs were more democratic than the scheme used in *Engel*. Students participated in the selection of the verses to be read. A variety of Bible translations was used. The prayer used was not composed by public officials but was taken from the Bible. Despite this somewhat more free-spirited approach, the Court concluded that the programs violated the establishment clause.

In reaching these conclusions, the Court began to develop a more refined analytical framework for determining establishment clause violations. What was needed were analytical tools by which the presence of the three evils against which the establishment clause was directed (government ideological endorsement of religious or anti-religious views, government fiscal sponsorship of religion, and intermixture of religious and secular power) could be detected. The *Bible Reading Cases* spawned two such devices, the first two prongs of what is now known as the three-part *Lemon v. Kurtzman* test.[15] The Court in the *Bible Reading Cases* concluded that an establishment clause violation occurred if the government action was taken pursuant to a purpose of advancing or inhibiting religion, or, even if such an impermissible purpose were absent, a violation still could occur if the primary effect of the government's action was to advance or inhibit religion. Later the Court added a third detection tool that indicated that an establishment clause violation occurred if the government's action led to excessive entanglement between government and religion. This entanglement could take the form of administrative entanglement by which government bureaucrats conducted surveillance of the practices of religious institutions or interfered with their decision-making process. It could also take the form of political entanglement in which various religions competed for larger shares of the government financial pie by injecting religious issues into political campaigns.[16] These detection devices are correlates of the evils of ideological endorsement, financial sponsorship and intermixture of government and religion. Where a purpose or effect of advancing religion is found there is also likely to be government fiscal aid, ideological approval or church-state power sharing.

In the *Bible Reading Cases*, the Court found that the Pennsylvania program had an impermissible purpose of advancing religion and the Maryland plan had a primary effect of advancing religion.[17] Pennsylvania's purpose of advancing religion is seen in (1) the inclusion of the

Bible reading as part of the curriculum, (2) the participation of state-paid teachers in planning and execution of the exercise, and (3) holding the exercise on premises paid for by tax-raised funds.[18] Maryland was more subtle. It claimed that its goals were more secular. It sought to teach moral values (a goal important to any civilized society) and appreciation of good literature, of which the Bible was certainly a good example.[19] However, the Court concluded that even if the state's goals were genuinely secular, the program had a primary effect of advancing religion since it sought to achieve those goals through religious means when secular means were readily available.[20] Why single out the Bible as an example of good literature by making it the only work read aloud daily to the entire student body when other examples of good literature also were available?

The Court hastened to add that it was not banishing the Bible from the school system. That great work can occupy a legitimate place in the education system. The Court stated:

> Nothing we have said here indicates that such study of the Bible or of religion, when presented objectively as part of a secular program of education, may not be effected consistently with the First Amendment. But the exercises here do not fall into those categories. They are religious exercises, required by the States in violation of the command of the First Amendment that the Government maintain strict neutrality, neither aiding nor opposing religion.[21]

Thus study of the Bible could form a part of a comparative religion or literature course. In such a milieu, it would not be the subject of worship; it would not be the tool of proselytization. It would not be recommended as the sole fountainhead of truth. It would be studied in comparison to other religious and secular sources. Religion has been a major force in the history of this country as well as the rest of the world. Presumably, the *Bible Reading Cases* would permit the study of the impact of religion on history so long as it was approached in an objective, non-evangelizing manner.

The reaction to the *Engel* and *Bible Reading Cases* in South Carolina was varied but largely critical. Criticism of the first decision, *Engel*, was especially vehement. In Charleston, an editorial in the *News and Courier* concluded with a broadside aimed at the Supreme Court. It stated:

> At the risk of being held in contempt, we submit this fervent daily prayer: God save us from the Supreme Court.[22]

Other editorials argued that the Supreme Court had misconstrued the intent of the framers of the First Amendment. The *Charleston Evening Post* concluded that "[t]he amendment was designed to effect separation of church and state, but most Americans doubtless feel that banning a non-denominational prayer goes beyond the intent of the amendment."[23] The *News and Courier* espoused a similar interpretation of the doctrine of separation of church and state when it argued that "[o]ur government must be neutral as to denomination, but not to religion itself."[24] The general theme was that since no one was forced to say the prayers and the government only endorsed broad, non-denominational religious concepts, no constitutional wound was inflicted by the New York Regent's Prayer.

In Columbia, *The State* commented that:

> The constitutional requirement of separation of Church and State is indeed to be protected, and it will be. Be [But?] across America today is many a man and woman who will feel there is an increasingly urgent need for protection from some of the trends in contemporary adjudication.[25]

These observations may reflect a view that the decision, instead of safeguarding the separation of church and state, threatened that principle by erecting obstacles to free exercise of religion in a setting (schools) that formed the focal point of the lives of most children. By contrast, the *Spartanburg Herald* did not view the *Engel* decision as posing such a threat. An editorial argued that:

> It is a mistake to label the ruling as an action against prayer. It is an action against requiring prayer in the public schools by official edict.[26]

The reaction of ministers to the *Engel* decision was also varied but largely condemnatory. The Reverend Waites R. Haynsworth, executive secretary of the Protestant Episcopal Diocese of South Carolina, said:

> I am opposed to the ruling prohibiting prayers in school.

> Religion has always been a vital part of the structure of our nation, and we still need to emphasize it. The children of parents opposed to religion are just a tiny minority, and they could be given something else to do during the devotional period.[27]

The Reverend J. Roy Robinson, an officer of the Charleston Ministerial Association and pastor of the Citadel Square Baptist Church, said that he saw no conflict between the doctrine of separation of church and state and non-denominational religious observances such as recitation of the Lord's Prayer and Bible reading in the schools.[28] Lutheran minister Reverend William R. Summers called the *Engel* decision ". . . shocking and frightening."[29]

The reaction of the Right Reverend Joseph Bernardin, Chancellor of the Catholic diocese of Charleston, and later Cardinal and Archbishop of Chicago said that:

> With this new Supreme Court ruling it would seem that secularism has now been made part of the official program of our public school system. This is to be regretted.[30]

By contrast Rabbi N. L. Rabinovitch of Brith Sholom Beth Israel vigorously supported the *Engel* ruling when he observed that:

> Religion is the prime responsibility of the home and the churches. As a personal thing, whenever any sectarian interest is involved, I feel very strongly that such prayers have no place in public schools.[31]

The *Baptist Courier*, published by the South Carolina Baptist Convention, took a cautious "wait-and-see" approach. It concluded that:

> It is easy for people to form opinions hastily, and it is dangerous to do so. Just now, we are not ready to comment beyond a brief statement. We believe prayer to be such a sacred and personal matter that it is not to be regulated in any way by government. As it now appears, the decision dealt with only one question, the legality of a prayer composed officially to be used in public schools. We do not know how widely the decision against such prayers may be applied; but it is evident that the principle of Separation of Church and State is endangered by any official action by a school board prescribing a particular prayer to be used. The content of the prayer would not be the issue.[32]

Later in the summer of 1962 a *Baptist Courier* editorial argued that:

> Freedom of religion must be protected. A free church in a free state, or separation of church and state, is the proper relationship. A school that is supported by public funds should, therefore, never become an agency for the establishment and propagation of religion. That is not the responsibility of public schools.[33]

However, at the 1964 annual meeting not long after the decision in the *Bible Reading* cases, the South Carolina Baptist Convention adopted two resolutions. The first measure, called the Asbury Resolution, endorsed the practice of saying ". . . voluntary prayers in public schools," and the second provision, the Lawton Resolution, was a broad reaffirmation of the principles of religious freedom and opposition to the establishment of religion by any level of government.[34]

Together the resolutions constitute a theological ink-blot test in which the viewer can see what he wants. Neither *Engel* nor the *Bible Reading* cases forbade voluntary prayer that was not part of a school-sponsored exercise. If the resolution merely endorsed the right of students to take the initiative to pray on their own, without having the practice become an officially-sanctioned rite, then there would be no bruising clash between the resolution and the *Engel* and the *Bible Reading* decisions. If the approval of "voluntary prayers in public schools" was meant to endorse either officially-composed prayers as in *Engel*, or a school-designated time for Bible reading and recitation of the Lord's prayer as in *Abbington v. Schemp*, which is voluntary only in the sense that the student can opt-out of the ceremony, then the Asbury Resolution does contain at least a philosophical clash with the Supreme Court decisions. The Supreme Court opinions concluded that an officially sanctioned religious observance (even though an attempt was made to be non-denominational, and the student, upon parental request, could withdraw from the ceremony) still violated the establishment clause principle against government endorsement of religious concepts even if the opt-out provision avoided a free exercise clause violation.

A month after the *Engel* opinion, the *South Carolina Methodist Advocate* featured commentaries that viewed the decision as having a positive effect that enhanced opportunities for free exercise of religion by limiting state involvement in spiritual matters. An article written by Bishop Paul Hardin, Jr., stated that:

> Since the decision was made I have talked with some of the most competent lawyers in the country and they are agreed that *the Court did not say that there could be no prayers offered in schools or other acts of religious worship. The Court merely ruled that the state can not require a prescribed prayer.* I see a vast distinction between this and ruling out any or every semblance of worship. Indeed, if we Protestants were in the minority in this country, or if some other faith had control of our Government, we would be the first to resist any effort on the part of the state, through any of its agencies, to require us to pray an unacceptable prayer.
>
> . . . .
>
> *Perhaps this decision of the Supreme Court will serve a useful purpose in that it will shake us from our lethargy and remind us in the most forceful way that fathers and mothers must once again teach and practice religion in the home, and that the Church must meet her spiritual responsibilities.*[35]

In the same issue, the editor of the *Advocate*, A. McKay Brabham, Jr., wrote a lengthy editorial. He stated in part that:

> We are frank in saying that we do not find ourselves disturbed by this decision.
>
> On the contrary, we are much encouraged to think that, with this decision as a fresh precedent, the Supreme Court in the future will have ample basis for declaring unconstitutional any and all laws which may be passed which shall provide government support of parochial schools or otherwise intrude the life of the church (any church) upon that of the state.
>
> In the meantime, we think it well to keep in mind that merely commanding a teacher to recite a prayer will no more advance the cause of true religion than commanding a true Christian not to pray will prevent the transmission of Christian love, mercy and grace to all who come in contact with him or her.
>
> Our public schools were not devised to teach religion.

> They were the outgrowth of an earnest desire which was born in a Protestant setting, that every person should be sufficiently educated to learn for himself that Word which would lead him to his eternal Salvation.[36]

Such views did not by any means represent the universal approach of the Methodist church. In an earlier issue, the *Advocate* noted that the influential Methodist publication *World Outlook* called the Supreme Court ruling a "Bad Error."[37]

In an editorial in the *South Carolina Lutheran*, David R. Poole argued that the opinion could have a positive impact on religion by alerting Christians to the fact that proselytization was their responsibility and not that of the state. Poole stated:

> The public schools are no agencies of evangelism for the Christian churches, nor for any other organized religion.
>
> Yes, maybe — just maybe — this court decision will wake us up to the fact that we and not our public schools are responsible for the Christian training of our children.[38]

A prominent Episcopalian commentator had a different view. The Constitution did not require such a strict divorce of church from state. In an interview with *The State* Dr. George V. Johnson, editor of the *Episcopal Churchman*, stated that:

> The whole concept of our constitution is based on religious principles. To endeavor to separate religion from the principle of American government is to deny the foundations upon which our founding fathers built the Constitution.[39]

This opinion that not only is there no high wall separating church and state but that government is inextricably rooted in religious principles echoed views expressed by an earlier Episcopal leader, Dr. J. Adams, in 1833.[40] Doctor Adams concluded that:

> The people of the United States have retained the Christian Religion as the foundation of their civil, legal and political institutions; while they have refused to continue a legal preference to any one of its forms over any other.[41]

Dr. Johnson's more modern perspective did not claim an exclusively Christian rooting of our governmental system as did his nineteenth, century predecessor. However, both statements reflect a belief that religion is so ingrained in the character of the people of the nation and state that attempts to achieve a total separation of church and state inevitably will fail.

If the religious denominations were puzzled as to what direction they should take in reaction to the decision, so were the school officials. The *Engel* and *Bible Reading Cases* caused school officials throughout the country to reexamine their religious observance practices. In 1964 the South Carolina superintendent of education asked the state attorney general for an opinion outlining what forms of religious observances were permitted in the schools in the wake of the Supreme Court decisions. In response, the attorney general issued an opinion which was largely a careful and accurate appraisal of the *Engel* and *Bible Reading Cases*.[42] However, the black letter summary at the beginning of the opinion is somewhat misleading if read out of context. It states:

> (1) The reading of the Bible and the recitation of the Lord's Prayer when required by the law or the ruling of the school authorities as a religious procedure is violative of the First Amendment of the United States Constitution.
>
> (2) The study of the Bible for literary or historic purpose and not involving religious services and *the voluntary reading of the Bible or the recitation of the Lord's Prayer in the absence of any State or school requirements are not violative of the constitutional provisions and are permissible.*[43]

The misleading portions of the summary have been placed in italics by the author of this volume. The statement is misleading in that it could be read to mean that public school prayer recitation and Bible reading, even though sanctioned by the authorities, is permissible so long as there is some mechanism by which the students whose parents do not wish to participate can withdraw. A passage in the *Engel* case quoted above clearly says that the voluntary nature of the officially composed and sanctioned prayer did not make it constitutionally valid.[44] The voluntary quality of the observance might help rebut charges of free exercise clause violations but not allegations of breach of the establishment clause which do not require coercion. Viewed in another light, however, the statement is accurate. Nothing in *Engel* or the *Bible Reading Cases* forbids voluntary, privately initiated prayer that is not disruptive of the school's learning atmosphere and which is not instigated or endorsed by the school or made a part of its official program. In *Board of Education of the Westside Community Schools v. Mergens*[45] we shall later see the Supreme Court more directly address the role of student-initiated Bible clubs as part of school extracurricular periods that permit a wide variety of activities from which the students can freely choose the ones in which they will participate. In the interim between the *Bible Reading Cases* in 1963 and the *Mergens* case in 1990, the Court confronted several other cases in which the introduction of religious observances or materials into public schools was governmentally initiated. These practices fell afoul of the prong of the *Lemon* test which forbids government action that has the purpose of advancing religion.

In *Stone v. Graham*[46] the Court considered a Kentucky law which required the posting of the Ten Commandments on the walls of each classroom in the public school system. The state futilely took several steps to avoid an establishment clause violation. To obviate the evil of state financial support of religion, funds for acquisition of the plaques were raised by private donations rather than through taxes. To negate any possible finding that the Ten Commandments were posted with a view to advancing religion, each copy of the Commandments was accompanied by a statement that said:

> The secular application of the Ten Commandments is clearly seen in its adoption as the fundamental legal code of Western Civilization and the Common Law of the United States.[47]

The Court noted that it was not required to accept the state's avowed purpose as the real reason prompting the posting of the Ten Commandments. The actual reason clearly was the advancement of religion. This is seen by the fact that not all of the Commandments deal with secular crimes such as killing and stealing. Several focus on religious principles such as the admonition not to worship idols. Even though the Court did not focus on this point, it also could have been noted that even if the purpose were genuinely the secular one of explaining the origins of our legal system to students, the primary effect of the law was religious since it used only a religious source to explain the formation of a jurisprudence which drew from many secular as well as religious concepts.

The Court noted that the Kentucky program was not distinguishable from those struck down in the *Bible Reading Cases* merely because the Commandments were not recited orally as was the Lord's Prayer in those cases. The invalid purpose of advancing religion remained. The Court also questioned the state's success in removing the taint of government fiscal sponsorship of religion since, even though the copies of the Commandments were purchased with private funds, the state expended money to administer the program.[48]

The Court once again emphasized that it was not banishing the objective study of religion from the classroom. It stated that:

> This is not a case in which the Ten Commandments are integrated into the school curriculum, where the Bible may constitutionally be used in an appropriate study of history, civilization, ethics, comparative religion, or the like.[49]

Justice Rehnquist vigorously dissented, arguing that the Court had no business substituting its own view of what the *real* purpose of the Kentucky legislature was in enacting the legislation as compared to its *expressed* intent.[50]

Proponents of school prayer gained hope from a 1983 case, *Marsh v. Chambers*.[51] *Marsh* was not a school prayer case but dealt with a challenge to the long-time practice of the Nebraska legislature in opening each session with a prayer rendered by a chaplain paid with public funds. The Court's ruling was based on history and the original understanding and practices of the framers of the First Amendment rather than the purpose, effect, entanglement doctrine used by the court since *Lemon v. Kurtzman*. A good case could have been made that the Nebraska legislature's practice clearly violated the establishment clause by providing government financial support for a religious function. In dissent, Justice Brennan argued that the purpose of the practice was clearly religious -- to obtain divine guidance for legislative deliberations.[52] He also argued that the primary effect of the practice was religious since it linked religion with the power and prestige of the state, and it created intense social pressure on legislators who wished to be successful lawmakers to conform to the practice even though theoretically they could absent themselves.[53] Furthermore, entanglement between legislative and religious officials was inevitable since they would confer about who was to be selected as chaplain and what the contents of the prayers would be.[54] In Brennan's view such mutual surveillance by church and government authorities, involving the joint wielding of spiritual and secular power, was inappropriate under the doctrine of separation of church and state.

To the majority, these arguments based on the Court-created purpose, effect, entanglement doctrine were less important than the original intent of the members of the First Congress in drafting the First Amendment. In ascertaining how the framers of the First Amendment viewed the religious clauses, actions by them that were contemporaneous with the passage of the First Amendment furnished significant clues. The Court noted that almost simultaneously with the passage of the Bill of Rights, the First Congress adopted a policy of opening sessions with prayers led by chaplains paid with government funds. This practice had been followed consistently by the Congress and was also the tradition in Nebraska and many other states.[55] Since the framers did not regard the practice as obnoxious to the establishment clause, why should the Supreme Court take a different view? An unarticulated concern of the Court also may have been the enforceability of a contrary ruling. How would the Court appear in the public eye if United States Marshals were sent to legislative chambers throughout the country to stop prayers? Would this be considered an act hostile to religion which would be a deviation from the neutral position which the Court should take in church-state issues?

Any comfort school prayer proponents could derive from the *Marsh* case was short-lived. The original understanding of the framers provided no clues as to how the school prayer issue should be handled. Public schools were more scarce in 1789 than they are today. No one has brought forth laws or resolutions passed by the First Congress on school prayer issues. School children are more impressionable than mature legislators and more avidly seek peer approval through conformity. School-sponsored religious observances would exert greater pressure on children to conform even if there were excusal provisions.

The Court returned to the *Lemon* purpose, effect, entanglement approach in lieu of the historical or original understanding technique in the 1985 case of *Wallace v. Jaffree*.[56] In the *Wallace* case, the Court considered the validity of an Alabama statute ". . . which authorized a period of silence 'for meditation or voluntary prayer.'"[57] The Court began by reaffirming the long line of precedents that have held that the First Amendment religious clauses' standards were incorporated into the due process clause of the Fourteenth Amendment which applied those principles to state and local governments.[58] It viewed the district court's findings that the First Amendment establishment and free exercise clauses did not apply to the states, and thus Alabama had the right to establish a state religion, to be novel, spurious and beyond the power of a district judge governed by Supreme Court precedent.[59] It did not need to proceed any farther than the first prong of the test. It concluded that the moment-of-silence law had been adopted with a purpose of advancing religion.[60] This conclusion was based on several characteristics of the language and legislative history of the law. These included the following:

(1) statements made by the senator sponsoring the bill, and the governor who signed it, indicating that the purpose of the act was to "return voluntary prayer" to the public schools.[61]

(2) the bill under attack amended an earlier provision that provided only for a moment of silence for meditation by adding the clearly religious phrase ". . . or voluntary prayer."[62]

(3) the statute was part of a series of laws passed by the Alabama legislature within a short span of years that wove a tapestry of regulations returning prayer to the classroom.[63]

The state argued that the law merely served the purpose of guaranteeing a student's free exercise of religion right ". . . to engage in voluntary prayer during an appropriate moment of silence during the schoolday."[64] The Court, at least by implication, seemed to agree that there was such a right but it concluded that it was adequately protected by the earlier law providing only for a moment of silence without specifying that it be used for prayer.[65] This may have been a hint by the majority that a simple moment-of-silence law, with no reference to prayer, which did not carry the burden of a legislative history indicating that its purpose was to return voluntary prayer to the classroom, might pass constitutional muster. This hint was made more explicit in the concurring opinions of Justices O'Connor and Powell.[66] Justice O'Connor noted that a moment-of-silence law has much less of a tendency to endorse particular religious views, or even religion in general, than does an officially composed prayer as in *Engel* or recition of the Lord's Prayer aloud as in the *Bible Reading Cases*. During a moment of silence, a student can think about whatever secular or religious subject he or she likes. No orthodoxy is prescribed.[67] Whether a simple moment-of-silence law, containing no reference to prayer, would be valid would depend not only upon whether or not the legislative history revealed a purpose of advancing religion but also upon the way in which it was administered. A neutral law could be given religious content in a particular classroom.

Of the three dissents filed in *Wallace*, that of Justice Rehnquist was the most vigorous.[68] He denied that the framers ever intended the First Amendment to require strict government neutrality toward religion. Church and state could never live in water tight compartments. He stated that:

> The Framers intended the Establishment Clause to prohibit the designation of any church as a "national" one. The Clause was also designed to stop the Federal Government from asserting a preference for one religious denomination or sect over others. Given the "incorporation" of the Establishment Clause as against the States via the Fourteenth Amendment in *Everson*, States are prohibited as well from establishing a religion or discriminating between sects. As its history abundantly shows, however, nothing in the Establishment Clause requires government to be strictly neutral between religion and irreligion, nor does the Clause prohibit Congress or the States from pursuing legitimate secular ends through nondiscriminatory sectarian means.[69]

This view may well gain adherents in the future as conservative disenchantment with the *Lemon* test grows.

Encouraged by the hint in the majority opinion and the more explicit language in the O'Connor and Powell opinions in *Wallace*, that a school moment-of-silence law that was uncluttered by a legislative history revealing a purpose of advancing religion, or by the use of religious terminology, might pass the hurdles of the *Lemon* test, members of the South Carolina Senate in 1988 fashioned a bill that stated:

(1) the public school day is filled with hectic activity and demanding challenges for students and teachers; . . .

(2) it is appropriate at the beginning of the school day to observe one minute, free of the multiple distractions that intrude on the educational process during which students and teachers can contemplate the challenges of the upcoming day and assume a frame of mind that promotes the proper atmosphere for learning and teaching.[70]

This bill passed the Senate but ran into difficulties in the House because of fears that it violated establishment clause standards.[71] This prompted a sponsor of the bill, Senator Addison G. "Joe" Wilson, Republican of Lexington County, to request an opinion from the state attorney general concerning the bill's constitutionality.[72] The Attorney General, Travis Medlock, responded with an opinion that concluded that the bill was valid on its face but warned that even a bill not explicitly espousing a constitutional purpose of advancing religion could be applied in such a manner as to have the invalid result of advancing religion.[73] The Attorney General observed that the bill was distinguishable from that struck down in *Wallace* since it did not use the word "prayer" or any other religious language. The South Carolina bill was further distinguishable from the invalid Alabama measure in that it did display a clear secular purpose, i.e., to put the students in a frame of mind to focus seriously on their studies. The opinion cautioned, however, that in *May v. Cooperman*, the United States Court of Appeals for the Third Circuit had invalidated a New Jersey law that also did not mention the word "prayer" or other frankly religious terminology.[74] The Third Circuit affirmed the district court's conclusion that a moment of silence had ". . . no legitimate pedagogical value . . .," and it further observed that the "legislators' tendered secular purpose — to provide a transition from non-school life to school life — was . . . pretextural. . . ." and that the real purpose was to provide an opportunity for prayer for those who chose to use the time in that fashion.[75]

Despite the favorable attorney general's report, the 1988 bill never emerged from the House. In 1989 the Senate passed a similar measure.[76] Senator Nell Smith opposed the bill, noting that:

> I have spoken in opposition to S - 508. There has not been, nor is there now, any law which prevents a teacher from having a period of silence in his or her classroom in any school in South Carolina.
>
> In addition, any student has the personal right and privilege to pause for a moment of silence and contemplation should he or she so desire.
>
> It concerns me when legislation is proposed that mandates an action which is currently the right and privilege of any student or citizen.[77]

A possible implication of her remarks was that the only purpose that would be served by a moment-of-silence law that permitted people to do what they could already do was to provide an opportunity for prayer and thus advance religion. Opponents of the bill had to resort to such conjecture, because the sponsors had been careful to avoid the kind of over-heated religious rhetoric that had doomed the Alabama law in the *Wallace* case.

Senator Caldwell Hinson, Democrat of Lancaster, stated that "[i]t's hectic on the bus rides and in the halls. . .[w]e need some mechanism for the teachers to get those students calmed down and in the right frame of mind."[78]

Despite these attempts to avoid telltale signs of a religious purpose, the measure again became bogged down in the House after passage by the Senate.[79] Perhaps the failure of the legislature to pass the bill prompted Reverend Melvin Padgett to lament in a letter to the editor of *The State* that:

> Almost 30 years have passed since our Supreme Court justices first found that God had no place in our schools and that Bible study and prayer would no longer be tolerated.
>
> . . . .
>
> Today, our children are not allowed even a silent *minute* before class for fear they may say a prayer or meditate on God. They have not been taught, or encouraged, to have a blessing at school before lunch, and many never hear one at home.[80]

In addition to its invalidation of public school religious exercises as violating the *Lemon* case rule that state action should not be designed to achieve the advancement of religion, the Court was scrutinizing state curriculum policies under the same standard. In 1968, in *Epperson v.*

Arkansas[81] the Court struck down a state statute which forbade the teaching of any scientific theory that held that mankind descended from a lower order of animals. The Supreme Court concluded that the law was intended to endorse a literal interpretation of the Book of Genesis view of the origins of the world and banish any contrary opinion from the classroom. In the Court's view, this was a significant deviation from the neutral position that governments must maintain in theological disputes.

In 1987, a more subtly crafted law designed to achieve somewhat the same purpose as that struck down in *Epperson* was held to be invalid in *Edwards v. Aguilard.*[82] In that case the Court considered a Louisiana law which required that whenever the theory of evolution-science was taught in the public school classrooms its study must be accompanied by consideration of a creation-science view which argued that the earth and life on it were created by a supernatural being. The law would also require the converse: the teaching of creation-science must be balanced by a study of evolution. Proponents of the law argued that creation-science was not a religious doctrine but a scientific approach, supported by careful research. They contended that teaching creation-science was not a means of advancing religion but a method of increasing academic freedom by presenting more than one theory concerning the origin of life to the students. The doctrine of evolution was not unassailable truth but a theory that was best considered in competition with its leading rival, creation-science. Unlike the law struck down in *Epperson,* the Louisiana law did not banish evolution from the classroom. In fact, it guaranteed that it would be considered along with creation-science. It did not require that either view be presented, but if one were presented, so must the other be. Students and teachers were not required to believe either theory. The concepts were merely presented for consideration.

Despite this attempt to show that the law was designed to achieve the secular purpose of academic freedom, the Court concluded that the real purpose was the advancement of the creation-science view which the Court considered a primarily religious doctrine, centering around the concept that earth, life and mankind were created by a supreme being. The Court dismissed the attempts by the law's proponents to argue that it was designed to achieve academic freedom. It actually reduced academic freedom by requiring that if evolution science were taught, it must immediately be met by a countervailing view. The proponents of the law argued, however, that what they meant by a secular academic freedom purpose was not guaranteeing the discretion of the instructor, to teach whatever he or she wanted but guaranteeing that students were in possession of all of the evidence and not just a one-sided evolution-science approach. The Court concluded that although this may sound like a balanced secular goal, the legislative history of the law and the administrative structure that had been created to support it were heavily skewed toward the creation-science view. Comments by legislative sponsors of the measure demonstrated that the purpose was the advancement of the essentially religious creation-science view. In addition, the program provided for the production of creation-science teaching materials but not for evolution-science teaching materials. It provided for protecting teachers who were creation-science advocates from adverse personnel action. No comparable protection was provided for the teachers of evolution-science. The advocates of the measure argued that this approach was not really one-sided but just did what was necessary to redress the entrenched position of evolution-science proponents. Despite these contentions the Court concluded that the law was designed to advance a religious doctrine over its rivals.

Justice Scalia, joined by Chief Justice Rehnquist, filed an energetic dissent. He not only disagreed with the Court's conclusion that the law was designed to achieve a religious purpose, he contended that the purpose prong of the *Lemon* test was not rooted in the language of the Constitution but was the Court's own invention and was highly subject to manipulation. Reliance on legislative history as a means of determining whether or not a law is designed to achieve a religious purpose results in the Court's becoming lost in a quagmire of subjective judgments as it tries to sort out the multi-hued motives that prompt different legislators to support or oppose a bill. One might respond to this argument, however, by noting that similar difficulties confront conservative judges who attempt to rely on the original intent of the framer. Which framers' intents should govern — those in Congress adopting the First Amendment, or those in the ratifying state legislatures — or those who later adopted the Fourteenth Amendment in Congress and the state ratifying bodies?

The Court from *Engel* to *Edwards* had consistently hammered home the message that the establishment clause could be violated by non-coercive actions, designed to advance religion, by providing it with ideological endorsement, financial or administrative support. This view is not by any means the unanimous approach of Supreme Court justices. This is most clearly seen in Justice Kennedy's dissent in the 1989 case of *County of Allegheny v. American Civil Liberties Union.*[83] In that case a highly fragmented Court dealt with the validity of two government-sponsored holiday displays. One display, a creche scene erected in a prominent location in the county courthouse during the Christmas season, and bearing a sign reading *Gloria in Excelsis Deo,* was struck down as an invalid endorsement of a religious point of view by the government. The message that a reasonable observer would see in the display was that those agreeing with the doctrines represented by the nativity display were favored members of the political community, but those who disagreed were second-class citizens. The other display, erected on government property in front of the city-county administration building consisted of a Christmas tree, a Jewish menorah, and sign posted by the government celebrating freedom and the diversity of views in this country. Unlike the creche display, which stood alone in isolated religious splendor, this display, consisting of symbols conveying a variety of secular and religious messages, merely represented a neutral celebration of the winter holiday season rather than an endorsement of a religious view that a reasonable observer would conclude was the one that should be adopted by those who wished to be treated as full members of the political community.[84]

Justice Kennedy considered both the creche display and the Christmas tree, menorah, liberty sign display to be valid under the establishment clause.[85] He did not accept the distinction made between the establishment and free exercise clauses which holds that although the free exercise clause requires government coercion to be violated, the establishment clause can be violated by more subtle action, such as government ideological endorsement of particular religious views or religion in general. To Kennedy, government coercion or proselytization (intense government-created social pressure to adopt religious views) is essential to the violation of both clauses.[86] Government action that does not involve coercion or proselytization but merely accommodates religion by passively recognizing its role in society does not constitute establishment of religion to Justice Kennedy. This view, like Justice Rehnquist's belief that the establishment clause does not require that the government take a strict view of neutrality toward religion, may gain adherents in the future. However, the view that the establishment clause may be violated by non-coercive endorsement of particular religious views, or religion in general, is deeply embedded in the case law discussed above. It must be remembered, however, that the establishment clause principle that government should adopt a posture of neutrality toward religion means that not only should government not endorse religion, it should not be hostile to religion either.

When the government opens its facilities to a variety of views and modes of expression, they should be open to peaceful religious expression as well as other varieties of speech. In 1990, the United States Supreme Court applied this doctrine to the public schools in *Board of Education of the Westside Community Schools v. Mergens.*[87] The *Mergens* case dealt with congressional legislation extending to the public high schools the principles applied to state-supported colleges by the Supreme Court in *Widmar v. Vincent.*[88] In *Widmar,* the Court concluded that the University of Missouri at Kansas City could not exclude from school facilities religiously oriented extracurricular clubs when those facilities had been made available to a wide variety of other forms of extracurricular activities. By permitting use of its facilities by a wide array of clubs, the university had created a limited public forum dedicated to free speech. The forum was limited in the sense that it was not open to the general public, but it was open to most segments of the university community. Once such a forum has been created, the government cannot exclude from it particular speakers for reasons based on the content of their speech unless there is a compelling reason to do so. Such a compelling reason normally does not exist unless the speech poses a palpable danger such as incitement to violence or serious disruption of the school's normal functions. The university offered as a compelling reason for excluding religious clubs from its limited public forum the argument that letting such clubs use the facilities would result in an establishment of religion. The Court rejected this argument, noting that admitting religious clubs to the facilities would not constitute endorsement of religion since clubs would be only a part of a great rainbow of choices available to the students.

Singling out religious clubs for exclusion from a public forum might itself violate the posture of neutrality that government should have toward religion and constitute an act hostile to religion. Permitting religious club use would not serve a purpose of advancing religion. It merely adds to the already great variety of views expressed in the forum. Because of the potpourri of views expressed in the forum, the primary effect of permitting religious club access would not be encouragement of religion. The Court also concluded that allowing religious clubs to use university facilities would not result in the entanglement of church and state power. The Court did not elaborate on this point, but perhaps it was significant that with young adult college students it would not be necessary for a faculty advisor to be present at such meetings and thereby risk a public employee being swept into religious activities. The Court did emphasize that excluding religious clubs might actually increase entanglement because the university would then be obliged to make judgments concerning which forms of expression are religious and which are not. Furthermore, religious club exclusion would require constant university surveillance of clubs to ferret out religious content.[89] The Court emphasized that the establishment clause did not exist in a vacuum. It should not be interpreted with such single-minded zeal as to undermine free exercise of religion or freedom of speech. Religious speech is entitled to compete in the marketplace of ideas along with ideas inspired by secular political, economic and philosophical concepts.

Could the rationale of *Widmar* be extended to public schools with a younger student body? The *Mergens* case dealt with a congressional attempt to open high school extracurricular periods to student religious organizations. In *Mergens,* the Court considered the meaning and constitutionality of the Equal Access Act by which Congress required that any public secondary school that received federal funds and that had created a limited open forum by which it allowed extracurricular student organizations to meet on school premises before or after the regular instructional hours must give equal access to that forum without regard to the political, religious, or philosophical content of the speech at such meetings.[90] Mergens, a student at Westside High School, arguing that the school had created such a limited open forum for extracurricular clubs, sought equal access to school facilities for a Bible club. Although the club eventually was permitted to meet informally on school premises during the after-school extracurricular period, the club never gained equal access to school equipment such as bulletin boards and the public address system. As a result, club members, through their parents, brought suit seeking declaratory relief that the club had been improperly denied use of school facilities, and injunctive relief directing the school to grant the Bible club access on a par with other student extracurricular organizations. When the case ultimately reached the Supreme Court, it was confronted with two questions, one statutory and the other constitutional:

(1) had Westside High School created a limited open public forum for student extracurricular clubs so that under the statute it was obligated to give the Bible club equal access;
(2) if it had created such a limited open public forum, would admission of Bible clubs to it violate the establishment clause?

The Court concluded that the high school had created such a forum and that it had not granted the Bible club equal access to its use. The school did not permit partisan advocacy groups, whether political or religious, to use school premises during the after-school extracurricular period. The clubs that used the facilities were largely noncontroversial hobby or public service clubs. These included a chess club, a stamp collecting club and a club for those interested in water sports. The Court concluded that the use of school facilities by such clubs was enough to trigger the equal access requirement. Even though it could be argued that creation of a constitutional limited public forum, such as that to which the religious clubs were ordered to be admitted in *Widmar,* might require a forum dedicated to controversial speech, the statutory standard was different. It did not demand that the school must have opened its facilities to advocacy groups before equal access was required. The use of such facilities by any extracurricular group, controversial or not, would trigger the equal access obligation. An extracurricular club was one that did not directly relate to courses, was not required by an instructor, was not graded, and was not a vehicle for carrying out school-wide policy. Organizations such as the stamp and chess clubs fit the definition. Thus the equal access standard had been activated. Had the Bible club been denied equal access? Yes, even though it eventually had been permitted to meet informally on school premises, it had never been treated on a par with other clubs with regard to access to bulletin boards, the public address system, or school newspapers.

The Court then addressed the constitutional issue. If Bible clubs were admitted to a limited open forum, would this constitute an establishment of religion? The Court concluded that it would not. In arriving at this view, the Court utilized the three-part purpose, effect, entanglement test. Granting equal access to religious clubs would not serve a purpose of advancing religion even though religion might receive some incidental benefit. Since the Equal Access Act was designed to open school premises to a variety of political and philosophical as well as religious groups (assuming a limited open forum had been created) the purpose was a neutral, secular one. Under the second prong of the test, the Court concluded that admission of religious groups to the forum would not have a primary effect of advancing religion. This was not only because student participation was voluntary and students could choose from a variety of secular as well as religious organizations, but also because any religious effect of equal access was diluted by the fact that faculty members would attend the meetings only in an order-maintenance, property-protecting role and not as advisors who would actively participate in the meetings. This low profile faculty participation would reduce the chances that permitting access by Bible clubs to school premises would be perceived as endorsement of the beliefs of club members. This restriction on the faculty role also would reduce the need for surveillance of the clubs by other school officials to insure that teachers were not espousing religious doctrine. The possibility of entanglement of religious and school authorities, and the need for surveillance, was further reduced by the fact that clubs could not be directed or controlled by persons or groups (such as churches) that were not members of the school community. As in *Widmar*, the Court concluded that denying access to clubs with religious content in their meetings would actually increase the need for official surveillance of the clubs.

The *Mergens* case is factually distinguishable from the *McCollum* case with which we began the discussion of this line of authority. Unlike *McCollum*, the students in *Mergens* would have a choice among a variety of secular as well religious organizations, rather than a stark choice between religious instruction and regular school duties. Also, since the clubs met after regular instructional hours, there was even less chance that the compulsory school attendance nudged the students toward participation. As we have seen throughout this section, the establishment clause can be violated by non-coercive action by which a state endorses religious views, but that possibility also was reduced by the smorgasbord of choices given the students. Even though the high school students in *Mergens* were younger than the college students in *Widmar*, they would be able to perceive that the mere addition of religious clubs as part of an array of choices that included secular organizations in no way provided official endorsement of religious beliefs.

The *Mergens* opinion undoubtedly will give rise to concerns that schools, once they permit extracurricular clubs, even the most innocuous and noncontroversial, must allow disruptive fringe groups to enjoy equal access. However, the schools would still be permitted to exclude groups that are materially and substantially disruptive to the school's learning environment.[91] In his *Mergens* dissent, Justice Stevens argued that even though the benefits of a true public forum should be extended to religious as well as other clubs, such a forum was not created under the Constitution or the statute by permitting noncontroversial clubs, such as a stamp club, to use school premises. Thus, unless a school gave access to advocacy groups, it would not be confronted with the choice of admitting fringe groups or closing the forum.[92]

Article 10, section 5, of the South Carolina Constitution of 1868, after forbidding religious organizations from controlling public school funds, went on to state ". . . nor shall sectarian principles be taught in the public schools." Such explicit language is not found in the current state constitution. However, the establishment clause of the First Amendment of the United States Constitution, and presumably also the comparable antiestablishment language of Article 1, section 2, of the current state constitution, forbids instruction or observances that endorse particular religions, religion in general or which deviate from the neutral by being hostile to religion. Coercive government action is not required to violate such standards, but merely creating a well-stocked ideological bazaar, in which the student can conduct the exploration process toward discovering his or her own beliefs taps into the well-spring of American tradition. It is questionable whether the approach permitted in *Mergens* — creating an ideological market place of secular and religious activities from which students can choose during extracurricular period — will satisfy those who favor having the government play an active role in shaping the moral standards of society.[93]

The question of what is the proper role of religion in the public schools dramatizes more than any other issue the debate over the proper relationship of church and state that has formed the major focus of this volume. Based on our discussion of this question, as well as our inquiry into other problems posed by the interaction of government and religion, let us now examine the varied patterns which the church-state relationship may take.

NOTES

1. Walz v. Tax Comm'n, 397 U.S. 664, 90 S. Ct. 1409, 25 L. Ed. 2d 697 (1970).

2. Illinois *ex rel.* McCollum v. Bd. of Educ., 333 U.S. 203, 68 S. Ct. 461, 92 L. Ed. 649 (1948).

3. 333 U.S. at 211.

4. 333 U.S. at 211. *And see* Everson v. Bd. of Educ., 330 U.S. 1, 67 S. Ct. 504, 91 L. Ed. 711 (1947).

5. Zorach v. Clawson, 343 U.S. 306, 72 S. Ct. 679, 96 L. Ed. 954 (1952).

6. 343 U.S. at 315.

7. Engel v. Vitale, 370 U.S. 421, 82 S. Ct. 1261, 8 L. Ed. 2d 601 (1962).

8. 370 U.S. at 422.

9. 370 U.S. at 423-24.

10. 370 U.S. at 430.

11. 370 U.S. at 431.

12. 370 U.S. at 441 (Douglas, J., concurring).

13. *Engel*, 370 U.S. at 441-42.

14. School Dist. of Abington v. Schempp, 374 U.S. 203, 83 S. Ct. 1560, 10 L. Ed. 2d 844 (1963).

15. *See* Lemon v. Kurtzman, 403 U.S. 602, 91 S. Ct. 2105, 21 L. Ed. 2d 745 (1971).

16. *See* Lemon V. Kurtzman, 403 U.S. 602, 91 S. Ct. 2105, 29 L. Ed. 2d 745 (1971); Walz v. Tax Comm'n, 397 U.S. 664, 90 S. Ct. 1409, 25 L. Ed. 2d 697 (1970); and Tilton v. Richardson, 403 U.S. 672, 91 S. Ct. 2091, 29 L. Ed. 2d 790 (1971).

17. *Bible Reading Cases*, 374 U.S. at 223.

18. 374 U.S. at 205-11.

19. 374 U.S. at 223.

20. 374 U.S. at 224.

21. *Bible Reading Cases*, 374 U.S. at 225.

22. The News and Courier, Jun. 29, 1962 at 10-A, cols. 1-2.

23. Charleston Evening Post, Jun. 27, 1962 at 2-B, cols. 1-2.

24. The News and Courier, Jun. 27, 1962 at 8-A, cols. 1-2.

25. The State, Jun. 27, 1962 at 12-A, cols. 1-2.

26. The Spartanburg Herald, Jun. 27, 1962 at 4-A, cols. 1-2.

27. Charleston Evening Post, Jun. 27, 1962, at 4-C, cols. 1-3.

28. Charleston Evening Post, Jun. 27, 1962, at 4-C, cols. 1-3.

29. Charleston Evening Post, Jun. 27, 1962, at 4-C, cols. 1-3.

30. Charleston Evening Post, Jun. 27, 1962, at 4-C, cols. 1-3.

31. The News and Courier, Jun. 26, 1962, at 1-B, col. 8.

32. The Baptist Courier, Jul. 12, 1962 at 2-3.

33. The Baptist Courier, Aug. 30, 1962 at 2.

34. 1964 Convention Annual, S.C. Baptist Convention, Columbia, S.C. at 185-86.

35. South Carolina Methodist Advocate, Jul. 26, 1962 at 2. (emphasis in original).

36. South Carolina Methodist Advocate, Jul. 26, 1962 at 3.

37. Quoted in the South Carolina Methodist Advocate, Jul. 12, 1962 at 11.

38. South Carolina Lutheran, September 1962 at 4.

39. The State, Jun. 27, 1962, at 1B, col. 2.

40. *See* a Sermon Preached By Reverend Doctor J. Adams, President of the College of Charleston, On February 13, 1833, Before the Convention of the Protestant Episcopal Church of the Diocese of South Carolina, 12-13 available at the South Caroliniana Library University of South Carolina, Columbia, S.C.

41. *Id.*

42. *See* 1964 Opinions of the Attorney General of South Carolina, No. 1668, April 10, 1964 at 107-10.

43. 1964 Opinions of the Attorney General of South Carolina, No. 1668, April 10, 1964 at 107 (emphasis added).

44. *Engel*, 370 U.S. at 430.

45. Bd. of Educ. of Westside Community Schools v. Mergens, 495 U.S. ____, 110 S. Ct. 2356, 110 L. Ed. 2d 191 (1990).

46. Stone v. Graham, 449 U.S. 39, 101 S. Ct. 192, 66 L. Ed. 2d 199 (1980).

47. 449 U.S. at 40 n.1.

48. 449 U.S. at 42.

49. 449 U.S. at 42.

50. 449 U.S. at 43-45 (Rehnquist, J., dissenting).

51. Marsh v. Chambers, 463 U.S. 783, 103 S. Ct. 3330, 77 L. Ed. 2d 1019 (1983).

52. 463 U.S. at 797 (Brennan, J., dissenting).

53. 463 U.S. at 798 (Brennan, J., dissenting).

54. 463 U.S. at 798-99 (Brennan, J., dissenting).

55. 463 U.S. at 788-92.

56. Wallace v. Jaffree, 472 U.S. 38, 105 S. Ct. 2479, 86 L. Ed. 2d 29 (1985).

57. 472 U.S. at 40.

58. 472 U.S. at 48-61.

59. 472 U.S. at 41, 48-61; *and see* Jaffree v. Bd. of School Comm'ns, 554 F. Supp. 1104 (S.D. Ala. 1983) *rev'd,* 705 F.2d 1526 (11th Cir. 1983). The Court then returned to the purpose, effect, entanglement analytical scheme it had ignored in *Marsh.* (472 U.S. at 55-56).

60. 472 U.S. at 56-61.

61. 472 U.S. at 57, 60.

62. 472 U.S. at 59.

63. 472 U.S. at 58-59.

64. 472 U.S. at 59.

65. 472 U.S. at 59.

66. *See* 472 U.S. at 66 (Powell, J., concurring) and 472 U.S. at 70-74 (O'Connor, J., concurring).

67. *Wallace*, 472 U.S. at 72-73.

68. 472 U.S. at 90-114.

69. 472 U.S. at 113.

70. The State, Apr. 12, 1988, at 1A, cols. 3-5.

71. *See* DIGEST HOUSE AND SENATE RESOLUTIONS, 1987-88, S-660, pt. 2, at 229 (showing that the bill passed the Senate but was tabled by the House committee).

72. The State, Apr. 12, 1988, at 3-A, cols. 5-6.

73. 1988 Opinions of the Attorney General of South Carolina, Apr. 11, 1988 at 107-10.

74. May v. Cooperman, 780 F.2d 240 (3rd Cir. 1985) *appeal dismissed sub nom.* Karcher v. May, 484 U.S. 72, 108 S. Ct. 388, 98 L. Ed. 2d 327 (1987).

75. 780 F.2d at 251-52.

76. *See* SOUTH CAROLINA SENATE JOURNAL 1989, May 15, 1989, S-508 952-53.

77. SOUTH CAROLINA SENATE JOURNAL 1989, May 15, 1989, S-508 952-53.

78. The State, Mar. 16, 1989, at 11-A, cols. 1-2.

79. DIGEST HOUSE AND SENATE BILLS AND RESOLUTIONS, 1989-90, S-508, pt. 2, at 145-46.

80. The State, Jul. 21, 1989, at 10-A, cols. 4-5 (emphasis in original).

81. Epperson v. Arkansas, 393 U.S. 97, 89 S. Ct. 266, 21 L. Ed. 2d 228 (1968).

82. Edwards v. Aguillard, 482 U.S. 578, 107 S. Ct. 2573, 96 L. Ed. 2d 510 (1987).

83. County of Allegheny v. American Civil Liberties Union, 492 U. S. 573, 109 S. Ct. 3086, 106 L. Ed. 2d 472 (1989) (Kennedy, J., dissenting).

84. *See also* Lynch v. Donnelly, 465 U.S. 783, 104 S. Ct. 1482, 79 L. Ed. 2d 804 (1984) (upholding the display of a government-owned and maintained creche in a private park during the winter holiday season, since it was surrounded by a variety of secular symbols).

85. *Allegheny*, 492 U.S. at 655-79, 109 S. Ct. at 3134-46.

86. 492 U.S. at 659-65, 109 S. Ct. at 3136-39.

87. *Mergens*, 495 U.S. _____, 110 S. Ct. 2356.

88. Widmar v. Vincent, 454 U.S. 263, 102 S. Ct. 269, 70 L. Ed. 2d 440 (1981).

89. 454 U.S. at 272, n. 11.

90. *Mergens*, 495 U.S. at ____, 110 S. Ct. at 2371.

91. 495 U.S. at _____, 110 S. Ct. at 2366-67 ***and see*** Tinker v. Des Moines Indep. Community School District, 393 U.S. 503, 509, 89 S. Ct. 733, 738, 21 L. Ed. 2d 731, 739 (1969).

92. 495 U.S. at _____, 110 S. Ct. at 2383-93 (Stevens J. dissenting).

93. Parents dissatisfied with the secular nature of public schools have another alternative besides private schools and seeking religiously oriented extracurricular activities under *Mergens*. S.C. Code Ann. § 59-65-40(A)(1)(a) provides that parents can teach their children at home if the parents meet reasonable educational qualifications validly related to the home schooling process. In Lawrence v. South Carolina State Board of Education (Opinion No. 23526, December 9, 1991), the state Supreme Court concluded that the state had the power to "impose reasonable standards on home schooling programs" but that the standards must be validly related to the home instruction process.

Even the option of educating children at home where religion could be made an integral part of the instruction did not alleviate the pressure to include prayer as a regular feature of the public school day. Perhaps inspired by growing judicial and political conservatism, the South Carolina State Board of Education on December 11, 1991 adopted a resolution "encouraging prayer in the public schools of South Carolina." The board stated that pupils "need the inspiration, motivation and discipline of the religious values on which our country was founded." The State, December 13, 1991, p.1A, 24A.

CHAPTER TEN

PATTERNS OF CHURCH AND STATE RELATIONSHIPS

The historical account of church-state relations contained in this volume reveals several styles or modes of relationship between secular and religious authority. These modes continually struggle and interact with each other to be the prevailing pattern. They do not appear, disappear or reappear according to any cycle or predictable rhythm. No one mode is ever entirely absent. No one mode is ever entirely prevalent, but different eras may bear the stamp of one more than another.

These patterns include the following:

(1) Dominance by a Narrow Political-Religious Elite

The attempt by a narrow group of politically and economically powerful elites to impose their standards on the rest of the population often involves the use of religion as a tool for maintaining public order. This pattern is found in early South Carolina colonial history in such events as the creation of the Anglican Church establishment which was supported by money from the public treasury, religious qualifications for voting and holding public office, and by rigid Sunday laws that mandated the cessation of secular work, travel and recreational activities on the officially-endorsed day of worship.

(2) Forming a Broader-Based Establishment Permitting More Religious Diversity

In South Carolina, the dominance of the narrow elite was never fully successful. It foundered on the rocks of economic necessity. A measure of religious freedom was needed to induce new settlers to uproot their lives in the Old World and seek something better in the new. The replacement of European religious suppression by its colonial counterpart was not attractive. The result was that interwoven with the attempts by a narrow elite to impose its religious standards on others was the counterpoint: the economic necessity for *diversity*. The vast reaches of North America would have to be filled from diverse sources — Anglicans, Huguenots, German Lutherans, Catholics, Baptists, and Presbyterians.[1] Disintegration of the attempts at Anglican dominance was precipitated not only by the need to stock the new land with settlers, but ultimately by the perception that an intimate church-state relationship could retard rather than encourage the spread of religion because it could result in reducing religion to being a mere political apparatus of the elite — a device for gaining and maintaining political control. This is seen in the control by a secular commission over church affairs beginning in early eighteenth-century South Carolina. The cynical attitude produced by the use of religion as a political tool undermines the moral authority of the established church.

Furthermore, the intimate mutual embrace of church and state can lead to a severe deterioration of the position of the established church if its political patron falls out of favor. Such was the case with the Anglican church which found its privileged position undermined as the Revolution that led to a split of the colonies from England also led to the loss by that church, as the one most intimately identified with that country, of its privileged position as the sole established church. A colony faced with war with its imperial parent could not afford to give second-class treatment to its large non-Anglican Protestant population. This military and political necessity gave non-Anglican Protestants the leverage to extract admission into the exclusive precincts of the establishment as a price of vigorous support of the Revolution. Thus the attempt of a narrowly-based elite to impose its religious standards on the colony disintegrated, and this led to an attempt in the Constitution of 1778 to redefine the religious elite in broader terms that could successfully maintain an established position.

This attempt to forge a *new, more diverse, consensus* out of the wreckage of the established church led to the replacement of the old Church of England establishment by a general Protestant establishment. The legal privileges of a corporate body, such as the right to own property as an entity, sue and be sued, and perpetual existence, were reserved to Protestant Christian organizations that adhered to a set of religious principles prescribed by Article 38 of the Constitution of 1778. Although a large measure of religious freedom was enjoyed by other groups such as Catholics and Jews, their status still was not equal to that of Protestant organizations whose religious principles were constitutionally endorsed by the state. Thus the religious elite was redefined in a broader fashion than the earlier Anglican establishment, and this reformulated religious consensus obtained constitutional approval of its ideology, but it did not obtain support by imposition of taxes or coerced forms of worship.

(3) The Free Market Place of Religious Ideals

Even this redefined and broadened establishment proved to be too narrow. Dominance by this new religious-government coalition was swept aside by the nationwide constitutional reforms that culminated in the adoption of the Bill of Rights, including the First Amendment provisions prohibiting the Congress from establishing an official religion or interfering with the free exercise of religion. Influential local political figures such as Charles Pinckney, who were also prominently involved in national constitution making, brought their influence to bear in South Carolina in the drafting of the Constitution of 1790. That document's movement in Article VIII, section 1, away from a general Protestant establishment toward *a state with broad principles of religious freedom and no officially endorsed church* was aided by the Revolutionary War experience in which Catholics and Jews proved to be loyal citizens who could be trusted with religious freedom and who deserved such practical tools of operating a viable religious organization as the right to incorporate.

The religious freedom provisions of Article VIII, section 1, of the Constitution of 1790 insured ". . . the free exercise and enjoyment of religious profession and worship, without discrimination or preference . . ." with the proviso that liberty of conscience should not be construed to ". . . excuse acts of licentiousness, or justify practices inconsistent with peace or safety of this state." This article embodies a theory of a *free market place of religious ideals* from which a citizen can make his or her own choice so long as it does not result in action injurious to the rights of others or to public order.

Thus in early South Carolina history we saw an attempt by a narrow-based religious and political coalition to impose its ideology upon the colony through government fiscal support of the favored religion, fortified by religious qualifications to participate in the political process and laws imposing standards of Sunday decorum. This form of establishment ultimately failed and was succeeded by a broader-based but still ideologically select establishment which in turn was succeeded by a complete disestablishment and the adoption of a system by which an individual could define his or her own relationship with God, so long as the individual's choice from the religious market place of ideals did not involve actions disruptive of public safety or the rights of others. Systems of church-state relations that are characterized by the grant of privileged positions to certain beliefs and organizations are doomed to failure in a country populated by immigrants and the descendants of immigrants drawn from a variety of religious traditions, especially when the waves of immigration are followed by other waves drawn from ever-broadening sources. Attempts to define the national, state or even local consensus that is a prerequisite for any establishment to succeed are bound to fail or to produce a meaningless, bland form of religious pablum.

Elements of the establishment survived into the nineteenth and twentieth centuries in the form of the intricate Sunday closing laws that ultimately were portrayed as secular health-safety measures. However, they became progressively pockmarked with exceptions designed to serve various commercial interests such as railroads, textile mills and the recreation industries. Ideology does not always surrender to economic forces, but when government attempts to prescribe human moral decorum in prolix detail the venture often proves to be unsuccessful. Government can effectively prohibit the cruder forms of misconduct such as acts of violence, fraud, larceny and betrayal of the public trust. Government can set the moral tone of society by the exemplary conduct of its business. Temporarily and sporadically, government might succeed in controlling the details of individual behavior patterns — but enduring principles of morality must come from within the individual. Such moral principles are often fortified by membership of the individual in private groups such as churches or other organizations with an ethical orientation. The desirable orientation of government to such groups is one of even-handedness and nondiscrimination.

Government has a proper role to play in insuring that individuals and private groups have the freedom to define their own attitudes toward religion. This is especially true in a setting such as the public schools in which the government controls the general environment. Court decisions, such as *Westside Community Schools v. Mergens*,[2] that permit schools to create extracurricular periods during which the students can choose from a variety of religious and secular activities without official coercion to accept, or government endorsement of, particular religious views enhance rather than reduce the chance that the individual will find an enduring moral compass rather than a superficial outward conformity that provides little guidance once the government pressure toward orthodoxy is relaxed, as it invariably will be.

Religion is entitled to have equal access to public forums created by the government. However, religious organizations should not seek to become the special favorite of government, dependent on its fiscal largess. Such dependency invariably demeans religion and reduces the effectiveness of its role in society in the following respects:

(A) Religion is a moral critic of government as it is of every other aspect of society. Just as within government there is a concept of separation of powers between the executive, legislative and judicial branches whereby each branch checks and balances the power of the other, similarly, in society at large, religion serves as a countervailing power to major forces such as industry, the media, academia and government. It makes government examine the moral underpinnings of its policy. The effectiveness of this role is diluted if religion must timidly mind its words for fear of offending the keeper of the key to its financial well being. Government funding exacts a bureaucratic price. The early eighteenth-century church commissioners in South Carolina kept close watch on such internal church functions as the allocation of power within the congregations and the design and location of church buildings. Such government entanglement with its affairs robs the religious organization of its right of privacy. In addition, the identification with certain tax sources can place religion in a morally compromising position as was the case with the use of funds derived from the tax placed on the importation of slaves to finance the construction of a steeple.

Not only does the violation of the concept that secular and church power should be separate dilute the effectiveness of the church as moral critic of government and society, it concentrates too much power in too few hands. The fifth-century Pope Galasius I captured this separation of powers concept graphically in his "two swords" metaphor. Because of the weakness of human nature, including the tendency to abuse power, he believed that the sword of secular power should never be wielded by the same hands as the sword of spiritual power.[3]

(B) The moral weight of the criticism of government is reduced if religion is viewed by the rest of society as just another supplicant for government funds or just another species of economic enterprise with the same motives of cupidity as anyone else.

(C) Reliance upon government funding makes religion fat, sleek and lazy. It become lethargic and less involved in the routine care of its parishioners and others in need. This would be true even if no particular denomination is favored but an earnest attempt is made to dispense funds in an even-handed fashion. Government fiscal resources are not infinite. Any government funding of religion, no matter how well intended, invariably would place government officials in the position of having to weigh the comparative ideological worth of the applicants, a process that would spawn a political whirlwind that would make it more difficult for the diverse elements of our society to work together.

Benjamin Franklin was an eloquent proponent of the theory that churches should survive on their own merits without being artificially propped up by the government. He stated that:

> When a religion is good, I conceive that it will support itself; and, when it cannot support itself, and God does not take care to support it, so that its professors are obliged to call for the help of the civil power, it is a sign, I apprehend, of its being a bad one. . . .[4]

To guard against such consequences of a cozy fiscal relationship between church and state, Article XI, section 4, of the current South Carolina Constitution forbids the use of state or local funds or credit to grant direct aid to educational agencies controlled in whole or in part by religious organizations. Such a limitation is particularly appropriate with regard to church-related educational institutions. When one person's tax funds are diverted to another's religion, this makes the taxpayer an involuntary contributor to a religion that is not necessarily his own. Even if the taxpayer were allowed to earmark the funds on a tax form so that they would go to a religious or secular educational institution of his own choosing, the government would become even more of a monitor of the very private act of charitable giving. In addition, a religious educational institution might be tempted to hedge its ideological fervor in order to avoid offending the government grant maker. When the direct recipient of the aid is not the religiously affiliated institution but a student attending it to pursue a primarily secular course of study, the danger of coercing taxpayers to contribute to religious education and the danger of tempting the religious institution to alter its ideological direction in order to qualify for grants are significantly reduced. In recognition of this reduced danger, Article XI, section 4, now no longer prohibits *indirect* aid to religious or other private educational institutions as did Article XI, section 9, of the original Constitution of 1895.

A more difficult question arises with regard to government fiscal aid to organizations that are affiliated with religious denominations but which perform functions that are not directly related to worship or sectarian instruction but which are useful in preserving the health and well-being of the general public. Such aid includes government grants to medical research centers and hospitals that serve patients without regard to their religious affiliation. Such aid is brought to bear at a point where government functions in pursuit of the general welfare legitimately intersect with the functions of religious organizations in pursuit of their doctrinal mandates to heal the sick. To what extent can government legitimately grant such aid without violating the principle that the state must not financially sponsor religious activities? Article XI, section 9, of the original Constitution of 1895, which forbade state or local government property, funds or credit from being used directly or indirectly to benefit colleges, schools, hospitals, orphanages or other institutions controlled wholly or in part by religious organizations, has been replaced in the current constitution by Article XI, section 4, which specifically prohibits only *direct* aid to educational institutions. No express prohibition is found in that provision of aid, whether direct or indirect, to religiously affiliated hospitals. However, the general principle prohibiting the government reestablishment of religion remains in Article I, section 2, of the South Carolina Constitution and the First Amendment of the United States Constitution. Under establishment clause principles discussed in the chapter on government financial aid to religious institutions, it might be constitutionally possible to grant aid to the secular functions of religiously affiliated institutions if such functions are sufficiently compartmentalized from the religious activities of the recipient and the recipient is not so pervasively religious that inexorable pressure would build to breach such compartmentalization.

Assuming that government aid to a religiously-affiliated organization is constitutionally permissible under such circumstances, a more fundamental question remains. Does the state constitution as presently structured strike the proper balance between an unrealistic absolute separation of church and state at one extreme and intimate entanglement of sectarian and secular authorities at the other? In general, the balance is properly calibrated. Even though the church-state relationship can be analogized to the separation of powers concept, and the church viewed as a moral check upon the powers of the state, and even though too cozy a relationship between church and state undermines that function, this does not dictate a consistently adversary relationship between church and state.

Just as the branches of the national and state governments which operate to curtail each other's tendencies to abuse power must often work in harmony to accomplish their tasks, the same is sometimes true of church and state. If a state in pursuit of its function of advancing the general welfare finds ready at hand a church-affiliated agency that can assist it in accomplishing those goals, there is no reason why the state should not fiscally assist that agency rather than going to the expense of duplicating its facilities. However, care should be taken that such assistance occurs only when the function is nonideological in content and does not place the state in the position of enhancing a religious organization's opportunities to proselytize.

The 1988 United States Supreme Court decision in *Bowen v. Kendrick,*[5] by approving the general contours of a federal program which not only permitted but required grant applicants to state how they would mobilize church as well as secular social service agencies in a program of counseling young people to engage in greater restraint in their social relationships, went too far in approving fiscal entanglement between church and state. The Court concluded that the program did not violate the establishment clause since its purpose was the secular one of solving the social and economic problems of teenage pregnancy. The Court also concluded that since the program was not designed to promulgate religious doctrines, and it contemplated a variety of governmental, private secular and religious grantees and subgrantees, its primary effect would not be to advance religion unless a particular grantee was so pervasively religious that any funds awarded to it would be diverted to sectarian purposes. If a religiously affiliated participant was capable of separating its secular from its sectarian functions and the government funds aided only its secular activities, the program would not have a primary impact of advancing religion. Assuming that a particular grantee was not pervasively religious, the government's grant monitoring to prevent use of the funds for religious purposes would not unduly intrude on the privacy of the religious organization. However, such reasoning failed to appreciate the unique nature of the services the grantee would be performing.

Such counseling programs, unlike medical research or hospital treatment, often will have a strong ideological content, and the government could find itself in the position of financing the transmission of religious messages. Even though the Court only approved the general approach of the program, and left open the possibility of striking down individual incidents of government funds being used to finance counseling that is primarily religious in content, the opinion permitted a wide degree of fiscal cooperation between church and state in an area highly prone to ideological content. The same goal of community-wide mobilization of government, private-secular, and religious organizations to fight serious problems such as teenage promiscuity and pregnancy, could be accomplished by simply coordinating efforts of all of these agencies without channeling government funds through religious agencies. Freedom of religion is best safeguarded by keeping church-state fiscal entanglements to a minimum.

Whenever either church or state uses the other to convey an important message, whether it be a prayer transmitted through the public schools or a government social doctrine disseminated through religiously affiliated grantees, the contents of the message will be changed, intentionally or unintentionally, subtly or crudely, to conform to the standards of the messenger. A religious message will become watered down. A secular program will take on a sectarian cast. When government funds are involved this metamorphosis is exacerbated.

Government has proven to be too clumsy and too preoccupied with its own agenda to serve as midwife at the birth of genuine spiritual belief as distinguished from the illusion of such belief that is produced by state-prescribed orthodoxy. The state may be no more successful in insuring that its citizens think clean thoughts than it is in mandating religious faith, but it may have a legitimate role to play in protecting its citizens, especially minors, from sexual exploitation, including invasions of privacy and abusive actions. The next chapter focuses on the constitutional issues accompanying the state's discharge of this task.

NOTES

1. *See* I D. WALLACE, THE HISTORY OF SOUTH CAROLINA at 33-47, 67-81, 142-78, and 336-51 (1934). A modern survey reveals the following pattern of religious adherence in late twentieth-century South Carolina: Roman Catholic = 5.7; Baptist = 46.5; Methodist = 15.6; Lutheran = 2.5; Presbyterian = 3.5; Pentecostal = 2.0; Jews = 0.3; Episcopalian = 2.0; Mormon = 0.6; none = 3.2; others = 18.1. *See* Research Report The National Survey of Religious Identification at p.11 (conducted 1989-90) (Director Barry A. Kosmin, The City University of New York, March 1991). Despite the predominance of mainline Protestant denominations, when the figures for the "other" category are combined with those of small groups, it becomes clear that South Carolina is far from being a state of monolithic religious beliefs.

2. Westside Community Schools v. Mergens, 495 U.S. ____, 110 S. Ct. 2356 110 L. Ed. 2d 191 (1990).

3. *See* G. SABINE, A HISTORY OF POLITICAL THEORY 194-95 (4th ed. rev. 1950) and R.W. CARLYLE and A.J. CARLYLE, VOL. I, A HISTORY OF MEDIEVAL POLITICAL THEORY IN THE WEST 190 (3d ed. 1928).

4. A. STOKES and L. PFEFFER, CHURCH AND STATE IN THE UNITED STATES at 41 (1964).

5. Bowen v. Kendrick, 487 U.S. 589, 108 S. Ct. 2562, 101 L. Ed. 2d 520 (1988).

CHAPTER ELEVEN

THE REGULATION OF OBSCENITY AND PORNOGRAPHY

Even with the demise of the formal established church in the late eighteenth century, and the decline in the late twentieth century in the rigidity of adherence to that faint echo of the established church, the Sunday closing laws, moral concepts retained a strong grip on the scope of freedom of expression that was permitted in South Carolina. One commentator has noted that "[m]ost religious southerners have . . . seen strict obedience to the moral law as prime evidence of a Christian society and have suppressed doubts they might have had about using the legal system to achieve that society."[1] Indeed, obscenity law in South Carolina traces its origins to late seventeenth- and early eighteenth-century statutes that were primarily directed at protecting church doctrines from blasphemous and profane criticism. The statutes had only indirect implications for the regulation of sexual decency apart from safeguarding religious orthodoxy.[2] As the concept of separation of church and state became more entrenched, government became more concerned with imposing regulations to uphold general standards of sexual morality than particular religious beliefs.

This concern became more acute when cheap printing methods were developed that made sexual material available to large numbers of people rather than just wealthy dilettantes. This trend was exacerbated by the development of inexpensive methods of reproducing pictures and by the invention of photography.[3]

(A) CORRELATES OF THE OBSCENITY LAWS: STATE CONSTITUTIONAL PROVISIONS REGULATING PERSONAL MORALITY

A climate fraught with the tempation of erotic pictures and books prompted enactment of constitutional safeguards for sexual decorum. Sexual morality gained constitutional stature in South Carolina in Article III, section 33, of the Constitution of 1895 which directed that no unmarried woman under fourteen could legally consent to sexual intercourse. The primary impact of this provision was to make the issue of consent irrelevant in rape trials in which the victim was under fourteen.[4] However, the provision also has the flavor of mandating a standard of personal morality and providing increased protection for young women. In a country in which the majestic generalities of the federal constitution often serve as the measuring rod against which state constitutions are evaluated, it is remarkable to find a state fundamental law that intermixes standards for the personal conduct of private citizens with provisions allocating power among the branches and guaranteeing civil rights to the people.

The age-of-consent provision was placed in the Constitution of 1895 at the request of the South Carolina Women's Christian Temperance Union which complained to the constitutional convention that South Carolina afforded less protection to women and girls from sexual assaults than other states. The group's petition to the convention noted the ". . . increasing and alarming frequency of assaults upon women and the frightful indignities to which even little girls are subject . . . ."[5] The Union sought to raise the age of consent from ten to eighteen, the age at which women legally could marry, but the convention settled upon fourteen.[6] Increasing the age of consent would make convictions easier to obtain when the defendant was charged with assault upon a young girl, and this presumably would deter such attacks.

Beginning in the early 1880's, the Women's Christian Temperance Union in South Carolina fought all forms of excessive behavior that it viewed as posing a moral threat. This movement included not only a campaign against the use of alcohol and tobacco but also sexually offensive expression. A prominent figure in the movement, Mrs. Sallie F. Chapin, organized a "Legion of Honor" which consisted of boys who had pledged temperance including a promise not to use profanity or remain in the presence of those who did, as well as a vow ". . . to hold as a sacred thing the reputation of woman and never allow a disparaging remark made of her in our presence."[7] Presumably pornography would be viewed as a particularly offensive form of "disparaging remark."

The 1895 Constitution also sought to insure sexual morality by completely forbidding divorces. Article 14, section 5 of the 1868 Constitution stated that "divorces from the bands of matrimony shall not be allowed but by the judgment of a Court, as shall be prescribed by law." This was replaced in Article XVII, section 3, of the original Constitution of 1895 by a provision completely forbidding divorces. Newspaper accounts of the debate reveal the remarkable degree that discussions of the provision revolved around interpretations of the Bible and the practical question of whether forbidding divorces would encourage or discourage adultery. D. S. Henderson urged the 1895 convention to replace the 1868 provision with one that would permit divorce only on the ground of adultery.[8] Under this motion, divorces would have been granted only by juries and the guilty party would not be permitted to remarry.

Henderson argued that to totally outlaw divorce would be uncivilized, but that adultery should be the only ground since that was the only one recognized in the Bible.[9] He argued that a complete prohibition of divorce would be ". . . an incentive to the vile, home-destroying crime of adultery."[10] However, I. W. Bowman argued that permitting divorce on the ground of adultery might lead to manipulation of the provision in order to facilitate obtaining a divorce. Presumably he meant that people would commit adultery to create grounds for divorce or would fabricate evidence that their spouse had committed adultery.[11] At any rate, he ultimately moved to completely forbid divorce.[12] The Bowman proposal was adopted by the convention.[13] In the preceding debate, the delegates brandished Biblical passages and theology like duelists.[14] The remarks of Senator R. B. Watson, as described in *The State,* illustrate the pronounced theological character of the debate.

> He held up a Bible and said this Scripture was clear as it could be. The majority of the people of South Carolina were believers in the Bible. He read what the Bible said. Do this [permit divorces] and you will shock the sensibilities of hundreds of Christians all over the State.[15]

Interspersed with such Biblical references were observations on what permitting divorces would do to sexual morality. W. C. McGowan called divorced women "married women without husbands" and argued that their presence in the community would lead to a sharp rise in adultery.[16] So intermixed were the observations on Biblical doctrine and sexual morality that with respect to the divorce issue church and state were again one.

Historian Daniel Hollis has observed that South Carolina remained the only state that did not grant divorce until a 1949 constitutional amendment. He also noted that church influence upon adoption and maintenance of the anti-divorce provision was "pervasive."[17] In 1949, an amendment to Article XVII, section 3, was adopted that allowed divorces ". . . on grounds of adultery, desertion, physical cruelty, or habitual drunkenness."[18] In 1969 the grounds for divorce were further liberalized to permit divorce on the ground of ". . . continuous separation for a period of at least three years," and the necessary separation time was reduced to one year in 1979.[19] Even with these concessions to the transitory nature of modern relationships, the South Carolina Constitution remains a document that seeks to regulate personal morality as well as to prescribe the balance of power among the branches of the government and to guarantee individual rights.

The constitutional standards are augmented by an array of statutes designed to strike at the source of temptation to betray standards of sexual morality. A major device for upholding moral standards in South Carolina has been the laws regulating the dissemination and possession of obscene material. However, such laws do not exist in a constitutional vacuum. They must be drafted in such a manner as to avoid undue intrusion on freedom of expression.

Article I, section 2, of the Constitution of South Carolina states that "[t]he General Assembly shall make no law . . . abridging the freedom of speech or of the press. . . ." The speech and press provisions of the First Amendment to the United States Constitution are identical except for inconsequential differences in punctuation and, of course, in the name of the government unit to which the prohibition against encroachments on freedom of expression applies. Because of this striking similarity in the wording of the state and federal constitutional provisions guaranteeing freedom of expression, and because federal constitutional standards on freedom of speech and the press have been incorporated into the Fourteenth Amendment's due process clause and applied to the states, federal and state constitutional law on freedom of expression in general, and the permissible scope of the regulation of obscenity and pornography in particular, have become closely interwoven.[20] Because of this intimate relationship of state and federal constitutional law concerning the clash between the use of police power to regulate "dangerous" expression and the guarantees of freedom of speech and press, the discussion of the control of obscenity and pornography in South Carolina must include the United States Supreme Court decisions and federal statutes that helped set regulatory styles. This development of federal law was itself preceded by decisions from other states, most notably Pennsylvania and Massachusetts.

(B) NINETEENTH CENTURY STATE AND FEDERAL REGULATION OF OBSCENITY

In the 1811 case of *People v. Ruggles,*[21] the famed New York jurist Chancellor Kent, in a case in which he approved the prosecution of the crime of blasphemy despite the abolition of the legal establishment of religion, observed that blasphemous remarks shared with obscene expression the quality of posing serious threats to widely accepted principles of social order. Other early nineteenth-century cases also viewed pornography as a threat to the general public morality and not just corruption of the individual.

In 1815, in *Commonwealth v. Sharpless,*[22] a Pennsylvania court ruled that an obscenity charge was not only indictable at common law but that a successful prosecution did not require that the pornographic material had been publicly displayed if it tended to corrupt morality in a manner that harmed the general public. Presumably this meant that the cumulative weight of one-by-one viewing could create inertia toward the general moral depravity of society or that individual viewers might be inspired to interact offensively with others. In addition, the court concluded that the requirement that indictments had to give the defendant concrete notice of the nature of the offense did not need to be carried to such lengths that a detailed description of the obscene material had to be entered in the court records.

In the *Sharpless* case, the defendant was charged with exhibiting to several persons in exchange for money ". . . a certain lewd, wicked, scandalous, infamous and obscene painting representing a man in an *obscene, impudent and indecent posture with a woman* to the manifest corruption and subversion of youth, and other citizens of this commonwealth to the evil example of all others in like case offending, and against the peace and dignity of the Commonwealth of Pennsylvania."[23] Even though the terms "lewd", "obscene," and "scandalous" are not defined, and no detailed description was given of the "indecent posture" in which the figures in the painting were arrayed, the judges concluded that a conviction would be valid so long as the "[t]he offense is described with reasonable certainty" and the jury is able to examine the material.[24] Since the prosecution was cast roughly in the form of a criminal libel proceeding, the court agreed that the painting must have been "published", i.e., shown by the defendant to someone else. However, a general public display was not necessary. A dissemination to several, or perhaps even one person, was sufficient so long as moral standards were breached in a manner that harmed the general public.[25]

In *Commonwealth v. Holmes,*[26] a Massachusetts court concluded that the state's courts of common pleas had jurisdiction over a charge that the defendant had published a "lewd and obscene" book entitled *Memoirs of a Woman of Pleasure.*[27] Like the Pennsylvania court in the *Sharpless* case, the Massachusetts tribunal held that it was not necessary to preserve the offending book and pictures in the court records. To insist upon inclusion of the obscene work in the court records would ". . . require that the public itself should give permanency and notoriety to indecency in order to punish it."[28]

An 1821 Vermont statute stated:

> That if any person shall, hereafter, print, publish, or vend any lewd or obscene book, picture or print, such person, on conviction, before the supreme court, shall be sentenced to pay a fine, not exceeding two hundred dollars.[29]

Not long after the promulgations of these state decisions and laws, Congress began to use its foreign trade powers to control threats to public morality coming from beyond the nation's borders. The Tariff Act of 1842 stated at section 28 that:

> The importation of all indecent and obscene prints, paintings, lithographs, engravings, and transparencies is hereby prohibited; and no invoice or package whatever, or any part thereof, shall be admitted to entry, in which any such articles are contained; and all invoices and packages whereof any such articles shall compose a part, are hereby declared to be liable to be proceeded against, seized, and forfeited, by due course of law, and the said articles shall be forthwith destroyed.[30]

Early United States Supreme Court cases focused primarily upon the authority of the national government under Article I, section 8, clause 7, to exclude obscene materials from the mails as a subsidiary power incident to federal government authority to establish post offices and post roads. These cases generally vindicated federal power to exclude obscene material from the mail, but they did not define what type of material was subject to proscription as obscene. In *Public Clearing House v. Coyne*,[31] the Court said that "[f]or more than thirty years not only has the transmission of obscene matter been prohibited, but it has been made a crime, punishable by fine or imprisonment, for a person to deposit such matters in the mails. The constitutionality of this law we believe has never been attacked. . . ."[32] The Supreme Court's definition of obscenity tended toward vague rhetorical flourishes such as the following statement found in *Rosen v. United States*,[33] which stated that:

> . . . Everyone who uses the mails of the United States for carrying papers or publications must take notice of what, in this enlightened age, is meant by decency, purity, and chastity in social life, and what must be deemed obscene, lewd, and lascivious.

Much of the impetus for combating obscenity through federal and state statutes in the late nineteenth century came from anti-vice crusader Anthony Comstock. Comstock's persistent lobbying efforts succeeded in getting the New York legislature to toughen its obscenity laws and helped persuade Congress to enact federal legislation curbing the use of the mails to disseminate obscenity.[34] An 1868 New York statute, espoused by the Young Men's Christian Association, and quickly utilized by Comstock as an anti-vice crusader, sought to control traffic in obscene and indecent materials by rewarding informers with a portion of the fines collected from violators.[35] An 1873 New York law waged a multi-front war against sexual immorality by attacking not only obscene literature but also contraceptive devices and drugs or procedures that induced abortions. This law stated:

> If any person shall sell, or lend, or give away, or in any manner exhibit, or shall offer to sell, or to lend, or to give away, or in any manner exhibit, or shall otherwise publish or offer to publish in any manner, or shall have in his possession, for any such purpose or purposes, any obscene book, pamphlet, paper, writing, advertisement, circular, print, picture, drawing or other representation, figure or image on or of paper, or other material, or any cast, instrument, or other articles of an indecent or immoral nature, or use, or any drug or medicine, or any article whatever, for the prevention of conception, or for causing unlawful abortion, or shall advertise the same for sale, or shall write or print, or cause to be written or printed, any card, circular, book, pamphlet, advertisement or notice of any kind whatsoever, stating when, where, how, or of whom, or by what means, any of the articles in this section hereinbefore mentioned can be purchased or obtained, or shall manufacture, draw, or print, or in anyway make any of such articles, every such person if of twenty-one years of age or over, shall, on conviction thereof, be imprisoned at hard labor for not less than three months or more than two years, and be fined not less than one hundred dollars or more than five thousand dollars for each offense. . . .[36]

More lenient penalties were applicable to violators who were under 21.

It is notable that this law reached not only commercial traffic in obscene and indecent goods, but also dissemination without charge. This would prevent informal networks of acquaintances from lending or giving pornographic material to one another. Like so many laws of the period, however, it did nothing to define "obscene," "indecent" or "immoral."

In the late nineteenth century, during the same era as the *Rosen* decision and Anthony Comstock's New York law, South Carolina's statutory prohibitions of the exhibition and publishing of obscene materials also seemed to assume that the type of material that was banned was self-defining. An 1885 statute stated:

> Section 1. *Be it enacted* by the Senate and House of Representatives of the State of South Carolina, now met and sitting in General Assembly, and by the authority of the same, That whoever knowingly imports, prints, publishes, sells or distributes any book, pamphlet, ballad, printed paper or other thing containing obscene, indecent or improper print, picture, figure or description manifestly tending to the corruption of the morals of youth, or introduces into a family, school or place of education, or brings, procures, receives or has in his possession any such book, pamphlet, printed paper, picture or ballad, or other thing, either for the purpose of sale, exhibition, to aid in a circulation, or with intent to introduce the same into a family, school or place of education, shall be punished by imprisonment not exceeding two years or by a fine not exceeding one thousand ($1,000) dollars, or both, at the discretion of the Court.
>
> Section 2. That whoever posts or exhibits in any public place any advertisement, show bill or other printed or written picture of an indecent or obscene character shall be guilty of a misdemeanor, and, upon conviction thereof, shall be punished by imprisonment not exceeding two years or by a fine not exceeding one thousand dollars, or both, in the discretion of the Court.[37]

Such statutes reflected the growing concern about the spread of sex-oriented materials, but their use of such general terms as "obscene," "indecent" and "improper" did little to inform the publisher or distributor of what was permissible. The term "improper" is capable of a multitude of interpretations. It could even include material that is objectionable for reasons having nothing to do with the depiction of sexual themes. For example, it could even include a politically unorthodox opinion. Such general terms leave the law enforcement officer free to impose his own subjective moral standards on society without sufficient guidance from the elected representatives of the people.

Several other features of the 1885 act are notable. Foremost among these are emphasis on the protection of family values. This is the same moral strain that ten years later prompted the insertion of an anti-divorce provision in Article XVII, section 3, of the original Constitution of 1895. A closely related theme is the protection of youth and the institutions in charge of their education from invasion of "obscene," "indecent," and "improper" material. As we shall see later in this chapter, the same goal pervades late twentieth-century statutes designed to protect minors from exposure to, or participation in the making of pornographic material because minors have not acquired the critical faculties necessary to make their own choices. It is this objective of protecting youth and the integrity of the family structure that is the most persistent refrain in South Carolina obscenity regulation.

Further evidence of the breadth of the statute is seen in its prohibition of private possession ". . . with intent to introduce the same into a family . . ." as well as commercial dissemination of obscene, indecent, or improper material. Section 2 of the 1885 law prohibits the posting of obscene and indecent show bills as a means of protecting the unwilling viewers from being confronted with material that may be difficult to avoid by simply choosing to look elsewhere. However, the range of the law is not limited to insulating the unwilling viewer but also prohibits private possession under circumstances that threaten the family or educational institutions. However, the breadth of the statute is limited by its state of mind requirements. The publication and dissemination of the material must have been made with knowledge that it had a manifest tendency to corrupt youth, and introduction of the material into a family or educational institution must have been done intentionally rather than inadvertently. The statute leaves unclear whether or not an adult who privately possesses material for his own perusal rather than for public dissemination or introduction into a school or family circle would be subject to punishment.

The 1885 obscenity law was introduced in the General Assembly by Representative William H. Brawley of Charleston.[38] In 1887 Brawley delivered a speech at the anniversary celebration of Erskine College and used that occasion to address a wide range of social problems including the need to maintain the strong moral character of the state. In describing the moral foundations upon which the state historically had rested, he stated that:

> But, above all, there was a dignified simplicity of manly character — a sacred and unchangeable love of home and all the tranquilizing, sanative influences of country life, a reverence for religion, a stability in the marriage tie, and homes full of grace and fragrant with all domestic virtues.[39]

Perhaps such sentiments prompted him to introduce the obscenity law. However, in the same speech, he showed a growing doubt about whether or not ". . . ascetic law-making in the supposed interests of more virtuous living . . ." could bring about a genuine improvement in character which was better achieved by ". . . the silent teachings of inborn purity. . . ."[40] However, such ambivalence toward controlling obscenity through legal sanctions was sometimes smothered by growing concern about the increasing problems created by modern methods of disseminating obscene materials.

Professors Lockhart and McClure have noted that increased impetus for the control of obscene materials arose during the twentieth century from the mass marketing of paperback books that made these works available to such a wide audience that there were fears of a general deterioration of the moral standards of the country.[41] The development of pictorial mass media, such as motion pictures and television, doubtless further alarmed the moral watchdogs. The need for a clearer understanding of the definition and legal status of obscenity became acute.

(C) THE *ROTH* CASE AND THE DEVELOPMENT OF THE MODERN DEFINITION OF OBSCENITY

In the 1957 case of *Roth v. United States*,[42] the United States Supreme Court came to grips with the need for giving the speaker, publisher, merchant, and viewer a clearer idea of what kind of material was obscene and to what extent such material could be regulated without running afoul of the constitutional standards guaranteeing freedom of expression.

In his majority opinion in the *Roth* case, Justice Brennan emphasized that material could not be banned as obscene merely because it dealt with sex. To be obscene the materials must treat sex in a manner designed to appeal to the prurient interest.[43] The Court utilized the American Law Institute Model Penal Code definition, replete with pungent, highly charged rhetoric in an effort to add substance to the vague phrase "appeal to the prurient interest." This standard stated that appeal to the prurient interest consisted of ". . . a shameful or morbid interest in nudity, sex, or excretion . . . [that] goes substantially beyond customary limits of candor in description or representation of such matters."[44] The authors of this definition seemed to attempt to make up for its lack of clarity by the emotional intensity of its language. Later, we shall see that South Carolina law incorporated the Model Penal Code description of appeal to the prurient interest as part of its definition of obscenity. The requirement that in order to be obscene, material must go "substantially beyond customary limits of candor . . ." was the forerunner of the later rule that the prosecution must prove that the material was patently offensive.

In determining whether or not the material appealed to the prurient interest, the courts were to consider the work as a whole rather than in isolated fragments which might appear to be more dangerous than they were in the context of the entire work.[45] The dominant theme must be to appeal to the prurient interest. In determining whether or not the material stirred the prurient interest, the courts were to judge the material's likely impact on the "average person" rather than its impact upon the most sensitive, most suggestible person at one extreme or the most jaded, world-weary cynic at the other extreme. "Contemporary community standards" rather than some halcyon age of moral utopia were to be used.[46] The Court's emphasis upon examining the predominant theme of the entire work and its impact on the average person was a studied departure from the nineteenth-century English approach declaimed in *Regina v. Hicklin*,[47] which permitted the suppression of a book when only half was obscene, the rest being a criticism of Catholic theology.

Some American courts, such as those of Massachusetts, expanded the *Hicklin* approach and would find a book to be obscene if selected passages tended to corrupt a vulnerable segment of society such as the youth of the state. For example, in *Commonwealth v. Friede*,[48] attorneys defending a person charged with selling Theodore Dreiser's *American Tragedy*, were unable to have the entire work introduced in evidence since only portions were alleged to be obscene.[49] In the 1913 case of *United States v. Kennerley*,[50] Judge Learned Hand considered the *Hicklin* standard to be so well entrenched that he was obliged to follow it. However, he suggested that it would be preferable to allow jurors to apply the moral standards of their own age rather than those of the mid-Victorian era. He further urged that society as a whole should not be deprived of material just because it might be offensive to the most sensitive or might lead to antisocial acts committed by the most perverted segments of society. The impact of the material on the average person would be preferable. He said:

> To put thought in leash to the average conscience of the time is perhaps tolerable, but to fetter it by the necessities of the lowest and least capable seems a fatal policy.[51]

The federal Court of Appeals broke with the *Hicklin* approach in *United States v. One Book Entitled Ulysses by James Joyce.*[52] These cases severed the psychological umbilical cord to the *Hicklin* case and prepared the way for the Supreme Court's total ouster of the old standard in *Roth.*[53]

The *Hicklin* standard made it possible for the censor to ban nearly any work treating sexual themes since most such material could provoke or offend some element of society. Granting the censor such a wide ambit of discretion would deprive the public of much material that would be useful in solving social problems or that would have value as thought-provoking literature or drama.[54]

In the view of the *Roth* Court, if the predominant theme of a work was to appeal to the prurient interest, it normally lacked social value. It was not an ". . . essential part of any exposition of ideas. . . ."[55] Lewd and obscene works did not contribute to the discussion of the pivotal issues of the day. Their minuscule social utility was heavily outweighed by their tendency to corrupt and provoke antisocial acts.[56] Obscenity had such an intrinsic quality of corrupting morals that the Court concluded that it was unnecessary to prove in each prosecution that material that met the definition of obscenity resulted in concrete social harm.[57] However, the Court sought to restrain the enthusiasm of the censor by cautioning that "[a]ll ideas having even the slightest redeeming social importance -- unorthodox ideas, controversial ideas, even ideas hateful to the prevailing climate of opinion . . ." are to be protected unless they encroach upon more important interests.[58]

The *Roth* Court concluded that works that displayed a dominant theme of appealing to the prurient interest as judged by their likely impact on the average person in the contemporary community were not protected by the First Amendment.[59] Despite the apparently comprehensive protection given by the broad First Amendment language to all forms of speech, the Court concluded that since most of the states that had ratified the First Amendment by 1792 placed restrictions on a variety of forms of speech, including profanity, it was unlikely that these states would have backed such a complete about-face in speech regulation that would have permitted no control over obscene speech.[60] Among the laws cited by the Court was South Carolina Act No. 202 of 1703, which forbade blasphemous and profane speech.[61] It should be noted, however, that profanity and blasphemy, as used in that statute, were given a meaning that referred to denying fundamental religious doctrines such as the truth of the concept of the Holy Trinity and that the Bible was inspired by God. Given this specialized meaning, the statute either proves too little or too much as a precedent for regulating obscenity. The statute's prohibition of religious dissent makes it a poor precedent for regulating sex-oriented speech. Its validity as a curb on religious speech was suspect under the broad religious freedom provisions in Article VIII, section 1, of the South Carolina Constitution of 1790. The *Roth* Court's conclusion that the original understanding of the framers of the First Amendment was that regulation of obscenity would be permitted is not entirely convincing.

The approach of the *Roth* case was to sustain prosecutorial efforts to restrict palpably harmful material but to protect material that contributed to the exchange of ideas. To avoid chilling the dissemination of useful material, the Court had to guard against chilling vigorous discourse by placing strict liability on those who unknowingly disseminated obscene material. A bookseller with a large stock, confronted with possible absolute liability for purveying obscenity, might choose to engage in self-censorship, withdrawing from the shelves any material dealing with sex, no matter how useful or innocuous. In *Smith v. California*,[62] the Court took steps to reduce this danger. The Court observed that applying strict liability to the dissemination of books invariably had the effect of driving from the market not only obscene works but also protected material that would contribute to the examination of social problems.[63] Thus the Court concluded that proof that obscene material was disseminated with knowledge of its contents was an essential part of the prosecution's case. The Court turned aside state arguments that such a demanding standard would lead to the successful frustration of virtually every prosecution by defendants making fraudulent claims of lack of knowledge of the obscene nature of material they had sold. The Court concluded that such dire consequences were unlikely since it was not insisting upon eye-witness testimony that a seller had knowledge of a book's contents. Reasonable inferences of such knowledge could be made from the circumstances in which the material was sold.[64]

The *Roth* case had a pro-prosecution flavor and sustained state and federal convictions. The *Smith* case, by insisting that knowledge of the obscene contents be an essential element of the prosecution's case in the trial of a bookseller, broadened the protection of sex-oriented speech. In a series of cases in the mid and late 1960's, the federal Supreme Court further strengthened the constitutional protection given such speech. The Court was deeply split on the issue of obscenity, and these protective measures often received far from majority support, but state courts were forced to include, as part of the basic obscenity test, standards that were endorsed by a minority of judges since their votes might prove to be pivotal in upholding or rejecting a conviction.

In *Jacobellis v. Ohio*,[65] Justices Brennan and Goldberg emphasized that the Court had a duty to make an independent factual examination of the material to determine whether or not it was obscene. The scope of free speech protection could not be made to depend so completely on the whim of juries.[66] The *Jacobellis* case also afforded the occasion for Brennan and Goldberg to move toward a requirement that in order to mount a successful prosecution the government must prove not only that the material as a whole appeals to the prurient interest of the average person in the contemporary community but that it lacks social value. In their view, a lack of social value was an independent requirement that must be met in order to prove that the material was obscene. The tendency of the material to corrupt and deprave -- its appeal to the prurient interest -- was not to be balanced against the social value of the material, so that if the likelihood of the material producing serious harm was strong enough, this would outweigh the social value and permit the material to be banned. No matter how intense the appeal to the prurient interest, the existence of social value would remove the material from the category of obscenity.[67] Two years later this approach would be developed further. In the *Jacobellis* case, Justices Brennan and Goldberg also insisted that the community standard used to determine whether or not the work was obscene must be a national rather than a local one. They observed that national standards governed the interpretation of other constitutional freedoms. A standard that varied from town to town, or county to county, would deter national publishers, motion picture producers, and distributors of candid work from nationwide distribution if they had to steer around the dangers posed by the shifting quicksand of a thousand local standards that might exist only in the secret hearts of as yet unformed juries.[68] By contrast, Chief Justice Warren, in dissent, prophetically argued for a local community standard such as that adopted by the Court nearly a decade later. He contended that a national standard would be impossible to define.[69]

The pivotal role that a lack of social value could play as an essential element in the prosecution's case is demonstrated by a 1966 case, *A Book Named "John Cleland's Memoirs of a Woman of Pleasure" v. Attorney General of Massachusetts*.[70] In an opinion joined only by Chief Justice Warren and Justice Fortas, Justice Brennan utilized a three-part test for determining when material was obscene. In this formulation, the lack of social value became an essential element that had to be proved by the government. No matter how overwhelming the proof on the other two elements, a failure to establish the absence of social value could sink the prosecution's case. Brennan described the test in the following terms:

> Under this definition, as elaborated in subsequent cases, three elements must coalesce: it must be established that (a) the dominant theme of the material taken as a whole appeals to a prurient interest in sex; (b) the material is patently offensive because it affronts contemporary community standards relating to the description or representation of sexual matters; and (c) the material is utterly without redeeming social value.[71]

The Supreme Court reversed the judgment of the state Supreme Judicial Court because the state court rejected an argument that in order to be obscene, material must be "unqualifiedly worthless."[72] It is important to note that the "utterly without redeeming social value" standard never enjoyed the support of more than three justices on the Court at any one time. Nevertheless, because of the unpredictable bounce that Court judgments on the question of obscenity sometimes took, it was impossible for state courts and legislatures, seeking to assure the validity of their laws, to ignore this standard.

Justice Brennan at this stage could be described as a liberal pro-speech balancer, *i.e.*, in determining whether material is unprotected obscenity, he balanced the government's need to regulate the material to avoid social harms against the damage such regulation would cause to freedom of speech, but his balancing process, especially because of such elements as the "utterly without redeeming social value" standard, was heavily skewed toward protecting speech. The pro-speech wing of the Court during the 1960's was rounded out by Justices Black and Douglas who purported not to engage in balancing at all. They were so-called absolutists who believed that all speech that was not closely intertwined with action deserved complete protection. Justice Black forcefully noted that ". . . I think the First Amendment forbids any kind or type or nature of governmental censorship over views as distinguished from conduct."[73] In another opinion, he implied that sex-oriented material also was entitled to absolute protection. He stated that ". . . this court is without constitutional power to censor speech or press regardless of the particular subject discussed."[74] Justice Douglas stated that:

> We have no business acting as censors or endowing any group with censorship powers. It is shocking to me for us to send to prison anyone for publishing anything, especially tracts so distant from any incitement to action. . . .[75]

The balancing process may be heavily influenced by the location and the purpose for which the obscene material is used, as well as by whether the state is attempting to curb dangerous conduct or to control the nature of a person's thoughts. This approach was most clearly seen in the Supreme Court's decision in the 1969 case of *Stanley v. Georgia*.[76] In that case the Court reversed a Georgia conviction of a man for possessing unquestionably obscene material in the privacy of his home. The government side of the balancing process was severely weakened because the state seemed to be less interested in regulating in order to stem antisocial conduct or commercial exploitation of obscenity that intruded on the lives of the unwilling viewer, and more interested in thought control, insuring that its citizens dreamed of pastoral meadows and babbling brooks rather than of erotic material. The Court noted that:

> . . . Georgia asserts the right to protect the individual's mind from the effects of obscenity. We are not certain that this argument amounts to anything more than the assertion that the State has the right to control the moral content of a person's thoughts. To some this may be a noble purpose, but it is wholly inconsistent with the philosophy of the First Amendment.[77] '

Even material that is clearly obscene may be possessed in the privacy of one's home. The need to protect the right to transmit and receive information joins with the right of privacy (especially within the innermost sanctum of one's residence) to erect a moat of constitutional guarantees around a person's home. The Court stated:

> If the First Amendment means anything, it means that a State has no business telling a man, sitting alone in his own house, what books he may read or what films he may watch. Our constitutional heritage rebels at the thought of giving government the power to control men's minds.[78]

The broad principles of the *Stanley* case have been significantly limited in later cases. The *Stanley* case may have recognized a person's right to possess a wide variety of material in the privacy of his home, even material that was obscene under the *Roth* standards. However, later cases refused to extend the zone of privacy protection to the luggage of an international traveler entering the country, an interstate traveler transporting obscene materials, or to a commercial motion picture theater that sought to attract an audience of consenting adults.[79] Much later, in the 1990 case of *Osborne v. Ohio*,[80] the Court refused to extend the right of privacy protection to a defendant who possessed in his home lewd photographs of nude minors, but the Court reversed his conviction on other grounds. The right of privacy to possess whatever one liked in his home was outweighed by the need to stop the exploitation of minors by child pornography at all of the interrelated levels of activity that contributed to such exploitation, including production, distribution, or private possession.

Despite the liberal banners displayed with such flamboyance by so many federal Supreme Court decisions in the 1960's, the decade did result in several important tools being added to the prosecution's arsenal. In *Ginzburg v. United States*,[81] the Court observed that in judging whether or not material that was on the borderline between being obscene or protected fell on one side of the line or another, the setting in which the material was presented to the potential user could be considered. The advertising that touted the erotic qualities of the material sometimes could tip the scales in the direction of finding that a work was obscene. If the distributor portrayed the material as being pervasively erotic, serving no purpose but to stir the viewer's prurient interest, the courts were entitled to take the distributor at his word. Advertising that pandered solely to the salacious interest of the potential purchaser could be influential in not only demonstrating the prurient nature of this material, but also in highlighting its offensiveness and demonstrating that it had no social merit. The Court also implied that the use to which the material was to be put might affect the outcome of the balancing process. Material that could form a useful ingredient in a psychiatric practice, and thus be protected in that context, could lose its protected qualities when it was presented to the public in a hard-sell advertising campaign that emphasized only the prurient.[82]

Another addition to the prosecution's weaponry came in *Mishkin v. New York.*[83] As noted in the earlier discussion of *Roth, supra,* that case departed significantly from the old English approach exemplified by the decision in *Hicklin, supra,* by focusing on the likely impact of the material on the average person in the contemporary community rather than upon the material's potential for arousing either the most suggestible or the most emotionally calloused elements of society. *Mishkin* created an important caveat from the *Roth* "average person" approach. In *Mishkin,* the Court noted that if the material was designed to appeal to the prurient interest of a particular deviant group and it did indeed have the qualities to arouse such a group, then the prosecution could succeed even though the works would have left the average person unmoved.[84] The case raised the bizarre possibility that (rather than wrestling with the likely impact of the material on the average person in the general population) a jury confronted with material tailored for a specialized audience, such as sado-masochists, must be concerned with determining what appeals to the "average" sado-masochist, an apparently self-contradictory term.

As the decade of the 1960's drew to a close the Court was so deeply fragmented among liberal balancers, free-speech absolutists and conservatives that it sometimes was unable to develop a consensus concerning why it was affirming or reversing a conviction. In this chaotic situation, the Court resorted to the so-called *Redrup* approach, named after its decision in *Redrup v. New York.*[85] In that case the Court reversed several convictions because in none of them did the material pose the kind of threat concerning which the government's regulatory power most legitimately could be exercised. The Court identified three forms of danger concerning which government regulatory power was most likely to be sustained. These consisted of the following:

(1) material disseminated to juveniles;[86]
(2) graphic material that was distributed in such a manner as to "... make it impossible for an unwilling individual to avoid exposure to it";[87] and
(3) material that was distributed in the commercially exploitative, heavy-breathing, hard-sell advertising manner that the *Ginzburg* case called pandering.[88]

(D) THE SOUTH CAROLINA COURTS APPLY THE *ROTH* DEFINITION OF OBSCENITY

It was onto a constitutional landscape marked by such faint and shifting guidelines that the South Carolina Supreme Court entered to apply state and federal constitutional standards to the regulation of allegedly obscene speech. In the 1970 case of *State v. Burgin,*[89] the South Carolina court ran aground in the unchartered seas of the *Redrup* opinion. The *Burgin* case involved a conviction of a Greenville magazine dealer for selling pornographic publications. At that time, the South Carolina Code of 1962 stated in a 1965 revision to section 16-414.1 that:

> Obscene means that to the average person, applying contemporary standards, the predominant appeal of the matter, taken as a whole, is to prurient interest among which is a shameful or morbid interest in nudity, sex or excretion, and which goes substantially beyond customary limits of candor in description or representation of such matters.

This language closely follows that used in *Roth, supra,* including that decision's approval of the "substantially beyond customary limits of candor" approach used by the Model Penal Code as a precursor of the requirement that in order to be obscene, material must be patently offensive. In affirming the conviction, the state Supreme Court apparently applied two additional standards enunciated by some members of the liberal wing of the United States Supreme Court but which never enjoyed majority support. The court decided that the community standard to be used in determining whether or not the predominant theme of the material was to appeal to the prurient interest, and that the publication went beyond customary limits of candor, was a national rather than a local community standard.[90]

In addition, the South Carolina court applied the test adopted by Justices Brennan and Fortas, and Chief Justice Warren, that in order for the material to be obscene, it must be "utterly without redeeming social value."[91] The South Carolina court determined that all elements of the obscenity test had been met. The publications displayed a predominant theme of appealing to the prurient interest and going beyond customary limits of candor by their graphic focus on the genital areas of nude females.[92] The magazines made ". . . no pretense of artistic value."[93] The state court concluded that the right of privacy applied in *Stanley v. Georgia, supra,* to reverse a conviction of a defendant for possession of obscene material within his home had no relevance to a commercial operation. The South Carolina court concluded that the zone of residential privacy recognized in *Stanley* ". . . put no shield around distributors of obscene materials."[94] Private possession was one thing. Commercial exploitation was a different and more harmful activity. As for the rights of a potential possessor, his right to possess and examine the obscene material in private did not imply a ". . . correlative right to acquire such material."[95]

The state court recognized that *Redrup, supra,* had listed three situations in which a state's regulatory interest was at its height: (1) dissemination of sex-oriented materials to juveniles; (2) thrusting material upon an unwilling viewer with little chance of escape; and (3) pandering material with hard-sell salacious advertising. It could be argued that none of those situations existed in *Burgin.* However, the state court concluded that the *Redrup* list was not an exhaustive itemization of situations in which a state could regulate sex-oriented material harmful to the community. This assumption, although perhaps understandable, proved to be incorrect.

The United States Supreme Court summarily reversed the *Burgin* conviction in an order that contained no explanation other than a citation to *Redrup*.[96] This cryptic opinion led to an equally brief response in which the state court reversed its affirmance of the conviction.[97] Little can be said with certainty about this brief exchange of fire between state and federal high courts. The most likely explanation arising from the United States Supreme Court's citation of *Redrup* is that since the defendant had not been engaged in one of the three most dangerous forms of disseminating obscenity itemized in that case, then the conviction was constitutionally invalid.

In *City of Greenville v. Bryant*,[98] the South Carolina Supreme Court was confronted with a trial court decision that upheld the city council's revocation of a bookstore's license because it was selling obscene publications. The court quickly disposed of a flurry of objections to the city council's procedures and the narrow scope of the trial court's review of the council decision. The state supreme court refused to countenance the defendant's objections that the council had considered publications at the revocation hearing that had not been listed in the notice of the proceedings that had been sent to the defendant. Since the defendants had failed to make a timely objection at the council hearing to the incompleteness of the notice, their belated arguments could not be heard. The defendants further contended that the trial court erred by conducting its review solely on the basis of the record compiled at the council hearing without conducting a new trial or permitting the introduction of new evidence. The state supreme court concluded that the defendants were not entitled to a new evidence-gathering proceeding since they had agreed earlier that the trial court review would be conducted entirely on the basis of the record compiled by the council. The court then approved the definition of obscenity used by the city as being substantially the same as that used by the state. The city defined as obscene material that met the following standards:

(a) The dominant theme of the material or printed matter taken as a whole appeals to a prurient interest in sex;

(b) The material or printed matter is patently offensive because it affronts contemporary community standards relating to the description or representations of sexual matters; and

(c) The material or printed matter is utterly without redeeming social value.[99]

The state supreme court concluded that the publications sold by the defendants met these standards since:

> They contained pictures in which both nude males and females are shown together in varied positions to actually portray or suggest sexual activity. The predominant, in fact sole appeal of the publications is to a prurient interest in sex. No one would be so naive as to suggest that the publications or the pictures contained therein serve any artistic or moral purpose. Their sole purpose is to debase.[100]

The city's definition of obscenity, like that used by the state in *Burgin, supra*, incorporated the liberal, pro-speech rule that in order to be obscene the material must be "utterly without redeeming social value." This approach had been adopted by three justices in *Memoirs v. Massachusetts, supra*.[101] Despite its lack of support by a majority of the federal Supreme Court, state and local governments probably considered it necessary to embrace the standard in order to insure that their laws would be upheld by a highly fragmented United States Supreme Court. Thus, the city and the state supreme court were using a definition that was reasonably up-to-date and attempted to take account of most of the United States Supreme Court factions that might be inclined to reverse convictions. However, it missed one angle. The state supreme court failed to take account of the United States Supreme Court's reversal of its *Burgin* decision in 1971. Apparently the United States Supreme Court had reversed the state *Burgin* decision since the case did not involve dissemination of material to juveniles, unconsenting adults, or involve pandering through hard-sell, salacious advertising. These three factors, emphasized in the *Redrup* case, *supra*, as the most appropriate circumstances in which state and local governments could regulate obscenity, were no more present in the *City of Greenville* case than they had been in *Burgin*. However, there was no United States Supreme Court action in the *City of*

Greenville case. Perhaps the state court in *City of Greenville* was being prophetic by anticipating later cases such as *Miller v. California*,[102] in which the federal Supreme Court did not limit valid obscenity prosecutions to the three situations emphasized in *Redrup*.

Just at the height of the confusion wrought by the summary reversal of its *Burgin* decision by the United States Supreme Court with no more than a sphinx-like citation to *Redrup* to give guidance to the state court, the South Carolina Supreme Court decided *State v. Watkins*.[103] The *Watkins* case involved the conviction of a motion picture exhibitor for showing a film called *Anomalies*, which graphically depicted a variety of unusual sexual practices. At the time of the conviction, the state was using the same definition of obscenity as described in *Burgin, supra*. This definition embraced the approach followed by Justices Brennan and Goldberg in *Jacobellis v. Ohio, supra*, that the relevant community standard to be used in determining whether or not the material appealed to the prurient interest, and went substantially beyond customary limits of candor, was a national and not a local one.[104] However, the South Carolina Supreme Court applied this standard in a manner that in reality made it not only a local standard but the standard of that segment of the citizenry most actively troubled with the problems posed by obscenity. The difficulties of defining a national standard were becoming more and more apparent. The state supreme court sustained the conviction despite the fact that the prosecution did not introduce evidence of a national standard but instead relied on testimony from members of the local community who had been actively concerned with obscenity issues. When the defense objected to the testimony of two local residents to the effect that the films went substantially beyond customary limits of candor in the community, the state supreme court concluded that an adequate foundation for the testimony had been laid and that the trial judge had not abused his discretion in admitting it. To support its conclusion that the testimony of the two witnesses had been admitted properly the state supreme court noted that:

> Both of these witnesses appear to have been actively affiliated with local churches and with groups such as the Kiwanis Club, Chamber of Commerce, school board, etc. They testified that they had had occasion during the past year to discuss, with numerous persons living and working in the communi-

ty, the current treatment and representation of sexual matters in books, newspapers, magazines and motion pictures.[105]

This approach emphasized not only a local community standard but a standard filtered through what some might call the local conservative elites — church leaders, chamber of commerce members, etc. However, the court noted that the jury, presumably selected from a wide segment of the community, was the ultimate decision-maker concerning what the community standards were and the jurors could rely heavily or not at all on the testimony of such local leaders.[106] The state was not required to produce evidence concerning community standards but could depend upon the jury's knowledge of community values.[107] The court injected a liberalizing note into its view of community standards. Since such standards were to be contemporary, they were to be dynamic and evolve as society changed.[108]

The state supreme court stuck very close to the *Roth* case approach in discussing the burdens that must be met by the prosecutor. It was not necessary that the prosecutor produce specific evidence that the material alleged to be obscene produced concrete harm. Proof that the material met the *Roth* obscenity standards, as modified in *Memoirs* and other cases, made the material harmful *per se*.[109] This appraisal of the prosecution's responsibilities with regard to demonstrating the harmfulness of the material was the same as that used by the United States Supreme Court in the *Roth* decision, *i.e.*, once a category of speech had been deemed sufficiently dangerous to fall into an unprotected category, it was unnecessary to produce concrete evidence of its harmfulness in each prosecution.[110]

The South Carolina court rejected the defendant's argument that the South Carolina obscenity definition was invalid in that it did not embody the United States Supreme Court mandate that in order to be obscene, material must be patently offensive. The court concluded that the "substantially beyond customary limits of candor" approach used in South Carolina was even more exacting than the federal standard and was thus valid.[111]

The South Carolina court then addressed the requirement that in order to be obscene the material must be utterly without redeeming social value. The court correctly noted that this standard had not been endorsed by a majority of the United States Supreme Court.[112] Because of this lack of majority support for the "utterly without redeeming social value" requirement, the state court was understandably ambivalent about it. It could not be ignored. It must be used in some fashion to insure the validity of state law in the face of a deeply divided Supreme Court in which each vote was important. In *Watkins* the state court seemed to treat the "utterly without social value" factor less as an element that must be proved by the prosecution and more as something approaching an affirmative defense by which a defendant could rebut the prosecution's case on the first two elements (appeal to the prurient interests; patent offensiveness) by demonstrating that the material contained social value. The state supreme court approved the trial judge's charge to the jury on the "utterly without social value" standard when it stated:

> This [trial judge's charge] was quite proper. *But not because "utterly without redeeming social value" is an element of "obscenity."* We understand "utterly without redeeming social value" to be the ground for not affording obscenity the protection of the First Amendment.[113]

Whether the prosecution had to prove a lack of social value as an element of its case, or whether the defense proved that such value did exist and could rebut an otherwise effective showing of obscenity, or the standard existed in a vague limbo between being a prosecutorial element or an affirmative defense, it was apparent that disenchantment with the factor was growing. The disenchantment would reach fruition in the United States Supreme Court's decision in *Miller v. California*.[114]

In the meantime, the defendant in *Watkins* attempted to prove that the film under attack, *Anomalies*, did have social value. He attempted to demonstrate that the picture conveyed several valuable ideas including the following: (1) that what society considered an anomalous, or perverted sex act often depended upon social circumstances rather than the inherent nature of the act; (2) that people should be educated about sex; (3) that Americans should cease repressing sexual urges since such pent-up desires often exploded into violence.[115] The court was satisfied with the fact that the jury had viewed the film and that its verdict had implicitly rejected these contentions of social value. The supreme court had made an independent examination of the picture but it was reluctant to disturb the conclusions of a jury familiar with community standards.[116]

Under the standards announced in *Smith v. California, supra,* it is necessary for the prosecution to demonstrate not only that the defendant published, sold or disseminated obscene material, but that he did so with knowledge of its obscene nature. Under the South Carolina Code of 1962, section 16-414.1(d), the *Smith* standard was followed, but "knowingly" was defined as:

> . . . having knowledge of the contents of the subject matter or failing after reasonable opportunity to exercise reasonable inspection which would have disclosed the character of such subject matter.

The defense argued that because under state law knowledge of the obscene nature of the material could be demonstrated not only by showing that the defendant had actual knowledge of the contents of the material but also by proving that the defendant had failed to exercise a reasonable opportunity to inspect the material, an impossible burden was placed on defendants, especially those with large stocks. The supreme court rejected this contention without elaborating upon its reasons.[117]

The defendant's final assault on the state obscenity law was more successful, but it did not save him from conviction. He asserted that the statute violated the Constitution of South Carolina by delegating legislative authority to a private body, the Motion Picture Association of America, by exempting from prosecution motion pictures carrying the Association's seal of approval.[118] The defendant argued that such a delegation to a private party violated Article 3, section 1 (powers of the legislative branch), and Article 1, section 8 (separation of powers doctrine). The supreme court agreed that legislative power was improperly delegated to the Association. In addition, the delegation of power was defective in other ways. Even if legislative power is delegated to a public agency, the authority must be granted with sufficient guidelines from the legislature concerning how the authority is to be exercised. The legislature should set the general policy to be applied by the delegatee, the principal means by which the policy is to be effectuated, and a fair procedure by which all sides that are likely to affected by the policy have an opportunity to be heard.[119] The delegation of legislative authority to the association did not meet these standards. However, the court concluded that this infirm portion of the statute was severable from the remainder of the law and did not render provisions of the obscenity statute that were crucial to the defendant's conviction invalid.

(E) THE *MILLER* CASE REFORMULATES THE DEFINITION OF OBSCENITY

Shortly after the South Carolina court rendered the first *Watkins* decision, the United States Supreme Court promulgated a significant reformulation of the obscenity test in *Miller v. California*.[120] The *Miller* case represented an evolutionary refinement of the *Roth* approach rather than a bold revolutionary charting of a new course. The Court had grown increasingly restless with the *Redrup* approach of summarily reversing state convictions unless the offense involved dissemination to juveniles, or non-consenting adults or involved hard-sell, salacious advertising. The *Miller* Court noted that:

> In the absence of a majority view, this Court was compelled to embark on the practice of summarily reversing convictions for the dissemination of materials that at least five members of the Court, applying their separate tests, found to be protected by the First Amendment.[121]

The state courts and legislatures deserved the greater guidance that would be given by a new test supported by a majority of the Court.

The new test was a lineal descendant of the *Roth* formula. The Court reiterated that restrictions on sex-oriented speech should be "carefully limited" to avoid intrusion on the dissemination of ideas. However, some elements of the test eased the prosecution's burden. The Court compressed this combination of pro-speech and pro-prosecution qualities into the following three-part inquiry concerning whether or not the material was obscene:

> (a) whether the "average person, applying contemporary community standards" would find that the work, taken as a whole appeals to the prurient

> interest . . .; (b) whether the work depicts or describes in a patently offensive way, sexual conduct specifically defined by the applicable state law; and (c) whether the work, taken as a whole, lacks serious literary, artistic, political, or scientific value.[122]

The Court rejected the approach of *Memoirs v. Massachusetts, supra,* with regard to the third prong of the test. The Court noted that the requirement that the prosecution must prove that the material was "utterly without redeeming social value" had never enjoyed the support of more than three justices in any one decision.[123] Apparently the burden of proof with regard to element three remained squarely on the prosecution's shoulders. Even if the prosecution demonstrated that the material appealed to the prurient interest and was patently offensive, a valid conviction could not be obtained unless it was demonstrated that the material lacked serious value. The Court offered medical texts as an example of works that under the new standards might contain graphic, offensive treatments of sexual conduct but which still would not be legally obscene because they possessed significant value. The Court did little more to define what it meant by serious value. It considered whether or not material had serious value to be a question of fact that would be left to the ". . . jury system, accompanied by the safeguards that judges, rules of evidence, the presumption of innocence, and other protective features provide . . . ."[124] A further fleeting glimpse into the murky meaning of serious value was given when the Court emphasized that the primary thrust of the First Amendment was to protect this vigorous exchange of "*ideas*" in "*political debate*" rather than graphic depictions of sexual conduct that serve no other purpose than commercial exploitation.[125] The concept remained a very subjective one that gave little notice to the speaker concerning what he could and could not say.

The *Miller* Court did not explain whether or not literary, artistic, political and scientific value composed an exhaustive or a merely suggestive list of the kinds of value that could save patently offensive, prurient depictions of sexual material from being obscene and losing their status as protected speech. Equally unclear was whether the term *serious value* could refer only to solemn, straight-faced discussions with utilitarian, social problem-solving qualities. Could a work have serious value when its only redeeming quality was humor or escapist, purely entertainment value? If the work did nothing to train doctors, solve the national debt or push back the frontiers of science but gave the audience a few hours of carefree diversion, would it have serious value? The tone of the *Miller* Court's discussions is that in order to have serious value, a work must have a resolute, problem-solving quality, but that is by no means a clear conclusion.

What is clear is that the serious value must pervade the material ". . . taken as a whole."[126] A spurious gloss of "value" tacked on at the end to insulate the material from obscenity charges would no longer afford protection. The prosecution would have an easier task. No longer would it have the impossible task of anticipating every conceivable form of value, no matter how minuscule, that the defendant might raise.

Next to the demise of the "utterly without redeeming social value" approach, the most significant development in the *Miller* decision was the resolution of the puzzle of whether or not the community standard that would be used in determining whether the material appealed to the prurient interest or was patently offensive would be a national or a local community standard.

In *Jacobellis v. Ohio, supra,* Justices Brennan and Goldberg had advocated a national community standard, while Chief Justice Warren opted for a local community approach.[127] The South Carolina court in *Watkins I, supra,* while giving lip-service to the national-standard approach in order to safeguard the state law from invalidation by a highly fragmented federal Supreme Court, applied the community standard rules in a way that more closely resembled a local than a national approach. In *Miller,* the United States Supreme Court came down clearly on the side of the local community standard as the frame of reference by which appeal to the prurient interest and patent offensiveness was to be determined.[128] The Court concluded that although the basic constitutional right of free speech would not vary from community to community, what appealed to the prurient interest and what was graphically offensive were questions of fact that could be influenced by local conditions. The country was too large and diverse to make a uniform, national standard feasible. Furthermore, the Court stated that ". . . this diversity is not to be strangled by the absolutism of imposed uniformity."[129] Maine and Mississippi should not be compelled to tolerate risqué material acceptable in New York and Las Vegas; nor should the latter be forced into the more straight-laced mold of the former.[130]

Reliance on the jury system as the primary mode of fact-finding virtually preordained that the jurors be allowed to rely to some extent on the mores of their local community. However, appellate courts retain the obligation to make an independent review of the constitutional issues and facts in an obscenity case to insure that local standards do not become so oppressive that they curb the vigorous exchange of ideas.[131] A local community standard poses obvious difficulties for a nationwide distributor of publications, films or videotapes. He must either find a means of ascertaining the myriad subtle variations in thousands of local standards and develop expensive means of adapting the product to each market it enters or use a most-conservative-common-denominator approach. He could play it safe by using the standards of the most conservative community in which the product would be marketed, or by restricting marketing to a narrow range of "liberal" localities. In any event, a play-it-safe approach may retard the vigorous dissemination of ideas as well as the offensive depiction of conduct.

Although the substitution of the *lack-of-any-serious-value* approach for the *utterly-without-redeeming-social-value* standard made the prosecutorial task easier, another aspect of the *Miller* test tightened the standards that had to be met in order to achieve a valid conviction. To be obscene, a work must be patently offensive. Although the *Miller* decision did not introduce the phrase, it took a tough, demanding stance in defining "patently offensive." By requiring that a work be not only offensive but patently offensive before it could be labeled obscene, the Court gave breathing room for free speech. Scarcely any work, apart from the most bland and uninspired, fails to offend in some respect. Merely requiring that material be offensive in order to qualify as obscenity would give too much freedom to law enforcement authorities to impose their personal standards on society at large.

As a prelude to giving examples of the kind of material that would be patently offensive, the Court noted that it was no business of the federal judiciary to prescribe detailed codes that states must follow.[132] However, the examples do illuminate the constitutional standards. The Court exemplified the meaning of "patently offensive" by describing it as:

(a) Patently offensive representations or descriptions of ultimate sexual acts, normal or perverted, actual or simulated;

(b) Patently offensive representations or descriptions of masturbation, excretory functions, and lewd exhibition of the genitals.[133]

Thus, merely depicting a nude figure is not obscene. To be patently offensive the work must depict "sexual conduct."[134] A passive, immobile nude figure no matter how much it might stimulate the imagination of an individual viewer would not be obscene. Genitals must not only be depicted but must also be shown to be functioning in a manner appealing to the prurient interest. The Court further described "patently offensive" conduct as "hard core."[135] This is an often used but never clearly defined term. The author of this volume offers the following provisional definition for the reader's consideration. "Hard core" material displays repeated sexual actions, graphically focusing on the physical manipulation of genitalia more than emotional reactions. These physical manipulations are described in minute detail rather than in a general impressionistic manner. Of course, even such minute descriptions of sexual conduct would be protected under the *Miller* approach if they possessed serious value.

The *Miller* opinion emphasized that the state law, either in the obscenity statute itself or in authoritative court constructions of the statute, must specifically define the forms of sexual conduct, the graphic depiction of which would be patently offensive.[136] A speaker, publisher, or distributor must have concrete notice of what he can and cannot say so that he will not engage in the self-censorship that people often exercise when criminal laws regulating speech are ambiguous and the speaker must be silent to be sure that he is safe from arrest.

To Justice Brennan, however, this seemingly tough definition of patently offensive material that required the prosecution to focus its efforts on hard core depictions of sexual conduct did not go far enough in protecting vigorous expression. He stated that "[o]f course, the Court's restated *Roth* test does limit the definition of obscenity to depictions of physical conduct and explicit sexual acts"[137] but even further limitation was needed. Brennan had been the author of the original *Roth* test that sought to steer a middle ground between those conservatives who would defer to the prosecutor's discretion unless it was grossly abused and the absolutist who would protect all forms of speech, no matter what the message, so long as the speech was not accompanied by dangerous conduct. Not only did he have no sympathy for the Court's reconstruction of the *Roth* test in *Miller,* he also was disillusioned with the *Roth* approach that he had fathered. He no longer believed that it was possible to define obscene expression with enough precision for it to be fair to make that form of expression unprotected and thus subject to prosecution or other form of censorship. A speaker who cannot know with reasonable certainty what he can and cannot say will be intimidated into silence. To reduce the impact of this intimidating effect, Brennan argued that obscenity should be prohibited only in a narrow range of circumstances when the state's interest is at its height. These circumstances occur when there is a need to protect juveniles and unconsenting adults.[138]

In *Paris Adult Theatre I v. Slaton,*[139] decided on the same day as *Miller,* the Court delineated the goals that could legitimately be pursued in regulating obscenity. The Court agreed that states had strong interests in protecting juveniles from exposure to graphic sexual material that they were not mature enough to assimilate. It further agreed that states had a legitimate responsibility to protect unconsenting adults from invasion of their right of privacy by persistent exposure to explicit sexual material that they had no reasonable chance of avoiding. However, the majority in *Slaton* rejected Brennan's contention that these were the only legitimate goals a state could pursue in regulating obscenity.[140] The *Slaton* decision noted that state regulations of obscenity could pursue goals such as:

(1) ". . . the quality of life and the total community environment . . ." and ". . . the tone of commerce in the great city centers . . .";

(2) ". . . the public safety."[141]

The Court noted that studies indicated that there was ". . . at least an arguable correlation between obscene material and crime."[142] The Court admitted that there was no conclusive scientific proof linking exposure to obscenity and antisocial conduct such as rape or sexual assault. Indeed, the controversial Report of the Commission on Obscenity and Pornography, submitted to the President in 1970, concluded that there was no firm evidence linking exposure to erotica to the perpetration of antisocial acts. A dissenting opinion, known as the Hill-Link Report, found that a causal connection between intensive exposure to obscenity and sex crimes did exist.[143]

In the *Slaton* opinion, the Supreme Court concluded that the disagreement as to whether or not obscenity was causally linked to antisocial acts did not prohibit legislation that assumed that there was such a causal connection since such an assumption was not unreasonable.[144] Legislatures are not limited to passing laws that are based entirely on principles that are capable of scientific proof.[145] Underneath the Court's quiet language was a struggle for ascendancy among basic constitutional principles. When the factual premises underlying the regulation of speech are in doubt, but not entirely absent, should the Court resolve close questions by deferring to the judgment of the state legislature, thus vindicating a dual sovereignty system in which states, as well as the federal government, have significant police powers? Such an approach also vindicates separation of powers principles in which the Court yields to popularly elected assemblies as the primary legislative authority. The contrasting approach is that when the factual basis for the regulation of any form of expression is subject to dispute, the Court should err on the side of vindicating speech. Even though our legislative system would suffer from an advanced form of gridlock if legislation had to be based on conclusively demonstrated facts, substantial evidence should undergird the regulation of speech.[146]

The majority's conclusion that a state could validly regulate explicit sexual material that was not likely to be exposed to juveniles or unconsenting adults but might lead to antisocial acts or a decline in the quality of life in residential neighborhoods or commercial centers resulted in the Court's upholding Georgia's regulation of adult theaters even though they made some effort to warn patrons of the general sexual orientation of the pictures which awaited them within the theaters. The right of privacy, which *Stanley v. Georgia, supra,* had extended to one who views avowedly obscene material within the cloister of his home, does not extend to the patron of a commercial theater.[147] A patron of an adult theater could interact with others viewing the films at the same time. At the conclusion of the films, the viewer, now in a state of excitement, might, upon leaving the theater, commit antisocial acts. As speculative as this scenario might seem, perhaps it underlies the Court's distinction between a person's right to view what he wishes in the privacy of his home and the more restricted rights of a patron of a commercial theater. Limiting the freedom of the patron or film exhibitor at a commercial theater was not pursuing the illegitimate goal of thought control that had been so thoroughly denounced in *Stanley v. Georgia,* but was instead pursuing a state's legitimate interests in protecting the quality of life from the sleazy, deleterious influence of commercial exploitation of obscenity. Furthermore, the state was pursuing its interest in protecting its citizens from physical acts of sexual aggression.

In addition to more clearly delineating the goals that a state validly could pursue in regulating obscenity, the *Slaton* opinion also clarified the nature of the evidence and proof that could be used in such cases. The *Slaton* decision reaffirmed the faith the Court had placed in a jury of laymen and women to decide whether or not the material under adjudication appealed to the prurient interest. It was not error for the state courts to fail to require the prosecution to submit expert testimony that the films were obscene. The films were placed in evidence. The pictures themselves are the best evidence of whether or not the elements of the obscenity test have been met. Juries normally do not need an expert to translate what the jurors can see for themselves. The Court did not rule out the use of expert testimony. However, it did observe that obscenity trials did not lend themselves to the use of expert testimony as readily as did areas more capable of precise scientific proof. Indeed, the Court observed that the spurious use of experts in obscenity trials ". . . made a mockery out of the otherwise sound concept of expert testimony."[148] The Court reserved judgment on whether or not expert testimony might be required in a trial in which the material in question was directed at deviant groups concerning which the average juror would have little understanding.[149]

In addition to these observations on evidentiary standards, the Court also offered guidance concerning the due process optimum in obscenity cases. *Slaton* involved a civil complaint filed by state prosecutors in order to obtain an adjudication that certain films shown in *Paris Adult Theatre I* were obscene and that the theatre should be enjoined from exhibiting them. The film exhibitors were given an opportunity in a full adversary proceeding to rebut the allegations of obscenity. No criminal indictments would be brought prior to such a civil adjudication of obscenity. The United States Supreme Court praised this procedure as providing a healthy level of due process. The only improvement it suggested that would have made the procedure even more meritorious was the addition of a mechanism by which an exhibitor could initiate proceedings to determine in advance of showing the film whether or not it would fall afoul of obscenity laws.[150]

In *Slaton* the Court also offered valuable guidance concerning the scope of freedom that states would have in enacting obscenity regulations. The Supreme Court stated that:

> It should be clear from the outset that we do not undertake to tell the States what they must do, but rather to define the area in which they may chart their own course in dealing with obscene material.
>
> This court has consistently held that obscene material is not protected by the First Amendment as a limitation on the state police power by virtue of the Fourteenth Amendment.[151]

The states were not free to censor protected speech which did not meet the *Miller* definition of obscenity, nor to suppress even obscene speech by procedures that trampled on a publisher's or distributor's rights to a fair hearing, but apart from that the details of the regulation were left to the state legislature. Presumably the states could even grant greater protection to speech than that stipulated in the *Miller* case minimum standards.[152]

As we shall note in more detail later, the South Carolina courts have adhered closely to the *Miller-Slaton* formula. However, Oregon, with state constitutional provisions containing wording distinctly different from the federal First Amendment, has charted its own course in a manner that provides for more protection for sex-oriented speech. Article 1, section 8, of the Oregon Constitution states that:

> No law shall be passed restraining the free expression of opinion, or restricting the right to speak, with, or print freely on any subject whatever, but every person shall be responsible for the abuse of this right.

In *State v. Henry*,[153] the Oregon Supreme Court seized upon the state constitutional language granting freedom of expression ". . . on any subject" as a basis for concluding that even sex-oriented speech that was patently offensive, appealed to the prurient interest, and lacked serious value, was protected expression.[154] This interpretation of the state constitution's language was fortified by the court's reading of state and national history which it concluded failed to reveal that pornography traditionally had been regarded as a form of speech that posed such dangers to society that it was stripped of protection.[155] It was not the proper business of the state to weave uniform moral raiment in which to dress its citizens.

Even though obscenity was protected speech under the Oregon Constitution, the court seemed to leave the door ajar for reasonable time, place and manner regulations that would protect children and unconsenting adult viewers but which afforded reasonable access to such materials to the consenting adult.[156]

The South Carolina courts have more faithfully followed the path blazed by *Miller*.

(F) THE SOUTH CAROLINA COURTS APPLY THE *MILLER* CASE OBSCENITY STANDARDS

The South Carolina Supreme Court's decision in *State v. Watkins*[157] was in the United States Supreme Court pipeline at the time the *Miller* and *Slaton* decisions were rendered. The United States Supreme Court vacated the state court's decision in *Watkins* and remanded it to the state system for reconsideration in light of the reformulation of the obscenity standards in *Miller* and *Slaton*.[158] Such high court action does not necessarily imply that it views the state court's action to be out of step with the new approach. It merely gives the state court an opportunity to reassess its conclusions under the revised standards.

In *Watkins II*, the South Carolina Supreme Court concluded that the state obscenity laws remained valid under the *Miller* reformulation of the obscenity test.[159] The South Carolina obscenity laws applied to the kind of prurient, patently offensive, hard-core depictions of sexual conduct that *Miller* said were subject to state regulation. It was true that the South Carolina law contained explicit language stating that even though a work appealed to the prurient interest and was patently offensive, it would not be considered unprotected, obscene speech unless it lacked social value.

However, the state trial judge had charged the jury that in order to convict it must find that the film was utterly without redeeming social value. Even though that version of the social value test had never been adopted by more than three justices at any one time, the trial judge had given the defendant the benefit of this liberal charge that erected a high standard for the prosecution to meet. It was true that since the trial court's charge and its affirmation by the state supreme court in *Watkins I*, the United States Supreme Court had refashioned the social value element. However, the new standard only required the prosecution to prove the absence of serious social value. The defendant could not complain that a standard more favorable to him than the new serious value rule had been utilized at his trial.

The state court noted further that the *Miller* case had rejected any pretense that appeal to the prurient interest and patent offensiveness were to be judged by a national community standard, another approach that earlier had received minority support on the court. In a way, the *Miller* rejection of the national approach in favor of a local community standard was a vindication of the state supreme court's approach in *Watkins I* in which it had embraced a national community standard as one would a prickly porcupine -- holding it at a comfortable distance. Even though the state supreme court gave perfunctory bows to a national standard, the court had sustained a conviction in which the prosecution only presented evidence of local standards.

The South Carolina law also met the *Miller* standards that required clear notice to a speaker, publisher, or exhibitor of the kind of material that would be subject to the obscenity laws. *Watkins I* had demonstrated considerable disenchantment on the part of the South Carolina court with the *Redrup* emphasis on confining obscenity regulation to material exposed to juveniles, unconsenting adults, and material touted by hard-sell advertising. In a sense, the *Miller* and *Slaton* cases' approval of the regulation of obscenity to preserve the quality of life and curb antisocial acts was part of the same conservative jurisprudential tapestry as *Watkins I*. *Watkins II* virtually invited the state legislature to amend the obscenity laws to take advantage of the *Miller-Slaton* cases' jettisoning of the "utterly without redeeming social value" and national community standards.

Unsatisfied with the reaffirmation of his conviction, the defendant knocked on the door of the United States Supreme Court again. The high court rejected the appeal for lack of a substantial federal question.[160] Justice Brennan dissented from the dismissal of the appeal, arguing that the United States Supreme Court had failed to exercise its obligation to independently review the facts in order to determine whether or not the film was obscene. When there is any reasonable possibility that the speech involved was protected, the Supreme Court should not defer so readily to the jury's fact-findings. Furthermore, the defendant's conviction had been affirmed by the state court in *Watkins II* on the basis of a new, local community standard concerning which the defendant had not been permitted to introduce evidence. More and more, Brennan became an isolated voice speaking to an increasingly deaf audience preoccupied with law and order.

(G) THE SOUTH CAROLINA COURTS INTERPRET THE FAIR PROCEDURE, REASONABLE SEARCH AND SEIZURE RULES

The definition of obscenity does not exist in a procedural vacuum. Even if the definition strikes a good balance between the state's need to regulate explicit sex-oriented expression to guard against antisocial conduct, exposure of explicit material to minors, invading the privacy of unconsenting adults, and the physical deterioration of neighborhoods and commercial districts, these goals must be pursued with procedural fairness and search and seizure techniques that conform to the standards of the Fourth and Fourteenth Amendments. In *State v. Thompkins,*[161] the South Carolina Supreme Court wrestled with the standards of fairness in procedure and reasonableness in searches and seizures. In *Thompkins,* two Charleston County policemen purchased tickets and were admitted to the Chateau Theatre. The next day they appeared before an impartial magistrate and presented an application for a search warrant. The application was accompanied by an affidavit that gave a detailed description of the films to be seized, including various acts of oral sex and lesbianism. The warrants were issued and the films were handed over to the officers by the exhibitor upon service of the warrant. At their trial, the defendants sought to suppress introduction of the films into evidence because the names of the films had been omitted from the affidavit and warrant. The South Carolina Supreme Court concluded that the warrants were valid despite the omission of the film names since the detailed descriptions of the scenarios, and the lack of difficulty the exhibitor had in ascertaining which films were requested, indicated that the officers' discretion as to where they could search and what they could seize had been appropriately limited.

The court also rejected defense contentions that it was necessary to have an adversary hearing prior to the seizure of the material. The court concluded that a pre-seizure adversary hearing was not required if (1) the seizure was pursuant to a valid warrant issued by a neutral magistrate upon a finding of probable cause that a crime had been committed and that evidence connected to the crime was on the premises to be searched, and (2) a prompt post-seizure hearing on the question of whether or not the material is obscene was available upon request of an interested party.[162] The court cited *Roaden v. Kentucky*.[163] It will be recalled that the United States Supreme Court in *Paris Adult Theatre I v. Slaton* had praised the Georgia procedure that afforded an adversarial hearing prior to the issuance of an injunction against exhibition of allegedly obscene films. The South Carolina court made no reference to the *Slaton* case comments, but it implicitly assumed that such elaborate proceedings were not a necessary prelude to all varieties of adverse actions against an exhibitor but were optimum procedures that a state did not have to adopt. To the defendant's complaint that the state law permitted destruction of seized films without a proper hearing, the court replied that this view was erroneous since no such destruction could take place until after a full trial or guilty plea and the exhaustion of appeals.

The court in *Thompkins* rebuffed defense arguments that the South Carolina obscenity test was so vague as to fail to give adequate notice to the speaker concerning what he could and could not say, and so broad as to prohibit exhibition of innocuous sex-oriented material as well as that likely to cause serious harm. The court merely noted that the South Carolina courts had fully adopted the *Miller* test for defining obscenity. The trial court's charge was an accurate distillation of the *Miller* standards. The trial court instructed the jury that:

> In determining whether or not the movies were obscene, you, the jury, must find beyond a reasonable doubt the following: That the dominant theme of the movies taken as a whole, appeals to the prurient interest of nudity, sex or excretion; that the movies are patently offensive . . . because they affront the

> contemporary community standards relating to the description or representation of sexual matters; that the movies taken as a whole lack serious literary, artistic, political or scientific value.[164]

The court then confronted arguments that the state law did not adequately meet the requirements that before one could be validly convicted of selling, distributing or exhibiting obscene material he must have *knowledge* of its obscene character.[165] The court concluded that it was valid to find that a defendant had knowledge of the obscene nature of the material even in the absence of proof that he had *direct knowledge,* if he had had a reasonable opportunity to inspect the material but had failed to take advantage of that opportunity. The court noted, however, that the defendants in *Thompkins* did not have standing to raise this issue since it was clear that they had actual knowledge of the character of the pictures.[166]

Two films were involved in the *Thompkins* prosecution. The defendant asserted that the trial court had committed error by failing to require the jury to make separate findings for each film with regard to whether or not it met the elements of the obscenity test. The court tersely replied that such a special verdict form was unnecessary since the defendants had been charged with exhibiting obscene films and a finding that any one of the two was obscene would support the conviction. The court observed that the defendant had failed to offer proof that the two films were in any way different with regard to the proof of their obscene qualities.[167] The court's approach seems to shift the burden of proof from the prosecution to the defendant by assuming that if one film is shown to be obscene, the other one must be also unless the defendant proves that it is not. This would permit the law enforcement authorities to destroy both even though the jury has not explicitly found both to be obscene. Furthermore, it misconstrues the unit of expression that is to be appraised in determining whether or not material is obscene. Under the *Miller* test, a work is to be judged as a whole. Not only would this seem to mean that a work could not be judged by isolated fragments, it also would seem to mean that the deficiencies in the prosecution's case on whether or not work *A* meets the obscenity test should not be allowed to be remedied by proof that work *B* meets those elements. To the untrained minds of the jurors, such a mental process in which the qualities of one work mix in mulligan stew fashion with those of another to form an inchoate mixture, might seem quite appropriate unless the jury is given the guidance of special verdict forms which require separate findings for each film.

(H) THE UNITED STATES SUPREME COURT LIMITS THE LOCAL COMMUNITY STANDARDS

The *Thompkins* decision emphasized the primacy of the jury in determining whether or not a particular work met the elements of the *Miller* test. The pivotal role of the jury was quite true, but shortly before the *Thompkins* decision, the United States Supreme Court in *Jenkins v. Georgia*[168] reminded us that the jury's discretion was not unbounded and that a court had a duty to make an independent appraisal of the facts to guard against cases in which no reasonable jury could find the material to be obscene. The will of the jury was not absolute but must conform to constitutional standards protecting free expression. The *Jenkins* opinion reaffirmed the Court's preference for a local rather than a national community standard as the vantage point most compatible with reliance upon the jury as the principal fact-finder. However, a national circumference of free speech protection was drawn around that local standard so that an ultra-conservative local norm could not deeply infringe upon freedom of speech to accommodate local moral folkways.

The *Jenkins* case involved a film exhibitor who had been convicted of showing the film *Carnal Knowledge* in Albany, Georgia. *Carnal Knowledge* was a serious film that explored the problem of how a shallow, manipulative attitude could create barriers to finding love as distinguished from carnal desire. Several well-known critics listed it among the best motion pictures of the year in which it was released. It did portray sex including brief scenes of intercourse. These scenes were fleeting and impressionistic rather than lingering and graphic. Even though the jury concluded that the picture was obscene, the United States Supreme Court refused to accept this result. In an opinion by Justice Rehnquist, the Court reiterated that even though the jury remained the primary fact-finder, even in obscenity cases, when freedom of expression was involved the appellate courts had an obligation ". . . to conduct an independent review of constitutional claims when necessary."[169] After conducting its independent review, the Supreme Court concluded that *Carnal Knowledge* was not patently offensive. The Court recalled that *Miller* had given as examples of patently offensive depictions of sexual conduct "representations of ultimate sexual acts" or of "masturbation, excretory functions, and lewd exhibition of genitals."[170] *Carnal Knowledge* did contain scenes involving ultimate sexual acts but these were not presented graphically because ". . . the camera does not focus on the bodies of the actors."[171] Furthermore, "[t]here is no exhibition whatever of the actors' genitals, lewd or otherwise, during these scenes."[172] Even if a properly charged jury concluded that such depictions were obscene, the findings would not be acceptable. Thus, although the South Carolina court was correct in reaffirming the vital role the jury plays as fact-finder in obscenity cases, that role is played on a stage designed according to constitutional principles of free expression.

The *Jenkins* decision also helped clarify the dimensions of the local community, the standards of which were to be used by the jury in determining whether or not the material appealed to the prurient interest of the average person and was patently offensive. A state could designate a particular geographical area, including the statewide community used by California in *Miller*.[173] However, the state would not be forced to designate a particular geographical unit as the local community norm. It could simply instruct jurors to apply community standards without further defining what the community was.[174] In *Hamling v. United States*,[175] decided contemporaneously with *Jenkins*, the Court applied the local community standard to a prosecution under a federal law and noted that in the absence of further delineation in the statutes, the local community might be considered to be the area from which the jury was drawn. The Court noted, however, that evidence from other areas might be introduced to use as a measuring rod against which the local community could be compared.[176]

The *Jenkins* case retained the local community standard as a pivotal part of the obscenity definition but reined it in by mandating that conservative local standards could not label as pornographic material that clearly was not patently offensive. This process of whittling down the scope of the local community standard culminated years later in 1987, when the United States Supreme Court decided, in *Pope v. Illinois*,[177] that the local community standard should be applied only to the parts of the *Miller* test that require that in order to be obscene, material must appeal to the prurient interest and be patently offensive. The third element of the test, which requires that the prosecution prove that the material as a whole lacks serious literary, artistic, political or scientific value, was to be judged according to an approach without geographical roots, a reasonable-person standard.

This approach affords more room for creative experimentation. Even if a majority of the members of the local community in which the obscenity offense allegedly occurred would consider the material in question to be lacking in serious value, if that abstract paragon, the reasonable person, would find serious value, then the prosecution's case would fail. This would seem to encourage intellectual interaction throughout the country by reducing fear that a parochial standard could squelch unfamiliar ideas. The reasonable-person approach also avoids the difficulty the *Miller* Court found in a national standard: the impossibility of pinpointing a national consensus in such a varied country. The use of an abstraction — the reasonable person — avoids the necessity of identifying an actual consensus. Close upon the heels of the *Pope* decision, the South Carolina legislature amended the state's obscenity statute so that it requires that in addition to proving that a work appeals to the prurient interest and is patently offensive, the prosecution must demonstrate that ". . . to a reasonable person, the material taken as a whole lacks serious literary, artistic, political, or scientific value. . . ."[178]

The *Jenkins, Pope* and *Thompkins* cases dealt with the evolving standards concerning what is protected speech and what is obscenity that is stripped of constitutional safeguards. However, much of the routine work of appellate review of obscenity convictions deals with matters of statutory interpretation and evaluating the sufficiency of the evidence. For example, in *State v. Browder*,[179] the South Carolina Supreme Court reviewed the convictions of employees of a shop that showed sex-oriented films. The court struck down their convictions under charges that they had placed obscene material on public display. There had been no showing that the material was visible to anyone other than the patrons who sought to see it. However, the court sustained convictions of the employees for disseminating obscene material by making change for patrons who wished to use the coin-operated screening rooms. Even though the employees had no ownership interest in the business or building, they were still covered by the statute as persons who provided or rented obscene materials.[180] The case is a straightforward statutory interpretation that, although not reaching conclusions with which everyone would agree, does not betray a predisposition to strain its reasoning to either uphold or reverse convictions.

The validity of South Carolina laws under the *Miller* case definition of obscenity constituted merely a quickly disposed of preliminary question in the *Thompkins* case before the court went on to consider more pressing issues of procedural fairness. In the *Browder* case, the obscenity definition hovered dimly seen in the background as the court focused on questions of statutory interpretation. In the early to mid 1980's, the South Carolina courts and regional federal courts refocused their attention on the state's compliance with the *Miller* standards for identifying obscenity.

(I) DEFINING THE "PRURIENT INTEREST" AND "PATENTLY OFFENSIVE" ELEMENTS OF THE OBSCENITY TEST

This renewed interest in the obscenity definition was spawned by the South Carolina statute's elaboration of the basic three-part *Miller* obscenity standard. In an effort to give clearer notice concerning what was meant by appeal to the prurient interest and patent offensiveness, the General Assembly used examples and adjectives suggested by, but not strictly a part of, the *Miller* approach. The 1982 case of *State v. Barrett* began the process of evaluating these variations upon the *Miller* theme.[181] The *Barrett* case dealt with challenges to section 16-15-260(b) and (c) of the 1976 South Carolina Code that defined appeal to the prurient interest as meaning ". . . a shameful or morbid interest in nudity, sex or excretion [that] is reflective of an arousal of lewd and lascivious desires and thoughts." The defendants in *Barrett*, accused of criminal prosecutions under the obscenity laws, alleged that the definitions fatally departed from the *Miller* standards in using the phrase "lewd and lascivious desires and thoughts." The South Carolina Supreme Court concluded that far from rendering the statute invalid the phase erected a tough standard to be met by the prosecution.[182] The South Carolina standard not only demanded that the material alleged to be obscene created sexual arousal but also that the prurient interest be preternaturally lurid. This holding anticipated the later United States Supreme Court decision in *Brockett v. Spokane Arcades,*[183] which emphasized the need for state statutes to define obscene material as provoking more than the normal, healthy interest in sex.

A more significant challenge was launched against the section 16-15-260(c) definition of patent offensiveness as requiring that in order to be obscene material must be ". . . obviously and clearly disagreeable, objectionable, repugnant, displeasing, distasteful or obnoxious to contemporary standards of decency and propriety within the community." The court summarily rejected defense contentions that the language "... standards of decency and propriety within the community" skewed the local community standard toward the more prudish element rather a cross-section of the community.[184] However, this was an issue that would not go away. The same defense arguments resurfaced later in the federal case *Olson v. Leeke.*[185]

The *Barrett* decision rejected arguments that the South Carolina obscenity definitions lacked the precision necessary to meet the *Miller* requirement that in order to comply with due process clause standards that speakers, publishers and distributors be given clear notice concerning the type of material prohibited under the state's obscenity laws. Absent such clear notice, speakers would engage in self-censorship of material that was actually protected under constitutional standards if they feared that state authorities might suppress it anyway. The South Carolina court noted that some unavoidable imprecision in the definitions was tolerable. Some room must be left for juries to define and apply local community standards.[186]

The *Barrett* case is also notable for the South Carolina Supreme Court's conclusion that obscenity was a form of speech that was unprotected under the state as well as the federal Constitution.[187] Because of the nearly identical wording of the free speech and press provisions found in Article I, section 2, of the South Carolina Constitution and the First Amendment of the United States Constitution, this harmonization of their standards is plausible.

In *Olson v. Leeke,* the Fourth Circuit of the United States Court of Appeals confronted a federal habeas corpus challenge to a conviction under the South Carolina obscenity laws. The court was confronted with an issue raised earlier in *Barrett,* i.e., that using ". . . contemporary standards of decency and propriety within the community" resulted in defining "patently offensive" according to the life-style of the puritanical elites of the community rather than a more tolerant cross-section. In an opinion by Senior Judge Clement Haynsworth, the court admitted that the Court of Appeals for the Fifth Circuit, embracing the states of the lower south, had overturned a similar approach in *Red Bluff Drive-In Inc. v. Vance,*[188] because the standard created a bias against tolerance for a wide range of speech. However, the Fourth Circuit observed that such intolerance was obviated in the South Carolina approach by court interpretations and other portions of the same provision, section 16-15-260(c) of the 1976 Code, which required that in order to be patently offensive, the material must be ". . . obviously and clearly disagreeable, objectional, repugnant, displeasing, distasteful, or obnoxious. . . ."[189] This language seemed to require that in order to be obscene a work must be so strikingly repulsive that the community at large, not just the hypersensitive prudish elements, would be offended. This left breathing room for a considerable variety of speech. Nonetheless, it can still be argued that the statute so over defines patently offensive as to leave the juror awash in a sea of adjectives from which he or she can choose the language most closely fitting his or her subjective preferences which may or may not leave much breathing room for speech.

In *State v. Pee Dee News Co., Inc.,*[190] the South Carolina Supreme Court considered additional language in the South Carolina statutes designed to clarify the meaning of patently offensive and thus discharge its due process duty under the *Miller* standards of specifically defining the kind of material that would violate the obscenity laws.[191] The obscenity statute labeled as being patently offensive depictions of certain specified forms of sexual arousal. The defendant, Pee Dee News Company, which had been convicted of distributing obscene material, contended that the language was still unconstitutionally overbroad in that it prohibited the distribution of material that did not pose the dangers that works meeting the *Miller* standards would create. The court concluded that the language under attack was valid in that it was merely a more specific illustration of an example given in *Miller* itself as meeting patent offensiveness requirements.[192] The *Miller* case had listed as patently offensive material that contained ". . . lewd exhibition of the genitals,"[193] and the South Carolina law gave detailed descriptions of the meaning of that phrase.

However, despite this favorable finding concerning the constitutionality of the statute, the South Carolina court reversed the conviction because of prosecutorial misconduct. In cross-examination of a defense expert witness, the prosecutor had posed questions that implied that he possessed and was going to produce evidence linking the material distributed by the defendants to rapes that had occurred in the local area. Since such evidence was never forthcoming and the trial judge had not acted to curb the prejudicial effect of such wide-ranging cross-examination, the supreme court reversed the conviction.

In *Vernon Beigay, Inc. v. Traxler*,[194] the United States Court of Appeals for the Fourth Circuit faced a problem which the South Carolina Supreme Court had addressed briefly in the *Brockett* case, supra, i.e., did the South Carolina statute's definition of appeal to the prurient interest sweep overbroadly by prohibiting material that only aroused the normal healthy sex instinct? The South Carolina Code of 1976, section 16-15-260(b) defined prurient interest as meaning "... a shameful or morbid interest in nudity, sex or excretion ... reflective of an arousal of lewd and lascivious desires and thoughts." The plaintiff, a video store operator who had brought suit to enjoin Greenville County officials from enforcing the law, first contended that the provision was vague and confusing to distributors because it gave two contradictory definitions of appeal to the prurient interest, one emphasizing the morbid and shameful, and the other emphasizing the provocation of lewd and lascivious desires.

The court harmonized the allegedly contradictory provisions by concluding that in order to appeal to the prurient interest a work must cater to interest in both the morbid and shameful and the lewd and lascivious.[195] This reasoning foreordained the answer to the second and more fundamental question of whether or not the statute was overbroad as prohibiting material that merely aroused a normal interest in sex. The court reasoned that the statute's insistence that in order to be obscene, the material must provoke not only a morbid and shameful but also a lewd and lascivious interest in sex, meant that the law did not prohibit distribution of harmless material that aroused only normal sexual desires.[196] The court of appeals' reasoning in the 1986 *Vernon Beigay, Inc.* case was compatible with that of the United States Supreme Court in *Brockett v. Spokane Arcades* decided a year earlier.[197]

In the *Brockett* case, the Supreme Court concluded that a Washington state statute that defined appeal to the prurient interest as arousal of lasciviousness and lust should be declared partially invalid insofar as those terms might be interpreted to ban material that provoked only a normal, healthy interest in sex. By emphasizing that the state law required the prosecution to demonstrate that the material appealed to the morbid and shameful, the court of appeals signified that the Washington statute was distinguishable from an invalid law that prohibited works that aroused only a normal, healthy interest in sex.

The *Brockett* decision, even though it was concerned with the first prong of the *Miller* test, appeal to the prurient interest, also wrought a subtle change in the second element of the test, patent offensiveness. In giving examples of the type of material that would be patently offensive, the *Miller* decision referred to". . . [p]atently offensive representations or descriptions of ultimate sexual acts, *normal* or perverted, actual or simulated."[198] Assuming that depictions of "normal" sexual acts primarily arouse healthy, rather than morbid interests in sex, it may be that the word "normal" was edited out of the *Miller* example by *Brockett.*

Thus, graphic depictions that arouse normal sexual instincts may now be permissible, though perhaps subject to regulations concerning the time, place and manner in which they are presented. However, the Court's approach assumes that there is some general understanding of what are normal, healthy instincts with regard to sex as distinguished from morbid and shameful. Since this is a topic upon which people do not always talk freely and frankly, it would be difficult, if not impossible, to develop a standard of normalcy by which to measure the offensiveness of material.

(J) SHOULD THE NATURE OF THE AUDIENCE AFFECT THE SUSCEPTIBILITY OF THE MATERIAL TO REGULATION?

The Fourth Circuit in *Vernon Beigay* was not as charitable toward another provision of the South Carolina statute as it was toward the definition of appeal to prurient interest. Sections 16-15-280(1) and (4) of the 1976 Code stated that:

> In any prosecution for an offense involving dissemination of obscenity . . . , evidence shall be admissible to show:
>
> (1) The character of the audience for which the material was designed or to which it was directed.
>
> . . . . and to show:
>
> (4) What the predominant appeal of the material would be for ordinary adults or a special audience and what effect, if any, it would probably have on the behavior of such people.

The federal court agreed with defense contentions that these provisions were unconstitutional in that they permitted punishment for the dissemination of innocuous, constitutionally protected speech as well as for distribution of obscene, truly dangerous material.[199] The quoted provision departed from the *Miller* test in that it permitted the prurient appeal of the material to be judged not by its impact on the *average* person in the community but by its ability to arouse a "special audience" if such a group is the target of the marketing of the material. Thus, works that had little chance of inspiring the average person to antisocial acts but which might dangerously provoke a deviant group could be subject to censorship under this standard. Such an approach might harken back to the pre-*Roth* standards of *Regina v. Hicklin, supra,* which permitted courts to appraise material by its impact on the most sensitive elements of society. *Roth* and *Miller* rejected this standard as giving the censor virtually unfettered discretion to use subjective standards to ban much useful material since almost every publication or work of art offends someone. In addition to its departure from the *Roth-Miller* average-person approach, the Fourth Circuit concluded that the *same* provisions of the South Carolina statute overly emphasized prong one of the *Miller* test (appeal to the prurient interest) to the point that it might permit conviction of persons who disseminate materials with prurient qualities even though the materials are not patently offensive, or they possess enough serious value to save them from being obscene. The court concluded, however, that these defective portions were severable from the rest of the statute, which appeared to be valid. Thus, it was unnecessary to declare the entire statute unconstitutional.

The Fourth Circuit's conclusions made sense -- judging material by its appeal to deviant or highly suggestible groups seems inconsistent with the average-person approach. However, formidable precedent, unmentioned by the federal court, can be marshaled in favor of the portions of the statute that were invalidated in *Vernon Beigay*. Some of these precedents are cases decided after *Roth* adopted the average-person standard but before *Miller* adopted its reformulation of the three part *Roth* test. However, these cases continue to be cited and do not relate to the portions of the test that were the focus the *Miller* changes. In *Mishkin v. New York*,[200] the Court said that when a work is tailor-made for a deviant group its impact can be judged by its capability of arousing the members of that group rather than the general public. It strains logic, however, to try to picture the "average" members of a deviant group, such as sado-masochists, and to seek to determine whether or not the material would arouse such a person. In *Ginsberg v. New York*,[201] the Court observed that a state could ban material intended for dissemination to juveniles if it appealed to the prurient interest of juveniles and was patently offensive and lacked value according to society's standards of what was suitable for minors. Such material could be kept out of the hands of juveniles even though it could not be banned from dissemination to adults. A post-*Miller* case, *Erznoznik v. City of Jacksonville*[202] reaffirmed the *Ginsberg* conclusion that the state's regulatory powers were enhanced when children were likely to be members of the audience, but the Court insisted that the state clearly demonstrate that the material under attack was likely to harm children.

Five years after *Miller*, the United States Supreme Court in *F.C.C. v. Pacifica Foundation*[203] sustained the power of the Federal Communication Commission to regulate the time of the broadcast of material that was indecent in that it failed to conform to the accepted standards of society but was not graphic, prurient material under the *Miller* definition of obscenity. Such material, often consisting of so-called "dirty words," was material that was protected by the First Amendment from complete censorship. However, the Court noted that the time and circumstances of the broadcasts of such material could be regulated so that the broadcasts would occur when children were less likely to be in the audience. However, the Court later cautioned in *Sable Communications of California v. Federal Communication Commission*,[204] involving government regulation of "dial-a-porn," that the regulation of such indecent material to protect children should be conducted in a manner that did minimal damage to the dissemination of protected material, and that adults should not be deprived of such indecent (as distinguished from obscene) material merely to protect children when reasonably effective alternatives were available that would not involve depriving adults of the material.[205]

Paris Adult Theatre I v. Slaton,[206] decided the same day as *Miller*, also indicated that the nature of the audience might be considered in determining whether or not the use of expert witnesses might be necessary to insure a fair trial. The Court noted that in most obscenity trials such witnesses were unnecessary with regard to the appeal to the prurient interest question when the jury was given an opportunity to view the material and make up its own mind. However, the Court observed that it was possible that when the material under adjudication was designed for a deviant group, a jury drawn from the community at large might not be able to make an accurate determination of whether or not the material would arouse the targeted group. In such circumstances, the use of an expert witness to guide the jurors concerning the emotional impact of the material on the deviant group might be helpful to insure a fair trial.[207]

Thus, the approach that the South Carolina statute took in measuring the prurient appeal of the material in light of the nature of the audience was not such rank heresy as the Fourth Circuit's rather cursory discussion in the *Vernon Beigay* decision might indicate. However, the decision does indicate the self-contradictions inherent in an analytical system that simultaneously purports to limit its frame of reference for determining appeal to the prurient interest to the average person but allows consideration of the special interests of deviant groups or the unique need children have for protection from graphic sexual material. This approach raises unanswered questions about law enforcement techniques. If a particular set of materials would appeal only to a deviant group, should dissemination be prohibited to society at large or only to the deviant group? If the later option is chosen, would this mean testing would-be purchasers of sexual material for signs of deviancy? If considering the nature of the target audience leads us down that road, perhaps the strict adherence to the average-person standard, illustrated by the *Vernon Beigay* decision, is desirable.

(K) CIRCUMVENTION OF SEARCH AND SEIZURE LIMITATIONS BY UNDERCOVER OFFICERS MAKING PURCHASES

We have noted that in most challenges to the constitutionality of the South Carolina obscenity statutes the state law escaped either unscathed or with minor damage resulting from brief portions of the statute being declared invalid, but the superstructures of the laws remained intact. In addition to this largely unbroken string of success with regard to challenges to the South Carolina law's definition of the kind of material that is obscene, and thus not constitutionally protected speech, the courts also have considered the validity of obscenity law enforcement techniques challenged under provisions of the Fourth Amendment to the United States Constitution and their counterparts in Article I, section 10, of the South Carolina Constitution. These provisions protect the people against unreasonable searches and seizures, and they provide that no warrants shall be issued except upon a finding of probable cause that a crime has been committed and that evidence of fruits and instrumentalities of the crimes are likely to be found on the premises or persons to be searched. The warrants are to be issued only upon oaths or affirmations "particularly describing the place to be searched and the person or thing to be seized."[208]

The search and seizure provisions' requirements for a showing of probable cause before a magistrate, and the use of a warrant specifically describing the place to be searched and the items to be seized, have been circumvented by a law enforcement technique whereby police officers in civilian dress enter a store suspected of selling obscene material. The officers, posing as regular customers of such an establishment, examine the materials offered for sale to the public, purchase items which they believe to be obscene, and then, usually after consultation with other officers, arrest the sales clerk and/or owner. In the *Barrett* case, *supra*, the South Carolina Supreme Court ruled that the technique did not violate constitutional standards or statutory provisions in sections 16-15-270(a), (c), (d) of the South Carolina Code of 1976 which provided for a judicial determination of the pornographic nature of materials prior to seizure. The statute further provided that such searches and seizures of allegedly obscene material normally were to be pursuant to a warrant issued upon a finding of probable cause that the material was obscene. However, section 16-15-270(g) explicitly preserved the power to acquire the material through purchase. In the *Barrett* case, the court concluded that when a vendor offered his goods for sale to the general public, he waived any reasonable expectations of privacy in the materials.[209] The examination of merchandise in a store open for businesses was not a search and the purchase of goods offered for sale was not a seizure. The constitutional and statutory requirements for a judicial determination of the probable obscenity of the material prior to its acquisition by law enforcement authorities were not triggered by a mere purchase.[210]

Three years after the *Barrett* decision, the United States Supreme Court in *Maryland v. Macon*[211] used similar reasoning to uphold police acquisition of allegedly obscene material by a purchase without a preceding judicial determination of the obscene nature of the material or the issuance of a warrant. In the *Macon* case, a police officer in civilian attire entered a Hyattsville, Maryland, adult bookstore, sampled the magazines offered for sale, and purchased two magazines, which he believed to be obscene, with a marked fifty-dollar bill. After showing magazines to the two other detectives waiting outside the store and agreeing with them that the materials were obscene, officers returned to the store and arrested the clerk. The officers repossessed the marked fifty-dollar bill from the cash register but did not return the change that the officer had received when he made the purchase. The trial court rejected the defense motion to exclude the magazine from evidence as illegally seized materials. The state appellate court reversed, but the United States Supreme Court agreed with the trial judge.

The Court began by reaffirming the principle that the Fourth Amendment erects especially high roadblocks to the search and seizure of expressive materials such as books, magazines and films. The standards requiring that searches be conducted pursuant to a finding of probable cause and under the authority of a warrant describing with particularity the premises to be searched and the material to be seized must be applied with "scrupulous exactitude" when the target of the search is material that is "presumptively protected" by the First Amendment.[212] This strict standard, going beyond the already stiff requirements applied by the Fourth Amendment to any search and seizure, is used when expressive material is the subject of the search and seizure, because the Court fears that without such vigorous hurdles search and seizures, often accompanied by the destruction of materials, would have the same impact as a prior restraint imposed upon the publication or distribution of such materials.[213] However, the Court concluded that such concerns do not apply when the materials are not acquired by search and seizure but by purchase from a vendor who invites the public to examine and buy his wares.[214] The Court observed that "a search occurs when 'an expectation of privacy that society is prepared to consider reasonable is infringed.'"[215] When a merchant knowingly exposes his wares to the public for sale, he has no reasonable expectation of privacy in those goods. Continuing in this vein, the Court noted that "[a] seizure occurs when 'there is some meaningful interference with an individual's possessory interests' in the property seized."[216] When the material was obtained by a purchase, there was no "meaningful interference" with the seller's possessory interest. He agreed to the transaction. The Court brushed aside, as it would an irksome gnat, the defendant's arguments that since the officers had repossessed the marked fifty-dollar bill that they had used for the purchase and kept the change that they had received from the defendant, this deviation from the terms of service offered by the seller demonstrated that there had been an interference with the owner's possessory interest. The Court concluded that even if it accepted this premise, it could at most lead to excluding the marked bill from evidence and not the magazines, which were the most damning evidence against the defendant. Stripped of all rhetoric, this conclusion demonstrates a view that commercial pornographers not only have reduced privacy rights but diminished possessory rights as well.

When the police employ search and seizure techniques rather than an undercover purchase, the state courts rigorously scrutinize the procedure to insure that all constitutional and statutory standards have been met. In *State v. Hall*,[217] the court was confronted with a situation in which Darlington police officers obtained copies of four motion pictures by purchase from the defendant adult video store. The circuit judge concluded that the tapes were obscene and issued a warrant for seizure of copies of those pictures and "additional and like suspect material."[218] Under this vague authorization, the police seized copies of forty-five other motion pictures. These tapes were never the subject of the prosecution which focused on the four pictures obtained by purchase. The state Supreme Court ordered that the other forty-five tapes must be returned to the defendant because the warrant did not comply with the standards of the Fourth Amendment of the United States Constitution and with state standards. A state statute requires that:

> (e) Any warrant or order of seizure shall describe with particularity the premises to be searched and identify the material to be seized by name, title or fair description. . . .[219]

The vague phrase "additional and like suspect material" obviously did not meet these standards. The term "suspect material" left the officers free to apply their own subjective views as to what was offensive. A search and seizure warrant should be a well-aimed rifle shot, not a blast of grape-shot that sprays the innocuous and dangerous with the same lethal indifference.[220]

(L) REGULATING INDECENT MATERIAL BY ZONING RULES RATHER THAN TOTAL CENSORSHIP

Our discussion has focused on state and local regulatory power over obscene expression, an unprotected form of speech that graphically and offensively depicts sexual conduct in a manner that appeals to the prurient interest of the average person in the local community and lacks serious value. Our focus now shifts to state and local regulatory power over sex-oriented expression that fails to meet the *Miller* case definition of obscenity and thus is protected speech. For example, what are the state and local government's law enforcement powers with regard to nude dancing which although sexually suggestive and prurient does not graphically and offensively depict sexual conduct? Since such expression is not without First Amendment protection, and thus legislators may conclude that a complete ban is not the best approach, what less intrusive regulatory measures may be taken?[221] Zoning regulations are a possibility. In *Young v. American Mini Theaters Inc.*,[222] the United States Supreme Court upheld a Detroit zoning ordinance that forbade so-called adult theaters from locating within "1,000 feet of any two other regulated uses. . . ."[223] The Court reasoned that since the ordinance did not totally ban such forms of expression from the community but only regulated the time, place, or manner in which such expression could be disseminated, the law did not have to pass the strict examination to which censorship laws were subjected. A different result occurred in *Schad v. Borough of Mount Ephraim*,[224] in which the local government banned not only nude dancing but all other forms of live entertainment, including everything from plays and concerts to more risqué performances. The Court struck down the law as an overbroad enactment that banned dangerous and innocuous material alike.

The Court in *Schad* observed that the ordinance ". . . prohibits a wide range of expression that has long been held to be within the protections of the First and Fourteenth Amendments," and it further held that it was improper to ban an entertainment program ". . . solely because it displays the nude human figure."[225] In order to justify such a sweeping ban, a strong government interest must be served by the law, and it must be narrowly drawn so as to achieve those goals while doing only minimal damage to free expression. The *Schad* decision found the local government's interest in a sweeping ban of live entertainment to be both flimsy and unsupported by the evidence. The borough argued that one of its chief goals was to create a light commercial zone in which the residents of the borough could meet their immediate needs without having to endure the disadvantages of heavy commercial use. The Court observed that this goal could not be given much weight since the borough did not consistently pursue it. The local government did permit commercial use that went well beyond the residents' immediate needs.[226] The borough next attempted to justify its live entertainment ban as useful in alleviating the need for ". . . parking, trash, police protection and medical facilities . . ." as activities peculiarly associated with such entertainment. The Court rejected this goal as insufficient to justify the sweeping ban of live entertainment since evidence had not been produced that such entertainment would spawn more critical parking, trash, and police protection needs than would other commercial uses, such as restaurants, that were not subject to the ban.[227]

The Court refused to approve the validity of the ordinance under the less stringent standards applicable to laws that did not totally ban a particular form of expression but only regulated the time, place, or manner in which it could be displayed. Even if such laws are less closely scrutinized than a censorship ordinance, they must still be supported by a substantial government interest and be narrowly drawn.[228] To meet such a test, a zoning law must show that the use excluded from a particular area was incompatible with the normal uses to which the area was devoted. No such evidence was furnished in *Schad*.[229] A reasonable time, place, manner restriction should also insure that the use that is banned from a particular area is reasonably available elsewhere in the community unless the material is obscene and subject to total ban. This standard was not met since the ban applied throughout the community.[230] The ordinance was in fact a total ban masquerading as a time, place, manner regulation. It met neither the strict scrutiny standards to which such total exclusions of a form of expression are subjected nor the more indulgent, but still demanding, standards by which time, place, manner regulations are judged.

Local regulatory authorities were more successful in gaining Court approval of their system for controlling sex-oriented but protected speech in *City of Renton v. Playtime Theaters*.[231] In that case, the city forbade adult motion picture theaters from being within 1,000 feet of (1) any residential zone, (2) family residence, (3) church, (4) park, or (5) school. The plaintiff, Playtime Theaters, sought a declaration that the ordinance violated First and Fourteenth Amendment standards, and it also sought an injunction against enforcement of the law.

The Supreme Court sustained the law, characterizing it as a true time, place, manner regulation rather than a lightly disguised total ban such as the ordinance in *Schad*.[232] Regulations that are designed to control speech based on its content or point of view are presumed to be invalid. They can be justified only by the most compelling government goals implemented by means narrowly crafted to achieve those goals with minimal damage to free expression. Speech that is obscene or poses a clear danger of violence may be subject to such regulations if the probability of harm is clearly demonstrated. By contrast, regulations that do not totally ban a presumptively protected form of expression but only seek to regulate the time, place or mode of expression to minimize its intrusion on the rights of other persons or other significant interests are viewed more benignly by the courts. Time, place, manner regulations must be content-neutral – not giving particular points of view favored times or locations in order to enhance their impact. They should pursue substantial government goals. The goals necessary to justify such regulations need not reach the compelling level necessary to justify total bans or content-based regulations. Such regulations must insure that the harm to free expression does not sweep too broadly. Accordingly, reasonable alternative avenues of communication must be left open.[233]

The ordinance in *City of Renton* met this standard. The city had a substantial interest in preserving the quality of life in its boundaries.[234] Commercial traffic in sex-oriented material might clash harshly with the operations of a school, park or church, or the quiet one expects in a residential neighborhood. The commercial blight that sex-oriented businesses attract might seriously diminish the quality of life.[235] The ordinance was not designed to smother unpopular speech but was crafted to curb the undesirable "secondary effects" of commercial traffic in sex-oriented material. These adverse secondary effects include crime, damage to the profitability of more traditional businesses and harm to the quality of life in both residential areas and commercial districts.[236] Such ordinances aimed at the adverse secondary effects of sex-oriented speech are content-neutral time, place, manner regulations that may be viewed with a more benign eye since the targets of such regulations leave telltale physical signs of deterioration in the area. Such regulations directed at speech resulting in physically perceptible reduction in the quality of life may be less susceptible to manipulation by an administrator who simply wants to banish what he does not like. However, the term "secondary effects" is so broad and the cause and effect relationship between a particular form of expression and the physical deterioration so difficult to demonstrate that it may be quite easy to manipulate the standard to achieve the administrator's personal agenda.

Having noted that the goal of preserving the quality of life in the city against the deterioration caused by adult theaters being too close to the specified sensitive uses was a substantial enough government purpose to support the regulation, the Court then asked had the city met the second element of the time, place, manner regulatory standards? Were alternative locations available at which the theaters had a reasonable chance of reaching their audience? Yes. The Court noted that 520 acres, more than 5% of the land in the city, would still be open to adult theater or comparable uses.[237] The plaintiff complained that none of this land was then for sale and that it was unlikely that it was a realistic alternate location for them. The Court concluded that the Constitution did not require it to insure that plaintiff would actually conclude a deal at a reasonable price. That the theater company would have to fend for itself in the real estate market did not mean that reasonable alternate locations were unavailable.[238]

Perhaps inspired by the favorable result given local control of sex-oriented businesses through zoning laws, the Richland County Council adopted a similar approach in 1987 which was sustained by the South Carolina Supreme Court in *Centaur Inc. v. Richland County*.[239] The ordinance mandated that sex-oriented businesses be confined to the general commercial zones (C-3) and that they be 1,000 or more feet from parks, schools, churches, residential areas or any other sex-oriented establishment. Article 8A-2(16) of ordinance No. 1609 of Richland County defined a sexually oriented business as ". . . an adult arcade, adult bookstore or adult video store, adult cabaret, adult motel, adult motion picture theater, adult theater, escort agency, nude model studio, or sexual encounter center." Adult bookstores and video stores are those which sell or rent products displaying "specified anatomical parts" in a graphic and provocative fashion described in detail in the ordinance.[240] Sex-oriented businesses must obtain a license from the county zoning administrator who must issue the license within 30 days unless he finds that the applicant is disqualified because he is underage, delinquent in taxes, the premises do not pass a health and safety examination or other disqualifying facts are found to be present.[241] The administrator also could deny the license if the applicant failed to "... provide information reasonably necessary. . ." to evaluate the application.[242] Licenses could be revoked if drugs were used or prostitution took place on the premises.[243] Existing valid sex-oriented businesses that were located within 1,000 feet of a church, school, residential district, or park, are given two years within which to phase out their activities at their old premises and find a new location that conforms to the zoning rules.[244] The ordinance also regulated the structures of the premises in order to avoid their use for prostitution.[245]

The introductory section of the ordinance stated that it was not the purpose of the law to legitimize the dissemination of obscenity that was unprotected under constitutional free speech standards. Nor was it the intent of the ordinance to prohibit adult access to sex-oriented but not obscene materials. Instead, the ordinance sought ". . . to promote the health, safety, morals, and general welfare of the citizens of the county, and to establish reasonable and uniform regulations to prevent the continued deleterious location and concentration of sexually oriented businesses within the county."[246]

The plaintiff, Centaur Inc., operated two adult bookstores in Richland County. It attacked the validity of the statute as exceeding the county's authority as a local government and as infringing on the plaintiff's rights of free expression. The state supreme court quickly found that the regulations fit neatly within the county's statutory powers as a local government to enact land use regulations to promote the health, convenience, safety and morals of the public.[247] With regard to the claims that the ordinance violated the plaintiff's free speech rights, the court invoked the *Young v. American Mini Theaters, supra* and *City of Renton v. Playtime Theaters, supra,* precedents to sustain the measure as a content-neutral time, place, manner regulation.

The Richland County ordinance, like the regulations in *City of Renton,* was not designed to censor the content of speech but instead sought to control the secondary effects of sex-oriented speech that caused a deterioration in the quality of life and created a physical atmosphere incompatible with such sensitive uses of land as parks, schools, churches and residential areas. As a content-neutral time, place, manner regulation the ordinance had to meet the substantial government interest test applied in *City of Renton,* rather than stricter compelling interest rules applicable to laws that sought to totally ban a form of expression or which sought to favor speech expressing certain points of view. Controling the deleterious secondary effects that resulted from locating sex-oriented businesses close to sensitive uses such as schools and residential neighborhoods met the substantial interest test. The state supreme court did not explicitly delineate the analytical system in such detail, but its heavy reliance on *City of Renton, supra,* and *Young, supra,* made these points clear implications of the opinion. The undesirable secondary effects that were the target of the ordinance were not delineated. However, among the objectives may have been a desire to protect school children, whose critical faculties have not yet formed, and unconsenting adults, who do not enjoy being propositioned, from being swept into the sexually pervasive atmosphere. The question is -- is the influence of such sex-oriented businesses on the surrounding community so pervasive that the adult passerby can no longer protect him or herself by exercising the option, mentioned in *Cohen v. California*, of averting one's eyes from the offensive material?[248] Does the passerby become such a captive audience that the law must step in to protect him or her? The conclusion in *Centaur* was that the ordinance was designed to guard the health, safety and morality of the public and that this purpose was substantial enough to justify the ordinance. The *Centaur* opinion also concluded that the ordinance met the second element that a time, place, and manner regulation must meet in order to be valid. Reasonable alternative locations were available to which the adult stores could move.

The South Carolina Supreme Court then considered the broad authority given the county zoning administrator to deny a license to a sex-oriented business when the applicant had failed to supply all the information that the administrator considered to be needed to evaluate the request for a permit. The court concluded that the meaning of this standard could be objectively determined. The administrator was not left at large to apply his own subjective opinions. However, the fact is, the ordinance never delineated what was meant by the "information reasonably necessary" standard.[249] However, the test of the ordinance with its emphasis on avoiding prostitution, drug use and sales, unsafe buildings, and financially irresponsible licensees perhaps supplied sufficient guidance to the official. In addition to arguing that the ordinance was too vague in setting the standards that must be applied by the administrator, the plaintiff argued that the regulations, even if legitimately directed at controlling the secondary effects of sex-oriented businesses, did not meet the requirement that time, place, manner regulations of speech must be narrowly tailored so that the harm to free expression is minimized. In particular, the plaintiff alleged that the county zoning administrator's powers to suspend a license for thirty days for such conduct as permitting gambling, excessive use of alcohol on the premises, or refusing to admit inspectors, as well as the administrator's authority to revoke a license if the permittees furnished false information or knowingly permitted drug use or prostitution on the premises, were too sweeping and arbitrary.[250] Without further explanation, the court simply announced that the regulatory measures were no broader than they needed to be to accomplish the council's purposes.

This analysis was based on a 1989 United States Supreme Court formulation in *Ward v. Rock Against Racism.*[251] The *Ward* decision considerably strengthened the hand of local law enforcement officials who wished to use time, place, and manner regulation to make public performances less intrusive on the lives of those in the surrounding community. In upholding New York City rules requiring concerts in a portion of Central Park, near picnic sites and residential areas, to use a government electronic system that controlled the volume and mix of sound, the Court observed that since the rule was a neutral regulation of the *manner* in which speech was disseminated, it would not have to meet the strict scrutiny hurdles that a content-based regulation would encounter. Rather than demonstrate that the government was serving a compelling interests by means that were the least intrusive ones that could achieve the goals, the government only would have to prove that it was pursuing valid interests by means that would accomplish those goals more efficiently than would alternative techniques of control. Thus, the Court in the *Ward* case shifted its priorities away from insuring that time, place, manner regulations were narrowly tailored in order to minimize the harm to free expression. Instead, it permitted speech control mechanisms so long as they were more efficient than other means. The Court's focus jumped suddenly from speech protection to efficiency enhancement. This greatly expanded governmental freedom in selecting time, place, manner techniques for controlling expression that was likely to intrude on the rights of others or the quality of life. With subjective, ill-defined goals such as "quality of life" being decreed legitimate and the validity of the means chosen to pursue them more dependent on their efficiency than the extent to which they are likely to harm expression, it is likely that most time, place, manner regulations will be sustained.

The *Centaur* decision next addressed the validity of the "amortization" procedure by which existing sex-oriented businesses that were located too close to schools, parks, churches or residential areas had two years to phase out operations at their old location and find a new place conforming to the zoning standards. The plaintiff contended that the requirement that stores that did not conform to the zoning standards must move within two years after August 1, 1987, was an unconstitutional taking of its property. The Court concluded that the burden was on the challenger to show that an amortization period was unreasonable. The Court made no distinction between amortization rules applicable to ordinary commercial uses and those applicable to a business involving expressive material such as books, magazines and video tapes. The Court stated that the amortization law was presumptively valid and that this presumption could be surmounted only if the challenger proved that its loss outweighed the public benefit flowing from the regulation. Centaur had not discharged this burden. It had presented no proof of economic damage to its business that would result form the forced relocation other than some evidence that it had made improvements to its current building that would be rendered moot by the move. By contrast, the county had presented extensive evidence of the harmful impact of sex-oriented businesses on the nearby community.

The court refused to consider the plaintiff's contention that the ordinance was unconstitutionally vague in describing the establishments subject to its sanctions as those that had "... principal business purposes" of purveying materials displaying specific sexual acts or anatomical parts.[252] The state supreme court concluded that since the phrase clearly applied to Centaur's operations, it had no cause to complain of a lack of notice. In addition, the plaintiff had no standing to assert that the "principal business purpose" standard gave insufficient notice to other businesses, not parties to the case, concerning whether or not their operations would be subject to sanction. In order to make arguments that a law is vague or overbroad with regard to a third party, the challenger must demonstrate that the chilling effect on protected expression produced by the statute is "real and substantial" rather than marginal and speculative.[253]

When the "indecent" speech takes the form of a live performance involving public nudity, the courts may be willing to permit the use of more drastic law enforcement tools than zoning regulations.

(M) REGULATING THE MODE OF INDECENT EXPRESSION: THE CASE OF THE NUDE DANCER

Not only can indecent speech be regulated by zoning techniques that delineate the appropriate locations for such expression in order to minimize harm to the surrounding community, the manner by which such speech is disseminated can be regulated if the law does not restrict the essential nature of the message sought to be conveyed. In *Barnes v. Glen Theater Inc.*,[254] the Supreme Court sustained an Indiana public indecency law that forbade public nudity, including nude dancing. Unlike the law struck down in the *Schad* case, *supra*, this statute focused on public nudity, and did not create a sweeping ban on all forms of live entertainment.

A nightclub and a theater featuring such performances, and several dancers from the establishments, filed suit to enjoin enforcement of the law as a violation of their rights of free expression under the First Amendment of the United States Constitution. The Supreme Court upheld the law in a five-four ruling. Chief Justice Rehnquist wrote the lead opinion for himself and Justices O'Connor and Kennedy. Justices Scalia and Souter concurred in separate opinions. The Chief Justice concluded that ". . . nude dancing of the kind sought to be performed here is expressive conduct within the outer perimeters of the First Amendment, though we view it as only just marginally so."[255]

Even though nude dancing was entitled to a modicum of constitutional protection, the Indiana statute did not transgress the First Amendment rights of the clubs or the performers. At the heart of this conclusion was the nature of the speech. Even though the expression was erotic it was not the kind of graphic display of sexual conduct that constituted obscenity and thus received no constitutional protection. It was indecent speech of a symbolic nature. This means that the message was not conveyed by verbal means but by conduct — the symbolic mode of the dance. When speech is transmitted through conduct rather than the printed or spoken word it may be subjected to more intense regulation because of the greater likelihood that such action-oriented expression may provoke harmful conduct or otherwise seriously endanger the community. If symbolic speech conveys a message capable of being understood by an audience it may receive constitutional protection despite the greater propensity of action, as distinguished from verbal expression, to cause injury or interfere with the rights of others. If the symbolic, action-oriented speech carries a political or social message, it may receive a high level of constitutional shielding.[256] Erotic entertainment is not placed on as lofty a pedestal as political symbolic speech.

Since the form of expression involved was symbolic, action-oriented speech, rather than that of a purely verbal nature, the lead opinion utilized the analytical approach of *United States v. O'Brien*,[257] which upheld a federal law forbidding symbolic speech in the form of draft card burning. In *O'Brien* the Court held the government to a less stringent standard than it would have used if the speech had not been so action-oriented. It did not require the government to demonstrate that it was pursuing a compelling state interest by means that were necessary to its achievement and which intruded no more than necessary upon free expression. The *O'Brien* Court formulated the following test to apply to the regulation of symbolic speech:

> (1) Is the regulation "within the constitutional power of the Government" in that the conduct involved is of a type normally controlled by the state?
> (2) Does the regulation further "an important or substantial government interest"?
> (3) Is the government interest or goal "unrelated to the suppression of free expression"?
> (4) Is the "incidental restriction" on First Amendment rights "no greater than essential to the furtherance of that interest"?[258]

The lead opinion concluded that the Indiana law satisfied the test. The Chief Justice observed that "[p]ublic indecency statutes are of ancient origin and presently exist in at least 47 States."[259] Thus, the form of conduct controlled by the law is one traditionally and widely subject to state regulation.

Is the state's purpose in regulating the law a substantial one? Yes. The statute serves the goal of protecting "societal order and morality."[260] The lead opinion elaborated upon the importance of the state's purpose by noting that "[p]ublic indecency statutes such as the one before us reflect moral disapproval of people appearing in the nude among strangers in public places."[261] The Chief Justice also concluded that the law met part three of the test. The government's purpose in regulating public nudity was unrelated to the suppression of free expression. The law was not a subterfuge for censoring a particular message. The Chief Justice was skeptical that nude dancing conveyed any message. The lead opinion rejected the contentions of the dissenters that the state was attempting to censor a particular point of view: the erotic message.[262] Furthermore, the law was no more intrusive on the right of free expression than was necessary to achieve the substantial goals of the state. An erotic message could still be conveyed ". . . so long as the performers wear a scant amount of clothing."[263] Even assuming the dancing had a "communicative element, it was not the dancing that was prohibited, but simply its being done in the nude."[264] Any loss in the clarity of the erotic message would be minimal.

Justice Scalia also voted to uphold the Indiana statute but did so in a separate opinion that took an even broader view than Rehnquist about the state's power to regulate in order to achieve moral goals.[265] To him, it was unnecessary to make the state satisfy the demanding *O'Brien* standard. The law was directed at a general form of conduct — public nudity. It applied to, but did not target, public nudity, such as dancing, that might be considered expressive conduct. Since the government's purpose was to regulate conduct, not censor a message, the law did not have to serve an important goal, a standard that Scalia rejected as not being in the text or tradition of constitutional law. The state only had to assure the Court that it was serving a legitimate purpose in a rational manner. The government had met that standard.

Scalia's most sweeping vindication of government power was in his assertion that regulation to achieve moral goals did not have to be linked to the prevention of palpable harm. Thus the dissent's contention that the nude dancing caused no harm since only consenting adults were present was irrelevant, as were contentions that no clear causal link could be demonstrated between such performances and criminal conduct such as sexual assaults and prostitution. He concluded that "[o]ur society prohibits, and all human societies have prohibited, certain activities not because they harm others but because they are considered, in the traditional phrase, 'contra bonos mores' i.e., immoral."[266]

Scalia's approach and the lead opinion's "societal order and morality" standard give the government law enforcement tools of remarkable potency and flexibility. However, these standards also are remarkably subjective. Permitting punishment of acts that are under Scalia's hypothesis harmless but immoral leaves no concrete basis for judging what expressive acts are impermissible since different law enforcement officers and juries may have different views of what is immoral. The standard may shift erratically from case to case and from jury to jury as decision-makers enshrine their personal viewpoints in the law. Furthermore, there is no guarantee that speech regulation to achieve subjective moral goals will be limited to the sex-oriented speech area. It is not inconceivable that political speech with an unpopular viewpoint could be labeled as immoral. Justice Souter, however, provided a more palpable method for determining when expressive conduct is subject to regulation.[267] He found it unnecessary to rely on subjective standards of morality because he saw nude dancing as being associated with concrete and harmful secondary effects such as prostitution, sexual assault, and other criminal activity.[268] Souter, however, did not require proof of a direct causal connection between the nude dancing and the harmful secondary effects. It was enough if the nude dancing and the injurious secondary effects were correlates. Where you find one you find the other, even though you cannot prove that one produces the other.[269] A state has a substantial interest in forestalling such harmful secondary effects so long as the intrusion on free expression is no broader than necessary.[270]

Justice White led a group of dissenters that included Justices Marshall, Blackmun and Stevens.[271] To the dissenters, dancing is a key mode of expression that can convey emotions and ideas that cannot be captured by mere words.[272] A nude dance cannot be described as mere conduct subject to censorious regulation. To Justice White nudity may be an integral part of the ideas and emotions conveyed.[273] The state's regulation of nude dancing in lounges cannot be justified as merely a part of a general regulation of offensive conduct. Since only consenting adult viewers are present at the performances in the plaintiffs' lounges, it is unlikely that anyone will be offended.[274] The state has admitted that it will not apply the public indecency statute to nudity in operas such as *Salome* or musicals such as *Hair*.[275] Thus, the application of the law to the plaintiffs must be because of the state's desire to censor the erotic message conveyed by the plaintiffs. Such a content-based regulation must be subjected to the strictest scrutiny. The government must demonstrate that it has a purpose to justify the regulations that is not merely legitimate or important. It must be compelling. The regulation must be no more intrusive upon the right of free expression than is necessary to achieve the government's compelling goal.[276] The dissent does not view the state's purpose as the lofty one of achieving societal order and morality but a rather petty purpose of dictating matters of taste and style best left to the individual.[277] Even if the state's goal were deemed to be a compelling one, the means it has chosen create unnecessarily broad inroads on the right of free expression. Narrower means are available to attack the harmful secondary effects of nude dancing. Such performances could be banished to areas specially zoned for that purpose. The state simply could prosecute the harmful effects rather than the expressive element of the conduct. For example, the state could prosecute those guilty of prostitution or sexual assault rather than the dancing. The state could even use the liquor control authority under the Twenty-first Amendment to prevent alcohol from being served where nude dancing occurs.[278] Such rifle-shot regulations are preferable to the shotgun-blast ban on an entire form of expression — nude dancing.[279] The dissenters clearly viewed the approach of the Rehnquist and Scalia opinions as preparing fertile ground for creation of a thought police.

The deep division within the Court with regard to the need to regulate indecent but not obscene forms of speech, such as nude dancing, has not spilled over to the more poignantly injurious practice of child pornography, with regard to which the Court has a more nearly unified pro-regulation approach.

(N) PROTECTING CHILDREN

In assessing the susceptibility of speech to regulation, courts may take into account both antisocial conduct that is likely to be provoked by the speech and antisocial conduct that went into the creation of the material. When material is both the product of and is likely to produce antisocial conduct, it becomes particularly vulnerable to regulation. In no form of speech is this more evident than child pornography, which victimizes a segment of society unable to make informed, independent choices. In the 1982 case *New York v. Ferber,*[280] the United States Supreme Court recognized extensive state power to control material portraying children involved in sexual acts. Producers and distributors of such material can be subjected to prosecution even though their wares do not meet the traditional three-part obscenity test announced in *Miller v. California, supra. Ferber* cordoned off child pornography as a form of speech that was unprotected by the First Amendment when it consisted of "... works that *visually* depict sexual conduct by children below a specified age."[281] In the Court's view, such material derived much of its danger from involving children in the performance, or a realistic simulation of the performance of sexual acts such as intercourse, masturbation or bestiality. A mere verbal description, although it may appeal to the prurient interest of the pedophile, would not have the added danger possessed by *visual* depictions of sexual acts which involve children as participants in the production of such material. The participation of children in the creation of visual depictions of their involvement in sexual acts very likely would precipitate several significant harms to those or other children. Among the most serious risks posed by child pornography are:

(1) the likelihood that viewers would be stimulated to commit child abuse;

(2) the permanent psychological scarring of children who participate in making such material. This psychological damage could take several forms such as the minor involved in making the material becoming a child abuser when he or she becomes an adult, or the child becoming incapable of leading a normal sexual life upon reaching adulthood;

(3) the continuing invasion of the child's privacy for years to come as a result of a permanent visual record having been made of his or her participation in sexual performances.[282]

Since such harms are the likely byproduct of the participation of children in the making of pornographic material, it is not necessary that such works meet the *Miller* test in order to fall into the pit with the other unprotected forms of speech. Even if the material does not appeal to the prurient interest of the average person in the community, even if the material lacks the graphically detailed qualities that the *Miller* test demands of obscenity, even if only fragments of the material (rather than the predominant theme of the entire work) depict sexual acts, the degrading depiction of the child participating in the production of such material has left its scars. These scars remain even if the material arguably has some serious literary, artistic, political or scientific value.

The Supreme Court was unanimous in labeling visual depictions of children engaged in sexual acts to be an unprotected species of expression. Even though it was possible to speculate that the New York child pornography statute under attack by criminal defendants in *Ferber* could sweep so broadly as to suppress scientifically valuable material used in a manner that was not harmful to children, such conjectural overbreadth did not render the statute invalid. Claims that particular examples of child pornography had serious value and that application of the statute to them was unconstitutionally overboard would be handled on a case-by-case basis.[283] The Court was plainly skeptical that it would ever be presented with child pornography with such significant value that the Court would be justified in overlooking the propensity of such material to cause serious harm to children.[284] Justice Brennan was perhaps marginally more willing than the rest of the Court to at least entertain the possibility that child pornography existed that both possessed serious value and was unlikely to harm children.[285]

South Carolina obscenity laws were amended in 1987 to reflect the United States Supreme Court's conclusion in *New York v. Ferber* that visual depictions of children engaged in sexual activity were unprotected expression. Section 16-15-395 created the offense of "first degree sexual exploitation of a minor. . . ." This provision stated that:

> (A) An individual commits the offense of first degree sexual exploitation of a minor if, knowing the character or content of the material or performance, he:
>
> (1) uses, employs, induces, coerces, encourages, or facilitates a minor to engage in or assist others to engage in sexual activity for a live performance or for the purpose of producing material that contains a visual representation depicting this activity;
>
> (2) permits a minor under his custody or control to engage in sexual activity for a live performance or for the purpose of producing material that contains a visual representation depicting this activity;

(3) transports or finances the transportation of a minor through or across this State with the intent that the minor engage in sexual activity for a live performance or for the purpose of producing material that contains a visual representation depicting this activity;

(4) records, photographs, films, develops, or duplicates for sale or pecuniary gain material that contains a visual representation depicting a minor engaged in sexual activity.[286]

Section 16-15-405 defines the offense of "[s]econd degree sexual exploitation of a minor . . ." and provides that this felony is committed by a person who, knowing the nature of the material:

(1) records, photographs, films, develops, or duplicates material that contains a visual representation of a minor engaged in sexual activity; or

(2) distributes, transports, exhibits, receives, sells, purchases, exchanges, or solicits material that contains a visual representation of a minor engaged in sexual activity.

The second degree offense of recording and photographing or otherwise reproducing a visual depiction of a child engaging in a sexual act is presumably less serious than its first degree counterpart because it is not necessarily committed for pecuniary gain. The second degree offense of distributing, transporting, selling, or otherwise trafficking in such visual portrayals of children engaged in sexual acts would seem to encompass not only those who engage in commercial trafficking of child pornography but also private networks of people who circulate such material for private personal perusal rather than sale.

First degree offenses are punished by imprisonment of "not less than three years nor more than ten years."[287] The strict, no-nonsense nature of the sanctions for first degree exploitation of minors is further seen in the prohibition of suspending any portion of the minimum sentence or of paroling the offender prior to service of the minimum sentence.[288] The second degree offense is punishable by imprisonment for "not less than two years nor more than six years," and no portion of the minimum sentence may be suspended nor may parole be granted until the minimum sentence has been completed.[289]

In 1991 South Carolina added the offense of third degree exploitation of minors to take advantage of the United States Supreme Court decision in *Osborne v. Ohio* that permitted states to prohibit the private possession of child pornography.[290] The decision not only extended the reach of child pornography statutes into the possessor's home but also reconstructed the *New York v. Ferber* definition of what constituted unprotected depictions of children in sexually explicit poses. The approach of the Supreme Court in *Ferber* was to permit states to punish the production, sale and distribution of visual portrayals of children engaged in "sexual conduct."[291] The South Carolina Code provisions prohibiting the sexual exploitation of children curb specified activities related to the production, sale and exchange of material that visually depicts children engaged in "sexual activity."[292] The *Ferber* test and the South Carolina Code approach both emphasize the visual portrayal of minors engaged in sexual activity. By contrast, the *Osborne* case approved a statute which the state courts construed to prohibit the possession or viewing of pictures of minors involved in "lewd exhibition" of their genitals, or pictures that graphically focused on the genitals of minors. Thus, in order to qualify as unprotected child pornography, material need not visually depict minors engaged in sexual *conduct* or *activity*. Lewd exhibition of, or graphic focus in the pictures upon the child's genitals is sufficient even if the child is in a passive state. Apparently the assumption was that the psychological damage to the child in making such photographs, the likelihood of provoking the viewer or producers of the material to child abuse, and the continuing invasion of the child's privacy flowing from the embodiment in relatively permanent pictorial form of the minor engaged in sexually explicit poses would occur whether or not the scenes involved sexual *conduct* or merely the portrayal of the child in a passive but sexually explicit posture. The new South Carolina provision, however, does not go as far as *Osborne* would permit since it prohibits the possesion of ". . . material that contains a visual representation of a minor engaging in sexual activity."[293]

Not only did the *Osborne* case shift the emphasis of the child pornography definition from the necessity of providing visual depictions of sexual activity toward pictures composed of lewd exhibitions of, or graphic focus upon, the genitals of a minor, it also identified a zone of vulnerability in the moat of privacy that *Stanley v. Georgia, supra,*[294] erected around the ability to view obscene material in the sanctuary of the home. *Stanley* held that even though the material was clearly obscene, and thus normally unprotected by the First Amendment, if it were possessed or viewed in the home, the right of privacy supplied the shield of protection that the free expression clauses of the First Amendment did not. Furthermore, one had a right to receive information in his home even if that information was obscene. The private nature of the viewing reduced the harm to society. The chances that the viewer would interact violently or offensively with others were reduced from what they would be had similar scenes been viewed in a bar or a crowded theater. The private nature of the possession reduced chances that offensive material suddenly would be thrust upon an unwilling viewer. In view of this low potential of harm to society, the state of Georgia in *Stanley* was left with little more than officiously controlling the purity of the defendant's thoughts as a regulatory goal.

In *Osborne*, the pictures of a nude minor in sexually explicit poses were seized in the defendant's home pursuant to a valid search warrant. The Supreme Court in *Osborne* ultimately reversed the defendant's conviction because of failure of the trial judge to charge that a lewd exhibition of the genitals of a minor, rather than a mere portrayal of nudity, was an essential element of the offense. However, the court gave approval to state attempts to punish the private possession of child pornography. The Court reasoned that the need to protect the privacy of the viewer was outweighed by the need to protect minors from the child abuse, psychological scarring, and permanent invasion of their privacy arising from the existence of pictures of them in sexually explicit poses.[295]

Unlike the government objectives in *Stanley*, the state's goals in *Osborne* were not thought control but protection of children from palpable harms that resulted from their participation in the making of child pornography. The Court concluded that the state could reasonably assume that in order to wage an effective campaign against child pornography, it was necessary to fight a multi-front war, a war that attacked not only the procurement of children to appear in such pictures, and their production, distribution and sale, but which also punished the ultimate consumer. As long as a moat of privacy protected the viewing and possession of child pornography, the market for such wares would remain and the incentive to produce them would continue.[296] Prohibiting possession of such materials prods the owner to destroy them and thus halts the continued invasion of the privacy of the child who is portrayed in the picture.[297]

The *Osborne* opinion is marked by the willingness of the United States Supreme Court to approve a form of judicial activism that seems unusual in light of the Court's current conservative composition. This activism consisted of a judicial rewrite of the state statute involved in *Osborne* in order to save it from invalidation on grounds that it was overbroad in that it prohibited all varieties of depictions of nude children. Literally construed, the statute would have prohibited the possession of nude pictures of a toddler by doting grandparents or family friends.[298] The state courts engrafted upon the statute requirements that the pictures not be mere portrayals of nude minors but that they must involve lewd exhibitions of, or graphic focus upon, the genitals of children.[299] Described in this manner, the pictures were more likely to appeal to potential child abusers than to the benign relative or family friend. The willingness of the courts to narrow the statute to cover only lewd or graphic depictions of the genitals of minors was prompted by the statute's exemption of such a wide variety of educational, medical, scientific, and cultural uses of pictures of nude children that the statute could properly penalize only sexually lewd displays.[300]

In dissent, Justice Brennan contended that the so-called narrowing construction given the statute by the courts did little to cure the constitutional infirmity of an overbroad law that punished innocuous as well as injurious scenes of nude children. In fact, engrafting the terms *lewd exhibition* of and *graphic focus* upon genitals onto the statute added layers of verbal fog that one must navigate in order to determine whether or not he is breaking the law.[301] Overbreadth is not cured by vagueness.

Even though it deals with the specialized field of child pornography, the *Osborne* decision raises intriguing questions concerning whether or not it signals a shift in the regulation of obscenity in general. In *Miller v. California*,[302] the Supreme Court, in defining the requirement that material be patently offensive, said that the material must involve "sexual conduct." However, in giving examples of patently offensive material, the Court listed along with depictions of several varieties of sexual acts the "lewd exhibition of genitals."[303] Does the *Osborne* case mark the beginning of a shift in general obscenity law away from an emphasis on sexual conduct toward lewd exhibition of, or graphic focus on, genitals that may involve only passive poses and no conduct, or does *Osborne* merely reveal a reformulation of the child pornography definition away from the *New York v. Ferber* emphasis on visual depictions of sexual conduct by minors toward a standard permitting sexually explicit but passive displays to be deemed unprotected? The same question can be asked with regard to the right of privacy. Is *Osborne* a first step toward abandoning the *Stanley v. Georgia*[304] rule that even obscene material can be possessed in the privacy of the home, or does it just allow invasions of the zone of privacy when the material is child pornography?

The *Osborne* decision concerned the expanded police powers of the state when children participate in the making of sexually explicit pictures. The state also has greater regulatory power when children are the audience for, rather than participants in, the making of sexually-oriented material. In *Erznoznik v. City of Jacksonville*,[305] the United States Supreme Court stated that "[i]t is well settled that a State or municipality can adopt more stringent controls on communicative materials available to youths than on those available to adults." Earlier, *Ginsberg v. New York*[306] stipulated that regulatory measures designed to protect children from viewing materials harmful to them should use the basic framework of the obscenity test but vary it so that it could more accurately detect material that might be harmful to minors. For example, with regard to the first element of the test it must be rephrased to inquire whether or not the material appeals to the prurient interest of children. Under this approach, works could be suppressed as to children that could not be kept out of the hands of adults. Overbroad regulations that ban material from adults in order to avoid exposure of the material to children should be avoided if more narrowly crafted techniques could be utilized that would keep the material from children without depriving the adult audience of access.[307]

The theme of the *Ginsberg* case was that since children had not developed the critical faculties to make their own decisions with regard to what they should or should not view, the state was justified in acting to protect them. However, the *Erznoznik* case cautioned that even with regard to minors, state or local governments can not sweepingly ban all portrayals of nudity no matter how innocuous or educationally valuable. In the *Erznoznik* opinion the Court stated, in striking down an ordinance that prohibited the exhibition in outdoor drive-in theaters of films depicting any form of nudity, that:

> In this case, assuming the ordinance is aimed at prohibiting youths from viewing the films, the restriction is broader than permissible. The ordinance is not directed against sexually explicit nudity, nor is it otherwise limited. Rather, it sweepingly forbids display of all films containing *any* uncovered buttocks or breasts, irrespective of context or pervasiveness. Thus it would bar a film containing a picture of a baby's buttocks, the nude body of a war victim, or scenes from a culture in which nudity is indigenous. The ordinance also might prohibit newsreel scenes of the opening of an art exhibit as well as shots of bathers on a beach. Clearly all nudity cannot be deemed obscene even as to minors.[308]

To avoid such overbreadth and focus regulatory measures squarely upon material that would be injurious to children as viewers, the *Ginsberg v. New York* approach of requiring that child protection laws meet each element of the obscenity test, adapted to gauge the impact of the material on minors, should be followed. The South Carolina statutes have conformed to these standards. The statute prohibiting the dissemination of harmful material to minors contains the following definition section:

> (1) "Harmful to minors" means that quality of any material or performance that depicts sexually explicit nudity or sexual activity and that, taken as a whole, has the following characteristics:
>
> > (a) the average adult person applying contemporary community standards would find that the material or performance has a predominant tendency to appeal to a prurient interest of minors in sex; and
> >
> > (b) the average adult person applying contemporary community standards would find that the depiction of sexually explicit nudity or sexual activity in the material or performance is patently offensive to prevailing standards in the adult community concerning what is suitable for minors; and
> >
> > (c) to a reasonable person, the material or performance taken as a whole lacks serious literary, artistic, political, or scientific value for minors.[309]

Laws designed to keep sexually explicit material from children, when it meets such a test designed to gauge the danger of the material to minors, have enjoyed wide support across the ideological spectrum of the Supreme Court. Even Justice Brennan (who in his dissent in *Paris Adult Theatre I v. Slaton* rejected as hopeless attempts to define obscenity with enough precision to give due process notice to publishers and distributors as to what was and what was not permissible) was in favor of retaining laws to protect children from graphic sexual material since they could not adequately protect themselves because they were not yet "'possessed of that full capacity for individual choice which is the presupposition of the First Amendment guarantees.'"[310]

Under the South Carolina Constitution, an additional ingredient has been added to the analytical process. Article I, section 10, of the state constitution for the most part duplicates the United States Constitution's Fourth Amendment provision against unreasonable searches and seizures. However, it adds a significant feature not found in its federal counterpart. Section 10 also protects the people against ". . . unreasonable invasions of privacy. . . ." The drafting committee that proposed this explicit protection of privacy made no specific mention of an intent to protect sex-oriented material within the home. It stated that "[t]his additional statement is designed to protect the citizen from improper use of electronic devices, computer data banks, etc."[311] However, the committee continued with a statement that invites the judiciary to apply the core concept of protecting privacy from government encroachments that use techniques not yet invented or in vogue at the time of the drafting of the provision. The committee report stated that "[s]ince it is almost impossible to describe all of the devices which exist or which may be perfected in the future, the Committee recommends only a broad statement on policy, leaving the details to be regulated by law and court decisions."[312] Thus it is conceivable that a state court applying the South Carolina right of privacy provision could give the same degree of privacy to the possession of child pornography that the *Stanley* case gave to the possession of adult pornography, even though the *Osborne* case failed to recognize such possessory rights under federal standards.

Another interpretation of the South Carolina right of privacy provision is possible. Even though the general tenor of section 10 is to protect citizens against invasions of the right of privacy by government, it is not beyond the realm of possibility to interpret the provision as also containing an invitation to the legislature, under the ". . . details to be regulated by law . . ." language used in the drafting committee report, to enact statutes protecting another right of privacy, that of the child, from invasion by the pornographer.

(O) REFOCUSING THE OBSCENITY TEST

The law is replete with difficult to apply but useful standards that employ vague, abstract terms or demand proof that intangible, elusive mental attitudes existed at the time that certain injuries occurred. Tort law uses the concept of the reasonable man or "reasonably prudent person" as a frame of reference to determine when a person's conduct has been negligent.[313] A party seeking to prove that certain crimes or torts were committed must demonstrate that the alleged perpetrator acted intentionally or with reckless disregard for the safety of others, or with some other level of mental culpability.[314]

As slippery as these concepts are to apply, they by no means approach the enigmatic, protean qualities of the test used to define obscene expression. The obscenity test is littered with indefinable fictional beings or groups such as the "average person," and "contemporary community" which are used as guideposts by which the sexual-arousal potential of books, films and other material is measured.[315]

The test also asks the adjudicator to traverse several psychological labyrinths such as the requirements that the material appeal to the "prurient interest" and be "patently offensive." Fact-finders often struggle futilely to determine whether a particular person charged with a crime or tort had the requisite state of mind necessary to prove the offense. The task is infinitely more difficult when laws such as those regulating obscenity do not require that the court determine the *actual* psychological impact of the material at some particular time in the past but instead demand that it assess the *potential* of the work for provoking such elusive emotions as being offended or aroused sexually. The difficulty of making this decision is further exacerbated because the psychological status to be explored is not that of a real person but that of an abstraction such as the average person in the contemporary local community.

When we add to this formula of uncertainty the fact that these determinations generally are made by juries who sit only for one or a few cases and then disperse, usually without having given reasons for their conclusions, the unpredictability of obscenity law is further increased. Such vagueness and uncertainty furnishes fertile ground for judges and jurors to apply their own personal prejudices concerning what is and is not obscene. The speaker, publisher or film-maker receives scant guidance as to what are permissible and impermissible forms of expression. The prosecutor is left at sea concerning what are proper targets of law enforcement efforts. Despite these difficulties with crafting a workable obscenity test, an absolutist approach, totally abandoning the regulation of sex-oriented speech, appears to be unacceptable in view of the harm such material can bring in the form of violent reactions or the invasion of the privacy of unconsenting adults and children. What, then, are the appropriate parameters for the regulation of sex-oriented expression?

Outside the specialized enclave of sex-oriented speech, the forms of expression that are most vulnerable to intense government regulation are those that are violent in themselves or those which display a clear likelihood of immediately provoking or inciting violence.[316] Violence leaves a trail of palpable, concretely observable consequences. Determining whether or not expression that is not itself violent presents a clear and immediate likelihood of inciting or provoking violence requires making more subtle judgments involving assessing such intangibles as the intent of the speaker to provoke violence or the presence of a reasonably foreseeable likelihood that personal insults would move a listener to a violent response.[317] However, even such subtle appraisals are anchored to the core concept of violence — its actual presence, or its probable future occurrence. As difficult as such judgments are to make, they do not involve heaping intangible upon intangible as lavishly as does the obscenity test in its use of the psychological measurement concepts of appeal to the prurient interest and patent offensiveness, and in its use of abstract beings or groups, such as the average person, contemporary local community, and reasonable person, as frames of reference against which the psychological impacts of the speech can be measured. Rather than a common core concept, such as the relationship of the speech to violence, the obscenity test charges off into three divergent directions -- the potential of the material to arouse sexual emotions, its potential to offend, and its value to society. If this hydra-headed monster were replaced with an approach which focused more on the concept of violence, this area of speech regulation would become less of a specialized analytical enclave and more in alignment with the main channel of free expression analysis. Such a shift in legal vantage point obviously would not eliminate opportunities for the regulator to impose his personal moral standards upon society at large, but it reduces the range of such opportunities. Such an approach would shift the prosecutorial emphasis toward sex-oriented expression that urges or explicitly approves violent sexual activity such as rape, assault and sado-masochistic practices when the speech occurs under circumstances that make it likely to provoke harmful action.

However, changing the prosecutorial priorities to focus upon violence-related sexual expression can not be a complete test. The use of children in making sex-oriented expression poses a grave danger even if the material produced does not explicitly urge or applaud violent actions. Serious harm can also be inflicted by the public exposure of explicit, though not violence-oriented, sexual expression to non-consenting adults as well as children. The common harm underlying both the use of children in making sex-oriented materials and disseminating unwanted sexual-material to adults is that those swept into such activities are robbed of their individual choice. The children, even when they may seem to consent, are robbed of individual volition by having choices pressed upon them which they are not mature enough to make. The non-consenting adult, when confronted with the pervasive exposure of explicit sexual material that can not be avoided by averting one's eyes and ears, has his or her individual preferences overridden by those who have decided to bombard the public with unwanted material. A vast difference exits between such public dissemination of explicit, sex-oriented speech, whether violence-related or not, and the private use of material that is of sexual interest but is neither violence-oriented nor involves the depiction of children in an explicit sexual context. Thus prosecutorial emphasis with regard to sex-oriented speech should be placed upon: (1) speech that urges or approves sexual violence, and (2) expression that invades the freedom of choice of someone other than the speaker by either: (a) imposing such material upon unconsenting adults who are unable to take reasonable evasive measures, and (b) expression that is the product of pressuring or cajoling children, too immature to make their own decisions, into participating in the making of sex-oriented material. The second prong of this approach emphasizes modes of expression that deny others the freedom of personal choice. Speech that neither threatens substantial physical danger nor denies others the freedom of personal choice but invokes intense emotional reactions, whether devoutly religious, viscerally sexual or intensely political, is best left to informal means of social control by the development of mores and traditions rather than formal legal sanctions.

Law is modestly successful in controlling dangerous action. It lacks the subtlety necessary to be keeper of the soul. Faith and moral discipline can be found through personal spiritual quests and the communion of voluntary groups rather than by adhering to a legal litany.

NOTES

1. *See* M. BLOOMFIELD, LAW: FAMILY AND RELIGION, ENCYCLOPEDIA OF SOUTHERN CULTURE 800 (Wilson and Ferris eds. 1989).

2. *See* Act No. 74 of 1691, 2 S.C. STATUTES AT LARGE 68-69, (Cooper 1837) *and see* Act No. 202, 2 S.C. STATUTES AT LARGE 196-97 (Cooper 1837). *See also* Roth v. United States 354 U.S. 476, 483 n.11 (1957).

A similar approach was taken by a 1711-12 Massachusetts statute. It stated:

> And whereas evil communication, wicked, prophane, impure, filthy and obscene songs, composures, writings or prints, do corrupt the mind and are incentives to all manner of impieties and debaucheries, more especially

> when digested, composed or uttered in imitation or mockery of devotion or religious exercises, -

Be it further enacted by the authority aforesaid,

> That whosoever shall be convicted of composing, writing, printing or publishing of any filthy, obscene or prophane song, pamphlet, libel or mock-sermon, in imitation or [*in*] mimicking of preaching, or any other part of divine worship, every person or persons offending in any of the particulars aforementioned shall be punished by fine to her majesty not exceeding twenty pounds, or by standing on the pillory once, or oftener, with an inscription of his crime, in capital letters, affixed over his head, according to the discretion of the justices in quarter sessions.

I ACTS AND RESOLVES OF THE PROVINCE OF MASSACHUSETTS BAY, 1692-1714, chapter 7, Sects. 18-19, passed March 19, 1711-12; published March 26, 1712 (emphasis in original).

Like the early colonial South Carolina statutes, the Massachusetts law was directed primarily at language and conduct showing disrespect for religion rather than at graphic depictions of sexual conduct that had no explicit anti-religious message. However, the use of words such as "obscene" and "debaucheries" may indicate that the law could have been used to punish non-religious, sex-oriented expression. Both the South Carolina and Massachusetts laws imply a blending of religious and secular moral concepts to a degree that strikes the modern reader, steeped in the tradition of separation of church and state, as unusual, but which was apparently commonplace during colonial times.

3. *See* I Attorney General's Commission on Pornography, Final Report 240-43 (1986) (U.S. Department of Justice).

4. State v. Haddon, 49 S.C. 308, 27 S.E. 194 (1897) *and see* State v. Gilchrist, 54 S.C. 159, 31 S.E. 866 (1899).

5. JOURNAL OF THE CONSTITUTIONAL CONVENTION OF THE STATE OF SOUTH CAROLINA 1895, Session of September 19, 1895 at 172-73.

6. *Id.*

7. *See* J.L. Mims, *Unrecorded History of South Carolina Woman's Christian Temperance Union From 1881-1901* at 24-25 (undated pamphlet).

8. *See* JOURNAL OF THE CONSTITUTIONAL CONVENTION OF THE STATE OF SOUTH CAROLINA, Session of September 30 at 290 (1895).

9. The State, October 1, 1895 at 5, col. 5.

10. *Id.*

11. *Id.*

12. JOURNAL OF THE CONSTITUTIONAL CONVENTION OF THE STATE OF SOUTH CAROLINA, Session of September 30 at 290 (1895).

13. *Id.* at Session of October 1, 1895 at 293.

14. *For example, see* the exchange between Lieutenant Governor W. H. Timmerman and Dr. W.C. Smith who based their debate entirely on differing interpretations of the Bible. The State, October 1, 1895, at 5, col. 5. *Note especially* the column headlined "From a Biblical Standpoint."

15. The State, October 2, 1895 at 1, col. 2, at 2, col. 1.

16. *See* The State, October 2, 1895 at 2, col. 1.

17. Hollis, *The Role of the Church in South Carolina History*, 4 JOURNAL OF THE SOUTH CAROLINA BAPTIST HISTORICAL SOCIETY 1, 15 (November 1978).

18. 1949 S.C. ACTS AND JOINT RESOLUTIONS (STATUTES AT LARGE) 138.

19. *See* 1969 S.C. ACTS AND JOINT RESOLUTIONS (STATUTES AT LARGE) 74, *and see* 1979 S.C. ACTS AND JOINT RESOLUTIONS (STATUTES AT LARGE) 2-3.

20. *See* Gitlow v. New York, 268 U.S. 652 (1925) the case which applied the federal Constitution's First Amendment freedom of speech and press guarantees to the state and local government by making the assumption that those standards had been included in the broad term "liberty" used in the Fourteenth Amendment's due process clause that was intended to apply national standards of fairness to state governments and their political subdivisions.

21. 8 Johnson (New York Common Law Reports) 290, 293-94 (1811). The author would like to thank Professor Robert Wilcox for calling this reference to his attention. Early English decisions such as the Sir Charles Sydlyes Case, 1 Keble 620 (K.B. 1663) tended to deal with obscene actions, sometimes accompanied by an assault, rather than offensive language or art. Sir Charles was convicted of displaying himself naked on a balcony while pouring bottles of urine upon curious on-lookers.

22. 2 Pa. (Sergeant and Rawle) 91 (1815).

23. *Id.* at 91-92 (emphasis in original).

24. *Id.* at 99-100.

25. *Id.* at 102, 105.

26. 17 Mass. 336 (1821).

27. *Id.*

28. *Id.* at 337.

29. 1821 VT. LAWS ch. 1 § 23.

30. Tariff Act of 1842, 27th Congress, 2nd Session, section 28, 5 U.S. STATUTES AT LARGE 566-67.

31. 194 U.S. 497 (1904).

32. 194 U.S. at 508, *see also Ex parte* Jackson, 96 U.S. 727 (1877) for a general discussion of the federal postal power.

33. 161 U.S. 29, 42 (1896).

34. *See* Bremmer, *Editor's Introduction,* A. COMSTOCK, TRAPS FOR THE YOUNG XII-XIV (1967); *see also* R. Johnson, Reform, Vice, and the American Way 67-73 (Unpublished Doctoral Dissertation University of Wisconsin 1973); *and see* H. BROUN and M. LEECH, ANTHONY COMSTOCK, ROUNDSMAN OF THE LORD 128-33, 279 (1927) [hereinafter cited as H. BROUN and M. LEECH].

35. *See* Chapter 430, 1868 N.Y. LAWS 856-858. *See* H. BROUN and M. LEECH at 82-83.

36. Chapter 777, 1873 N.Y. LAWS 1183-84.

37. Act No. 181, 19 S.C. STATUTES AT LARGE 334 (1885) (emphasis in original). The statute retained this general form for many years. *See* S.C. CODE ANN. 16-414 to 16-421 (1962). In 1965 a new statute was passed and obscenity was defined in terms similar to those used in Roth v. United States, 354 U.S. 476 (1957) discussed *infra.* *See* Act No. 265, S.C. STATUTES AT LARGE 470-72 (1965). The new statute removed references to "indecent" and "improper" material and focused on obscenity. The 1965 act basically followed the Roth case approach of considering material to be obscene if its predominant appeal was to the prurient interest of the *average* person in the contemporary community and it went "... substantially beyond

customary limits of candor ..." in its depiction of "... nudity, sex or excretion." Prurient interest included but was not limited to a "shameful or morbid interest" in such subjects. *See* section 1(a) of Act No. 265 S.C. STATUTES AT LARGE 470-72 (1965). However, the Act decreed that if the material were "... designed for a specially susceptible audience" its predominant appeal should be judged with reference to that unique audience. The 1965 law also stated that if the material is distributed to "... minors under sixteen years of age, predominant appeal shall be judged with reference to such class of minors." *Id.* A 1966 amendment deleted the provision for deviating from the "average person" standard when the material was intended for "... a specially susceptible audience" but retained the variable standard for minors. *See* Act No. 914, S.C. STATUTES AT LARGE 2273 at Section 1(a) (1966). These provisions were codified as S.C. CODE ANN. § 16-414.1 (Michie and Co. 1962 and 1975 Cum. Supp.) The 1965-66 statutes also modernized the South Carolina approach to obscenity by including among the material that could be considered obscene, contemporary media products such as motion pictures or ". . . any recording, transcription or mechanical, chemical or electrical reproduction." *See* Act No. 265 S.C. STATUTES AT LARGE 470-472 (1965) at 1(b). The 1965 law reduced the penalties for violating the act to a fine of one hundred dollars or imprisonment for no more than thirty days. *See* Act No. 265 S.C. STATUTES AT LARGE 470-472 (1965) at section 8. The 1966 amendment returned the sanctions to imprisonment for no more than two years or "a fine not exceeding one thousand dollars or both." Act No. 914 S.C. STATUTES AT LARGE 2275 at section 3 (1966).

38. *See* 1885 S.C. HOUSE OF REPRESENTATIVES JOURNAL 126 (December 3, 1885), 138 (December 4, 1885), 322 (December 18, 1885), 332 (December 19, 1885). *See also* 1885 SENATE JOURNAL 429 (December 23, 1885).

39. *See* address by William H. Brawley, Erskine College, June 29, 1887 at 9 (available at the South Caroliniana Library, University of South Carolina, Columbia, S.C.).

40. *Id.* at 17-18.

41. *See* Lockhart and McClure, *Literature, The Law of Obscenity, and the Constitution,* 38 MINN. L. REV. 295, 302-304 (1954).

42. Roth v. United States, 354 U.S. 476 (1957).

43. 354 U.S. at 487.

44. *Id.* at 487, n.20. *See also* ALI Model Penal Code, Tentative Draft 6, p.1 section 207.10 (1957).

45. 354 U.S. at 488-89.

46. *Id.* at 489.

47. L.R.-3 Q.B. 360, 371, 378 (1868).

48. 271 Mass. 318, 171 N.E. 472 (1930).

49. *See also* Commonwealth v. Buckley, 200 Mass. 346, 86 N.E. 910 (1909).

50. 209 F. 119 (D.C.N.Y. 1913).

51. 209 F. at 121.

52. 72 F.2d 705 (2d. Cir. 1934).

53. For general discussions of the pre-*Roth* case law, *see* T. EMERSON, THE SYSTEM OF FREE EXPRESSION 468-71 (1970) and L. TRIBE, AMERICAN CONSTITUTIONAL LAW 904-08 (1988).

54. *Roth*, 354 U.S. at 489.

55. 354 U.S. at 485 quoting Chaplinsky v. New Hampshire, 315 U.S. 568, 571-72 (1942).

56. 354 U.S. at 484-88.

57. *Id.* at 486.

58. Beauharnais v. Illinois, 343 U.S. 250 (1952); *see also Roth*, 354 U.S. at 484.

59. 354 U.S. at 481.

60. 354 U.S. at 482-83.

61. Act No. 202 of 1703, 2 S.C. STATUTES AT LARGE 196-97 (Cooper 1837).

62. 361 U.S. 147 (1959).

63. *Id.* at 152-53.

64. *Id.* at 154.

65. 378 U.S. 184 (1964).

66. *Id.* at 187-90.

67. *Id.* at 191.

68. *Id.* at 192-95.

69. *Id.* at 200.

70. 383 U.S. 413 (1966). [Hereinafter known as *Memoirs v. Massachusetts*].

71. 383 U.S. at 418.

72. *Id.* at 419.

73. Ginzburg v. United States, 383 U.S. 463, 481 (1966) (Black, J., dissenting).

74. Mishkin v. New York, 383 U.S. 502, 516 (1966) (Black J., dissenting).

75. Ginzburg v. United States, 383 U.S. 463, 492 (1966) (Douglas, J., dissenting).

76. 394 U.S. 557 (1969).

77. 394 U.S. at 565-66.

78. 394 U.S. at 565.

79. *See* United States v. 37 Photographs, 402 U.S. 363 (1971) (international traveler); *and see* United States v. 12 200 Ft. Reels of Film, 413 U.S. 123 (1973); United States v. Orito, 413 U.S. 139 (1973) (interstate transportation); *and see also* Paris Adult Theater I v. Slaton, 413 U.S. 49 (1973) (adult audience commercial theater).

80. 110 S. Ct. 1691 (1990).

81. 383 U.S. 463, 465-72 (1966).

82. 383 U.S. at 472-74.

83. 383 U.S. 502 (1966).

84. 383 U.S. at 507-10.

85. 386 U.S. 767 (1967).

86. *Id.* at 769.

87. *Id.* at 769

88. *Id.* at 769.

89. 255 S.C. 237, 178 S.E.2d 325 (1970) *rev'd* 404 U.S. 806 (1971), 257 S.C. 506, 186 S.E.2d 523 (1972) *conforming to reversal* by U.S. Supreme Court.

90. 255 S.C. at 246, 178 S.E.2d at 327, citing Jacobellis v. Ohio, 378 U.S. 184 (1964).

91. 255 S.C. at 246, 178 S.E.2d at 327, citing Jacobellis v. Ohio, 378 U.S. 184 (1964).

92. 255 S.C. at 247, 178 S.E.2d at 328.

93. *Id.*

94. 255 S.C. at 247, 178 S.E.2d at 327.

95. 255 S.C. at 250, 178 S.E.2d at 329.

96. 404 U.S. 806 (1971).

97. State v. Burgin, 257 S.C. 506, 186 S.E.2d 523 (1972).

98. 257 S.C. 448, 186 S.E.2d 236 (1972).

99. 257 S.C. at 455, 186 S.E.2d at 238.

100. 257 S.C. at 455, 186 S.E.2d at 238-39.

101. 383 U.S. 413, 419 (1966).

102. 413 U.S. 15 (1973).

103. 259 S.C. 185, 191 S.E.2d 135, *vacated* 413 U.S. 905 (1973), decision conforming to vacation order in 262 S.C. 178, 203 S.E.2d 429 (1973). For convenience, the South Carolina court's decisions in *Watkins* will be known as *Watkins I* and *II*.

104. 259 S.C. at 195, 191 S.E.2d at 140.

105. 259 S.C. at 193, 191 S.E.2d at 139.

106. 259 S.C. at 196, 191 S.E.2d at 140.

107. *Id.*

108. 259 S.C. at 193, 191 S.E.2d at 139.

109. 259 S.C. at 194, 191 S.E.2d at 139.

110. *Roth*, 354 U.S. 476, 486-87 (1957).

111. 259 S.C. at 199, 191 S.E.2d at 142.

112. 259 S.C. at 199, 191 S.E.2d at 142.

113. 259 S.C. at 200, 191 S.E.2d at 142 (emphasis in original).

114. 413 U.S. 15 (1973).

115. 259 S.C. at 196-97, 191 S.E.2d at 140-41.

116. 259 S.C. at 197, 191 S.E.2d at 141.

117. 259 S.C. at 201, 191 S.E.2d at 143.

118. Section 16-414.9 of the 1962 S.C. CODE (Supp. 1975).

119. 259 S.C. at 202-03, 191 S.E.2d at 143-44; *see also* South Carolina State Highway Department v. Harbin, 226 S.C. 585, 594, 86 S.E.2d 466, 470 (1955).

120. 413 U.S. 15 (1973).

121. 413 U.S. at 22, n.3.

122. 413 U.S. at 24, (citations in the original have been omitted).

123. 413 U.S. at 24-25.

124. *Id.* at 26.

125. 413 U.S. at 34-35.

126. 413 U.S. at 24.

127. 378 U.S. at 192-95, 200.

128. 413 U.S. at 30-34.

129. 413 U.S. at 33.

130. 413 U.S. at 32-33.

131. 413 U.S. at 25; *and see* Jenkins v. Georgia, 418 U.S. 153, 160 (1974).

132. 413 U.S. at 25.

133. 413 U.S. at 25.

134. 413 U.S. at 24.

135. 413 U.S. at 27.

136. 413 U.S. at 24, 27.

137. *See* Paris Adult Theatre I v. Slaton, 413 U.S. 49, 99 (1973) (Brennan, J., dissenting).

138. Paris Adult Theatre I v. Slaton, 413 U.S. 49, 70-113, especially at 112 (1973) (Brennan, J., dissenting).

139. 413 U.S. 49 (1973).

140. 413 U.S. at 57.

141. 413 U.S. at 57-58.

142. 413 U.S. at 58.

143. *See* REPORT OF THE COMMISSION ON OBSCENITY AND PORNOGRAPHY 31-32, 463-64 (New York Times Books 1970).

144. 413 U.S. at 60-61.

145. *Id.*

146. 413 U.S. at 108-112 (Brennan, J., dissenting).

147. 413 U.S. at 65.

148. 413 U.S. at 56, especially at n.6.

149. *Id.*

150. 413 U.S. at 55, especially at n.4.

151. 413 U.S. at 53-54.

152. *See* Pruneyard Shopping Center v. Robins, 447 U.S. 74 (1980) (holding that a state constitution could grant greater protection to shopping mall pamphleteers than that required by the federal Constitution).

153. 302 Or. 510, 732 P.2d 9 (1987).

154. 302 Or. at 514-15, 732 P.2d at 11 (1987).

155. 302 Or. at 521-25, 732 P.2d at 15-17 (1987).

156. 302 Or. at 525, 732 P.2d at 18 (1987).

157. 259 S.C. 185, 191 S.E.2d 135 (1972).

158. 413 U.S. 905 (1973).

159. 262 S.C. 178, 203 S.E.2d 429 (1973).

160. 418 U.S. 911 (1974).

161. 263 S.C. 472, 211 S.E.2d 549 (1975).

162. 263 S.C. at 481, 211 S.E.2d at 552 (1975). The court cited Roaden v. Kentucky, 413 U.S. 496 (1973).

163. 413 U.S. 496 (1973).

CHAPTER ELEVEN—NOTES

164. 263 S.C. at 483-84, 211 S.E.2d at 553. *See also* City of Columbia v. Moser, 280 S.C. 134, 311 S.E.2d 920 (1983) in which the court held that a statutory definition of "lewd" was unnecessary since that term had a commonly understood meaning.

165. Smith v. California, 361 U.S. 147 (1959).

166. 263 S.C. at 484-85, 211 S.E.2d at 554.

167. 263 S.C. at 486-87, 211 S.E.2d at 555.

168. 418 U.S. 153, 160-61 (1974).

169. 418 U.S. 160 citing Miller v. California, 413 U.S. at 25.

170. 418 U.S. at 160 citing *Miller,* 413 U.S. 25.

171. 418 U.S. at 161.

172. 418 U.S. at 161.

173. 418 U.S. at 157.

174. *Id.*

175. 418 U.S. 87, 105-06 (1974).

176. *Id.*

177. 481 U.S. 497 (1987).

178. S.C. CODE ANN. 16-15-305 (Lawyer's Co-op. 1976 and 1990 Supp.).

179. 277 S.C. 206, 284 S.E.2d 775 (1981).

180. The *Browder* case interpreted sections 16-15-390 and 16-15-260(j)(4) of the SOUTH CAROLINA CODE 1976 (Lawyers Co-op. and 1980 Supp.).

181. 278 S.C. 92, 292 S.E.2d 590, *cert. denied,* 459 U.S. 1021 (1982).

182. 278 S.C. at 95, 292 S.E.2d at 592 (1981).

183. 472 U.S. 491 (1985).

184. 278 S.C. at 96, 292 S.E.2d at 592 (1985).

185. 744 F.2d 1061 (4th Cir. 1984) *cert. denied,* 471 U.S. 1053 (1985).

186. 278 S.C. at 96, 292 S.E.2d 592 (1982).

187. 278 S.C. at 93, 292 S.E.2d at 591 (1982).

188. 648 F.2d 1020 (5th Cir. 1981).

189. 744 F.2d at 1062.

190. 286 S.C. 562, 336 S.E.2d 8 (1985).

191. S.C. CODE ANN. §16-15-260(d)(2) (Lawyers Co-op. 1976).

192. 286 S.C. at 564, 336 S.E.2d at 9 (1985).

193. *Miller,* 413 U.S. at 25.

194. 790 F.2d 1088 (4th Cir. 1986).

195. 790 F.2d at 1093-94.

196. 790 F.2d at 1094.

197. 472 U.S. 491 (1985).

198. *Miller,* 413 U.S. 15, 25 (emphasis added).

199. 790 F.2d at 1094-95.

200. 383 U.S. 502, 508 (1966).

201. 390 U.S. 629 (1968).

202. 422 U.S. 205, 212-14 (1975).

203. 438 U.S. 726 (1978). To constitute indecent speech under a South Carolina law prohibiting the operation of a motor vehicle displaying an obscene or indecent sticker, decal, or emblem that is visible to the public, the material need not meet the appeal to the prurient interest element of the obscenity test but must meet the patent offensiveness and lack of serious value standards. Act No. 443 S.C. CODE ANN. §56-5-3885 (Law. Co-op. 1990).

204. 492 U.S. 115 (1989).

205. *But see* Pinkus v. United States, 436 U.S. 293 (1978) which implied that the presence of children in the community normally should not affect the determination of whether material intended for a general adult audience would appeal to the prurient interest of the average person.

206. 413 U.S. 49 (1973).

207. 413 U.S. at 56 n.6.

208. S.C. CONST. OF 1895 art I, § 10 (as amended). The wording of the South Carolina provision is nearly identical to the Fourth Amendment but makes significant additions that explicitly protect the people from "... unreasonable invasions of privacy ..." and require that warrants particularly describe not only the "person or thing to be seized" but also "information to be obtained" by invasions of privacy that may not amount to a seizure under traditional law. So far these right of privacy provisions have played no part in obscenity cases that have dealt largely with commercial distributions, but they could be significant when the charges involve private possession in the home or some other location at which an individual or small group has a reasonable expectation of privacy.

209. 278 S.C. at 98, 292 S.E.2d at 593 (1982).

210. *See also* The State v. Oxendine, 268 S.C. 328, 233 S.E.2d 118 (1977) *and see* Olson v. Leeke, 744 F.2d 1061, 1062 (4th Cir. 1984).

211. 472 U.S. 463 (1985).

212. 472 U.S. at 468 citing Stanford v. Texas, 379 U.S. 476, 485 (1965) and Lo-Ji Sales, Inc. v. New York, 442 U.S. 319, 326 n.5 (1979).

213. 472 U.S. at 470.

214. *Id.*

215. 472 U.S. at 469 quoting United States v. Jacobsen, 466 U.S. 109, 113 (1984).

216. 472 U.S. at 469 quoting United States v. Jacobson, 466 U.S. 109, 113 (1984).

217. 293 S.C. 331, 360 S.E.2d 323 (1987).

218. 293 S.C. at 332, 360 S.E.2d at 324 (1987).

219. S.C. CODE ANN. §16-15-270 (Law. Co-op. 1976 and Supp. 1985).

220. *See also* State v. Simmons, 272 S.C. 465, 252 S.E.2d 572 (1979) reversing a conviction based on a warrantless seizure.

221. *See* Schad v. Borough of Mount Ephraim, 452 U.S. 61, 65-66 (1981).

222. 427 U.S. 50 (1976).

223. 427 U.S. 50, 72-73.

224. 452 U.S. 61 (1981).

225. 452 U.S. at 65-66.

226. 452 U.S. at 72-73.

227. 452 U.S. at 73-74.

228. 452 U.S. at 68.

229. 452 U.S. at 74-75.

230. 452 U.S. at 75-76.

231. 475 U.S. 41 (1986).

232. 475 U.S. at 46.

233. 475 U.S. at 46-51.

234. 475 U.S. at 50.

235. *See* 475 U.S. at 48.

236. 475 U.S. at 49.

237. 475 U.S. at 53.

238. *Id.*

239. 301 S.C. 374, 391 S.E.2d 165 (1990).

240. Richland County Ordinance No. 1609, Article 8A-2(2).

241. *Id.* at 8A-5.

242. *Id.*

243. *Id.* at 8A-10.

244. *Id.* at 8A-12.

245. *Id.* at 8A-13.

246. *Id.* at 8A-1.

247. S.C. CODE ANN. § 4-9-30(9) (Law. Co-op 1976 and Supp. 1990).

248. 403 U.S. 15 (1971).

249. Richland County Ordinance No. 1609, Article 8A-5(3).

250. *See* Richland County Ordinance No. 1609, Article 8A-9 (Suspension) and 8A-10 (Revocation).

251. 491 U.S. 781, 799, 109 S. Ct. 2746, 2758 (1989).

252. Richland County Ordinance No. 1609, Article 8A-2(2).

253. Citing Young v. American Mini Theaters, 427 U.S. 50 (1976); State v. Smith, 275 S.C. 164, 268 S.E.2d 276 (1980); and Basiardanes v. Galveston, 682 F.2d 1203 (5th Cir. 1982). For cases in which the phrase "principal business purpose" withstood attacks that it was unconstitutionally vague *see* Dumas v. City of Dallas, 648 F. Supp. 1061, 1076 n.42 (N.D. Tex. 1986), *aff'd sub nom.* FW/PBS Inc. v. City of Dallas, 837 F.2d 1298 (5th Cir. 1988), *rev'd on other grounds*, 493 U.S. 215 (1990).

254. 1991 WL106079 (US).

255. *Id* at 4.

256. See Texas v. Johnson, 491 U.S. 397 (1989) and United States v. Eichman, 496 U.S. ___, 110 S. Ct. 2404, 110 L.Ed. 2d 287 (1990) striking down laws that forbade flag burning that was a form of criticism of the government.

257. 391 U.S. 367, 376-77 (1968).

258. See *O'Brien supra* at 376-377. *See also Barnes supra* at 4-5.

259. *Barnes, supra* at 5.

260. *Barnes, supra* at 5.

261. *Barnes, supra* at 5.

262. *Barnes, supra* at 6.

263. *Barnes, supra* at 6.

264. *Barnes, supra* at 7.

265. *Barnes, supra* at 8-13.

266. *Barnes, supra* at 9, Scalia J., concurring.

267. *See Barnes, supra* at 13-17.

268. *Barnes, supra* at 13-14, Souter J., concurring.

269. *Barnes, supra* at 15-16, Souter, J., concurring.

270. *Barnes, supra* at 14-16.

271. *Barnes, supra* at 17-22.

272. *Barnes, supra* at 22.

273. *Barnes, supra* at 19.

274. *Barnes, supra* at 18.

275. *Barnes, supra* at 18.

276. *Barnes, supra* at 19-20.

277. *Barnes, supra* at 20.

278. The Supreme Court has held that states under their Twenty-first Amendment liquor control authority can forbid nude dancing at locations where alcohol is served. Even non-obscene nude dancing could be banned under this power. *See* California v. LaRue, 409 U.S. 109 (1972) and New York State Liquor Authority v. Bellanca, 452 U.S. 714 (1981). However, some state constitutions may choose not to utilize the full Twenty-first Amendment police power. The result may be that laws forbidding the sale of alcohol at locations at which nude dancing occurs may run afoul of state constitutional free expression provisions. *See* Bellanca v. New York State Liquor Authority, 54 N.Y.2d 228, 429 N.E.2d 765 (1981) *cert. denied* 456 U.S. 1006 (1982); *see also* Harris v. Entertainment Sys., Inc., 259 Ga. 701, 386 S.E.2d 140 (1989) *and see* Cabaret Enterprises, Inc. v. Alcoholic Beverages Control Commission, 393 Mass. 13, 468 N.E.2d 612 (1984). A 1991 Amendment to S.C. CODE 61-9-410(4) forbids bottomless dancing on premises at which alcohol, beer or wine is served. *See also* 1991 Amendment to S.C. CODE 61-5-60 adding subsection (d) (license revocation).

279. *Barnes, supra* at 20.

280. 458 U.S. 747 (1982).

281. 458 U.S. at 764 (emphasis original).

282. 458 U.S. at 756-64.

283. 458 U.S. at 767-73.

284. 458 U.S. at 762-63.

285. 458 U.S. at 775-76.

286. S.C. CODE ANN. §16-15-395 (Law. Co-op. 1976 and Supp. 1990).

287. S.C. CODE ANN. §16-15-395(D) (Law. Co-op. 1976 and Supp. 1990).

288. *Id.*

289. S.C. CODE ANN. § 16-15-405(D) (Law. Co-op. 1976 and Supp. 1990).

290. _____ U.S. _____, 110 S. Ct. 1691 (1990). *See* R130 of 1991 adding S.C. CODE § 16-15-410(A).

291. 458 U.S. at 764.

292. S.C. CODE ANN. §§ 16-15-395 and 16-15-405 (Law. Co-op. 1976 and Supp. 1990).

293. *See* R130 of 1991 *supra.*

294. 394 U.S. 557 (1969).

295. _____ U.S. _____, 110 S. Ct. at 1696 (1990).

296. 110 S. Ct. at 1696-97 (1990).

297. *Id.*

298. 110 S. Ct. at 1698 n. 9 (majority opinion) and at 1760 (Brennan J., dissenting).

299. 110 S. Ct. at 1695.

300. 110 S. Ct. at 1694-95.

301. 110 S. Ct. at 1708.

302. 413 U.S. 15, 24-25 (1973).

303. *Id.*

304. *Stanley*, 394 U.S. 557.

305. 422 U.S. 205, 212 (1975). In Todd v. Smith, 1991 WL 149823 (SC 1991) the supreme court sustained a summary judgment in behalf of the city of Myrtle Beach, the city manager, and the director of its Convention Center, in a damages suit brought by an artist who had been directed to remove his painting of a nude woman from an exhibition in the inner lobby of the Convention Center. The court majority did not reach the merits of the plaintiff's contentions that his free speech rights had been infringed because he was forced to remove a non-obscene painting from the exhibit. In the view of the majority, monetary damages could not be recovered against the city under the federal civil rights statute, 42 U.S.C. 1983, since the removal directive was not issued pursuant to city policy but was the act of

individual officials. Damages against the officials would not be justified since they are protected by a qualified immunity. Justice Toal (joined in the result by Justice Chandler) agreed that the qualified immunity protected the officials but contended that the city was subject to a damages action since the directive to remove the painting received the acquiescence, if not the express approval, of the city. With regard to the merits of the plaintiff's free speech arguments, she concluded that since the city had designated the inner lobby of the Convention Center as a limited public forum for art work, paintings could not be barred from it because of their content unless there was a compelling reason to do so and the means chosen to pursue that goal were minimally intrusive on First Amendment rights. She concluded that the protection of children from a non-obscene (but perhaps indecent) painting might constitute a compelling goal. However, the means used to achieve that goal (a total ouster of the painting from the Center) may have been too intrusive upon the artist's free expression rights. The city should have considered a less harmful enforcement tool such as putting the painting in a room accessible only to adults. More evidence was needed rather than summary judgment on behalf of the city.

306. 390 U.S. 629 (1968).

307. Sable Communications of California v. Federal Communications, 492 U.S. 115 (1989).

308. *Erzonznik*, 422 U.S. at 213.

309. S.C. CODE ANN. § 16-15-375 (Law. Co-op. 1976 and Supp. 1990).

310. 413 U.S. at 107 (1973) (Brennan, J., dissenting) (quoting Ginsberg v. New York, 390 U.S. 649-50 (1968) (Stewart, J., concurring)).

311. Final Report of the Committee to Make a Study of the South Carolina Constitution of 1895 at 15 (1969).

312. *Id.*

313. 3 F. HARPER, F. JAMES, O. GRAY, THE LAW OF TORTS, 389-393 (1986).

314. *See* R. PERKINS and R. BOYCE, CRIMINAL LAW 826-80 (1982) *and see* W. LA FAVE and A. SCOTT JR., CRIMINAL LAW 212-42 (1986) *and see,* P. KEETON, D. DOBBS, R. KEETON, D. OWEN, PROSSER AND KEETON ON THE LAW OF TORTS 173-93 (1984).

315. Miller v. California, 413 U.S. 15, 24-25 (1973).

316. *See* Brandenberg v. Ohio, 395 U.S. 444 (1964) (distinguishes speech that incites immediate violence from that which merely advocates an abstract doctrine of violence).

317. *See* Chaplinsky v. New Hampshire 315 U.S. 568, 572-75 (1942) (used some of the same terminology in defining fighting words as is used in the obscenity test. Specifically the Court asked — is the speech of such "slight social value as a step to truth" and so likely to provoke the average person to retaliation that it is deserving of little or no protection by the First Amendment?).

TABLE OF CASES

City Council of Charleston v. Benjamin, 98-105, 107, 113, 138, 151

City of Columbia v. Moser, 400

City of Gaffney v. Putnam, 228, 231-32, 258

City of Greenville v. Bryant, 329-30

City of Renton v. Playtime Theaters, 365-66, 368

Cohen v. California, 369

Committee for Public Education & Religious Liberty v. Nyquist, 182, 198

Commonwealth v. Buckley, 394

Commonwealth v. Friede, 319

Commonwealth v. Holmes, 313

Commonwealth v. Sharpless, 312-13

County of Allegheny v. American Civil Liberties Union, 103, 285, 296

Dalli v. Board of Education, 255

Davis v. Beason, 210-11, 217, 254

Dumas v. City of Dallas, 404

Durham v. McLeod, 179-82, 198

Eason v. Witcofskty, 127, 143

Edwards v. Aguilard, 283-84, 295

Edwards v. South Carolina, 225, 257-58

TABLE OF CASES

INDEX

www.ingramcontent.com/pod-product-compliance
Lightning Source LLC
LaVergne TN
LVHW050146080826
844660LV00002B/96

* 9 7 8 0 8 7 2 4 9 8 3 3 4 *